AFGHANISTAN

A MODERN HISTORY

Monarchy, Despotism or Democracy? The Problems
of Governance in the Muslim Tradition

ANGELO RASANAYAGAM

I.B. TAURIS

LONDON · NEW YORK

In memory of my Father,
Who filled our house with books;

For my Mother,
Who has loved and cherished me;

And for dearest Anandi,
Who shares my life.

Reprinted in 2009 by I.B.Tauris & Co Ltd
6 Salem Road, London W2 4BU
175 Fifth Avenue, New York NY 10010
www.ibtauris.com

In the United States of America and Canada distributed by Palgrave Macmillan, a
division of St Martin's Press, 175 Fifth Avenue, New York, NY 10010

First published in 2003 by I. B. Tauris & Co. Ltd.
New edition published in 2005
Reprinted in 2007
Copyright © 2003, 2005 Angelo Rasanayagam

ISBN 978 1 85043 857 1

A full CIP record for this book is available from the British Library
A full CIP record for this book is available from the Library of Congress

Library of Congress catalog card: available

Typeset in Goudy Old Style by A. & D. Worthington, Newmarket, Suffolk
Printed and bound in India by Replika Press Pvt. Ltd.

Contents

Angelo Rasanayagam was Chief of Mission for the UN in Iran and a number of other countries, before becoming Director of the UNHCR in Peshawar, Pakistan. He now lives in Geneva.

'Well written, succinct, accessible, analytical, objective and balanced – this is one of the best introductions to the history of modern Afghanistan available to the general public.' – Baqr Moin, Head of the BBC Persian Service

'A very readable history of modern Afghanistan.'
– *Asian Affairs*

'Angelo Rasanayagam ... restore(s) the balance in this competent history of modern Afghanistan.'
– M.E. Yapp, *Times Literary Supplement*

'An excellent history book.'
– Simon Henderson, *International Affairs*

'This is the most clear, accessible, and informative single volume available for general audiences. ... Highly recommended.'
– *Choice*

'Excellent – a veritable textbook, and a reference source for anyone interested in Afghanistan.'
– Dr Thomas Withington, Jane's Intelligence Review and King's College London

Foreword

Angelo Rasanayagam's scholarly analysis of the Afghan imbroglio reads like a novel. Given the complexity of Afghanistan's history for the average reader, particularly in the West, this is no mean achievement. Rasanayagam manages to seize the thread of this beleaguered country's repeated upheavals to walk the reader through the events leading up to September 11, 2001.

This book should be required reading for those who are weary of stereotypes and who feel the need to understand the confusing factors that led to the destruction of the World Trade Center. Tracing Afghanistan's tragic history, from the nineteenth century geo-political 'Great Game' to what the country faces today, the book reveals the successive impact of foreign troops and mercenaries, modern weapons and land mines, war by proxy and drugs, all of which have compounded the corruption and infighting in what remains a tribal and feudal society.

Can Afghanistan emerge, Phoenix-like, as a viable and stable state, despite (or because of) US involvement and future 'pipeline politics'? In the last few decades Afghanistan has faced the imposition of a ruthless communist regime, following the monarchy and the short-lived Daoud republic, only to have the resulting chaos of warlords and infighting replaced by an obscurantist and retrograde foreign import known as the Taliban. Can a return to the wisdom of the traditional *jirgas* overcome the fragmentation, the destruction and the appalling suffering after so many years of conflict?

If bilateral and international humanitarian and developmental assistance is to produce lasting results, those in charge, and particularly the donors and the public at large, will benefit greatly from reading Angelo Rasanayagam's book and reflecting on its lucid and far-reaching analysis.

Prince Sadruddin Aga Khan
Former UN Coordinator for Afghanistan
and UN High Commissioner for Refugees

Preface and Acknowledgements

The idea for this book had its origins in my proximity to the tragic human fall-out of the Afghan saga: initially, when serving in 1985–86 as the first chief of mission of the United Nations High Commissioner for Refugees (UNHCR) in the Islamic Republic of Iran, a country that was generously playing host at the time to over 2.2 million Afghan refugees; and later, as head of the UNHCR Office in Peshawar, Pakistan, in 1991–93. In Pakistan, on the eve of the withdrawal of Soviet troops in 1989, the influx had peaked to over 3.2 million refugees. In 1992, after the fall of the communist Najibullah regime, 1,274,000 Afghan refugees in Pakistan repatriated voluntarily with UNHCR assistance, with a further 358,000 returning in 1993. The question that I asked myself at the time was: what kind of country were these refugee victims of war and foreign occupation returning to? I began work on the present book in answer to that question.

The year 2001 marked the centenary of the death of the Afghan Amir Abdur Rahman Khan. With the arrival of the Taliban on the Afghan scene, the state that he had created against great odds foundered, leaving only a territory fought over by rival factions – a sorry spectacle that would have broken the Iron Amir's heart. Seen from this tragic perspective, the great advantage of writing an analytical history of Afghanistan over the last 120 years is that the record acquires a built-in structure, consisting of a beginning, a middle, and an end. This answered to the Aristotelian recipe for unity of action in a Greek tragedy, or as the irreverent English poet Philip Larkin expressed it, 'a beginning, a muddle and an end'.

Since the publication of the book, two dear friends associated with its production have sadly passed away. The distinguished author of the Foreword, Prince Sadruddin Aga Khan, was the High Commissioner I had the honour to serve during the first eight years of my career with UNHCR. He was one of the first to be informed of my book project and took a special interest in its progress. He was the first to receive a copy of the completed manuscript and graciously undertook to write the Foreword after I had found a publisher. He was taken ill later that year, succumbing in the spring of 2003. Sergio Vieira de Mello, a cherished friend for over 30 years, was killed in Baghdad in the summer of 2003, bringing an exceptionally brilliant career in the service of the United Nations to a tragic and untimely end. I had conveyed to him my fears regarding his assignment, not on account of the physical risks – that would never deter Sergio – but because of the political risks of UN involvement in the Iraqi quagmire. But Sergio was a consummate practitioner of the art of the possible. And that I believe was what made him a prime target for his assassins. In replying to my advice, he said: 'I still cherish our youthful ideals for a better world.'

I am grateful to the many friends, colleagues, and acquaintances, too numerous to mention, who have unknowingly helped shape my thoughts and ideas. In Peshawar, I am indebted to the many informal conversations I had with my counterparts, senior Pakistani government officials, with first-hand knowledge of Afghan affairs, who were long and closely associated with UNHCR in the management of the multi-faceted programmes of assistance to the then largest refugee population in the world. My thanks also go to Nancy Hatch Dupree, the widow of the great Louis Dupree, whose store of material on Afghanistan was made freely accessible to me, and to UNHCR and NGO staff who brought back snippets of interesting information from their frequent forays into the field, both in Afghanistan and in Pakistan.

Besides my considerable debt to Louis Dupree's substantial pioneering work on Afghanistan, as well as to the work of Ahmed Rashid in the writing of this book, I am also much indebted to Barnett R. Rubin's scholarly analysis of the more recent history in his books and essays. Mr Rubin has acquired an international reputation as a leading contemporary expert on Afghanistan, and I owe much to his valuable insights. While preparing the paperback edition of this book, I noticed with some embarrassment that while I had credited some of his contributions, in the text and endnotes to relevant chapters, I had failed regrettably to do so in some others, particularly with regard to Chapters 1 and 11. This edition gives me the opportunity to further acknowledge my debt to Mr Rubin's valued original research and to apologize to him at the same time for my previous omissions.

In Geneva, my special thanks go to Harish Kapur, Professor Emeritus of the University of Geneva, and to Wahid Tarzi. They both reviewed the drafts of initial chapters of the book, and offered valuable comments, Wahid Tarzi's being drawn from his special 'insider's knowledge' of the Afghan monarchy, and Professor Kapur's from the viewpoint of a professional historian. During a visit to Australia, I called on Professor Amin Saikal, Director of the Centre for Middle Eastern and Central Asian Studies at the Australian National University in Canberra. He gave me some useful guidance and copies of some texts in his possession.

I owe a special debt of gratitude to two dear friends: Frances Bennet-Papazafiropoulos, head of the English section of the editorial and translation services of the International Labour Organization in Geneva who, despite a heavy workload, was painstakingly thorough in her editing of the entire manuscript during her hard-won leisure hours; and to Lily Papandropoulos of the International Red Cross who very obligingly translated some German texts into English. I also wish to express my appreciation of former UNHCR colleagues who have assisted, chiefly by making available to me documents bearing on my researches. They are Sergio Vieira de Mello, Daniel Bellamy, former head of the Afghan Desk, and Siri Wijeratne, a former chief of mission in Kabul. I owe a special debt to John Andrew of UNHCR who inducted me into the mysteries of word-processing after I had acquired, with some trepidation, a personal computer on his advice. Without a PC, I could not have produced this book.

Last but not least, I greatly benefited from the constructive dialogue with Turi Munthe, my editor at I.B.Tauris. He helped me to bridge the distance between author and reader with his insightful comments on content and form. I am also thankful to Turi for initiating a greenhorn into the somewhat opaque world of publishing.

Angelo Rasanayagam
Coppet (Vaud), Switzerland
July 2005

Afganistan and its Neighbours

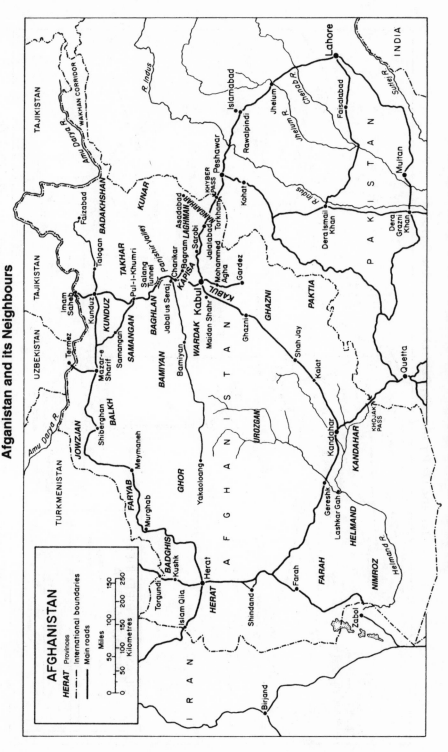

(Adapted from Ahmed Rashid, *Taliban*, I.B. Tauris Publishers, London and New York, 2000)

Gas and Oil Pipelines in Central Asia and the Caspian

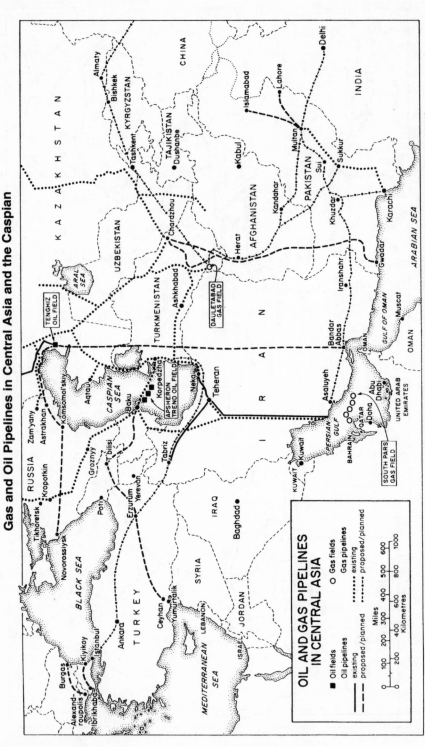

(With acknowledgements to Ahmed Rashid, *Taliban*, I.B. Tauris Publishers, London and New York, 2000)

Introduction: The Origins

In 1747 Ahmad Khan Abdali, a young Afghan warrior who had served in the army of the Persian conqueror Nadir Shah, won command in Kandahar of a confederation of the leading Pashtun tribes. To this event can be traced the emergence of Afghanistan as an autonomous and recognizable political entity. Ahmad Khan went on to found a dynastic empire, the borders of which, by the time of his death in 1772, extended from Central Asia and Kashmir to the Arabian Sea, and from eastern Persia (Khorasan) to the Indian Punjab. It was the largest west Asian empire of its time after that of the Ottoman Turks. This imperial enterprise was made possible by the waning power of the Persian Safavid dynasty to the west and the Indian Moghul Empire in the east.

Safavids and Moghuls had been rivals for control over Afghan territories since the sixteenth century. The Moghul base had been Kabul, the capital of the founder of the dynasty, Babur, a descendant of both Genghis Khan and Timur (Tamerlane). This youthful ruler of a small khanate in Ferghana in Central Asia had been driven out by the Shaybani Uzbeks in 1504. The Uzbeks, led by a soldier of fortune, Shaybani Khan, had captured the Timurid capital of Samarkand in 1500 and were absorbing the remnants of the Timurid Empire in Central Asia. They took Balkh and Kunduz in northern Afghanistan, and briefly held the splendid Timurid city of Herat before it fell to the Safavids, after Shaybani Khan was killed in battle in 1510. From Kabul, Babur, frustrated by the Uzbeks in his ambition of recreating the Timurid Empire of his forbears, set out on his conquest of India, culminating in his victory over the Afghan Lodi dynasty of Delhi at the battle of Panipat in 1526.[1] In 1558 Kandahar was wrested from Moghul control by the Safavids. The city and its environs subsequently changed hands several times, but at the beginning of the eighteenth century the area was firmly under Persian Safavid rule.

In 1709 Mir Wais Hotak, a Ghilzai Pashtun chief, led a successful rebellion against the Safavid governor of the province of Kandahar, a ruthless Georgian Christian apostate, known to the Afghans as Gurgin, who had tried to impose the Shi'ite brand of Islam on the staunchly Sunni Pashtuns. His son, Mahmud, went on to seize the Safavid capital, Isfahan, in 1722, and capture the Shah himself. The unspeakable sufferings inflicted on its hapless inhabitants by Mir Mahmud and his Ghilzai tribesmen, and the damage wrought on the beautiful capital embellished by Shah Abbas the Great, are still vividly recalled by Iranians. One of his many atrocities was to invite a large number of the notables of Isfahan to a banquet at the palace and have them slaughtered to a man. His bloody excesses caused his own followers to revolt, and they rallied to his cousin, Ashraf, whose father had been murdered by Mahmud. Ashraf proved to be an exceptional but ruthless military leader who was even able to defeat an Ottoman army which had sought to take advantage of the weakness of the Safavids by invading Persia.

Nadir Shah, a Chagatai Turk of the Afshar clan from the Safavid's Central Asian domains, was able to rally Persia around him in the name of his Safavid sovereign. In a series of victories, Nadir wrested control of Mashad (Khorasan) from the Abdali Pashtuns in 1729, defeated Ashraf and his Ghilzais in 1730, retook Herat from the Abdalis in 1732, overcame rebels in the Caucasus, and by 1736 was able to proclaim himself shah of Persia in place of an effete Safavid puppet. In 1738 he reasserted Persian suzerainty in Kandahar before undertaking his invasion of India in 1738–39.

For his Indian expedition, Nadir Shah had begun recruiting mercenaries from among both the Abdalis and the Ghilzais who between them made up all the tribes, sub-tribes, clans and sub-clans by which the Pashtuns identified themselves. Nadir had been much impressed by their fighting qualities in the course of his campaigns against them, and was astute enough to win them over through his generous treatment after their defeats. The Afghans became the elite corps of his army in which he placed his complete trust. This body of men, which included the young man who was to become Ahmad Shah, accompanied Nadir to India. Nadir Shah's partiality to the Afghans came eventually to be resented by his other followers and mercenaries (Persian, Georgian, Qizilbash and Turkmen), and was one of the principal causes of his assassination in 1747. The commander of his personal bodyguard of 4000 Afghans, and the guardian of his treasury, was Ahmad Khan Abdali, who was powerless to protect his king, greatly outnumbered as the Afghans were by the other contingents of Nadir's army. He and his men had to fight their way back from Isfahan to Kandahar.

After Nadir's death, his commanders dispersed to build mini-states of their own in the Persian lands. The fragmentation of political power and the rivalries of Afsharids, Bakhtiari, Qajars and Zands ended only in 1797, when a Qajar chief, Agha Mohammad Khan, became shah of Persia and founded a dynasty that lasted until 1925.

Ahmad Shah's ambitions to found an empire of his own may have been fired by his perception of the weakness of Persia and Moghul India, centred as these empires were on decadent courts and effete, self-indulgent rulers.

After his capture of Delhi, Nadir Shah had obtained not only the Peacock Throne and the most valuable of the Moghul treasures, including the fabulous Koh-i-Noor diamond ('the mountain of light'), as well as an immense amount of other loot, but also the cession to Persia of the whole region west of the Indus, including its chief city, Peshawar. Ahmad Shah would have considered himself the natural successor of Nadir Shah in the eastern Persian domains.

The long-term significance of Ahmad Shah's conquests is that they began the process that constitutes the subsequent political history of Afghanistan. The Abdali-led confederation of 1747 was by no means a state. It was a loose alliance of tribes sharing a strong Pashtun cultural identity. Their common aim was conquest, pillage, and the extraction of tribute from conquered peoples and territories.

Ahmad Shah had earned his credentials as an outstanding warrior chief in the service of Nadir Shah. He came from a small clan, the Saddozai branch of the Popolzai Pashtuns, themselves a major sub-tribe of the Abdalis, and was therefore acceptable in that his potential for advancing the interests of his own clan at the expense of the major Abdali clans appeared limited. Most importantly he derived his legitimacy by tribal consensus, from a Great Assembly (loya jirga) of representatives, elders and warriors of the various Pashtun tribes who enthroned him as padshah (king) in Kandahar. A sheaf of wheat or barley – a fertility symbol – was placed on Ahmad Shah's head and he was crowned Padshah, Durri-i-Dauran (Shah, Pearl of the Age). He is then said to have had a dream which inspired him to change his honorific title to Durr-i-Durran (Pearl of Pearls), thus becoming Ahmad Shah Durrani. Durrani became the name of the dynasty and the Abdali Pashtuns came to be known as Durranis. Ahmad Shah was in the traditional tribal context only a chief among equals. He also had some luck: in addition to Nadir Shah's personal treasury, he captured a rich caravan laden with treasures looted by Nadir Shah in Delhi that was on its way to Persia. This gave him a solid financial basis to reward his loyal followers and to secure the adherence of the Afghan chiefs who might not have otherwise accepted his leadership.

It is not easy to discern a coherent direction or pattern in the political history of Afghanistan after Ahmad Shah to show that it was set inevitably on the path to statehood, not to speak of nationhood. The first British envoy to the Afghan court, Mountstuart Elphinstone, who visited the Afghan ruler at his winter capital of Peshawar in 1809, had this to say of the dynastic successor:

> For the consolidation of his power at home he relied, in great measure, on the effects of his foreign wars. If these were successful, his victories would raise his reputation, and his conquests would supply him with the means of maintaining an army and of attaching the Afghan chiefs by favours and rewards: the hope of

plunder would induce many tribes to join him whom he could not easily have compelled to submit.[2]

Ahmad Shah was succeeded, not without the usual family and clannish intrigues, by a favourite son, Timur, who was his chosen heir. Timur Shah (1772–93) moved the dynastic capital from Kandahar, the traditional power-base of the Abdalis, to Kabul. Benefiting from his father's prestige, the Durrani Empire, although subject to intermittent revolts, remained largely intact for a period of 20 years, leaving the indolent Timur to devote his main energies to the care of his large harem. He fathered uncounted numbers of children, 36 by his legal wives alone. Twenty-three of these were sons, who could all, in the absence of a law of primogeniture in Muslim dynasties, individually lay claim to the succession. Success depended on how much support each could muster from influential tribal leaders and groups. Harem intrigues and poisonings could also play a decisive role.[3]

After Timur's death, fratricidal struggles for the succession continued for a long time, until a candidate with strong qualities of leadership appeared on the scene. This was Dost Mohammad, a scion of the powerful Barakzai branch of the Abdalis, the Mohammadzais. During this Afghan 'time of troubles', Ahmad Shah's empire disintegrated. Ibn Khaldûn's schematic analysis of the rise and decline of Muslim dynasties or states is very pertinent in this regard.[4] In the Afghan context, Louis Dupree called this process the cycle of 'fusion and fission'.

The internal power struggles within the Durrani ruling class had led to breakaway movements in the non-Pashtun components of the empire. The Mirs of Sind, the Khans of Baluchistan and the Uzbek Begs in the north escaped Kabul's control. External pressures and invasions aggravated the fissiparous trends. The Amir of Bokhara invaded across the Amu Darya to seize Balkh and support revolts against Pashtun hegemony. Punjab and Kashmir were lost to the rampaging Sikhs under Ranjit Singh who also destroyed the beautiful winter palace and gardens of Peshawar, so vividly described by Elphinstone, and reduced its governor, a brother of Dost Mohammad, to the status of a vassal. Thus when Dost Mohammad proclaimed himself amir in 1826, he effectively controlled only Kabul and Ghazni, while some other regions submitted to his nominal authority only intermittently when he was able to overcome them by force or through alliances.

A little over a century after Ahmad Shah had woven together a powerful Afghan confederation, a British general, Sir Henry Rawlinson, observed: 'The nation consists of a mere collection of tribes, of unequal power and divergent habits, which are held together, more or less loosely, according to the personal character of the chief who rules them. The feeling of patriotism, as known in Europe, cannot exist among Afghans, for there is no common country.'[5]

Ironically, it was European imperialism in Asia that gave Afghanistan a local habitation and a name. Robert Clive's victory at Plassey in 1757 had started Britain on its course of stumbling into an empire in India, in a fit of absent-mindedness, it has been said. It was a process made easier by Ahmad Shah's elimination of the Hindu Marathas as serious local contenders for paramount power in north India, in the vacuum created by the decline of Moghul rule. By 1849, the wars with the Sikhs, who had made themselves masters of the Punjab, brought the British into the territories west of the Indus, nominally under the suzerainty of the amir of Kabul. It was in fact Dost Mohammad himself who had appealed in 1836 for British help to restrain Ranjit Singh and his Sikhs.

The empire-building of the czars of Russia had begun under Peter the Great, and expanded dramatically under Catherine the Great, who took advantage of the declining power of the Ottoman Turks through territorial acquisition at their expense. In 1783 the Russians annexed the Crimea, which gave them control over the north coast of the Black Sea. Between 1800 and 1833 they pushed forward through the regions between the Black Sea and the Caspian, and began in 1834 to penetrate the Central Asian steppes north of the Syr Darya (Jaxartes).

It was the fear of Russian intrigues and ambitions in the region, which appeared to threaten Britain's interests in India, that provoked the British to undertake two major interventions in Afghanistan. The first was to thwart the Persians who, with Russian military support, attempted to retake Herat in 1838, and to replace the independent-minded Amir Dost Mohammad with the pliable Shah Shuja, who had spent 30 years as an exile in British India after his eviction from power in 1809. The second was in 1878 when, fearful of the spreading Russian influence in the region, advocates of the British 'forward policy' sent in troops to occupy Kabul, Kandahar and Jalalabad.

The first British military expedition, called the First Anglo-Afghan War, was futile and disastrous: the Persian siege of Herat was lifted before the pompously named 'Army of the Indus' crossed into Afghan territory. The British military occupation of Kabul from 1839 to 1842, to prop up an ineffectual and unpopular Shah Shuja, proved untenable because of the fierce hostility of the population and their increasingly effective armed attacks on the British garrison. The subsequent British retreat to Jalalabad, through narrow mountain defiles and passes in the harshest wintry conditions, with the long columns of soldiers and civilians being continuously shot at and ambushed by ferocious Ghilzai tribesmen from the surrounding hills, turned into a harrowing death march. The result was the almost total annihilation of some 9500 British-Indian troops, including 600 English officers and their wives and children, and some 12,000 Indian camp followers.[6]

This severe blow to the prestige of British imperial arms was bloodily avenged the next year by the sack of Kabul. The Second Anglo-Afghan War demonstrated to the British, as the Soviets found to their cost a century later, that it was easier to hold the cities than to control the countryside. As Sir Olaf Caröe stated, 'the object and result of these wars was to keep the relatively young Afghan state out of the orbit of czarist Russia and within that of India'.[7]

During this 'Great Game' as Kipling called it,[8] Afghanistan became a buffer state. The rivalries of the two imperial powers led them to contain each other by fixing 'strategic frontiers', which were later endorsed bilaterally in the Anglo-Russian Convention of St Petersburg of 1907, a treaty that was part of the realignment of European alliances constituting 'the march of folly' described by Barbara Tuchman that led to the First World War.

The terms 'Afghan' and 'Pashtun' have sometimes been used without distinction to refer to the inhabitants of a region that since very ancient times has been the crossroads of Asia. Invasions and migrations have left an extremely complex ethnic, linguistic, tribal and cultural patchwork that gives credence to the observation that there is no such thing as an Afghan. The Pashtuns referred to themselves as Pashtuns; the Persians were the first to call them Afghans.[9] While they were numerically in the majority and politically dominant, the Pashtuns are only one of the 20-odd distinct groups that coexist within the contemporary frontiers of Afghanistan. Louis Dupree listed and described 20 groups,[10] including their respective antecedents and habitats, from the dominant Pashtuns who speak Pashtu, followed by the Farsi-speaking Tajiks, the Turkic Uzbeks, to the smaller minorities. These latter are (in descending order of numerical importance): Hazara, Aymak, Farsiwan, Brahui, Baluchi, Turkomen, Nuristani, Kohistani, Pamiri, Kirghiz, Gujar, Moghol, Arab, Qizilbash, Hindus, Sikhs and Jews.[11]

PART I: THE BUILDING OF THE STATE

CHAPTER 1

The 'Iron Amir': Abdur Rahman Khan (1880–1901)

W hen Abdur Rahman was recognized as Amir of Afghanistan by the British in 1880 he had spent 11 years in exile in Samarkand and Tashkent, living on a generous stipend from the governor-general and commander of the Russian forces in Central Asia, General K. von Kaufman. He had been given the opportunity, however, as a guest of the Russians, to perceive that the greatest threat to Afghan independence came from the north. As he wrote in his autobiography:

> The Russian policy of aggression is slow and steady, but firm and unchangeable. ... Their habit of forward movement resembles the habit of an elephant, who examines a spot thoroughly before he places his foot upon it, and when once he puts his weight there is no going back, and not taking another step in a hurry until he has put his full weight on the first foot, and has smashed everything that lies under it.[1]

The new state had no choice but to follow a policy of neutrality. As Abdur Rahman himself said, 'How can a small power like Afghanistan, which is like a goat between two lions, or a grain of wheat between two strong millstones of the grinding mill, stand in the midway of the stones without being ground to dust?'[2]

The new amir was a grandson of the resilient Dost Mohammad, who had returned to Kabul as amir in 1843, after a self-imposed exile in India as a guest of the British who had ousted him in the first place.[3] The cornerstones of Dost Mohammad's policy were to restore internal Afghan unity, which had so eluded him during his previous reign, and to keep on friendly terms with the British. He reconquered Kandahar, Mazar-i-Sharif and the north, and reoccupied Peshawar after it was abandoned by the Sikhs during the two Anglo-Sikh Wars of 1845–46 and 1848–49. These wars had also resulted in the British occupation of Kashmir, which they sold in 1846 to the Hindu rajah of the adjacent autonomous state of Jammu, and in their permanent

1

annexation of the Punjab in 1849. In 1843, the British had also seized the turbulent realms of the Mirs of Sind, formerly tributaries of the amirs of Kabul. This gave them control of the Indus, and provided a convenient base of operations for their future incursions into Afghan territories west of the Indus.[4]

Since developments in Persia, Europe, India and Central Asia had a direct or indirect bearing on Afghan history before the accession of Abdur Rahman and during his reign, it is necessary to open a long parenthesis at this stage of the narrative.

In 1855 the British were concerned (as in 1838) by Persian designs on Herat, behind which they saw a hidden Russian hand, and by the uncertain outcome relative to west and Central Asia of the Crimean War which was then being fought. They therefore sought and obtained a treaty of friendship with Dost Mohammad. The Treaty of Peshawar of 30 March 1855 embodied three points: mutual peace and friendship, respect for each other's territorial integrity, and a commitment that the friends and enemies of one party were to be considered friends and enemies of the other. In October 1856 the Persians occupied Herat, with the collusion of the ruling Afghan Durrani prince of the Saddozai branch, hostile to the Mohammadzai ruler of Kabul, Dost Mohammad, who threatened his autonomy. The Persian aggression immediately precipitated a three-month war with the British in which the Persians were defeated, evacuated Herat, and agreed to abandon forever their irredentist claims to the area. Thus for the first time, imperial Britain, acting in its own self-interest, guaranteed Afghanistan's territorial integrity.

At the beginning of the Persian war, Dost was invited to Peshawar to sign a supplementary agreement under which he was to receive a subsidy of one lakh of rupees (£10,000) per month, for the duration of the war, in order to maintain an army capable of resisting aggression from the west and the north. It must be said that while the honourable Dost kept his side of the bargain, the British did not, as Dost and his successors were to discover to their cost. The sincerity of the amir's friendship for the British was put to a severe test when the so-called Indian Mutiny broke out in May 1857.

Many hotheads in Dost's entourage wanted him to assist their fellow Muslims who were revolting in British India. But the amir resisted. It may have been due to an ingrained Pashtun sense of honour – a promise was a promise to be kept. He may also have been keenly aware of British power based on its human and material resources, both in India and in Europe, where the Crimean War had ended in a Russian defeat. During the Mutiny, the amir reiterated to the British his pledge of non-interference.

Dost Mohammad died in 1863, a month after he had conquered Herat and realized his dream of Afghan unity. Dupree refers to a popular Afghan saying which would be a fitting epitaph: 'Is Dost Mohammad dead that there is now no justice in the land?' It would also be a telling comment on the situation that prevailed after his passing – another concrete illustration of Dupree's theory of 'fusion and fission'.

Dost Mohammad had outlived three of his favourite sons and had passed over his two oldest surviving sons, Afzal and Azam, to designate their younger half-brother, Sher Ali, as his successor. True to form, a fratricidal war followed, with Sher Ali defeating his two rebellious elder half-brothers, and then turning on his two full brothers and defeating them in a battle at which he lost his eldest son and heir. Meanwhile Afzal Khan's son, Abdur Rahman, who had fled to Bukhara after his father's defeat, raised an army in the north and defeated Sher Ali in three consecutive battles with the help of his uncle Azam. He then entered Kabul and placed his father on the throne in May 1866. When Afzal died in 1867, Azam succeeded him. But he soon alienated his nephew, and Abdur Rahman left Kabul for Mazar-i-Sharif and, after Sher Ali's reconquest of Kabul and Kandahar in January 1869 to re-affirm his former authority as amir, moved into a long exile in Russian Central Asia.

These last ten years of Sher Ali's rule were to prove decisive for the future of Afghanistan. Relying as his father did on his friendship with the British, he was overwhelmed by the local effects of external events over which he had no control. These events and developments affected in the long run not only the territorial integrity of Afghanistan and defined its future borders, but also the sovereignty of its rulers over their own territory.

The background to these developments was the steady expansion of the czarist empire eastwards beyond the Urals to the Pacific, and southwards to the Black Sea, the Caucasus and across to the Central Asian steppes. The empire-building had begun with Peter the Great (1672–1725), the first Russian czar or emperor, and continued inexorably under Catherine the Great (1729–96), who also transformed Russia into a European power to be reckoned with. She acquired more territory in the south by waging a series of successful wars against the Ottoman Turks. The Russian annexation of the Crimea in 1783 had given her control of the north coast of the Black Sea. By 1833 Russia had pushed forward towards the Caspian, coming into armed conflict on the way with the Persians. In that same year, after success in another war with the Turks, the Russians concluded the Treaty of Unkiar-Skelessi, which also imposed a virtual Russian protectorate over the Ottoman dependencies in the Balkans. Russia's pretext was the protection of the sultan's Christian Orthodox subjects, but her objectives were much more ambitious.

The roots of what came to be known as the 'Eastern Question' were the decline of Ottoman power and the efforts of some of the European powers, mainly czarist Russia, to take advantage of the situation to fulfil their own imperialist agendas. The Russians had already nibbled at and gnawed away the territories of the Ottoman sultan, who had now become the 'Sick Man of Europe'. There was a two-fold threat to the fragile edifice of the European balance of power, built up and carefully tended by statesmen, notably Metternich and Palmerston, after Napoleon's final defeat at Waterloo and the Congress of Vienna in 1815.

The first of these threats was the surge of nationalistic feelings among the restless Christian subjects of the sultan that not only threatened the peace but also invited outside intervention. As the majority of these Christians were affiliated to Orthodox churches organized along ethnic national lines, the Russians claimed that the Treaty of Kutchuk-Kainardji, concluded in 1774 after a military victory over the Turks that gave them freedom of navigation in the Black Sea and the right to send their merchant ships through the Bosphorus and the Dardanelles Straits, had also accorded them the right to make representations on behalf of the sultan's Christian Orthodox subjects.

This treaty was followed by others that registered further Russian gains at the expense of the Ottoman Turks: the Treaties of Jassy (1792) and Bucharest (1812) confirmed the annexations of the Crimea and of Bessarabia, and also gave the Russians control of the whole northern hinterland of the Black Sea between the Pruth and Kuban rivers. The 1812 treaty also extracted from the Turks the grant of a measure of autonomy to their provinces of Wallachia and Moldavia. Russian intervention in support of the Greek War of Independence, which began in 1821, had the Turks suing for peace, and led to the Treaty of Adrianople (1829), under which the Russians extracted more concessions: territory at the mouth of the Danube and in the Caucasus, a virtual Russian protectorate over Wallachia and Moldavia, autonomy for Greece, and to a lesser extent for the Serbs who had begun their revolt against Turkish rule in 1804.

In 1832 the Russians occupied the Dardanelles, purportedly in defence of the sultan against the forces of the Albanian Mohammad Ali, the talented and militant Ottoman governor of Egypt who had developed ambitions of his own. The Treaty of Unkiar-Skelessi of 1833 was a signal of Russian intentions to establish a virtual protectorate over the sultan's European provinces, and to wrest control from the Turks of the Dardanelles, which would have given their navy direct and untrammelled access to the warm-water ports of the Mediterranean for the first time.

These Russian actions, which were carried out unilaterally, thus threatened to unravel the whole fabric of the balance of power in Europe. Britain and Austria especially were determined to replace the bilateral provisions of the 1833 treaty with internationally endorsed regulations concerning the Straits. They succeeded in this by concluding the Straits Convention of 1841 to which Russia and Turkey were also parties, thereby setting a precedent for concerted international action on the Eastern Question. In so doing they

replaced the implicit Russian protectorate over the sultan's European domin-
ions with a general European protectorate that included Turkey. The main
idea was to ensure that the Ottoman Empire did not collapse, or, if it did,
that the outcome would not favour any single European state and endanger
the balance of power.

The next major Russian intervention in Turkish affairs led to the Crimean War in which, as a result of diplomatic miscalculations on the part of
Czar Nicholas I, Russia had to face an armed coalition of European states
arrayed against her in defence of Turkey. The Treaty of Paris (1856), which
ended the war, was a major setback for Russia: the return of southern Bessarabia to Turkey, the placing of Wallachia, Moldavia and Serbia under
international guarantees, and the interdiction of Russian naval vessels in the
Black Sea.

The Crimean War was also of major significance to nineteenth-century
Europe. It signalled the collapse of the Concert of Europe, whereby the
victors in the war against Napoleon – Britain, Russia, Austria and Prussia –
had cooperated to maintain the peace of Europe for four decades. The break-
up of the old coalition permitted the autonomous German and Italian states
to free themselves from Austrian influence and unite to become major
European powers and eventually imperialists in their own right.

The last major Russian intervention in Europe occurred as a result of a
general uprising in the Balkans against Turkish rule that led to a Russian
declaration of war against Turkey. The war of 1877–78 ended in a crushing
Turkish defeat. In the Treaty of San Stefano of 3 March 1878, the Russians
exacted a heavy price. In addition to the payment of a large indemnity, the
Turks were deprived of almost all their European possessions: the recognition
of the independence of Serbia, Montenegro, Romania (Wallachia and Moldavia) and of a Greater Bulgaria, and a Russian right to occupy Bulgaria for
two years. Turkey also had to cede to Russia the Danube delta, the Dobruja
region and four regions in the Caucasus.

Bismarck, the Prussian 'Iron Chancellor' of a consolidated German
Empire, was called upon to play the role of 'honest broker' at the Congress of
Berlin (June–July 1878), convened to deal with the implications of the latest
developments relating to the Eastern Question. The Congress was a turning
point in the history of Europe, as well as in world history, since it heralded
the beginnings of a generalized scramble for empire, especially in Africa, by
the major European powers, including Germany. But the Congress itself was
convened by the foreign minister of Austria-Hungary to curb Russian he-
gemonistic ambitions in the Balkans.

The Berlin Congress, while acknowledging the principle of national self-
determination for the Balkan peoples, also re-affirmed the principle that the
status of the Ottoman Empire and of its constituent territories was to be

jointly decided, and not through unilateral measures. The territorial dispensations adopted in Berlin were as follows: Serbia and Montenegro were accorded their independence, but their territory was reduced; Romania was declared independent, but Russia was allowed to retain Bessarabia (now Moldova), with Romania compensated by the addition of the Dobruja region; Bulgaria was divided into three parts, of which two (Eastern Rumelia and Macedonia) were allowed to continue under Turkish rule; Bosnia and Herzegovina were mandated to Austria-Hungary; and finally, in return for a guarantee covering Asiatic Turkey, Great Britain obtained from the Turks the use of Cyprus as a naval base.

Benjamin Disraeli, prime minister since 1874 and British plenipotentiary at the Congress of Berlin, was undoubtedly the star of the show, in Bismarck's words: 'Der alte Jude, dast ist der Mann' ('That old Jew, he's the man'). Disraeli had manoeuvred adroitly to prevent Russia from gaining any strategic advantages in the eastern Mediterranean. He succeeded brilliantly. Cyprus was a bonus. On his return to London Disraeli announced that the Congress of Berlin had brought 'peace with honour'.[5]

Disraeli was an unabashed imperialist and leading advocate of the 'forward policy' in India and Afghanistan.[6] But when he put an end to its European ambitions, Russia then turned with renewed vigour towards Asia, a *Drang nach Osten* (drive towards the East) that was to cause many a headache in the British chancelleries of London and Calcutta. Moreover, the full aspirations of some of the Balkan peoples were frustrated. Neither Disraeli nor Bismarck had much sympathy for the Balkan Slavs whom they considered violent trouble makers.[7] But their unfulfilled aspirations led to prolonged tensions that did not augur well for the European future: the assassin's bullet that triggered the First World War was fired in the Bosnian capital of Sarajevo.

It is interesting to note that the dispensations of the Congress of Berlin did not cover Russian territorial acquisitions at the expense of Turkey north and east of the Black Sea. What was not forbidden was therefore permitted. After their defeat in the Crimean War, the Russians resumed their steady advance from the Caspian to the Aral Sea, which they reached by 1864. They then proceeded further east by imposing their control over the Central Asian steppes north of the Syr Darya (Jaxartes), before penetrating southwards to the Amu Darya (Oxus). These rivers loosely defined the confines of the domains of the amir of Bukhara. In 1869 Russia had reduced the amir to vassal status, and had taken control of the cities of Tashkent and Samarkand. In 1872 the Russians moved into the territory of the khanate of Khiva bordering on Afghanistan. In 1876 they occupied the khanate of Kokand further east, which brought them to the borders of Chinese Sinkiang.

Such was the geo-political situation in Central Asia that confronted the Amir Sher Ali and the British in the last quarter of the century. The Great Game was on. When Disraeli became prime minister, the tacit policy of non-intervention in the internal affairs of Afghanistan ended, and was replaced by the 'forward policy', the blueprint for which had been prepared by Sir Henry Rawlinson in 1868 when the Russians were advancing towards the Oxus. Its main objectives, which were rejected at the time, were to occupy Quetta in Baluchistan, gain control of the Afghan area by subsidizing the amir as a British protégé, and establish a permanent British mission in Kabul to keep the Russians at bay. In 1876 Disraeli appointed Lord Lytton as viceroy of India to implement the new policy.

In 1876 Quetta was occupied and converted into a forward military base. An Indian Muslim had represented the British in Kabul since the reign of Dost Mohammad, and the Russians had sent a Muslim agent in 1875 as their representative at the court of Sher Ali. When the viceroy demanded that the amir accept a European-staffed mission in Kabul, Sher Ali refused on the grounds that the Russians might want reciprocal rights. The British reply was that they had received Russian assurances that Afghanistan was outside their sphere of interest – assurances treated with some scepticism by the amir and contradicted in a letter containing veiled threats and insinuations that he had received from the Russian commander in Central Asia, General von Kauf-man, which he passed on to the viceroy as his response.

In the meantime, developments were precipitated by the arrival in Kabul on 22 July 1878, a day after the signing of the Treaty of Berlin, of a Russian diplomatic mission led by General Stolietov without the authorization of Sher Ali. The timing was surely a coincidence, more as a response to the implementation of Britain's forward policy than to developments in Europe. Three weeks later the viceroy demanded that Sher Ali accept a British mission, to counter the Russian one. Sher Ali's response was delayed, as he had gone into the traditionally long period of mourning after the death of a son, his designated heir.

The British, with little understanding or sensitivity, accused him of procrastination, and sent in an officer, Major Louis Cavagnari, to herald the arrival of the mission led by Sir Neville Chamberlain. Permission was politely refused, but the refusal was considered a national insult to the British, who issued an ultimatum calling for an explanation by 20 November. The reply, which arrived on 19 October, was held to be unsatisfactory and the British launched a three-pronged attack into Afghan territory on 21 November. One column advanced from Quetta to Kandahar, another through the Khyber Pass into Jalalabad, and a central column, commanded by Sir Frederick Roberts, advanced through Kurram.

A desperate Sher Ali had concluded a defensive alliance with the Russians, and appealed for military assistance when the British invaded. When General von Kaufman refused, citing the daunting logistics of moving masses of men and materials over the Hindu Kush in winter, Sher Ali travelled to Mazar-i-Sharif with the intention of proceeding to St Petersburg to plead his cause in person with the czar. His attempts to proceed were blocked by the Russians, who advised him to make his peace with the British. It is possible that von Kaufman had already been apprised of the assurance given to London by St Petersburg that the Russian mission in Kabul would be withdrawn, since, after Berlin, war no longer threatened their two countries in Europe.

If this assurance was sincere or true, it would appear that the Second Anglo-Afghan War was a futile exercise as far as British interests were concerned.[8] But once a course of action is decided upon and undertaken, subsequent events take on a life of their own, generate their own momentum, and are driven by an inner logic, however undesirable or irrational the consequences. The three-pronged invasion of Afghanistan could not have been a hastily planned enterprise, launched at short notice. All that was needed was a pretext.

In February 1879 Sher Ali died in Mazar. His eldest son, Yaqub Khan, acting as regent in Kabul, signed the Treaty of Gandamak in May 1879 in order to forestall further British advances into Afghan territory. Yaqub had no choice. He was under pressure, and there was no organized internal resistance at this stage to stop the British forces. The main points of the treaty, disgraceful to Afghan eyes, were that the British would control Afghanistan's foreign affairs, with British representatives resident in Kabul and other cities whose security would be guaranteed by the amir. He also had to cede large areas west of the Indus – Kurram, Pishin and Sibi – and agree to the extension of British control to the Khyber and Michni passes.

This meant in effect the virtual secession of the Peshawar Valley and of other Afghan territories west of the Indus that, less than 15 years later, would serve the British in the demarcation of the Durand Line – thereafter the de facto frontier between Afghanistan and British India. In return for these concessions, the amir was to receive £60,000 a year and some vaguely worded guarantees of assistance in case of foreign aggression.

In July 1879 Cavagnari arrived with an escort to take up his functions as British Resident in Kabul. Surrounded by a hostile population, he was murdered in September by mutinous Afghan soldiers who had been assigned to protect him. In retaliation General Roberts moved from his base in Kurram and reached Kabul on 12 October 1879. Yaqub abdicated his throne and went into exile in India. Roberts then became the virtual ruler of Kabul, instigating a rule of terror that was bitterly resisted. The British forces found themselves under siege. In the meantime Abdur Rahman had crossed the

Oxus, and, with the help of the northern khans and begs who rallied to his cause, marched on Kabul, declaring himself amir in Charikar, north of Kabul, on 20 July 1880. The British had in fact endorsed him as a credible candidate for the amirate in Kabul. But meanwhile, on 27 July, the forces of the Afghan resistance under the command of Ayub Khan, another son of Sher Ali, that had gathered in Ghazni inflicted a disastrous defeat on the British in open battle at Maiwand, near Kandahar. The battle produced a famous Afghan heroine, Malalai, who, seeing the men faltering, used her veil as a standard and encouraged the warriors by shouting:

Young love, if you do not fall in the battle of Maiwand,
By God, someone is saving you as a token of shame.[9]

As before, the loss of British prestige could not be left unavenged. Roberts put together a mobile force that marched with remarkable speed from Kabul to Kandahar to defeat Ayub. For his superior generalship in the Afghan War, he was ennobled as Lord Roberts of Kandahar. In the British elections of April 1880, however, Disraeli's Tories had been defeated by Gladstone's Liberals. The new prime minister replaced Lord Lytton as viceroy, and it was decided to withdraw the remaining British forces from Kandahar in April 1881, much to the chagrin of the leading advocates of the forward policy. A new era in Afghanistan had begun.

The situation of Afghanistan is somewhat unique in the Muslim world. The territory owed its existence as a political entity to the rivalry between foreign imperialist powers who made it into a harmless buffer state. Technically it was never a colony, but the Treaty of Gandamak had imposed limitations on the amir's sovereignty. As the Great Game played itself out, the amir was forced to accept other infringements of his sovereignty.

The Russian advances in Central Asia continued, and followed their own logic in geo-political terms: south-west of the Oxus, the khanate of Khiva was subdued in 1881 in a horrendous scenario involving the wholesale massacre of the 6000 defenders of the Tekke Turcoman fortress of Goek Tepe, followed by the occupation of the Oasis of Merv in 1884 – causing an outbreak of 'Mervousness' in British imperial circles, according to some irreverent London wags – and the occupation of the Pandjeh Oasis in 1886.

The occupation of the Pandjeh Oasis provoked a crisis, since the area was traditionally an Afghan territory that paid tribute to the governor of Herat. Afghan troops in the area fought the Russians and were defeated. But as Britain had made itself responsible for the conduct of Afghanistan's foreign affairs, London informed St Petersburg that an attack would be considered a threat to Britain. But the threat was not followed up when the Russians occupied the Pandjeh, causing Abdur Rahman to complain that he could not rely on British assistance, despite their pledges, in his time of need. But during this so-called Pandjeh Incident, it was made clear to the Russians that any further advance south into Afghan territory, such as Herat, would amount to a casus belli. In fact Russian nationalist opinion called for the seizure of Herat as the first step in reaching the Indian Ocean and realizing the dream of a warm-water port, especially now that the Dardanelles was out of bounds.[10]

Eventually a joint Anglo-Russian boundary commission fixed the north-western frontier with Turkestan, as the whole of Russian Central Asia came to be called. In 1895–96 another commission, again without Afghan partici-pation, established the frontier in the north-east. Since the British did not want to be faced with a common frontier with Russia, they imposed Afghan sovereignty over the Wakhan Corridor in the High Pamirs, against the wishes of the amir who, as he said, had enough problems with his own people and did not want to be held responsible for 'the Kirghiz bandits' in the Wakhan and the Pamirs.[11] This inaccessible region of perpetual glaciers gave Afghani-stan a common frontier with China for the first time in history.

Alongside the Russian advances in Central Asia, the British were consoli-dating their hold on the nominally Afghan areas west of the Indus by bludgeoning the local Pashtun rulers and tribal chiefs into acquiescence, and by building a string of fortified outposts to keep out armed incursions into the valleys and plains of the frontier regions by raiders from the Afghan side who were outside the range of their punitive action. The Durand Line, a contentious issue in Anglo-Afghan relations (and later with Pakistan), was designed to bring stability to the frontier regions.

The external pressures on Afghanistan generated a kind of nationalism, not strong enough to forge a national consciousness, or a sense of national unity, but strong enough, together with its religion, to reinforce the tradi-tional Afghan spirit of independence. Islam brought together Afghans of all social classes in times of national crisis. But perceptions of what was in the national interest differed radically. For the backward, unlettered, rural masses, subject to the petrifying influence of malik and mullah, nationalism meant the conservation of a traditional way of life. The spirit of independ-ence took on a nationalistic dimension when the country was threatened by non-Muslim powers, British or Russian. Then resistance took on the specifi-cally religious aspect of a jihad (holy war) against 'infidels'. But there was another form of nationalism, actively pursued by the Kabul court and its associated bureaucracy, whose objective was to strengthen Afghan independ-ence through modernization. These different perceptions were to clash dramatically in the twentieth century.

In order to understand the characteristics peculiar to the Afghan state and society, it may be helpful to have recourse to the concept of 'spaces'.[12] The first was geographical space, the territory defined by external powers.

The second space was that occupied by the durable Durrani dynasty and the associated court aristocracy which, however tenuous its hold on the country as a central authority, was a focus for a national consciousness that could sometimes transcend internal rivalries and divisions. This space was considerably strengthened by Abdur Rahman through a ruthless indigenous version of the Bismarckian means of uniting the German states through 'blood and iron'.

The 'Iron Amir' himself described his task as putting 'in order all those hundreds of petty chiefs, plunderers, robbers and cut-throats. This necessitated breaking down the feudal and tribal system and substituting one grand community under one law and one rule.'[13] In almost continuous warfare during his 20-year reign, rebellions were punished by mass executions, or deportations such as the forced resettlement of thousands of Ghilzai Pashtun tribesmen, chief rivals of the dominant Abdalis in regions where they were neutralized in the midst of hostile Hazaras, Uzbeks, Turkmen and Tajiks.[14]

The amir then mobilized the Ghilzais in a jihad against the Shi'ite Hazaras, considered heretical, whom they plundered, displaced and sometimes sold into slavery. Tribe after tribe and ethnic group after ethnic group were subdued. He established a ruthless police force to subjugate suspected opponents and uncooperative officials. Recalcitrant Pashtun leaders were exiled. The pacification of the country was completed by the wholly gratuitous conquest of a remote mountain people in the north-east, the non-Muslim Kalash of Kafiristan (Land of the Unbelievers), who were forcibly converted to Islam. Their habitat was renamed Nuristan (Land of Light). Abdur Rahman tried to keep his countrymen isolated from the world, prohibiting Afghans from travelling abroad without authorization, and screening out alien influences that might undermine Afghan independence.

Lacking a viable resource base to finance his campaigns and impose his will, Abdur Rahman was dependent on the British for substantial supplies of arms and ammunition. In 1882 the British granted him an annual subsidy of 1.2 million Indian rupees, raised to 1.8 million rupees in 1893 when the Durand Line was demarcated, and to 1.85 million in 1897 at the time of the imposition of the Wakhan Corridor on the amir. These subsidies partially financed the recruitment of conscripts as troops, independent of the tribal levies, and who were accountable to the amir alone. Village and clan elders were also obliged to supply the amir with one eligible fighting man from groups of eight households, with the other seven households taxed to provide for his support. Armed with his powers of coercion, the amir was also able to expand his domestic tax base, by levying direct taxes on landowners.

Abdur Rahman also sought to legitimize his power in Islamic terms by assuming the role of *imam*, or spiritual leader of the Afghan *millat*, the geographical sub-division of the community of the Muslim faithful (the *umma*).

He linked his temporal power to his assumed religious role by insisting that as vice-regent of Allah, who appointed kings as shepherds to guard his flock, he derived his duties and responsibilities from the will of Allah and ruled by divine guidance. He claimed that as he was called upon to wage a holy war by unifying and strengthening the country against infidels, it was the duty of all good Muslims to support his efforts, for example by paying taxes.

In his self-proclaimed role of imam, the amir assumed the prerogative of *mujtahid*, or interpreter of the *shari'a*, thus depriving the *ulema* (theologians and jurisprudents) of their authority in religious matters. He took over the administration of the religious endowments (*waqf*) that had ensured the economic self-sufficiency, independence and power of the clerical establishment. The amir also set up ministerial departments to oversee the administration of justice and education, traditional monopolies of the clerics, thus turning the latter into paid servants of the state. As such they were ordered to undergo formal examinations to prove their suitability as state officials, a strategy aimed at controlling their numbers. These measures severely undermined the power of the ulema.

Abdur Rahman also sought to detach the khans and other dignitaries from their local ethnic and tribal ties through a mix of strategies. He split the major provinces into districts and sub-districts that did not correspond to tribal and ethnic territorial divisions. He appointed governors and administrators who were neither members of his immediate family, whom he kept at court in order to prevent them from creating political mischief in the provinces, nor indigenous to the regions they administered on his behalf. He decreed that all taxes collected locally were to be remitted to the centre.

Borrowing from the hierarchical system of state organization characteristic of the Ottomans and other Turkic peoples, Abdur Rahman tried to create an elite class of bureaucrats dependent on him alone and detached from their tribal or ethnic affiliations. The core of this elite was from the royal family and from among the leading chiefs of the Mohammadzai clan whose power-base was in Kandahar. The amir kept his own sons at court and also had other leading notables reside in Kabul, physically removed from their local power-bases and ethnic or tribal forces. These measures were designed to pre-empt the usual power struggles at the death of a ruler and ensure an orderly succession to the throne. Sons of influential families in the provinces were also brought to court as hostages for their fathers' good behaviour and to be trained to serve the state. Another innovation was the recruitment of slave boys (*ghulam bache*) from areas forcibly brought by the amir under his control and from leading non-Pashtun families, who were also trained, like the Janissaries in the Ottoman Empire, to man the state bureaucracy and officer the army. These were often married off to Mohammadzai women of the ruling class, to reinforce political loyalty through family ties.

As a concession to the Pashtun tradition of a loya jirga from which an Afghan ruler nominally derived his authority, the amir set up a national assembly consisting of aristocrats from the royal clan, village notables and landlords, and members of the ulema. Since he had no intention of sharing power, the assembly's role was purely advisory.

Lord Curzon, later to become a formidable viceroy of India, drew a vivid and balanced portrait of the complex and enigmatic 'Iron Amir', whom he visited in 1894 at his winter palace in Peshawar. During his two-week stay as a private guest of the amir, he had long and candid conversations with him that he recorded in his notebooks and later incorporated into a remarkable essay, in a collection that was published in 1923.[15] Curzon assessed him as follows:

> In the thirteen years that elapsed before my visit, the Amir had consolidated his rule over one of the most turbulent peoples in the world by force alike of character and of arms, and by a relentless savagery that ended by crushing all opposition out of existence, and leaving him the undisputed but dreaded master of the entire country. No previous Sovereign had ridden the wild Afghan steed with so cruel a bit, none had given so large a measure of unity to the kingdom; there was not in Asia or in the world a more fierce or uncompromising despot. ... [But] this terribly cruel man could be affable, gracious, and considerate to a degree. This man of blood loved scents and colours and gardens and singing birds and flowers. This intensely practical being was a prey to mysticism, for he thought he saw dreams and visions.

The amir was fond of quoting the Persian poet Sa'adi, and had an irrepressible sense of humour. On one occasion, writes Curzon, 'he put a man to death unjustly, i.e. on false evidence. Thereupon he fined himself 6,000 rupees, and paid the sum to the widow, who for her part was delighted at being simultaneously rid of a husband and started again in life.'

CHAPTER 2

The Afghan Monarchy

Abdur Rahman bequeathed a rudimentary national state to his son, Habibullah, who succeeded him in an uncontested transition, unusual in Muslim autocracies that had no laws of primogeniture, so well had his father cowed the potential opposition. The foundations of a state bureaucracy had been laid by Abdur Rahman through his policy of appointing provincial governors and other high officials on the basis of their personal loyalty. The policies of Habibullah, and after his assassination in 1919 of his progressive and modernizing son, Amanullah, created a new form of state bureaucracy, independent of the tribal or ethnic networks of power and authority. This new social group, urban and increasingly westernized with the opening of foreign-language schools in Kabul, occupied a third space, at a further remove from the traditional core of rural society, the local community or qawm.

The qawm could be the tribe, a clan or sub-clan, or a village, the power wielded by its traditional chiefs or elders being derived by consensus, and dependent on their ability to dispense patronage. The qawm was an autonomous and somewhat elusive network of relationships, in the eyes of which the state was an intrusion. This vast rural space is Afghanistan proper, and could be described as a community of interests, local and traditional, which, along with the multi-ethnic composition of the population, inhibited the development of a modern nation-state. The interaction of the competing forces of the state, symbolized by Kabul and its bureaucracy, and the qawm would constitute the political history of twentieth-century Afghanistan.

At the village level, the chief or malik was chosen by the male heads of families and represented the community to the state. Maliks were sometimes coopted by the state to serve as its representatives in the qawm. In such cases the malik's position became ambiguous. He could thwart the implementation of unpopular measures decreed by the state by taking evasive action, or he could use his official position to strengthen his personal influence and authority outside the traditional consensus. Either way, there was in such arrangements a potential for corruption, not necessarily seen as such by the qawm, since the bribing of state officials, tax evasion, complicity in the avoidance of military conscription and the like, were defensive actions of the traditional rural communities against the unwelcome encroachments of the state.

On a larger canvas, when provinces and districts were demarcated by the state for administrative and military purposes, a local notable or khan, drawn from the class of important landowners or tribal chiefs, could be nominated by the state to act as its representative in an administrative capacity. His authority or influence was also based on the consensus of the qawm, and sanctioned by his liberality and generosity - 'there is no khan without dastarkhan' (eating cloth), goes the Afghan saying. Such an appointment greatly enhanced the khan's capacity to dispense patronage, by drawing on the state's resources to the advantage of his qawm. He could extend his largesse, obtain state appointments and sinecures for relatives and loyal retainers, and so strengthen his own local power and prestige. In such ways, the conservative social structures rooted in the traditional rural communities of Afghanistan were able to infiltrate the state bureaucracy and its institutions and subvert them to their own interests, to maintain and strengthen the local status quo.

Habibullah (1901-19)

Habibullah's contribution to the process of modernization was not substantial, despite his personal fascination for Western technical inventions. He had the four official wives permitted by Islam, as well as 35 concubines, and sired some 50 children. His father had set up workshops with foreign help to manufacture shoes, soap and other articles for his harem and the ladies of the court. He had hired foreign technicians and advisers to assist in introducing new technology in some limited fields, such as mining. Habibullah commissioned an American engineer to build the country's first hydroelectric plant, to supply power to palaces and public buildings in Kabul. To indulge his passion for motor cars, he had a road built. Another of his private interests was Jules Verne, and he engaged a polyglot Afghan intellectual, Mahmud Khan Tarzi, to translate his science fiction into Persian.

Abdur Rahman had kept the traditional religious establishment on a tight leash, depriving it of its economic power or means of political influence, employing the measures described in the last chapter. In attempts to win over religious notables to counter harem intrigues upon his accession, Habibullah relaxed his father's policy, enabling clerics to regain some of their former power, and to influence the amir's decisions.

Habibullah's main contribution was to assert Afghan independence, and to remove the limitations on his country's sovereignty, such as the right of the government of British India to oversee his foreign relations, imposed by the Treaty of Gandamak in 1879. When he informed the viceroy of India, Lord Curzon, of his accession to the throne in 1901, that high-handed practitioner of the 'forward policy' used the occasion to extract further concessions before recognizing him as amir. With blatant effrontery Curzon replied that the treaty that the British had previously signed was a personal document, and that a new treaty had to be considered. In doing this he was flouting a basic principle of international law that the British, when it suited their purpose, had always insisted on: that treaties were between states, and not between rulers. He also refused the annual British financial subsidy on the same grounds. Habibullah shrewdly concluded that he had therefore no obligations under the existing treaty, and proposed opening diplomatic relations with a number of countries without prior consultations with the viceroy. To the persistent British demands for rail links from Quetta via Kandahar to Kabul, and telegraph links that would have tied his country to British India, and their attempts to restrict the transit through India of arms purchased by the Afghans, Habibullah responded with equal obduracy. He insisted on a new treaty that would acknowledge also his royal and sovereign status as ruler of Afghanistan 'and its dependencies' - the last phrase being a hint that he did not consider the Durand Line as an international frontier. The new agreement was signed in 1905. The arrears of the subsidy, amounting to £40,000, were also paid. Curzon resigned as viceroy later that year, to the applause of Afghan and Indian nationalists, as well as liberals in London.

Habibullah visited India in 1907 as a guest of the new viceroy, the liberal Lord Minto, and was received with due pomp and ceremony; indeed he was taken on the obligatory tiger shoot arranged by the British Raj for visiting dignitaries. He refused, however, to consider the provisions relating to Afghanistan in the St Petersburg Convention of 1907 as binding, on the grounds that his country had not been a party to the treaty.

When the Great War broke out, Habibullah resisted both internal and external pressures to abandon Afghan neutrality. When Ottoman Turkey entered the conflict, the sultan, nominally caliph of the Muslim world, declared a jihad against the 'infidel' Allies. Turkish propaganda conveniently overlooked the fact that the Hashemite guardian of the Islamic holy places, the sherif of Mecca, and his sons, were actively cooperating with the British through agents such as T.E. Lawrence to put an end to the Ottoman occupation of Arab lands in the hope of creating a unified Arab state. Turkey's own allies, Germany and the Habsburg Empire, were also 'infidel' states. These incongruities reached a high level of pantomime when the German kaiser was portrayed in the Turkish press wearing Arab dress and referred to as 'Hajji Wilhelm'.

Habibullah was embarrassed when a Turco-German mission arrived in Kabul in September 1915. They were accompanied by two virulently anti-British Indian nationalists, one a Muslim, the other a Hindu. The mission's objective was to persuade the amir to attack the British in India and the

Russians in Turkestan. Their plans called for the coordination of nationalistic uprisings in India, with simultaneous revolts by Muslims in Central Asia. In return the Germans undertook to provide the amir with a vast quantity of arms, and £20 million sterling in gold. The shrewd amir procrastinated, and began a correspondence with the British in India, indicating that in return for his neutrality they should relinquish their control of Afghanistan's foreign relations. Habibullah did not survive to see this last constraint on Afghan independence removed: he was assassinated during a hunting trip, another of his passions, in February 1919. The identity of his assailants remained a secret, but suitable scapegoats were found and executed.

Amanullah (1919–29)

Amanullah was the first Afghan ruler determined at all costs to pull his nation into the twentieth century. But he lacked the shrewd political sense of his father and grandfather. His clumsy and insensitive efforts to modernize the country came to grief and ended in anarchy. All this despite the fact that he had as a knowledgeable adviser Mahmud Khan Tarzi, one of the most remarkable of early twentieth-century Asian nationalists. It is possible that had Tarzi's advice been followed, Afghan history might have taken a different course.

Tarzi (1865–1933) was born in Ghazni. His father, a grandson of the Amir Dost Mohammad and therefore closely related to the ruling Mohammadzai family, was an eminent poet. Hence his appellation *tarzi* ('stylist' in Persian). The young Tarzi received a classical Persian education based on the study of Arabic and Persian literature, poetry and philosophy. When he was 16 the family was banished because of his father's critical views on the brutality of Abdur Rahman's policies. The family settled in Damascus, where the young Tarzi moved in Arab intellectual circles that had come under the influence of European ideas and values. He also came into contact with the Young Turks who were eventually to overthrow the sultan, following the dismemberment of the Ottoman Empire after the Great War, and to establish a secular republic.

Tarzi is inappropriately referred to in the literature as Mahmud Beg (*beg* being the Turkish equivalent of the honorific *khan*, derived from Mongol usage), because of his long stay in Ottoman lands. During his travels he had also come into contact with the Afghan religious reformer and political agitator, Jamal al-Din al-Afghani (1838–97). Afghani had been a minister at the court of the Kabul Amir. When his patron was ousted by Sher Ali in 1869, Afghani went on a long odyssey that took him to India and to European capitals, and to Cairo, Tehran and Istanbul, where he enjoyed the patronage of their respective rulers. In Paris he collaborated for a time with the Egyptian exile, Mohammad Abduh, in the publication of reformist Islamic periodicals that gave birth to the modernizing *salafiyyah* – a move-ment that was to become very influential among modernist intellectuals in some parts of the Muslim world. Abduh eventually broke with Afghani, whose ideas were often contradictory and who was incorrigibly given to political intrigue that was to get him often into trouble with his royal patrons. Abduh, however, was consistent in his efforts to reconcile Islam with the intellectual demands of a rational and scientific modernism that had enabled a dynamic and industrialized Europe to impose its will on vast areas of the Muslim world. His ideas had a special appeal for educated Muslims who wished to modernize their economically and socially backward societies without abandoning their Islamic faith and cultural heritage. One of them was Sir Sayyed Ahmad, who founded the Anglo-Oriental College in Aligarh, India, which exercised a great influence on forward-looking Muslim leaders of the sub-continent. Although his ideas departed in many important respects from the rigid interpretations of the shari'a by the orthodox ulema, Abduh was named Grand Mufti of Egypt on his return from exile, and eventually appointed to the Supreme Council of Al-Azhar University.

At the age of 25 Tarzi wrote his first book, *Travels in Three Continents*, after a tour with his father of Syria, Egypt, Turkey and France. It was purportedly a travelogue, but contained political satire. In the tradition of Montesquieu in his *Lettres persanes*, or of Voltaire who, in the guise of observations on foreign countries based on the accounts of the ubiquitous Jesuit missionaries of his day, obliquely satirized the monarchical and despotic France of the ancien régime, Tarzi used the device of a young Turkish liberal who spoke his mind concerning his experiences of the Ottoman bureaucracy. The manuscript was passed from hand to hand and published in 1915, when it was recognized as a plea for social justice in Muslim countries.

After the death of his father in 1901, Tarzi, as head of the family, ob-tained permission to visit Kabul to pay his respects to the new amir. Habibullah was impressed by his talents and requested Tarzi to end his family's exile. The family returned to Kabul two years later. Habibullah's son, Amanullah, then married a daughter of Tarzi, the charming Soraya, by his Syrian wife. In Damascus Tarzi had worked in the Ottoman secretariat of the Syrian province. Besides being proficient in Arabic, Persian and Turkish, he had a knowledge of Pashtu, Urdu and French. Habibullah appointed Tarzi to head a bureau of translations, mainly to render into Persian the works of Jules Verne. In 1911 Tarzi began publishing a bi-monthly newspaper, *Seraj-ul-Akhbar*, which became a vehicle for his critical views on imperialism, the need for the modernization of Afghan society, and on the resistance to change of Muslim clerics. His attacks on European imperialism struck chords in British India and in Central Asia. His more oblique criticism of the backward local scene made him vulnerable, and led to a strained relationship with Habibullah.

When his father was assassinated in 1919, Amanullah established his authority with the support of the army, after a brief revolt by one of his brothers. He then began to launch a series of internal reforms. But his first impulse was nationalistic. Urged on by Tarzi and his leading army generals, and with the support of tribal leaders, Amanullah declared war on the British. In this less-known Third Anglo-Afghan War of May 1919, known to the Afghans as their War of Independence, three Afghan columns marched against British India. One, led by General Nadir Khan, the future ruler, advanced beyond the Durand Line into Parachinar and Thal in the Kurram Tribal Agency of the North West Frontier Province of British India. Tribesmen on both sides of the Line, as well as deserters from the paramilitary British Frontier Scouts, rallied to the Afghan side. But the British brought in a new weapon. Military aircraft of First World War vintage dropped bombs on Kabul and Jalalabad. Both sides then began peace moves.

The initial negotiations for an armistice, to be followed by a peace conference, led to the Treaty of Rawalpindi in August 1919, largely dictated by the British, which left Afghanistan free to conduct its own foreign affairs. But the British concession was ambiguous, and the Afghans hedged their bets by sending a mission to the newly installed Bolsheviks in Moscow in October 1919. This visit had in fact been preceded by a Bolshevik mission to Kabul the previous month to negotiate the status of the still-disputed Pandjeh area in Turkestan, annexed by the czar in 1886, and to obtain Afghan support for the Bolsheviks in Muslim Central Asia in return for assistance against the British.

The Bolsheviks had represented themselves as champions of the colonial subjects of European and czarist imperialism, and held out hopes for their eventual independence. The formulation of a Bolshevik policy towards nationalist movements in colonial countries was discussed extensively in Moscow at the Second Congress of the Communist International (Comintern) in July–August 1920. The position taken by Lenin at the Congress was that the bourgeois nationalist stage must be passed before entering the stage of proletarian revolution. It was therefore the duty of communist parties to assist bourgeois-nationalist liberation movements in their struggle against imperialism, and even to form alliances with such movements. This was to define Soviet attitudes towards the national revolutions then taking shape in Ataturk's Turkey, Reza Shah's Iran, Amanullah's Afghanistan and Sun Yat Sen's China.

In September a Congress of Peoples of the East held in Baku brought together an array of Asian leftist revolutionaries from the Dutch East Indies to British India, to discuss the 'National and Colonial Question'. The Bengali communist M.N. Roy, with a more sceptical eye on his native India, took a radical view. He maintained that the nationalist bourgeoisie were essentially reactionary in character, and that the priority was to build up communist parties to organize the peasants and the workers, lead them to revolt against the bourgeoisie, and set up Soviet-style republics. The Congress in Baku appeared to have reached a compromise, but it was in fact Lenin's thesis that became the basis of Soviet theory and practice with regard to colonial peoples and territories until the dismantling of the Soviet Union itself.[1]

One of the Comintern's avowed objectives was to bring about the liberation of colonial peoples. The Comintern became in fact an instrument of Soviet foreign policy, later exploited with his habitual lack of scruple by Stalin, with the collusion of the nascent communist parties of Asia. In the meantime the Bolsheviks were reconquering Central Asia. Freed from their efforts in repressing anti-Bolshevik forces elsewhere in the former czarist empire, Red Army troops put an end in 1924 to the autonomy of the khanates of Khiva and Bokhara in Russian Turkestan. The Muslim resistance fighters called basmachis ('bandits' in Russian) were eventually defeated, with large groups of Turcomen, Uzbek, Tajik and Kirghiz fighters seeking refuge in northern Afghanistan with their families, thus significantly increasing the numbers of these ethnic groups in the north. Amanullah was sympathetic but powerless in the face of their pleas for help, caught as he was between his grandfather's 'millstones'.

On the domestic front, Amanullah's well-intentioned but unsubtle efforts, aimed at the wholesale transformation of an anachronistic society into a modern and secular state, were unsuccessful, and cost him his throne. In 1919 he had established a council of ministers, appointing Tarzi as the first foreign minister in Afghan history. In 1923 a constitution, modelled on the Persian constitution of 1906 and inspired also by the modernizing decrees of Mustafa Kemal Ataturk, was promulgated. The amir himself assumed the title of padshah (king) and made the office hereditary. Under pressure from conservative religious and tribal leaders, Amanullah was obliged to call the traditional loya jirga to review the constitution, and to amend some of its provisions, particularly those that restricted the wide discretionary powers of the religious judges (qazi).

Amanullah then began to decree a series of administrative, economic, social and educational reforms. His plans for the emancipation of women, compulsory education for all and coeducational schools angered the religious conservatives. In 1924 the unruly Mangal Pashtun tribesmen of Khost were stirred to revolt by a fanatical cleric called the Mullah-i-Lang. The rebellion was crushed a year later, but it was an ominous sign. Tarzi resigned in 1925, his advice on the need to proceed slowly and cautiously in the reform programme having been repeatedly ignored by Amanullah.

Meanwhile Amanullah's grandiose projects to turn Kabul into the capital of a modern kingdom bankrupted the treasury. Many projects were left unfinished. In 1927 he embarked on a grand tour of European capitals where he was dazzled by the achievements of the West. In Cairo he startled worshippers at a mosque by appearing in European dress complete with top hat. Amanullah also visited Turkey and Persia on his return journey, and was the first foreign ruler to visit the Soviet Union.

The architect of modern Turkey, Mustafa Kemal Ataturk, was sweeping away the centuries-old bureaucratic and religious resistance to change and forging a secular Turkish nation. Ataturk had warned Amanullah that no large-scale programme of political and social reform could be initiated without a strong and well-trained army, and a loyal and disciplined bureaucracy. In Persia Ataturk's example was followed by Reza Khan, a Russian-trained former Cossack officer who had overthrown the decadent and decrepit Qajar dynasty in 1925, and begun the forcible modernization of a tradition-bound society. Women were forbidden to wear the veil (chador), just as Ataturk had abolished the fez. Men were ordered to wear wide-brimmed hats, 'a device that was singularly designed to obstruct the rituals of Muslim prayer', as one writer said. Reza Shah had at his command a strong army and a subservient, centralized bureaucracy.

While Amanullah was making his grand tour, photographs of Queen Soraya, unveiled and wearing evening dress at European state receptions, were circulated in Afghanistan, arousing the wrath of the mullahs. The unveiling of Soraya in Europe provoked, it was reported, this reaction in Afghanistan: 'The King had turned against Allah and Islam.' He was also reported to be bringing back from Europe 'machines to make soap out of corpses'.[2]

After his return to Kabul in July 1928 Amanullah announced a series of reforms before a loya jirga composed of the country's leading tribal and religious leaders. He called for (a) the establishment of a Western-style constitutional monarchy, a cabinet of ministers, an elected lower house, and a nominated upper house (so far so good, except that such concepts would have been incomprehensible to the tribal and religious members of the loya jirga); (b) the separation of religious and state power – a perennially prickly issue in Muslim countries, as will be examined later; and (c) the emancipation of women, enforced monogamy, compulsory education for all, and coeducational schools. Had these proposed reforms been implemented, they would have cut into the very roots of conservative society in predominantly rural Afghanistan.

The loya jirga (itself a very ancient version of direct democracy, somewhat similar to the traditional landesgemeinde of the older Swiss-German cantons) rejected most of Amanullah's proposals. The king then convened a smaller loya jirga composed of loyalists, to approve those proposals that had been rejected, including the abolition of the *chadari* (veil). The wife of the British Minister in Kabul who was present on the occasion, wrote in her diary: 'The most dramatic moment of all was when Amanullah wound up an impassioned appeal to his people to free their women with a wave of his hand towards his Queen, saying, "Anyway, you may see my wife", and she pulled down her veil before the assembled multitude.'[3]

The writing was on the wall. In November 1928 Shinwari Pashtun tribesmen burned down the king's winter palace in Jalalabad – and for good measure, the British consulate – and marched on Kabul. In the north, a Tajik bandit known as Bacha Saqqao ('son of a water carrier') assembled a rag-tag force in the defence of Islam and marched on Kabul, forcing Amanullah to flee to safety in Kandahar, and to eventual exile in Italy. Amanullah had abdicated in favour of his elder brother, Inayatullah, who lasted three days before Bacha Saqqao and his ragged followers arrived in Kabul and subjected the city and its hapless inhabitants to a nine-month reign of terror. The looting, pillaging and arson, and the rapes perpetrated by the wild invaders, alienated even those religious leaders opposed to Amanullah, such as the influential Hazrat of Shor Bazar, the head of the Mujaddidi family and of the ancient Naqshbandiya Sufi order, who had first acclaimed the bandit as the 'Holy Warrior, Habibullah, Servant of the Faith'.

Armed opposition to Bacha Saqqao coalesced around two leaders. One was Ghulam Nabi Charki, the ambassador to Moscow, who with Soviet backing assembled a mercenary force from both sides of the northern border to march on Kabul and restore Amanullah. The other was the hero of the Third Anglo-Afghan War, General Nadir Khan, a member of the powerful Musahiban family from a collateral branch of the royal clan.[4] With the help of his four brothers and a tribal army assembled from both sides of the Durand Line (with the tacit collusion of the British it appears), Nadir Khan defeated the bandit forces and occupied Kabul in October 1929. Bacha Saqqao surrendered, but despite a pledge to spare his life and a promise of safe passage signed on a copy of the Koran by the victorious general, he was publicly hanged with his leading followers a month later.

Nadir Shah (1929–33)

Nadir Khan was proclaimed king by his tribal army. To legitimize his succession in the traditional Pashtun manner, he convened a loya jirga in September 1930 that proclaimed him king as Nadir Shah. The new king was a man of action. His first task was to bring the country firmly under his authority, carrying out measures ranging from conciliation to outright brutality, as in his handling of rebellious Tajiks in the north-east. He built up a regular army of 40,000 men. This replaced the tribal levies he had used to defeat Bacha Saqqao, but who in their turn had sacked Kabul in lieu of pay, a victory seen traditionally, as in the Arab *razzia*, as an invitation to loot. Nadir Shah replenished the treasury by collecting taxes with military efficiency. He built a road across the high treacherous passes of the Hindu Kush[5] that for the first time gave relatively easy access to northern Afghanistan, before the Soviets built the Salang Tunnel. He opened up the economy to private enterprise, giving great impetus to the development of a laissez-faire economy that thrived until the communist putsch in 1978. He coerced entrepreneurs to use their capital to drain the malarial swamps of the north and turn them into productive land.

Nadir Shah promulgated a new constitution in 1931 that, while containing some human rights provisions to satisfy the liberal sentiments of the pro-Amanullah faction, was in fact a reactionary document perpetuating the status quo ante, an autocratic monarchy allied to religious conservatism. His cabinet consisted of his brothers and other relatives. The government was in principle made responsible to a National Council selected from among its members by the loya jirga that had proclaimed him king in 1930. However, not only had the members of the council been vetted by the king before their selection, they also had to declare in advance their loyalty to the government.

The first article of the 1931 constitution decreed officially, and for the first time, that the religious law of the Hanafi school of Sunni Islam was the law of Afghanistan. In further acknowledgement of the power of religious leaders who had brought about the downfall of Amanullah, the king coopted them into the power structure by putting mosque imams on the government payroll, appointing relatives of influential religious figures such as the Hazrat of Shor Bazar to lucrative posts, and by establishing a special board of ulema to ensure that what was taught in schools conformed to Islamic values – an open-ended mandate that permitted the religious establishment to denounce whatever they disapproved of as 'un-Islamic'.

In November 1933 the king was shot dead by a high-school student in Kabul. The assassination may have been in settlement of a blood feud. The young cadet was the adopted son of General Ghulam Nabi Charki, who had been beaten to death the previous year by soldiers on the orders of Nadir Shah after an angry confrontation with the king at his palace. The Charki family were pro-Amanullah, anti-British, and avowed opponents of the king, whom they accused of being a man without honour who had usurped the throne from the grandson of Abdur Rahman. The Charki father had been one of the Iron Amir's favourite generals. A month before the king met his end, another Charki brother had been executed for his alleged part in an attack on the British Legation. The attack was carried out by a nationalist schoolteacher who confessed that his intention had been to kill the British Minister, force the British to interfere, and overthrow Nadir Shah.

Anti-British sentiment also appeared to be the motive for the assassination in Berlin the previous June of the Afghan Minister there, Mohammad Aziz, an elder brother of the king. Some observers linked the murder to the Charki–Musahiban feud. But there was also a perception that Nadir Shah leaned towards the British who, as was noted earlier, had allowed his passage through India and turned a blind eye to his mobilization of a tribal army from both sides of the Durand Line on his march to Kabul to overthrow Bacha Saqqao. The British had also granted him £170,000 on his assumption of power to enable his government to tide over the financial crisis resulting from Amanullah's extravagance.

It is of interest to note that the king's assassin, his brother's assassin in Berlin, as well as the school teacher who had attacked the British Legation, were all former students of the Amania School in Kabul founded by Amanullah (renamed the Najat or 'redemption' school by Nadir Shah). A clandestine irredentist movement committed to the return of Pashtun territory across the Durand Line also consisted of former students. In the years to come, students of such state schools in Kabul and in the principal towns coalesced into a new force in Afghan society – nationalistic, revolutionary, and alienated from the traditional spaces occupied by court, khan, qawm, malik and mullah.

This new force was never very numerous relative to the population. A modern school system had come late to Afghanistan. Students were sent abroad for the first time during Amanullah's reign. They were drawn from the wealthier families and were to become a forward-looking, modernizing elite, staffing the Kabul bureaucracy and the University after the Second World War. Due to the lack of qualified Afghans, the local foreign-language and other state schools were staffed by German, French and Indian teachers from whom the students could have imbibed subversive Western ideas. Nor were the students exposed to foreign influences a homogenous group.

The first institute of higher education, the Faculty of Medicine, which became the core of the future University of Kabul, was established in 1932. The University was to become a confused hotbed of dissent in the 1950s and 1960s, spawning liberals and progressives of all hues, including Marxists and outright atheists, as well as Islamists and other Muslim radicals. If there was one experience they had in common, it was that they were outsiders from underprivileged groups and minorities who felt that they had no place in the traditional establishment. Through their education they became a kind of middle class in a socially backward pre-industrial country that lacked a true middle class, and with no economic opportunities for such a class outside the limited confines of the state bureaucracy and army. They were to come into their own in the 1960s and 1970s. But as the blinkered slaves of imported ideologies, they invited unprecedented disaster.

Zahir Shah (1933–73)

The long reign of the French-educated Zahir Shah that began when he was 19 years old is aptly called 'the avuncular period' by Louis Dupree. Zahir Shah reigned, but his father's brothers governed. The elimination of the Charki family as a focus of serious opposition had ensured a stable transition, and the first 20 years of the Zahir Shah era were relatively peaceful on the domestic front. The king's uncle, Hashim Khan, who had been appointed prime minister in 1929, continued in that capacity until 1946, when he was replaced by his youngest brother, Shah Mahmud. In 1953 the latter was ousted in a palace revolution in which the king's cousin, who was also his brother-in-law, Sardar Daoud Khan, became prime minister.

The Second World War brought with it a challenge in the sphere of the government's foreign relations. Before the war, the Afghans had accepted economic assistance only from countries that were geographically remote enough (like Germany, Italy and Japan but not Britain and Russia) not to be able to influence their political independence. In 1936 the German government loaned DM 27 million in return for the purchase of arms. German advisers and technicians prospected for minerals and, with the Italians and Japanese, carried out irrigation projects. On the eve of the war the German presence was substantial.

In August 1940 Afghanistan, which had been admitted to the League of Nations in 1934, formally reaffirmed its neutrality. In October 1941 the British and the Soviets demanded the expulsion from Afghan soil of all citizens of the three Axis countries. A similar joint ultimatum to the Iranians, who had been slow to respond, had resulted in the invasion and partial occupation of Iran by British and Soviet forces in August 1941, and the forced abdication of Reza Shah who was replaced by his young son. There was of course more at stake in Iran: German agents had been very active there, Iranian oil was a precious resource for the Allies, and, with most of Europe occupied by the Nazis, a southern route to supply the beleaguered Soviets was a strategic necessity. But the Afghans considered the ultimatum an affront to their declared neutrality and to their traditional laws of hospitality. Some hotheads called for defiance, even war. In the end, a characteristic Afghan solution was found: the non-diplomatic personnel of all the belligerent nations were expelled.

When Shah Mahmud became prime minister in 1946, one of his first acts was to release political prisoners. There were other modest attempts to liberalize the regime, leading to the election in 1949 of a parliament in which some 40 per cent of the 120 members were educated, reform-minded Afghans who took their parliamentary duties seriously. According to the 1931 constitution, government ministers were in principle responsible to parliament for the policies of the government in general and of the ministries under their charge in particular. Ministry budgets had become a notorious source of graft and influence-peddling. Now when ministers were queried on their individual budgets, they sought refuge behind other provisions of the constitution that appeared to give parliament no jurisdiction over such matters.

However, the so-called 'liberal parliament' did open some windows. The enactment of laws permitting freedom of the press led to the appearance of newspapers and other publications whose favourite targets became the ruling family oligarchy and conservative religious leaders. A student union was formed at Kabul University that became a forum for free-wheeling debates and attacks on the status quo. A loosely organized political association called the Movement of Enlightened Youth also made its appearance during this period. Middle-class in origin and liberal in spirit, its manifesto called for the eradication of anachronistic customs and ideas, the grant of legal rights to women, the accountability of the government to parliament, the eradication of official corruption, the formation of political parties, economic development, and so on.

Such demands, it must be said, gave voice to a small minority of educated and reform-minded Afghans in urban areas, but found no resonance in the unlettered general population, subject to the traditional influences of malik and mullah, responsive only to the local concerns of their particular qawm, and utterly impervious to the secular issues that lay behind these demands. Thus, when the increasingly vocal opposition was perceived as a threat to the ruling oligarchy and the traditional vested interests, the government had no difficulty in clamping down on the reformists and imprisoning some of their more articulate elements. Samuel P. Huntington's comment is apt: 'Power which is sufficiently concentrated to promote reforms may be too concentrated to assimilate the social forces released by them.'[6] In the context of Afghanistan, the policies of Abdur Rahman, which allowed no uncontrollable social forces to be released, may have been vindicated. This problem is also faced by every autocratic regime, Pahlavi Iran and the Soviet Union being the most spectacular examples.

CHAPTER 3

Daoud's Modernization Programme and the Pashtunistan Issue (1953–63)

In September 1953 the king's cousin and brother-in-law, and son of the Musahiban uncle assassinated in Berlin in 1933, assumed power as prime minister with the tacit support of the royal family. The ambitious Daoud, who had formerly been minister of defence and was occupying the key military post of commander of the central forces in Kabul at the time of the palace coup, was an autocrat. He had had no patience with the liberal expressions of opinion aired during the prime ministership of Shah Mahmud that appeared, in the eyes of politically conservative Afghans like himself, as no more than attempts to overthrow the establishment. Political prisoners were not freed, and those who were, were released on condition that they ceased their anti-government activities. But Daoud was a fervent nationalist and a modernizer who had been frustrated by the slow pace of economic development under his predecessors.

Daoud's energetic efforts at modernization within the confines of a conservative and autocratic regime led to developments with ominous consequences for the future: the beginnings of the abandonment of the traditional Afghan policy of neutrality. The various strands of the web that led to this unacknowledged but palpable shift in policy are tangled and difficult to unravel even now, with the benefit of hindsight. It is relevant, at this stage, to cast some light on the circumstances prevailing at the time.

First and foremost, Afghanistan was in dire need of external economic and military assistance. The United States, which was in a position to help, was indifferent, or rather insensitive to the peculiarities of the Afghan situation after the British withdrawal from India had left the field open for the Soviets to exploit. Second was Daoud's aggressive espousal of the cause of Pashtunistan that had bedevilled Afghanistan's relations with the British-Indian successor state of Pakistan. These two factors were to bring about a wholly new dependency on the USSR.

The British withdrawal from India in 1947 and the attendant Partition of the sub-continent had made the Afghans vulnerable. The Afghan army at the time consisted of rag-tag groups of badly clothed and ill-equipped peasant conscripts, with an officer corps largely drawn from the Pashtun elite for want of better employment. The army's main role was to keep internal order and convey the impression that there existed a central government that was able to impose its authority throughout the country.

The Afghan minister of national economy, Abdul Majid Zabuli, had visited Washington in December 1948. According to a US diplomat with long experience in the region, Zabuli's mission was to make a special plea for the supply of weapons to defend Afghan territory in case of Soviet aggression in the wake of the British withdrawal from India, and to maintain internal security against tribal insurrections.[1] Afghan fears regarding the USSR were not without foundation, in view of what had occurred since 1945, and what was happening in eastern and southern Europe; furthermore, the communist parties of Asia, with Soviet support, appeared to be in the ascendant. The Afghans also confirmed their willingness, as in previous requests, to pay for arms and military training with their meagre resources. The US response was negative.

So was the US response to Afghan requests for economic assistance. When Zabuli was in Washington he also tried to obtain a loan to finance a development plan. Zabuli himself was a self-made capitalist, a pioneering entrepreneur who had set up an investment bank, later called the Bank-i-Melli, which had largely contributed to the beginnings of commercial agriculture (cotton in the Kunduz region) and industrial development in pre-war Afghanistan. Zabuli came to the US with a modest, well-conceived plan, with an integrated approach to economic development. The State Department shunted him off to the US Import-Export Bank, which offered instead to finance new contracts for an American engineering firm that had been commissioned by the Afghan government in 1946 to assist in the planning and implementation of a multi-purpose agricultural project in the Helmand Valley. Zabuli had little enthusiasm for putting all the Afghan eggs into one basket, but was forced by Shah Mahmud, his prime minister, to accept the offer for its potential political value. In a conversation with President Truman in Washington, Shah Mahmud is reported to have said: 'The Afghan government tends to think of the loan as of political as well as of economic importance, possibly increasingly so in the light of Soviet interest and offers of assistance to Afghanistan.'[2]

These Afghan demands for economic and military assistance from the United States were therefore highly political. In their concern to maintain their traditional neutrality and independence, the Afghans were only trying to bring into partnership, as they had done in the 1930s with Germany, Japan and Italy, a geographically remote world power that had the capacity to assist.

In October 1954 Mohamed Naim, the foreign minister (and Daoud's brother), went to Washington to appeal once again for military assistance.

The reply of Eisenhower's secretary of state, John Foster Dulles, was received three months later: 'After careful consideration, extending military aid to Afghanistan would create problems not offset by the strength it would generate. Instead of asking for arms, Afghanistan should settle the Pashtunistan dispute with Pakistan.'[3] In Dulles's Manichaean world view, Afghan neutrality meant 'non-alignment', a status that had no value to him at a time when he was busily forming military alliances like SEATO and the Baghdad Pact (later CENTO) to 'contain' the Soviet Union. Pakistan had joined SEATO in September 1954. It was to adhere to the Baghdad Pact a year later. Pakistan as a potential ally was not to be antagonized; Afghanistan was dispensable. To underline his point, and in a serious breach of diplomatic etiquette, Dulles sent a copy of his reply to the Pakistani government.

The outraged Daoud turned immediately to the Soviet Union, whose offers of military aid had long been rejected as a matter of policy. In December 1955, after their famous tour of India, Bulganin and Khrushchev visited Afghanistan – an unprecedented gesture towards a small and seemingly insignificant country. They not only offered to train and equip the Afghan army and air force, but also to grant economic assistance on a large scale – the first such Soviet programme in the so-called Third World. While in Kabul, the Soviet leaders also publicly announced Soviet support for the Afghan position on the Pashtunistan issue.

It was perhaps the headstrong Daoud's obsessive pursuit of the Pashtunistan issue that gave the Soviets the first opportunity for their economic penetration and subversion of Afghanistan. One concrete result of the ensuing confrontations with Pakistan was that they dramatized the landlocked country's extreme vulnerability: transit facilities for vital Afghan imports and exports through Pakistan and the port of Karachi were blocked or delayed. Soviet assistance to circumvent these threats to Afghan survival was prompt and psychologically effective. Abdur Rahman's 'elephant' had begun its 'slow and steady' advance. Its first victim was Afghan neutrality; its second, Afghan independence.

The Pashtunistan problem had originated with the demarcation by the British in 1893 of the Durand Line. The purpose of this demarcation had been both strategic and defensive: to delimit the respective spheres of influence of the amir of Kabul and of the British over the unruly Pashtun tribes on either side of the Line, and to discourage armed incursions into British India by wild raiding parties from the Afghan side. The substantial Pashtun population on the British side were nominally subjects of the amir. Nor could the British be said to have been actually administering at that time the whole of that vast territory west of the Indus. The 'pacification' campaigns against the fierce Pashtun tribesmen, in an era of jubilant Victorian jingoism, incidentally inspired a great deal of romantic literature, including Winston

Churchill's rather fanciful accounts of his youthful exploits in the Malakand campaign.[4]

In 1901 the British created the North West Frontier Province (NWFP), separating the Pashtun country west of the Indus from the province of Punjab. They divided the new province into the so-called 'Settled Districts', that is, the 'pacified' areas directly administered by the British, and five autonomous Tribal Agencies ruled by local khans or chiefs, with resident British political agents reporting, not to the governor of the NWFP, but directly to the viceroy's government in Calcutta.[5]

The Durand Line was not an 'international frontier' in the accepted sense and its status was not without ambiguity. The Anglo-Afghan Treaty of 1921 referred to the mutual interest of the contracting parties in the tribes residing close to their respective boundaries. But the special status of the autonomous Tribal Agencies placed them outside the pale of the mainstream political, economic and social developments in the rest of British India. In fact the Simon Commission Report of 1930 went so far as to say that 'British India stops at the boundary of the administered area'.[6]

Before Partition in 1947 the British sponsored a referendum in the Settled Districts of the NWFP, giving them the choice of joining either India or Pakistan. The overwhelmingly Muslim population of the Settled Districts voted to join Pakistan. In the five autonomous Tribal Agencies linked to the government in New Delhi by special arrangements, the British sponsored a jirga that also opted for Pakistan. The Afghan government objected to this procedure on the grounds that the Agencies belonged to the same category as the 562 self-governing princely states of British India that had been presented with a third option – becoming independent – an option that was not made available to the Tribal Agencies which, like the princely states, had never been directly administered by the British. Although the new state of Pakistan continued to respect the autonomous status of the Tribal Agencies, and even worked hard to placate the tribes with subsidies and a reduced military presence, the Afghans, supported at first by newly independent India, claimed that by denying the third option to the frontier Pashtun tribes, the Durand Line had been treated as an international border.

When Pakistan applied for United Nations membership in September 1947, Afghanistan, a fellow Muslim state, cast the only negative vote. The Afghans also revoked unilaterally the Anglo-Afghan treaties containing references to 'boundaries', and had this action endorsed by a loya jirga. So began a period of acute tension between the two neighbours. Although formal diplomatic relations were established in 1948, hostile Afghan actions and declarations on the Pashtunistan issue led Pakistan to retaliate on several occasions by subjecting the transit through its territory of vital Afghan imports and exports to bureaucratic delays and other obstacles.

The resulting economic hardships caused the Afghans to turn to the Soviets for help. The Soviet response was prompt: a four-year barter agreement was signed in July 1950, with the Soviets providing petroleum products, cement, cotton cloth and other essentials in return for wool, raw cotton and other Afghan products. The Soviets also agreed to the free transit of Afghan exports through their territory, and offered to invest in oil exploration. In 1952 the Afghans authorized the opening of a Soviet trade mission in Kabul, a facility that had always been denied before.

In early 1954, some months after Daoud had taken office, the Soviets loaned the equivalent of US$3.5 million for the construction of grain silos in Kabul and Pul-i-Kumri, and a flour mill and bakery in Kabul. This was the first Soviet loan to a neutral country in the Third World. Josef Stalin, who had employed more direct methods of extending Soviet power and influence, had not believed in providing material assistance to such countries. Loans for other infrastructure projects soon followed: $1.2 million for the construction of an oil pipeline across the Amu Darya, and three oil storage facilities; $2 million for road-building equipment, $2.1 million for an asphalt factory and equipment to pave the streets of Kabul. That same year, Czechoslovakia provided a credit of $5 million to build three cement plants and other projects – its first aid programme outside the Soviet Bloc.[7] During their December 1955 visit Bulganin and Khrushchev announced an outright gift of a 100-bed hospital for Kabul, and 15 passenger buses to ply the newly paved streets of the capital. These are examples of the small but highly visible projects that appeared as spontaneous and generous responses to meet real Afghan needs, but had in fact great psychological and propaganda value for the Soviets.

US economic assistance, when it began in 1956 in response to the Soviet economic offensive, provided essential but nearly invisible items and services: wheat, stored in the Soviet-built silos, and substantial investments in educational programmes, such as grants to Afghan students to study at American universities, and projects to expand and upgrade the local educational infrastructure and services. As Dupree commented: 'and so nine-tenths of the American aid sits, iceberg-like, below the surface, invisible to the journalistic eye'[8] – one might add, just like the American grain in the Soviet silos.

Another US project was an ambitiously modern airport in Kandahar that turned out to be a white elephant. The US also built a highway between Kabul and Kandahar. The Soviets built the Kandahar–Herat highway, and, most dramatically, an all-weather road linking Kabul with the USSR border that involved a spectacular feat of engineering – the construction of a tunnel that pierced the Hindu Kush for the first time in history. The Salang Tunnel, the road network and the airports would prove to be of immeasurable value to the Soviets in easing the logistics of their 1979 invasion.

The Afghan–Pakistani confrontations over Pashtunistan intensified in March 1955 when Pakistan announced the One Unit Plan to create the single province of West Pakistan, symmetrical to the existing single province of East Pakistan. The idea was to end the disparities between the east wing, which had a larger population, and the west wing, which, with four provinces, had a disproportionately greater representation in the national legislature, an equal number of seats having been attributed to each of the five former provinces.

For Daoud the One Unit Plan was a provocation, an attempt to treat the Durand Line as the official frontier and to absorb the Tribal Agencies into Pakistan. Although the Agencies were not included in the plan, their own self-governing khans feared that it was a move towards their eventual integration into Pakistan. In Afghanistan mobs staged violent demonstrations at the Pakistan embassy in Kabul, and attacked the consulates in Kandahar and Jalalabad. The country prepared for war. The government called a loya jirga that unanimously endorsed its demand for a plebiscite in the Pashtun areas of Pakistan. The Pakistanis countered by asking whether the Pashtun population on the Afghan side of the Durand Line would have the right to secede by voting for an independent Pashtunistan straddling the Line. Pakistan had scored a very valid point, underlining the essential weakness of the Afghan position.

The most prominent proponents of Pashtunistan in British India before Partition had been Dr Khan Sahib and his elder brother, Khan Abdul Ghaffar Khan. The latter was known as the Frontier Gandhi because of his ascetic habits, his alliance with the Mahatma's Hindu-dominated Congress Party in the anti-British civil disobedience campaigns of the 1920s and 1930s, and his leadership of a radical movement for Pashtun social reform called the 'Red Shirts' (the khudai khidmatgar). The Khan brothers had politically organized the NWFP so well that their party, the Frontier Congress, controlled the provincial legislature. Before the British held their referendum, the NWFP cabinet had voted to join India. It is possible that Indian Congress leaders had promised Pashtun autonomy within an independent India. As the British journalist George Arney pointed out, Pashtunistan meant different things to different people:

> To Ghaffar Khan, it may well have carried spiritual overtones. He had devoted his life, not just to independence, but to the moral regeneration of a people racked by blood feuds, bribery, family disputes and degrading social customs. To his fellow Pashtuns of the North West Frontier, Pashtunistan could mean anything from autonomy within Pakistan to complete independence. To the wild tribesmen straddling the Durand Line, it probably meant the splendid prospect of everlasting anarchy, without interference from north or south. To the rulers of Kabul, who

adopted the call for Pashtunistan with alacrity, it clearly implied the integration of Pakistan's North West Frontier Province into the Afghan state.[9]

If ethnic affinity was the basis of the case for a Pashtunistan, then logic demanded that such an autonomous or independent entity would also have to include the Pashtuns of Afghanistan. Afghan demands for a plebiscite could certainly not have encompassed Afghan Pashtuns who were the very basis of the Afghan state. Any expectations that Daoud may have had, that Pakistani Pashtuns would choose to be attached to Afghanistan in a plebiscite, were purely illusory. The NWFP had been under British rule for over 50 years, and the Pashtuns, especially the elite, had reaped the benefits of modernization. For instance, two public schools on the British model, Edwardes College and Ismailia College in Peshawar, had for several generations catered to the educational needs of the sons of tribal leaders, landowners and other Pashtuns of standing. The British had also favoured the recruitment of Pashtuns into the armed forces because of their proven fighting qualities, and they were thus well represented in the Pakistani officer corps. One of them, General Ayub Khan, was to take power in 1958, and, as president of Pakistan and a ferocious opponent of Pashtunistan, was to prove Daoud's nemesis.[10]

Although passions had cooled by September 1955, Daoud's closure of the border for a five-month period drove the desperate Afghans to seek Soviet help once again. At Daoud's request the 1950 transit and barter agreements were renewed. The visit of Bulganin and Khrushchev took place in December that year. This resulted in a US$100 million long-term development loan on very soft terms. By March 1956 numerous projects had been identified by joint Afghan–Soviet teams: two hydro-electric plants, three automotive repair and maintenance facilities, a road from Qizil Qala on the Iranian border west of Herat to Kabul, including the Salang Tunnel through the formidable Hindu Kush, a major air base in Bagram, three irrigation dams and canal systems, a fertilizer factory, and so on. The planning and implementation of these projects brought in large numbers of Soviet advisers and technicians. The Soviet economic penetration of Afghanistan had begun. Between 1956 and 1978 Afghanistan received a total of $1265 million in Soviet economic assistance, mostly in the form of loans, and an additional $110 million from the rest of the Eastern Bloc.

In 1955, at the height of the tensions over Pashtunistan, the Afghans had purchased $3 million worth of arms and military equipment from Czechoslovakia. After the Bulganin–Khrushchev visit, Soviet military assistance also began in earnest, with a loan of $32.4 million for the purchase of tanks, aircraft and arms, and for the construction of four military airfields. There is no doubt that Daoud's intent was to build up and equip armed forces that would be strong and effective enough to deter any external threats and maintain internal order during his determined efforts to modernize his economically and socially backward country, in the manner of an Ataturk or a Reza Shah. But the US refusal to be of assistance made him almost exclusively dependent on the Soviet Bloc. He may not have perceived the long-term implications of such dependence.

Between 1956 and the eve of the communist coup in 1978, Afghanistan also received the equivalent of $1240 million in military aid from the USSR, mostly in the form of credits. By 1978 some 3725 Afghan military personnel had been trained in the Soviet Union. In the words of an official document emanating from the US embassy in 1971: 'There is no effective organization within the military to counter or even catalog the long-term possibly subversive effects of the training of the many military officers who go to the USSR for stints as long as six years.'[11] In contrast, Afghan officers had taken a total of 487 courses in the United States, with smaller numbers trained in Egypt and India.

While Daoud worked with restless impatience to implement his programme of modernization of the Afghan economy, his efforts at social reform were cautious, circumspect and carried out with a minimum of publicity. This was especially true of his efforts to achieve the social emancipation of Afghan women. Amanullah's attempts to tamper with the tradition of *purdah* (the isolation of women) and the wearing of the veil had brought down on him the wrath of the mullahs.

But Daoud had gathered round him as advisers, jurists who had studied at the shari'a school of Kabul University, a faculty affiliated to the oldest extant seat of Islamic theological learning, the Al-Azhar University in Cairo. Some of them had gone on to complete their theological studies at Al-Azhar, and others had rounded off their training with secular legal studies at universities in the West. Daoud had his legal advisers carefully scrutinize each reform he contemplated, to ensure that it did not violate the religious law, the shari'a, as contained in the Koran and the canonical sayings (*hadith*) of the Prophet.

Once his advisers had concluded that purdah and the veil had no absolute justification in Islamic law, Daoud did not promulgate a decree but acted unofficially. During the ceremonies to celebrate the 40th anniversary of Afghan independence in August 1959, Daoud, other members of the royal family, and high-ranking civilian and military officers appeared on the podium to review a military parade. Their wives and daughters were also on the reviewing stand, but the women were unveiled. The effect on the Kabul populace was electrifying.

Before this very public event, Daoud had quietly tested the waters. A few years before, women singers and announcers had been employed for the first time by Radio Afghanistan: they could not, for obvious reasons, have been wearing the veil. But since they had to work in the company of men who were not their fathers, brothers or sons, there was a flurry of protests. In 1957 a delegation of Afghan women attended an international women's conference in Colombo, Ceylon. The next year a woman was included in the Afghan delegation to the United Nations in New York. Some months before the public unveiling, a number of women were recruited to serve as (unveiled) receptionists and stewardesses on the national airline, Ariana. There were no protests this time. Around the same time, young girls who had completed their studies at a high school in Kabul were asked to volunteer to work in a local pottery factory: 40 of them turned up armed with letters of consent from their families. Daoud's approach was not Amanullah's, but there was a new environment. Daoud had a trained army behind him, and a feared secret police.

When a delegation of religious leaders called on the prime minister to condemn the public unveiling, Daoud retorted that he would be the first to return his wife and daughter to purdah and the veil if the clerics could provide justification in Islamic law. When the mullahs then took to preaching against the regime in their mosques, the ringleaders were arrested. They were charged with treason for advocating the overthrow of the government, and with heresy: in traditional Islamic theory a de facto government rules by 'divine sanction' that can only be withdrawn or refused by his Muslim subjects if the ruler openly violates the laws of Islam. In practice, however, an autocratic ruler with strong powers of coercion at his command continues to have his way in spite of such theories.

The imprisoned mullahs had learned their lesson and were soon released. But as Dupree comments:

> Not all religious leaders accepted the voluntary abolition of the veil and other reforms, however, because each intrusion into their customary power erodes their secular influence. They oppose secular education, for in the past they have controlled the educational institutions; they call land-reform anti-Islamic, for they own large tracts of land in the name of waqf (religious endowments); they oppose a constitutionally separated church and state, for such a move diminishes their temporal power.[12]

Daoud demonstrated the new power of the central authority on two other occasions: firstly, when a tribal feud in the Khost area of Paktia province erupted into an armed conflict, during which an army officer was killed by mistake; and secondly, during riots in Kandahar. How the riots came about is particularly instructive. Year after year a charade was enacted when the governor of the province notified the local landlords about their obligations concerning the payment of taxes. After such meetings, the landlords or their representatives marched to the compound of a neighbouring mosque where they claimed sanctuary (bast), which by tradition protected them from government authority, until the governor gave up for the sake of peace. In

December 1959, after the meeting in the governor's compound, the land-lords found their habitual line of march to the mosque blocked by armed policemen. There could therefore be no recourse to bast this time. But the landlords, and religious leaders who had large land-holdings in the form of religious endowments, fomented anti-government riots that were quickly suppressed, with some bloodshed, by the police and the army. The new element in the Afghan context was the rapidity and effectiveness of the interventions of the Kabul government in Khost and Kandahar with the help of the newly mechanized army.

Daoud's realistic attempts to bring about the social transformation of his country were largely countered by his illusions with regard to the Pashtunistan issue. In September 1960 a local quarrel between rival tribal chiefs in the Pakistani frontier district of Bajaur erupted into a war, with the two governments taking sides. Pakistan used US-supplied military aircraft and weapons against armed incursions of tribal elements from the Afghan side, and US protests were haughtily ignored by the Pakistani president, Ayub Khan. In the course of the mutual recriminations that followed, Pakistan closed its consulates in Kandahar and Jalalabad, and demanded that the Afghans close theirs in Quetta and Peshawar. In September 1961 Daoud took the extreme measure of breaking off diplomatic relations with Pakistan and sealing off the border. It was the irrational move of a self-deluded auto-crat, explicable only by Daoud's irredentist obsession with 'Pashtunistan'.

Customs duties accounted for some 40 per cent of Afghan government revenues; these were lost during the 1961–63 closure of the border, and ministry budgets had to be slashed by 20 per cent. US aid projects, the implementation of which had received a big boost after President Eisenhower's visit to Kabul in December 1959, were threatened: several million dollars' worth of equipment and materials for the Kabul–Kandahar road gathered dust or eroded in Pakistani warehouses; the construction of new faculty buildings for Kabul University was curtailed; and a US gift of 8000 tonnes of wheat lay rotting in Peshawar warehouses. Private Afghan exporters and importers suffered the most. The bulk of Afghan exports that brought in precious foreign exchange were fresh and dried fruit and nuts. The national carrier, Ariana Afghan Airlines, of which a 49 per cent stake was held by a major US airline, chartered more aircraft and began an airlift to India, Afghanistan's most profitable customer for these products. But the truckers and smugglers on both sides of the porous Durand Line had a field day, despite the official closure of the land border.

While the Afghan government and legitimate business were the major losers – and there were some winners – the Soviets were the ultimate win-ners, a Pyrrhic victory as it turned out in the end. A few days after the border was closed by Daoud's dictat, the Afghan foreign minister flew to Moscow and negotiated an agreement for a major increase of transit facilities through the USSR, and for an airlift of the threatened fruit crop, mainly grapes, for sale there or elsewhere in the Soviet Bloc. By 1963 it appeared that the servicing of the Afghan debt to the USSR would exceed the total value of Afghan exports to that country. On 9 March 1963 Radio Afghanistan informed the country that the king had accepted Daoud's resignation.

CHAPTER 4

The Democratic Experiment (1963–73)

The most important announcement made by the new prime minister, Dr Mohammad Yousuf, appointed by the king, was to inform the public of the formation of a seven-member committee of experts to draft a new constitution. After nearly a year's work, the draft was submitted to the scrutiny of a broad-based Constitutional Advisory Commission of 29 persons under the chairmanship of the president of the National Assembly. When the commission's work was completed, a loya jirga composed of 452 members was convened in September 1964 to discuss and adopt the draft constitution. The Loya Jirga of 1964, an ancient Pashtun institution adapted to a modern national purpose, was the most representative of all such assemblies in Afghan history. Its members were drawn from across the whole ethnic, social, political and religious spectrum, including elected representatives of all non-Pashtun ethnic groups, women, and a solitary Hindu delegate from Kabul.

After the formal opening by the king, officially president of the Loya Jirga, Dr Yousuf was elected vice-president to preside over the daily sessions. The rules of procedure were read out and adopted with some amendments by a majority vote. The assembly then got on with its work, to the surprise of observers, in a serious and responsible fashion.

The draft constitution had been published in Persian, Pashtu, French and English. But the majority of the delegates were illiterate. Radio Afghanistan had for many weeks introduced and explained the major provisions of the draft. But the Afghans have a long tradition of being very articulate in their local shuras (councils). It is a truism that in non-literate communities, verbal skills, including a penchant for oral poetry, are well developed. Examples can be found in all ages and places, from Homeric times to pre-Islamic Arabia. The oratorical skills of unlettered refugee spokesmen have impressed international humanitarian aid workers and visitors in Afghan refugee camps in Pakistan. The 1964 Loya Jirga was therefore not a rubber-stamp assembly, with the delegates given a choice between a 'yes' or a 'no', but a genuine debating forum, where dissenters overruled by the majority were even permitted to have their opinions recorded in writing.

Amendments to some articles were proposed and adopted. Among the provisions of Title III, which spelled out a bill of basic human rights of the most liberal kind, was the paragraph: 'No Afghan shall be sentenced to banishment from Afghanistan' – a terrible fate for an Afghan whose sense of identity was rooted in his local community. But the Loya Jirga, remembering the collective punishment of forced resettlement meted out by Abdur Rah-man to rebellious Ghilzai Pashtuns, insisted on an additional phrase, 'or within its territory'. There was also a long debate on the meaning of the term 'Afghan'. It was explained to a female delegate that the term embraced both sexes, and to the delegates of ethnic minorities that Afghan did not mean Pashtun, as generally understood by the non-Pashtun minorities, but all inhabitants of Afghanistan.

Other interesting debates revolved around opposition by religious conser-vatives to the secular-oriented articles. In the matter of legislation, Article 69 stated that inclusive of the provisions of the constitution to be adopted, 'a law is a resolution passed by both Houses of Parliament and signed by the king. In the area where no such law exists, the provisions of the Hanafi jurisprudence of the Shar'ia shall be considered as law.' To objections that the shari'a had been placed in a secondary position, the secretary of the Jirga, Dr Musa Shafiq, a product of both Al-Azhar and Columbia universities and one of the chief legal architects of the draft, explained that another article ('There shall be no law repugnant to the basic principles of the sacred relig-ion of Islam') ensured the primacy of Islamic values under the constitution. Thus Islam was used, as Dupree observes, to overturn the arguments of the traditionalist opponents of the secular provisions.

Under Title VII of the draft, the definition of the judiciary as 'an inde-pendent organ of the state that discharges its functions side by side with the legislative and executive organs' provoked a heated debate. The traditionalist members defended the centuries-old Islamic system of the administration of justice by religious judges (qazi). But the inequities of both the old system and the mixed system introduced by Nadir Shah were bitterly attacked by many delegates. Their attacks were based on their personal reminiscences of judicial corruption, malpractice, or mere caprice on the part of religious judges.

At times the decisions of the poorly educated and penurious qazis were influenced by bribes. In the mixed system introduced by Nadir Shah, a sentence delivered by a qazi, condemning a thief to have his offending hand cut off in accordance with the shari'a, might be overturned by the local provincial administrator who sent the offender to prison instead. For an Afghan, deprivation of freedom in prison was a fate worse than death. Given the medieval conditions of Afghan prisons, losing a hand was preferable. If witnesses were not available to confirm the guilt of a man accused of a crime, confessions were extracted by means of the bastinado or other forms of torture. Dupree quotes one delegate: 'The judiciary only wanted victims; every crime had to be solved.'[1] The majority of the Loya Jirga voted for the new concept of an independent judiciary, with guarantees of individual rights.

Other subjects of vigorous debate were the provisions concerning the monarchy: the definition of those who could be considered to be members of the royal house, the provisions to ensure an orderly succession (a crucial necessity in Muslim monarchies), and an amendment introduced by the Jirga to exclude all members of the royal house from participating in politics.

The draft constitution also made provision for the formation of political parties, to be legalized formally by a separate enactment of the parliament which would be constituted after the general elections. The parliament (shura) was to be bicameral, with a fully elective lower house (Wolesi Jirga) comprising 216 members, and an upper house (Meshrano Jirga - House of Nobles) consisting of 184 members, a third of whom were to be elected by the 28 provinces, a third by the provincial councils, and the remaining third appointed by the king 'from among well-informed and experienced persons'.

The 1964 Afghan constitution was characterized by some writers as perhaps the finest in the Muslim world. It was adopted after extensive debate by representatives from across the whole spectrum of the heterogeneous population of Afghanistan. It promulgated in theory the principle of equality before the law of all men and women citizens of Afghanistan, their personal liberty, freedom of thought and expression, the protection of private property, freedom of worship for non-Muslims 'within the limits determined by law, decency, and public peace', the right to education and health, and the right to form political parties. But in fact it was only a blueprint for the development of a modern Afghanistan drawn up by a minority of enlightened Afghan intellectuals. The acid test was the development of the necessary institutions, which, as in all communities, societies, and nations, are the only guarantee of the kind of rights, human and civic, to which the 1964 constitution attested.

In the Afghan context, as in many other societies, the natural and harmonious development of civic institutions cannot be taken for granted. It is a long haul. The process took several centuries in the more or less homogenous nation-states of post-medieval Europe. The experience was to be repeated, more or less painfully, in post-colonial Asia and Africa, and in the newly independent states of the former Soviet Union, the efforts towards the creation of a 'civil society' being telescoped into a generation or two in ethnically heterogeneous states with diverse historical and cultural heritages.

After the adoption of the 1964 constitution, elections to the bicameral legislature were held, and the results announced the following year. The level of popular participation in the election was as follows: in the highly politicized urban centre of Kabul, 'about 15,000 of the 40,119 eligibles voted, but results from Ap-Kupruz, a sub-district in north Afghanistan, probably reflected more closely the national average: 3000 of the 19,003 eligibles voted.'[2]

In 1965 more than 90 per cent of the population of Afghanistan was estimated to be illiterate. The lack of popular enthusiasm for the new-fangled concepts and institutions, imposed from above by urban or foreign-educated intellectuals, showed how little relevance these had to the reality of the everyday lives of a predominantly rural and tradition-bound people. Afghans could therefore not be expected to be open and receptive to the potential benefits that their participation in the workings of the institutions could bring, leading to a transformation of their lives. Their faith was in their qawm. Their traditional distrust of the encroachments of the state - be it Durrani, Marxist or Islamist - would remain intact.

But there was a fundamental flaw in the constitution itself that made the institutions unworkable in practice from the beginning: the absolute separation of powers between the executive and legislative branches of government. Neither the prime minister, the head of government appointed by the king, nor any of his cabinet ministers, could be members of either house of parliament. After the king had approved the list of ministers proposed by the prime minister, the list was submitted for approval to the fully elective lower house (Wolesi Jirga), once the prime minister had outlined the government's policies in general to the house, which had the power of veto. Only after the prime minister had received a vote of confidence from the elected lower house would the king endorse the ministerial appointments. According to the constitution, the king was held 'not accountable' for his actions. An uncooperative lower house elected by universal franchise could not only block cabinet appointments but also legislative enactments proposed by ministers. The system would have proved unworkable even in well-established parliamentary democracies.

Dr Mohammad Yousuf, who had served as interim prime minister since Daoud's resignation in March 1963, was confirmed in that office by the king when the new legislature met in October 1965. Reform-minded members of the Wolesi Jirga had expected a complete break with the past, with a prime minister and cabinet ministers who had no connection with previous governments, many of whose members were identified with corruption and nepotistic practices. Their vociferous accusations, supported by student demonstrations in and outside the House, came to a head on 25 October 1965 when troops opened fire on a group of students shouting slogans outside the home of Dr Yousuf, killing three. Before the month was out, the popular and respected minister of education, Dr Mohammad Hashim Maiwandal, was appointed prime minister and requested to form a new government by the king.

As one writer observed: 'The bulk of the Wolesi Jirga's members merely fulfil the minimum requirements of sanity, literacy, and attainment of the 25th birthday'. Afghan politics in the New Democracy were 'the politics of the intellectuals not of the masses'.[3] Thus it was that students and educated and semi-educated Afghans, concentrated in Kabul and the larger urban centres, came to have a preponderant influence on the future course of events. As some 90 per cent of the educated minority were to be found in Kabul, the city's influence was decisive.

It is therefore pertinent to introduce at this stage reviews of the development of modern educational institutions in Afghanistan, the growth of the Afghan press and the emergence of informal political groupings, and the economic basis of the Afghan state. These are essential to an understanding of the forthcoming Afghan debacle.

The development of state-sponsored education

The first high schools established in Kabul with a modern curriculum were foreign-language schools. The first was Habibia College (1904), which was modelled on the elite college for Muslims in Aligarh, India,[4] and staffed by English-speaking Indian Muslims. During Amanullah's reign, and due to the efforts of Mahmud Khan Tarzi, a French-language high school, the Lycée Istiqlal, staffed by French teachers, was founded in 1923, followed by a German college, Amania, in 1924, and an English college, Ghazi, in 1928. Many of the more promising graduates of these elitist schools went on to attend universities in France and elsewhere in Europe on scholarships.

Members of the Musahiban family had lived in exile in France until the abdication of King Amanullah in 1928. Zahir Shah, his uncles and cousins, including Daoud, had been educated in France, and it is therefore not surprising that the beginnings of higher education in Afghanistan had a French connection. A Faculty of Medicine, affiliated to the University of Lyons, was established in 1932 under French government sponsorship, followed in 1938 by a Faculty of Law and Political Science, affiliated to the University of Paris.

Other faculties that were subsequently established reflected the changing political realities, internal and external, in their funding, staffing and institutional affiliations. Thus a Faculty of Science, set up in 1942, was affiliated to the Universities of Bochum and Bonn in Germany. The Faculty of Theology (1951) was bonded with the ancient Islamic University of Al-Azhar in Cairo. As the needs of modernization developed, other faculties were set up with foreign assistance: Agriculture (1956, University of Wyoming, USA); Economics (1957, Bochum-Bonn); Education (1962, Columbia University, USA, which also sponsored the Ibn Sina Teacher Training Institute in Kabul); and Engineering (1963, US Engineering Team, formed by a consortium of nine

US institutions). A Faculty of Letters, set up in 1944 without foreign assistance, was expanded in 1966 to include an Institute of Anthropology sponsored by the German University of Heidelberg. Ominously the last of the schools at the tertiary level, the Polytechnic (1967), had the USSR as its godfather.

In 1947 the University of Kabul was formally established, to serve as an administrative framework for the existing faculties. However, these faculties and the others subsequently constituted continued to function autonomously, with independent sources of funding and staffing, and in separate physical locations. In 1964 they were brought together in a single campus, constructed by a West German firm, with funds provided by USAID: 'the usual example of West Germans making friends while making money, a process generally foreign to Americans', as Dupree wryly comments.

Under Daoud the state school system had expanded, with the government establishing primary schools in many villages and districts, secondary schools in provincial centres, and secondary boarding schools in Kabul for students from certain regions that appeared to serve Daoud's geo-political ambitions. For instance the Rahman Baba and Khushal Khan schools enrolled sons of rural khans from the eastern Pashtun tribes, along the Afghan and Pakistani sides of the Durand Line respectively. Daoud had also established a military boarding school in Kabul that trained mainly eastern and Ghilzai Pashtuns for careers in the officer corps.[5]

According to UNESCO figures, cited by Barnett Rubin with some reservations, in 1950–51, there were 91,414 primary school students enrolled nationwide, 4908 in secondary schools and 461 at the tertiary level. In 1965 their numbers had grown to 358,037, 45,248 and 3451; in 1975 to 784,568, 93,497 and 12,256; and at the time of the communist take-over in 1978 to 942,787, 106,544 and 21,118. Such statistics are to be treated with caution, since they conceal as much as they reveal. In the case of Afghanistan, the task of arriving even at approximations of population figures is hopeless at the macro level. The experts at UNESCO who compiled statistics to the last digit at the micro level should be congratulated on their zeal. But the actual figures themselves do not really matter. What matters is that there was a substantial explosion in the student population in Kabul and elsewhere in Afghanistan that had far-reaching social, economic and political consequences in a socially backward and resource-poor country.

As Barnett Rubin observes: 'The foreign aid-funded growth of the educational system quickly multiplied the number of educated and semi-educated youth of village backgrounds, although these remained an isolated minority in a country where less than 10 percent of the population and 2 percent of the women could read and write.' With regard to Kabul University: 'As with other development projects, the various faculties grew according to the amount of foreign aid available to them, rather than according to any educational program or employment plan.'[6] Dupree, writing in the early 1970s, described the University as 'an institution with a student body, faculty, and a curriculum, but few extracurricular goals or activities, a perfect breeding-ground for political discontent. About half of the students from all parts of Afghanistan live in campus dormitories with few university-oriented activities (social clubs, athletics, professional clubs) outside the classroom.'[7] One foreign observer quoted by Rubin characterized the University dormitories, where 1200 students without family connections in Kabul lived in 1967, as a 'center of insurgents', and 'the generation that crowded into the secondary schools in the New Democracy period provided the core leadership for all sides in the war, although a few of the top leaders were older'.[8]

In fact the state-sponsored education system, both in the provinces and in Kabul, estranged the rural youth who went through the system. This youth was to become 'a stranger: a stranger to his own society, and even worse, a stranger to himself', according to Sayed Majrooh, a prominent Afghan intellectual quoted by Rubin. The young rural Afghans became *déracinés*, cut off from their roots, separated socially and emotionally from their largely illiterate kin group, and even from their own family members. In a 1967 survey of Kabul University graduates cited by Rubin, it was found that 62 per cent had fathers with minimal or no formal education.

In Kabul the experience of adolescent students from rural backgrounds, abruptly moved from an extended family or clan in an isolated village into a state boarding school, must have been destabilizing. Even more traumatic must have been the experience of university students who mixed with their peers from all over the country, as Rubin states, 'in a heady atmosphere of freedom from parental and family supervision'. Another novel experience for the students was that of attending coeducational institutions. In 1961 the various faculties had been opened to women, one of Daoud's major contributions to their emancipation.

The objective of the state-sponsored education system was to train young Afghans to staff the expanding bureaucracy and to help them attain the skills required by the state-directed modernization programme. Opportunities for employment in the private sector were almost non-existent, and virtually the only employment potential for high school and university graduates was to be found in state institutions. According to Rubin, there were 56,099 men and 6323 women employed by the government in 1974, with 35 per cent of the men and 69 per cent of the women working as teachers. The public service was expanded partly in order to employ graduates. But at the end of the New Democracy period, unemployment among university graduates was visibly increasing.

Although the education system offered rural youth career opportunities external to their qawm, even those who eventually found work in the centralized state infrastructure were thwarted and frustrated in their aspirations if they did not have the right family or other connections. Professional advancement depended less on merit or achievement and more on seniority and personal connections. Salaries were low, fostering corruption. With the decline in foreign aid in the New Democracy period, inflation reduced purchasing power, stirring further discontent.

Contributing to the Afghan brew of social and political ferment was the increasing number of young Afghans who had been sent abroad on scholarships to study at foreign universities or to receive technical or military training. Rubin states that in the early 1970s two-thirds of the teachers in the Law and Political Science Faculty of the University held degrees from French universities, and half the teachers in the Faculty of Theology (the shari'a faculty) had degrees from Al-Azhar in Cairo. These and other foreign-trained students had acquired fresh perspectives with which they could judge their backward nation. They would also be a source of recruits for progressive or radical political movements of all colours. Between 1956 and 1978 it is estimated also that some 5000 Afghan students attended Soviet academic institutions, and an additional 1600 received training in Soviet technical institutes. As will be seen, many of these students, like the officers of the Afghan armed forces trained in the Soviet Union, brought back with them, along with their academic and technical qualifications, a great deal of foreign ideological baggage that became dangerous to the future of Afghanistan.

The Afghan press and the formation of political parties

A rather elaborate Press Law was promulgated in 1965, in line with the constitutional undertaking to guarantee freedom of expression, but with provisions to safeguard 'the fundamentals of Islam, the constitutional monarchy, and other principles enshrined in the Constitution'.

Dupree lists 30 privately sponsored weeklies that appeared, disappeared and reappeared in the New Democracy period, not to mention numerous provincial newspapers and government-sponsored publications.[9] The financial basis of the independent publications was precarious, and since they relied exclusively on private funding, they appeared irregularly or closed down completely for this reason. The government sometimes clamped down on others when they expressed views that came perilously close to subversion, as happened during the relatively liberal regime of Prime Minister Shah Mahmud in 1946–52. One of the conspicuous failures of the democratic experiment was that the special legislation required by the new constitution to legitimize the formation of political parties was never passed.[10] The 1965 election campaigns had centred round personalities with local power-bases or influence, rather than on the basis of party platforms, and the next elections in 1969 were conducted on the same lines, in the absence of formally legalized parties.

The Wolesi Jirga (lower house) of 1965 was the most representative of the 12 Afghan parliaments that had sat since 1931. According to Louis Dupree, a first-hand observer, the interests and opinions of the members loosely coalesced into six identifiable groupings. There was a 'stick-in-the-mud' group of conservatives headed by traditional religious leaders; a group of Pashtun ultra-nationalists led by Ghulam Mohammad Farhad (known as Papa Ghulam), who was also the publisher of an influential weekly, *Afghan Mellat*; a group favouring free enterprise; a centrist group led by a poet, Khalilullah Khalili, that supported the king's progressive policies; a small group of articulate liberals led by Mir Mohammad Siddiq Farhang; and a tiny vocal group on the left, led by Babrak Karmal and his close friend, Dr Anahita Ratebzad, both elected from Kabul constituencies where they had a popular following. The latter had won one of the four seats reserved for women. Karmal and Ratebzad were both leaders of the student demonstrations that broke out at the opening sessions of parliament, as mentioned earlier. None of these informal groupings, except the leftists, were to achieve politically viable organizational structures at the national level.

Political expression in Afghanistan outside the elite ruling groups had first begun to take shape during the Shah Mahmud period. The manifesto of the reformist and nationalist Tehrik-i-Naujawanan Baidar (TNB), or Movement of the Enlightened Youth, has been briefly described at the end of Chapter 2. Its members were middle class in origin and exposed to Western ideas, either at the high schools and the University faculties in Kabul staffed by foreign teachers, or at universities abroad. While they were all nationalists and wanted reforms of one kind or another, some were irredentists who espoused the cause of Pashtuns on the other side of the Durand Line, some were Islamic radicals, and others were liberals and progressives, some avowedly Marxist.

The TNB was suppressed just before the palace revolution that brought Daoud to power as prime minister in 1953, and some of its more vocal leftists were jailed. Among these were the doyen of Afghan Marxism, Dr Abdul Rahman Mahmoodi, who had edited a Persian-language bi-weekly, the *Nida'-yi-Khalq* ('Voice of the People'), Mir Ghulam Mohammad Ghubar, who had edited another Persian bi-weekly, *Watan* ('Homeland') and had written a history of Afghanistan from the progressive point of view while in prison, and Mir Akbar Khyber, a dedicated Marxist who was the mentor of the young Karmal who was also imprisoned in 1953.[11]

The Marxists

It was in prison that Babrak became a committed Marxist and took the name Karmal ('Comrade of the Workers' in Pashtu) to dissociate himself from his elitist bourgeois background. His father had been a general and a provincial governor. After his release from prison in 1956 Karmal did two years of military service before resuming his studies at the University. He had been very active in the students' union, formed in 1950. By now, after his prison term, he had become a hero to reform-minded students. He used his prestige and his talents to recruit actively for the Marxist cause.

Noor Mohamed Taraki, who was later to become the leader of the 1978 communist coup d'état, was a writer who had become a Marxist through his contacts with Indian communists in Bombay, where he had worked from 1934 to 1937 as the representative of the leading Afghan capitalist entrepreneur, Zabuli. After his return from India he continued to work for Zabuli in Kabul, and took a degree in law and political science at the University. It was about this time that he began writing short stories, taking as his theme the exploitation of the Afghan peasantry by landlords. He was assistant editor of an Afghan news agency from 1951 to 1953. Despite his TNB involvement, he was not imprisoned but sent to the United States as the press and cultural attaché at the embassy in Washington. He was recalled by Daoud in 1953 after he had resigned from his post, following public declarations in the US and in Karachi of his opposition to the monarchical regime. According to his official biography, published during his time in power, he is said to have telephoned Daoud from Kabul airport and told him: 'I have returned. Should I go home, or to the jail?' Daoud did not imprison him, but all avenues to state employment were now closed to him. He eked out an impecunious existence by opening a private translation agency that also did some work for USAID.[12] But he resumed his political activities.

During his decade as prime minister, Daoud's growing relationship with the Soviet Union to further his own national ambitions did not extend to tolerance of its ideological disciples in his own country. Avowed Marxists like Dr Mahmoodi, who was also pro-Beijing, spent the entire Daoud decade in jail. Others like Khyber and Babrak Karmal were released in 1956 on condition that they did not persist in their political activities.

However, these committed left-wing intellectuals and activists began to meet in clandestine 'study circles'. These were informal groups, and membership did not extend beyond the coterie of like-minded friends and acquaintances of the organizers; they met in private homes. There were reportedly four of these in the early 1960s: a circle led by Taraki (a Ghilzai Pashtun); another led by Karmal (a Ghilzai Pashtun, although it has been alleged by his detractors that his family was of Tajik origin) and his mentor,

Mir Akbar Khyber, with Tajik and Hazara members; another led by Karmal and Badakhshi, a Tajik who recruited mostly students from his native province of Badakhshan; and a circle formed by another Tajik Panjshiri, with Tajik and Uzbek recruits. It is interesting to note how these small groups of left-wing activists were already dividing along the tribal and ethnic lines of Afghanistan, although they were a powerless minority on the political scene at the time.

The provision in the 1964 constitution concerning the eventual legitimization of political parties led members of the Marxist study circles to conclude that the time was propitious for the formation of a progressive party. In January 1965 30 of these men met at the house of Taraki to form the People's Democratic Party of Afghanistan (PDPA), or Khalq ('People') for short. The 'founding congress' elected a seven-member Central Committee, and four alternate members. Some important future leaders of the PDPA were not present: Khyber had been appointed instructor at the Police Academy; Anahita Ratebzad, Karmal's mistress, was attending to the dissolution of her marriage; and Hafizullah Amin was completing his studies in the United States.

The political programme of the PDPA was contained in documents and articles published in the party organ Khalq, which appeared for the first time in April 1966. The stated objective was to resolve 'the fundamental contradictions of Afghan society', which could only be accomplished through socialism, and by the constitution of 'a national government'. 'The political pillars of the national government of Afghanistan would consist of a united national front representing all the progressive, democratic and nationalistic forces, that is, workers, farmers, enlightened and progressive intellectuals, craftsmen, the petit bourgeoisie and national capitalists.'[13]

This statement was in keeping with the orthodox Leninist line, that in the post-colonial world, and in countries that had achieved independence under the leadership of 'bourgeois nationalist' parties, 'progressive forces' – i.e. local communist parties ideologically allied to the USSR – should seek to form anti-imperialist 'united fronts' that would bring about socialism through participation in a 'national democratic phase'.

But from its inception the internal organization of the PDPA, and hence the power structure, was based on the pure Stalinist model. Membership was not open, even to other professed Marxists, and candidates had to undergo a probationary period. The party hierarchy, consisting of a general secretary (the party leader), first secretary, politburo and central committee, reflected the Soviet pattern.

Without the legal cover of the yet-to-be-enacted legislation for the recognition of political parties under the constitution, the PDPA fielded eight candidates for the 1965 elections on a personal footing, of whom four won seats. Among those who were not returned were Taraki and Amin who had no personal influence in the constituencies they contested – unlike Karmal and Ratebzad.

At a very early stage of its existence the PDPA broke up into two distinct factions, one around Karmal, the other around Taraki, the party leader, and Amin. The differences were not ideological, but personal, reflecting their different social origins and their different approaches to revolution. There were uncommitted members who threw their weight behind one or the other, depending on their interests of the moment. Thus Badakhshi and Panjshiri, both Tajiks from Badakhshan and the contiguous Panjshir Valley in the north-east, played a game of musical chairs to make sure that they were not on the same side in the changing internal configurations of the PDPA.

The first indication of a break occurred when the party organ, Khalq, published by Taraki, was banned by the authorities in May 1966 after only six issues. Karmal is reported to have described the paper's red masthead as 'leftist adventurism', observing that 'instead of flying the red banner, we should have tried to re-assure Zahir Shah that we were not communists', thus indirectly criticizing Taraki. Karmal was a firm believer in the 'national democratic' road to socialism, while his opponents tended to be more doctrinaire. The infighting that followed within the PDPA, when each faction tried to get its own candidates elected when the central committee was expanded, led to a complete break in May 1967. Two parties calling themselves the PDPA were formed, each with its own central committee and general secretary (Taraki and Karmal), despite efforts by the Soviet embassy to get the two factions to resolve their differences. The Karmal faction came to be known as the Parchamis (parcham means 'banner') and the Taraki-led faction the Khalqis.

The formal rupture also led to the emergence of splinter groups based on ethnic affiliations, such as Badakhshi's Sitm-e-Melli that began to organize youth in Badakhshan against the Pashtun domination of Afghan politics. There was one radical Marxist study circle that had kept out of the PDPA. The group had formed a pro-Beijing party in 1966, led by a brother and a nephew of Dr Mahmoodi, three months after the latter's release from prison and his death. These communists, who came to be known as Maoists, condemned the 'social imperialism' of the Soviets and their local allies, and had, unlike the PDPA, a following among industrial workers. The majority of workers in the Kabul factories were immigrant Shi'ite Hazaras, looked down upon by the rest of the population as a kind of underclass, a lumpenproletariat. The Mahmoodis tried to organize them on an ethnic and religious basis, and are credited with leading most of the workers' strikes in the New Democracy period.

The Islamists

In 1965 a group of *ustads* (professors, teachers) met under the auspices of the head of the Theology Faculty of Kabul University, Gholam Mohammad Nyazi, to found the Jamiat-i-Islami (Society of Islam). The members of the Jamiat had no formal links with the traditional Afghan religious establishment of trained theologians and jurisprudents, the ulema, but were products of the government education system of state-controlled *madrasas* (religious schools), high schools and university faculties. Nyazi, who was elected president or amir of the Jamiat, was a product of Al-Azhar in Cairo, the oldest extant centre of theological learning in the Muslim world.

The term 'fundamentalism' has been used in the media and in the literature as a catch-all phrase to describe radical Muslim movements everywhere. As Bernard Lewis reminds us in a perceptive analysis of the Iranian revolution, the term 'fundamentalist' as applied to such movements is not only inaccurate but misleading. The term was first used in English early in the twentieth century to describe certain Protestant Christian groups in the United States that believed in the divine origin and literal truth of the Bible, as a counter to the growing influence of liberal theology and critical biblical studies.[14] As Lewis states, 'In principle, all Muslims believe in the literal divine origin and textual inerrancy of the Koran. No one within Islam has ever asserted otherwise, and there is no liberal theology or critical Koran study against which a protest or reaction might be necessary.'[15]

There is also a distinction to be made between what the French scholar Olivier Roy calls 'traditional fundamentalism' – the will to have the shari'a and only the shari'a as the sole law – and 'Islamism' or 'political Islam'. In the Afghan context, the uprisings against an intruding non-Muslim power (the British in the nineteenth century, the Soviets in the twentieth), or against a reformist government (Amanullah in 1928, Daoud in 1975, the PDPA in 1978), were traditionalist reactions whipped up by the ulema and the mullahs, and as such 'have been pervasive through modern Afghan history'.

But for Islamists, the shari'a is 'just a part of the agenda ... They address society in its entirety, in politics, economics, culture and law.' Their aims are highly political, to gain power and establish an 'Islamic state', divested of 'un-Islamic' laws and other trappings influenced by Western concepts and ideals. Socially they draw their leaders and adherents not from the unlettered classes, but from Western-type high schools and universities, particularly from technical institutes, as they argue that science and technology are ideologically neutral and not incompatible with Islam.[16]

Islamism owes its ideological origins to an Egyptian religious reformer, Hassan al-Banna, who founded the Muslim Brotherhood (al-Ikhwan al-Muslimin) in 1928. He attributed the social and political corruption prevailing in his country to the separation of political power from the imperatives of Islam, compounded by the pernicious inroads of the West. Egypt at the time was virtually a British protectorate, a strategic area that, since Disraeli's purchase of the khedive's shares in the Suez Canal Company and Lord Cromer's long pro-consulship, secured the route to their empire in India. With colonies and protectorates in and around the Persian Gulf, European imperialism was the dominant political force in the whole region. The founder of the Brotherhood was also an anti-imperialist and anti-Western nationalist.[17]

After the Second World War, in the context of a decadent and discredited monarchy and the sterility of Egyptian party politics, the Brotherhood flourished. Its leaders and activists sought to transform society through preaching, good works and education. They were well organized and well represented in factories, trade unions and schools. They also ran businesses, using the profits to finance their social welfare programmes for the needy. The Brotherhood had perhaps half a million adherents in the 1940s, mostly from the poorer classes, those least tainted by Western influences, and the most resentful. They were also active in Syria and Jordan.

But there were in the Brotherhood's philosophy some latent ambiguities. To the Islamists, religion and politics are inseparable, and any Muslim society that fails to live by the Koran and the shari'a is considered impious, flouting God's law. This may have invited the more radical elements to conclude that the ends justify the means. The teeming cities of Cairo and Alexandria were highly secularized, centres of cosmopolitan culture to some, dens of vice and corruption to puritanical Muslims and to the deprived social classes who formed the overwhelming majority of the Egyptian population. Tens of thousands of the landless rural poor were immigrating to the cities to live in slums and earn a precarious livelihood.

There was a poisonous mix of everything in Egypt that could offend nationalist, religious or moral sensibilities: the post-war presence of British soldiers in the country; the conduct of the French who treated their Suez Canal headquarters in Ismailia as if it were a Shanghai-style extra-territorial concession; the mimicry of European lifestyles by political and social leaders and the Westernized bourgeoisie; and the flaunting of wealth in an impoverished country by the ubiquitous foreigner and his privileged Egyptian imitators.

It is therefore not surprising that when the Brotherhood failed to transform Egyptian society through their teachings and good works, such purely religious and social activities came to be subordinated to a campaign to rid Egypt of secularism, corruption and foreign influence by force. Some members of the Brotherhood resorted to terrorism to achieve their ends, by murdering government officials, bombing cafés and the like. In December

1948 the government of Prime Minister Mohammad Nuqhrashi ordered the dissolution of the Muslim Brotherhood and imposed a ban on its activities. Three weeks later one of the Brothers assassinated Nuqhrashi. Shortly afterwards al-Banna himself was murdered, allegedly by King Farouk's agents.

The avowed aim of the Egyptian revolution of 1952, led by General Naguib and Colonel Gamal Abdel Nasser and his Free Officers, was the abolition of the monarchy, the political liberation of Egypt from British domination and the reassertion of Egyptian sovereignty over its whole territory, including the Suez Canal and its operations. But Nasserism also implied that there was to be no retreat from the modernization that Egypt, almost alone in the Muslim world, had undertaken since the time of Mohammad Ali in the nineteenth century. Thus a confrontation with the Muslim Brotherhood, which had gone underground since the 1949 ban but had resurfaced during the revolution, became inevitable.[18] In 1954 an assassination attempt on Nasser was followed by swift reprisals on the Brotherhood: six of its leaders were hanged, and about a thousand others imprisoned.

The Islamist ideology was also expounded on the Indian sub-continent by Abul Ala Maududi who founded the Jamiat-i-Islami (Society of Islam) in 1941. Rejecting the nationalist and secular ideology of Mohammad Ali Jinnah's Muslim League, Maududi insisted that God was the only source of sovereignty, and hence of all authority and of law: men had no right to pass laws in place of God. It followed from this that the sole purpose of an 'Islamic state', as opposed to a Muslim state governed by Muslims, was to apply the precepts of God.

The far-reaching implications of this were given extreme expression by an Egyptian Muslim Brother, Sayyid Qutb, who asserted that contemporary Muslim societies had reverted to *jahiliyya* (the pre-Islamic Arab conditions of ignorance and savagery), that it was therefore lawful to wage jihad against governments that were Muslim in name only, and that the leaders of such governments should be considered infidels (*kafir*) and named or denounced as apostates (a process called *takfir*). The penalty for apostasy in formal Islamic law is death. Qutb was executed by Nasser in 1956. It is probable that the assassins of Anwar Sadat, and the other Islamic groups such as the Groupe islamique armée (GIA) in Algeria that have included murder in their political agenda, were, and continue to be, inspired by Qutb's extreme doctrines.

The Afghan Jamiat had a shared ideology with the Indo-Pakistani Jaamat founded by Maududi. The Afghan party had no immediate impact on the politics of the New Democracy period. Its leaders, such as Nyazi, Rabbani and Sayyaf, were university teachers on the government payroll. But they served as a clandestine ideological umbrella for its student wing, the Organization of Muslim Youth, which operated openly, organizing demonstrations and fighting communists. Islamists won the student elections at Kabul University in 1970.

The foregoing is an outline of the ideological forces at play towards the end of Zahir Shah's reign and their broad alignments. In the same way that there had been a split in the Marxist PDPA between the Parchamis and the Khalqis, there was also a parting of the ways between the moderates and the radicals among the Islamists of the Jamiat. The pragmatic Burhanuddin Rabbani and his fellow Tajik, Ahmad Shah Massoud, believed in a longer-term strategy for the establishment of an Islamic state, including the infiltration of the army and the bureaucracy, as they felt that the Afghan people were not ready to overthrow the establishment. The more radical elements, like the detribalized Ghilzai Pashtun Gulbuddin Hekmatyar, favoured direct confrontation by means of popular uprisings. The Islamists as a whole were not only critical of the royal establishment, but also despised the tradition-bound ulema and opposed Pashtun nationalism and the idea of a Pashtunistan. There was also a latent fragmentation along ethno-linguistic lines in the Jamiat as in the PDPA.[19]

The economic and financial basis of the Afghan state

The extreme fragility of the Afghan economy is best illustrated in the table below, which covers the period up to the eve of the abolition of the monarchy in 1973, with 1952 taken as the base year.

Before the upheavals following the so-called Saur Revolution of April 1978, the population of Afghanistan was estimated at some 15 million. Eighty-five per cent of the people were either peasants who made a precarious living off the land, or nomads. The nomads subsisted chiefly on their herds of livestock, exchanging their products for the agricultural produce of the villages they passed through in their annual migrations. Some groups, such as those from among the eastern Pashtuns, ignored international frontiers during these treks. They were natural traders, and some even became money lenders to the sedentary farmers.

The domestic resource base of the Afghan state at its inception was very weak, too weak to be able to respond to the aspirations of its modernizing rulers and elite without considerable help from foreign sources. To begin with, the state lacked the administrative structures required to put in place an efficient and effective system of tax collection targeting landowners, farmers and owners of livestock. Even the tax base was limited, scarcely adequate to meet the additional requirements of social and economic development. There was also very little capital accumulation, the nation being hardly endowed with a class of industrial and commercial entrepreneurs. As noted earlier in this chapter, almost all employment outside the agricultural, pastoral and trading sectors was tied to state or state-related activities.

State revenues, state expenditures and sources of financing

	1952	1962	1972
Domestic revenues (millions of afghanis)	614	2123	6172
Direct taxes			
Land and livestock	18%	6%	1%
Corporate taxes	13%	9%	6%
Indirect taxes			
Foreign trade	40%	50%	46%
Other taxes	7%	3%	2%
Sales			
Domestic (petrol, tobacco)	10%	24%	22%
Natural gas exports	0%	0%	12%
Other revenues	12%	8%	11%
State expenditure (millions of afghanis)	830	2996	7789
Ordinary expenditure	(660)	(1850)	(5689)
Defence and security	38%	38%	29%
Debt service	0%	14%	19%
Other	62%	48%	52%
Development expenditure	(170)	(1146)	(2100)
Education	15%	6%	4%
Health	0%	1%	4%
Transport/communications	0%	58%	15%
Agriculture	0%	8%	45%
Industry and mines	0%	25%	16%
Other	85%	2%	16%
Sources of financing			
Domestic revenue	74%	29%	20%
Domestic borrowing	8%	17%	4%
Natural gas exports	0%	0%	7%
Foreign aid	18%	54%	69%

Source: Adapted from Maxwell Fry, *The Afghan Economy: Money, Finance, and the Constraints to Economic Development* (Leiden: E.J. Brill, 1974).
Some of these figures have been rounded off.

One notable feature of the evolution of the Afghan economy, as revealed in the table, was the steady decline of direct taxes on agricultural and pastoral activities as a proportion of domestic revenues. From 18 per cent of total revenues of only 614 million afghanis in 1952, they declined to 6 per cent and 1 per cent of total revenues of 2123 million and 6172 million afghanis in 1962 and 1972 respectively.

According to Maxwell Fry, the agricultural sector was thought traditionally to have contributed about 50 per cent of the total value of gross national product (GNP). In the 1920s the land tax alone had often amounted to 20 per cent of the crop. Apart from bureaucratic inefficiency in overseeing the effective collection of taxes in a country where such impositions always met with resistance, there had also been a relaxation, by Nadir Shah and the Musahiban ruling class, of the pressure on the more important landowners to pay up, as a concession to the south-eastern Pashtuns who had assisted them in their accession to power. Afghanistan's tax effort had become one of the lowest in the world.

However, Nadir Shah and his successors were more successful in encouraging the growth of an alternative source of state revenue, through direct and indirect taxes on joint-stock companies. These companies were chiefly engaged in trade, organizing the export of the valuable karakul sheep skins (produced by Central Asian refugees who had fled the Stalinist repression of the 1920s and 1930s and had settled in northern Afghanistan), fresh and dried fruits, cotton and wool. They operated largely under the aegis of the private Bank-i-Melli, established by the leading Afghan entrepreneur, Abdul Majid Zabuli. It was Zabuli who, as minister of national economy, had visited Washington in 1948 to seek US assistance in the financing of·a modest development plan.

The Bank-i-Melli had been granted far-reaching powers over the regulation of the currency and the economy and thus acted virtually as a semi-official central bank.[20] The direct and indirect taxes levied on the private companies and on private traders were relatively easy to collect, requiring little coercion, as the success of the operations of the small entrepreneur class depended on state patronage and on their personal links to the Musahiban ruling class.

Thus, again with reference to the table, corporate taxes accounted for 13 per cent, 9 per cent and 6 per cent of the increasing government revenues in 1952, 1962 and 1972 respectively, this revenue increase being mainly due to large injections of foreign aid. Indirect taxes on foreign trade moved from 40 per cent in 1952, to 50 per cent and 46 per cent in 1962 and 1972 respectively. Another source of state revenue that increased during the same period was the income from the local sales of imports, chiefly petroleum products and tobacco, which rose from 10 per cent of total revenues in 1952, to 24 per cent in 1962 and 22 per cent in 1972. A new source of income arose in the 1960s with the exports of natural gas from sites in the north developed by the Soviets.

Government revenues in 1952 amounted to only 614 million afghanis, out of a GNP estimated at 19,053 million afghanis. These comprised direct taxes on land and livestock (18 per cent), and taxes levied on private enterprises (13 per cent). Indirect taxes accounted for 47 per cent of total domestic revenues, of which the largest component was the tax on foreign trade (40 per cent). The net proceeds from sales of imported products, such as petroleum and tobacco, which were government monopolies, as well as other revenues, made up the balance of 22 per cent.

However, the gap between state revenues and state expenditures remained very significant between 1952 and 1972. The sources of financing of government expenditure in 1952 demonstrate the extreme vulnerability of the Afghan economy, and therefore of the Afghan state at that time. In 1952 total expenditure amounted to 830 million afghanis, with 80 per cent devoted to ordinary expenditure, including defence and security (38 per cent), and development expenditure on infrastructure and services, including education, accounting for the remaining 20 per cent. With 74 per cent of the expenditure financed from domestic revenues, the deficit was met largely by foreign aid (18 per cent), along with some limited domestic borrowing (8 per cent).

The state was thus utterly dependent on foreign assistance (grants and loans) for the development programmes initiated on a large scale after Daoud became prime minister in 1953. It was a time when the international political environment was favourable to Afghan aspirations. The Cold War was at its height, and the Afghans benefited from the competition between the Soviet Union and the United States for leverage in the Third World.

Between 1953 and 1973 Afghanistan received the equivalent of nearly US$2 billion in foreign economic assistance: US$1265 million and US$110 million from the USSR and the Eastern Bloc respectively, accelerated by the visit of Bulganin and Khrushchev in 1955; and US$527.87 million from the United States after President Eisenhower's visit to Kabul in 1956. The bulk of Soviet assistance came in the form of loans; 71 per cent of US assistance consisted of outright grants.

The bulk of the foreign assistance went into the highly visible projects of infrastructure development mentioned in Chapter 3. However, just before the communist coup d'état of 1978, the economic and social indicators relative to Afghanistan were the worst in the world. Per capita income was $157, with correspondingly low per capita figures for agricultural and industrial production, exports and energy production. It was the most backward country in the world with respect to energy consumption, with almost the entire rural population having no access to electricity. The country also ranked among the lowest in the world in terms of public health facilities, with one doctor for every 16,000 Afghans, 80 per cent of the doctors being concentrated in Kabul. Despite the efforts deployed by the state to expand the school system, the educational facilities were heavily weighted in favour of the urban population. On the eve of the communist putsch 76 per cent of Afghan children had not received any education, with no more than 4 per cent of rural girls having ever attended a primary school. Afghanistan occupied the 127th place in the world in terms of literacy.[21]

To sum up, the Afghan state has had two abiding characteristics. First, it harbours a predominantly peasant population practising a subsistence agriculture at the limits of physical survival. Some areas, particularly where the land could be irrigated, were more productive than others. The growing of wheat, the primary crop, could be supplemented by the cultivation of grapes and other fruits as a means of earning cash. Productivity declined where the altitude and harsh growing conditions reduced cultivable land to narrow valleys. The effects of a prolonged drought, such as occurred between 1969 and 1972, could be catastrophic, not only for peasant agriculture but for the grazing of livestock by nomadic groups that was also a mainstay of the subsistence economy.

Second, the Afghan state has been what Barnett Rubin calls the 'rentier state' par excellence.[22] A rentier is by definition one who derives unearned income from property or investment. Since the time of Amir Abdur Rahman, who received subsidies from the British to procure arms and create an army to maintain law and order, Afghanistan has been a rentier state, dependent almost entirely on foreign aid to develop its infrastructure. As shown in the table, by 1962 foreign aid accounted for 54 per cent of the financing of government expenditure. A road system was being built with Soviet and US funds, equipment and materials that would link Kabul to the north and to Kandahar and Herat. The new transport and communication links threw open the country in a way that had never been accomplished before. Not only could goods and people move more freely between the countryside and the larger urban centres, but the urban centres, predominantly Kabul, attracted rural migrants in large numbers. There were not only the expanding educational opportunities for youth but also state-related employment prospects in the infrastructure development financed through foreign aid. Any slowing down of foreign aid, as the country was beginning to experience in the late 1960s, would also be disastrous. As Rubin states more recently:

> In the 1970s Afghanistan had an economy bifurcated between a rural, largely subsistence economy and an urban economy largely dependent on a state that in turn drew most of its income from the international state system and market. Agriculture and pastoralism accounted for more than 60 per cent of GDP, and about 85 per cent of the population depended on the rural economy for its livelihood. As late as 1972, economists estimated that the cash economy constituted less than half of the total. This figure probably increased after the completion of the nation-

wide ring road and a rise in remittances from labor migration to Persian Gulf
countries after the 1973 oil price rise.[23]

CHAPTER 5

The Abolition of the Monarchy and the Daoud Presidency (1973-78)

T he underlying causes of the social ferment that characterized the New Democracy period have been examined in the previous chapter. The level of foreign grants and loans that had sustained the growth of what Rubin calls a 'rentier state' (that is, a state deriving unearned income from property or investment, but in Afghanistan's case from foreign aid) began to decline after 1965. This trend was reflected in the rising levels of unemployment and under-employment among high school and university graduates, and the frustration of their social aspirations. In 1968 student strikes that began in Kabul spread to provincial centres, where students who had returned to teach and work had become carriers of a new politically radicalized militancy. There was also a spate of workers' strikes for better pay and conditions in the few industrial centres around the country. The PDPA was to claim later that it had led 2000 meetings and demonstrations throughout the country between 1965 and 1973, and 'thus played a vital role in the political re-awakening of the masses'.[1]

During this period, there was a polarization of forces in Afghanistan. The traditional conservative elements strengthened their position in the 1969 elections to parliament. Tribal khans and other wealthier provincial notables, including landowners, had come to realize the potential for tapping into the resources of the state through influence-peddling in an elected body. With money at their command, they had their sons, nephews and other relatives elected. Outside parliament the political Islam of the Jamiat was still a clandestine movement, but its student activists in the Organization of Muslim Youth operated openly against the Marxists and won the student elections at the University in 1970. The publication in a Marxist journal, *Parcham*, of an 'Ode to Lenin', couched in the language of praise reserved for the Prophet, was a provocation that brought the battles off the campus and into the streets of Kabul. In 1971 the University was closed for six months as a result of the bitter confrontation between Islamic and leftist radicals. The Islamic backlash also took the form of attacks instigated by the mullahs on women wearing Western dress. They were also incensed by the campaigns for female literacy and women's rights led by the All-Afghanistan Women's Council. According to a senior leader of the Council interviewed by George Arney, the mullahs declared in 1971 that 'women should stay in the house. Reactionaries sprayed acid on women's faces when they came out in public without a veil. And when women wore stockings, they shot at their legs with guns with silencers.'

Finally, as Arney says, 'it was the more elemental forces of nature that put an end to the democratic experiment'. A drought that began in 1969 lasted for three years. The effects were catastrophic. The number of deaths during the famine of 1971–72 were variously estimated at 'between 50,000 and half a million', with the poorest regions, such as the highlands of the Hazarajat, most badly affected. After the failure of the second successive harvest, the government appealed for international assistance. When the help finally arrived, including 200,000 tonnes of wheat from the United States, much of it was squandered through pilfering, profiteering and a corrupt and ineffi- cient administration. Thousands of peasants lost their flocks through lack of fodder, or their lands to money lenders.

On 17 July 1973, when Zahir Shah was on holiday in Europe, the king was deposed by his cousin Daoud, who was also his brother-in-law. At his first press conference the veteran politician promised a revolution: 'whenever a nation verges on disaster, and corruption in government institutions reaches its highest, and hope for reform is totally lost ... then a resort to revolutionary reforms must take place'.[2]

One of Daoud's priorities during his previous ten-year tenure as a royalist prime minister had been to create a modern army, supplied with modern weaponry and led by trained officers. As we have seen in Chapter 3, his task was achieved largely with the assistance of the USSR. Daoud had also built up an officer corps loyal to himself by personally supervising the appointment of all middle and senior ranks and by favouring those from socially under- privileged groups who had no family connections of their own. Although a privileged member of the ruling class, his French education may have predis- posed 'the Red Prince', as he came to be known, to adopt Napoleon's dictum that careers should be open to talent.

But unfortunately for Daoud the 1964 constitution had excluded mem- bers of the royal family, however talented or accomplished, from public office. As a fervent Afghan nationalist and reformer, the strong-minded erstwhile prime minister could not have been expected to retire permanently from the political scene and cultivate his private garden. Since 1969 Daoud had been hosting informal seminars at his house to discuss and analyse Afghan realities. But he had no power-base, no party of his own. His seminars attracted reform-minded Afghans of all kinds: a motley group of liberals, dissidents and young officers from the armed forces who had been exposed to progressive ideas during their extensive training periods in the USSR. The

Russians had been wise enough to have had most of them undergo their professional training in the Muslim lands of Soviet Central Asia, where they must have perceived that communist and Muslim egalitarian ideals were not altogether incompatible.

Babrak Karmal, the son of one of Daoud's former generals, also became a frequent participant at these seminars, and the self-appointed president would have realized that Karmal's Parchamis had the cohesion and discipline that he would need to secure control of the civil administration and implement the reforms he had in mind. When he proclaimed the creation of the republic, Daoud described the previous decade as a period of 'false democracy which from the beginning was founded on private and class interests' and the constitutional monarchy as 'a despotic regime'.[3]

Besides declaring himself president and prime minister, Daoud also held the portfolios of foreign affairs and defence. He also nominated a 50-member Central Committee. Its full membership was never revealed, but was said to include leading Parchamis like Karmal, Dr Anahita Ratebzad and Noor Mohamed Noor, who were thought to be part of an inner circle of advisers. Karmal's open support for Daoud was consistent with his view, and with the prevailing Soviet line, that the road to socialist revolution lay in the politics of the 'united front': the participation of progressive social forces in 'a national democratic phase'.

As revealed by Rajah Anwar, Karmal downplayed the role of his own party. He considered that Daoud's revolution was carrying out the programme of the PDPA, and any independent party activity would be counterproductive. He hoped to use the ageing Daoud to advance the cause of his own revolution, but without linking Parchamis too closely to the regime. There were six closet Marxists in Daoud's cabinet, but known Parchamis did not take up any official positions. It was said that Karmal himself had tactfully refused Daoud's offer that he fill the post of deputy prime minister.[4]

On the other hand, numerous Parchami supporters and fellow-travellers were placed in the ministries and in the lower positions of the state bureaucracy. A Parchami 'military wing' headed by Noor was also created to follow up on contacts with progressive-minded army officers that had been made at Daoud's seminars. Another of Karmal's aims was to weaken the Khalq faction of the PDPA, with which he had been engaged in a bitter feud since the 1967 break-up. But the wily Karmal's honeymoon with the imperious Daoud did not last very long.

Daoud's commitment to reform was genuine, as shown by his agrarian programme. Ceilings were imposed on land holdings, and he set a personal example by redistributing his ancestral lands. But his reformism was tempered by the pragmatism of an experienced politician who knew his country well. Landlords were compensated for land expropriated by the state, and peasants who could not afford to buy the surplus received no special help. As he himself said soon after he assumed power: '[any] measure for the sudden overcoming of centuries of backwardness and the immediate reforming of all affairs is a futile and immature act'.[5] It was a warning that the doctrinaire Marxist revolutionaries could have done well to heed when they overthrew Daoud in 1978 and launched their frontal assault on the long-entrenched traditions, and on the complex economic, social and political interests and relationships that had enabled the predominantly rural Afghans to survive, and more, during their 'times of trouble'.

But Daoud himself had never been able to master his inherent autocratic bent in the treatment of those who appeared to defy his will. He was no democrat.[6] When he compromised, he sought to manipulate, and when he failed, he struck. The first to suffer his wrath were those who could have helped him most to achieve his cautious reformist programme. They included three prominent leaders of the New Democracy, Dr Mohammad Yusuf, Musa Shafiq and Hashim Maiwandal, who were arrested on some vague charges of conspiracy. In October 1973 the government released a report on the 'confession and suicide' of the respected Maiwandal. The report was prepared by the Interior Ministry headed by the pro-Karmal Faiz Mohammad. Rajah Anwar's account of this episode supports Khalq's later allegations that the mysterious 'suicide' could be traced to the Parchami interest in eliminating Maiwandal, who had returned from abroad to forge an alliance with Daoud.[7]

One major plank in Daoud's foreign policy was, as he expressed it, 'unfalterable' friendship with the Soviet Union. Another was his perennial interest in the Pashtunistan issue. When he took power new opportunities had arisen to revive his irredentist ambitions. At the end of 1971 the Bengalis of East Pakistan, who made up more than 50 per cent of the population of Pakistan as a whole, had broken away under their leader Sheikh Mujibur Rahman to create the independent state of Bangladesh. In the west the Pashtuns and Baluchis who had, like the economically exploited and impoverished Bengalis, long suffered the domineering, centrist policies of the Punjabi-dominated federal government, champed at the bit.

In 1973 the Baluchi provincial government formed by the opposition National Awami Party (NAP) was suspended by the federal prime minister, Zulfikar Ali Bhutto, the populist leader of the Pakistan People's Party (PPP). This action led to an armed insurrection by the Marri and Mengal tribes of Baluchistan, and the resignation in protest of the NAP ministry in the NWFP. The Pashtun opposition in the latter province took the form of terrorist attacks, one of which took the life of the local PPP leader, Hayat Mohammad Sherpao, who was promptly declared a Pashtun martyr of the federalist cause, with a new town in Peshawar district being named after him.

The situation in Pakistan held out opportunities for Daoud that he was quick to exploit. A camp was established in Kandahar for the training and arming of Baluchi 'freedom fighters'. A godsend was the arrival in Kabul of the general secretary of the NAP, the Pashtun poet Ajmal Khattak, seeking political asylum. Bhutto retaliated by organizing his own bomb blasts in Jalalabad and Kabul, and by encouraging Islamic and other anti-Daoud factions to stage armed insurrections in 1975. These turned out to be unco-ordinated and ineffective. They were ferociously repressed. Hundreds of Islamists were executed or imprisoned, or fled into exile in Pakistan.

Bhutto's objective was to force Daoud to the negotiating table. Bhutto had rejected a hare-brained scheme dreamed up by his generals, to make up for their humiliating defeat at the hands of India in former East Pakistan by invading and occupying some adjacent areas of Afghanistan. He used his canny knowledge of inter- and intra-tribal rivalries in Baluchistan to eventu-ally defuse the explosive situation there. He successfully prevailed on the USSR to use their influence on Daoud to settle the Pashtunistan issue. As he reminded Brezhnev during his 1974 visit to Moscow, the Pashtuns, Baluchis, Punjabis and Sindhis were also part of the population of three other neigh-bouring countries, and a break-up of Pakistan on ethno-linguistic lines would threaten the stability of the whole region. When he returned to Islamabad, Bhutto was able to boast, 'I have cut the string that flew the Afghan kite.'[8]

When Daoud left Moscow after his first visit as president in June 1974, all he had obtained for his pains were a moratorium on debt repayments, a further $428 million in development aid, and a lot of advice which he strongly resented. He was told to negotiate with Pakistan – Daoud's public attacks on that country's treatment of its minorities were censored by the Soviet press – and exhorted to strengthen his partnership with the Par-chamis. Daoud's disenchantment with Moscow had immediate effects both on his foreign and domestic policies.

The Shah of Iran had sent a number of helicopters to assist the Pakistan army in its anti-insurgency operations in Baluchistan. Iran had its own size-able population of Baluchis on its eastern borders, and the prospect of a 'Greater Baluchistan' could not have been entrancing. However, in 1974 Iran and Afghanistan had signed the Treaty of Helmand involving the construc-tion of a dam on the river to benefit both countries. Afghanistan was also to receive a billion-dollar loan, mainly for the construction of a railway from Kabul to the Iranian port of Bandar Abbas on the Persian Gulf.

The Shah could not have relished Daoud's abolition of the monarchy, but he was America's 'regional policeman', had developed grandiose pretensions of his own, and now served as broker in weaning the Afghan republican leader away from his dependence on the USSR. In 1975 the Shah doubled his offer of aid to $2 billion. (In fact only $10 million was ever paid, and the projected railway was never built.) Daoud also began approaching other oil-rich nations aligned with the US, such as Saudi Arabia, Kuwait and Iraq, for assistance, and arranged for officers of his armed forces to be trained in Egypt and India.

After his Moscow visit Daoud began easing out known Parchamis from his inner circle of advisers and his cabinet. Some 40 Soviet-trained army officers were also removed from their posts, including those who had assisted him in seizing power. The purge was completed in 1975, but many closet communists holding minor but sometimes sensitive posts in the administration and the armed forces escaped the net. These included some members of his own security service, most notably the Parchami commander of his presidential guard. As Anwar states, 'There is no doubt that Karmal was well and regularly briefed by his men in the government on Daoud's thinking, strategy and secrets.'[9]

In 1976 Daoud had to swallow the bitterest pill of all – the abandonment of his long-held dream of Pashtunistan. In June of that year he received Bhutto in Kabul and indicated his willingness to make peace with his neighbour. In August he visited Islamabad and agreed to the Durand Line as the international boundary between the two states, in return for Bhutto's undertaking to release the imprisoned NAP leaders. Face was thus saved on both sides. That same month, the US secretary of state, Henry Kissinger, arrived in Kabul to give his blessing and express his government's strong support for Daoud's initiatives which, he said, had improved relations between the states of the region. That practised panjandrum of patchwork realpolitik had got his equations wrong.

Within the next three years radical changes were to occur that profoundly altered the political configuration of the region and its future history. In Pakistan Bhutto's land reform and nationalization programmes in the name of a populist brand of socialism had alienated the powerful land-owning classes and the industrialists. The armed forces had also become disaffected: Bhutto had initiated reforms to bring them under civilian control and so curb the political role they had played in the past. In July 1977 his elected government was overthrown in a coup engineered by his army chief of staff, General Zia ul-Haq. Bhutto himself was imprisoned on charges of murder, found guilty and executed in April 1979. In Afghanistan Daoud was killed during the communist coup d'état of 27 April 1978 that came to be known as the 'Saur Revolution'. By 1978 Iran was in a state of virtual civil war, with mass demonstrations against the Shah being followed by bloody repression by the army and the secret police, the dreaded Savak, trained by the Americans. In January 1979 the Shah was forced to flee abroad. The Ayatollah Khomeini returned in triumph after his long exile to establish an Islamic republic. Except perhaps in Pakistan, these radical transformations had been brought about by profound social forces that had been at work for quite some time, and lying outside the ken of the superficial realpolitik of international diplomacy.

Daoud's veering away from the Soviet Union, which became more marked after a showdown with Brezhnev during a visit to Moscow in June 1977 and the purge of his Parchami supporters, had forced the two bitterly opposed factions of the PDPA to unite, after much bickering and under Soviet pressure. The role of conciliator was played by an Iranian Tudeh Party leader, Ehsan Tabari,[10] as well as by Indian communists with whom Taraki had formed links during his sojourn in Bombay. In July 1977 the two factions agreed to form a single administrative organization, with parity for Khalqis and Parchamis in a 30-member central committee. It was in reality a tenuous alliance, not a reunification, so great was the rift in the PDPA as was shown up a year later after it took power. The application of parity was to be confined purely to civilian posts in a future PDPA administration, and not to the armed forces.

After Daoud's purge Parcham's representation in the armed forces was weak, but the Khalqis' recruitment drive, spearheaded by Hafizullah Amin, had proceeded by leaps and bounds, especially after Daoud's 1973 coup. Amin, a Ghilzai Pashtun like Taraki, was a poor scholarship boy who was a student, like Karmal, of the Najat school, a hotbed of dissent since the 1930s, and went on to acquire a science degree at Kabul University and degrees in education at the universities of Columbia and Wisconsin. By the time he returned from the United States in 1965 he had become a fully fledged communist.[11] He was a brilliant organizer who had used his influential teaching positions, lastly as head of the Ibn Sina Teacher Training Institute, to recruit actively for the PDPA from among disaffected teachers and other cadres in Kabul and the provinces. He also found fertile ground among progressive-minded officers in the armed forces, nearly one-third of whom, including the bulk of the air force, had been trained in the Soviet Union before the communist putsch in 1978.[12]

One of the contentious issues between the two PDPA factions had been the Parchami support for Daoud. Khalq could argue that this was a betrayal of the true socialist cause and that their own hands were clean. Such a stand attracted progressive Afghans, especially in the armed forces, who became disenchanted with Daoud who, lacking a power-base after his purge of the Parchamis and his distancing himself from his erstwhile Soviet ally, was resorting to the age-old practices of nepotism and buying allies where he could. He was also moving towards a one-party dictatorship by banning all political activities and opposition newspapers and by setting up his own National Revolutionary Party. By 1976 Hafizullah Amin had brought his military wing to a point of preparedness where the Khalqis believed that they could 'with a certain number of casualties on the part of the armed forces topple the Daoud government and wrest political control'.[13]

The majority of professional and technical posts in the civilian administration were also filled by those trained in the Soviet Bloc. Between 1965 and 1978, some 750 Afghan graduates were sent to the USSR and returned with higher degrees. Some 850 Afghans had also graduated from the Kabul Polytechnic, set up in 1967 as a symbol of Afghan–Soviet friendship, and staffed by some 50 Soviet instructors. A total of 1096 Afghans had also completed their training at the Gaz Technicum in Mazar-i-Sharif and the Auto Technicum in Kabul, established in 1971 and 1974 respectively, and also staffed by Soviet instructors. It is instructive at this point to cite the words of Rajah Anwar from an Afghan government publication that assessed the Soviet influence on the literate sections of Afghan society on the eve of the Saur Revolution:

> With the assistance of the USSR (before April 1978) construction work started on 174 major projects in productive areas. ... For instance, 60 per cent of public sector production and 60 per cent of power generation was produced through Soviet-made plants. Similarly, 60 per cent of the major roads were constructed and asphalted with the help of the Soviet Union and 65,000 persons were trained in skilled and unskilled jobs. ... In the course of the development plans the government spent 70 billion afghanis, half of which (or more than 2.25 billion dollars) came from the Soviet Union.[14]

PART II: THE DESCENT INTO CIVIL WAR AND ANARCHY

CHAPTER 6

The 'Saur Revolution' (1978-79)

The so-called 'Saur Revolution' was in fact a military coup carried out by leftist officers of the armed forces under the direction of the PDPA without any popular participation. It is generally agreed by the two PDPA factions that the putsch was planned for the late summer of 1978. But it was precipitated by the murder of the Parcham ideologue, Mir Akbar Khyber, who was led out of his house and shot dead by two gunmen on the night of 17 April. The funeral procession organized by the combined PDPA turned into an impressive demonstration by some 15,000 mourners, with both Taraki and Karmal making incendiary anti-imperialist speeches, as it was believed at the time that the CIA had had a hand in the assassination.

The PDPA alleged, however, after it had taken power, that the murder had been arranged by Daoud in order to flush out PDPA leaders and activists and to gauge the extent of the support they commanded. This is a more plausible theory[1] since, in the days following the murder, Daoud had the army cantonments carefully watched before arresting Taraki, Karmal and a few other known leaders on the night of 25-26 April. Strangely enough, Hafizullah Amin was not taken at the same time as the others. His house was searched, but no incriminating documents were found, and he was placed only under house arrest, until he was taken to the detention centre on the evening of the next day.

The episodes that were crucial to the success of the planned coup appear entirely fortuitous; indeed it is doubtful that it could have been carried out had they not occurred in this way. In the first place, the delay in placing Amin under detention with the others cannot be explained. Amin was the most dangerous of the PDPA leaders and the delay, combined with other circumstances, equally fortuitous, turned out to be of crucial importance. When the police knocked on his door on the evening of 25 April, Amin handed over his written plan of operations to his wife, to be hidden under a mattress in the children's bedroom. The police did not find it, and after they left he sent his eldest son to Taraki's house to find out what was happening. The boy returned to report that Taraki had been taken away that evening. Taraki's arrest, which was expected, was the pre-arranged signal for the plan's execution by Khalqi officers in the armed forces.

But Amin, who was under house arrest, was in no position to pass on the plan to his courier, Faqir Mohammad Faqir, until Faqir himself arrived by chance at Amin's house on the morning of 26 April. Faqir had a low-profile position among the Khalqis and was not on Daoud's surveillance list. He was a frequent visitor at Amin's house and the police guards let him in as they mistook him for Amin's elder brother, to whom he bore a close physical resemblance. Thus Faqir was able to pass on Amin's written instructions to Syed Ghulabzoi, a junior officer in the air force, who had been designated in advance by Amin for the important task of briefing Khalqi officers in the air force and in the Fourth Armoured Corps based in Kabul on the details of the plan. On the evening of 26 April Amin was moved to a detention centre close to the presidential palace where the other PDPA leaders were being held pending a decision on their fate. In the meantime Amin had also been able to pass on a message through his son to another Khalqi activist, Engineer Zarif, with instructions to be transmitted to those responsible for the take-over of the radio station, once the coup got under way the following day.

Other episodes that greatly assisted the PDPA also turned out to be somewhat fortuitous. After the crackdown on the communist leaders, parties and entertainments were held in the cantonments to celebrate the arrests. According to a PDPA assessment quoted by Anwar:

> The Defence Minister had ordered that all armed forces detachments to be on a war footing and celebrate the occasion the next morning with folk dancing and meetings. This treacherous order proved very useful to the forces of the revolution, as the Khalqi elements participated in these meetings where they contacted their unit commanders for instructions without raising suspicion.

On the morning of 27 April a Khalqi officer of the Fourth Corps, Major Aslam Watanjar, called on his commander with a request to draw six shells for each of the 12 tanks in his unit so that it could be in combat readiness as instructed, to which the general readily complied. However, by adding a zero to the requisition order signed by his commander, Watanjar was able to draw sufficient ammunition to arm ten times that number of tanks. According to Amin's plan, a squadron of the air force from the Bagram air base was to buzz the presidential palace at noon. This was to be the signal for the Fourth Corps to move in on the palace.

But things did not go strictly according to plan. The senior rebel officer at the Bagram air base, Abdul Qadir, a Parchami and a former vice-commander of the Afghan air force during Karmal's brief honeymoon with Daoud, was to take over the base and command the entire air operation in Kabul. Instead, possibly confused or nervous, he locked himself in his office. The planned low sorties over the presidential palace at noon did not therefore take place until 4.30 pm, after a number of tanks from the Fourth Corps were rushed to Bagram by Watanjar to take over the base. Ghulabzoi and Asadullah Sarwari, a former officer and Amin's chief recruiter for the air force, had been at Kabul airport since morning. The failure of Qadir and his squadron to appear over the Kabul skies at noon prompted them to take over the airport with the help of two tanks dispatched by Watanjar.

In fact, the most important role in the coup was played by Watanjar and his Fourth Corps which had ringed Daoud's palace and fired the first shell, as planned, at the Kabuli 'hour of the cannon'. Traditionally, like Hong Kong's famous 'noon gun', the hour was sounded by the firing of a cannon. This was the signal for all the other tanks to enter into action despite the fact that the squadron from Bagram had failed to appear. Daoud brought to a stop the cabinet meeting he was chairing at the time, advising his ministers to escape from the palace and save their lives. Only the defence and interior ministers managed to escape in order to rally the loyalist forces they could muster, unsuccessfully as it turned out. The other ministers sought refuge at the royal mosque in the palace grounds. The sound of firing from the palace was the signal for Khalqi supporters everywhere to take over the armouries and command centres in Kabul, summarily shooting those officers who resisted and placing under arrest those who did not.

The fiercest resistance, however, was offered by the 2000-man presidential guard at the Arg palace commanded by a closet Parchami and, like Daoud and his royal clan, a Mohammadzai Pashtun who had evidently not been apprised of the coup.[2] The guard fought almost to the last man and the last round to defend the fortress-like palace before it was taken in the early hours of 28 April. Two infantry divisions also offered resistance. One of them tried to prevent the take-over of the radio station. But infantry was no match for an armoured force led by determined officers.

The rebel officers had no choice but to continue once they had started. The arrests of the PDPA leaders implied that their sympathizers in the armed forces had to take urgent action to forestall their own arrests and certain execution by Daoud. The palace meeting was called to discuss the fate of the arrested PDPA leaders, and there could have been no doubt that the penalty for treason would be death for all those involved if the coup failed. Daoud and his family were killed in a burst of gunfire after he drew a gun and wounded one of the rebel officers who had entered the palace in the early hours of the morning of 28 April to arrest him after the annihilation of the presidential guard.

But Daoud was still alive and fighting on the evening of 27 April when Qadir (in Persian) and Watanjar (in Pashtu) announced on Radio Kabul that a 'military council' headed by Qadir had taken power. This announcement was followed by the traditional Muslim invocation and then by a brief state-ment to the effect that future policy would be based on 'the preservation of the principles of the sacred teachings of Islam' and the 'promotion of the advancement and progress of our beloved people of Afghanistan'. Neither Marxism nor socialism were mentioned.

As was to be expected in the circumstances, there was much confusion in people's minds about what was really happening. The coup was carried out in a general atmosphere of indifference as far as the man in the street was concerned. The presidential guards at the palace resisted what they thought were reactionary right-wing elements in the armed forces who were opposed to Daoud's progressive policies. But the rightists themselves were confused and divided over the nature of the change. In Pakistan a member of the Mujaddidi family issued a press statement saying that 'Islam-loving' elements had taken power. The Soviet news agency, Tass, referred in the next three days to a 'coup d'état' rather than a revolution. Except for a strong note from his government protesting against the arrests of the PDPA leaders, which the Soviet ambassador was unable to deliver to the foreign minister on 27 April, there was no Soviet involvement in what was purely an Afghan affair, not-withstanding Cold War-biased Western reports to the contrary.[3]

There was even greater confusion for several years in the media and in the literature as to the relative weight of the roles played by the various PDPA actors in the putsch. The communist practice of rewriting history did not help. There was the Taraki version in the flattering biography of the 'Great Leader', the Amin version produced after the overthrow of Taraki, and the Karmal version that prevailed after the Soviet invasion and the assassination of Amin.[4]

Three days after the coup, the formation of a Revolutionary Council of the People's Democratic Republic of Afghanistan was publicly announced, with Taraki named as chairman and Karmal vice-chairman. According to Anwar, the Council consisted of 30 civilians drawn from the joint PDPA Central Committee, and five officers. The Council met on 1 May to choose a cabinet. Portfolios were evenly allotted to both Parchamis and Khalqis, with Taraki as prime minister, and Karmal, Amin and Watanjar as deputy prime ministers. The portfolios of Defence and Public Works were assigned respec-tively to two Parchamis, Abdul Qadir of the air force and Mohammad Rafi of the Fourth Armoured Corps, who were thus rewarded for the important roles they had played in the military operations.

But the power structure reflected in reality the outlines of an incipient struggle between Karmal and Amin, with the ineffectual and indecisive

Taraki in the background as a figurehead. What appeared on the surface as an equitable political balance was in fact a fearful symmetry, with the 'tiger' Amin, the actual architect of the revolution, waiting to pounce when the opportunity arose. As Anwar states:

> What the Party had done was to set up not one but three governments within the government in an effort to maintain what it thought was a political balance. Taraki was a sort of federal head of three governments. For the Khalq Ministers, Amin was the Deputy Prime Minister, while the Parchamite members of the cabinet were answerable to Karmal only. The (Khalqi) Watanjar controlled his (Parchamite) army colleagues, Qadir and Rafi. No Deputy Prime Minister was supposed to interfere in the working of the Ministries which were not under his direct control. In other words, these three mini-cabinets were three distinct and conflicting groups. They even used to hold separate sessions. Karmal had succeeded in wresting the army from Amin's direct control, whose portfolio (Foreign Affairs) was really a device to distance him from his former constituency, namely the armed forces.[5]

But Amin needed Parchami support at this stage because of their widespread presence as moles in the civilian bureaucracy during the Daoud presidency, while he himself had concentrated his efforts on infiltrating and subverting the armed forces.

The Revolutionary Council was soon replaced by a Soviet-style Politburo where all major decisions were taken. Amin was not a Politburo member, neither were the military members of the cabinet. The inclusion of PDPA-inclined officers in the civilian Central Committee had been a bone of contention between Parchamis and Khalqis since the reunification of the two factions in 1977. But after the coup, the astute Amin changed his previous position to argue cogently for the inclusion of the officers who had played such an active role and risked their lives in bringing the Daoud regime to an end. This he did in a document produced and circulated by the army's political department, which his own men controlled, before a meeting of the Politburo scheduled for 24 May.[6] This blow-by-blow account highlighted the role of Amin and the Khalqis in the revolution at the expense of Karmal and his Parchami followers, such as the commander of the presidential guard who had put up such a stiff resistance. The Parchamis, who now occupied half the cabinet posts, were painted as political opportunists, implying that they had been brought to power on the coat tails of the truly revolutionary Khalqis.

At the 24 May meeting the Politburo agreed, despite Karmal's opposition, to induct four officers into the Central Committee. Karmal's objections to the use of the term 'Khalq' to designate the victors without reference to the Parchami role were overruled by Taraki. The latter maintained that the term 'Khalq' was a true reflection of the party's unity, while Parcham was a symbol of factionalism. Karmal also proposed that the army pamphlet, with its exclusive reference to the Khalqis, be withdrawn and confiscated on the grounds that it would give rise to internecine feuds, and be replaced by a more representative account to be produced by the Politburo itself. On the issue of the pamphlet, which included for the first time flattering references to Taraki as the 'Great Leader' and the 'Great Teacher', the wily Amin had correctly concluded that if Karmal objected to the pamphlet, it would become evident to Taraki, who was susceptible to flattery, that he was not willing to accept Taraki as the 'Great Leader' of the unified PDPA or Khalq (People), as the party was named when it was founded in 1965.

When reading the history of the period before the Soviet invasion of December 1979, it is easier now, with the benefit of hindsight, to discern a pattern, a truly Machiavellian design on the part of Hafizullah Amin. His first objective was to get rid of Karmal, towards whom he bore a congenital hatred and with whose policy of a 'national front' he disagreed, and next, to over-throw his own leader, Taraki.

On the very first day of the coup two incidents occurred when the fight-ing was still going on in which Taraki had openly sided with Karmal rather than bowing to Amin's own views. After they were released from detention and taken to the radio station, Karmal expressed the opinion that until there was complete certainty that the revolution had succeeded, it was inadvisable to remain at the station where they would be sitting ducks. Amin vehemently opposed the proposal, asserting that at this critical juncture the party leaders should stay close to the officers and to the scene of action and take direct command of the fighting. The cautious Taraki agreed with Karmal and went with him and others to seek the relative security of the airport. Amin stayed back to organize a makeshift operations room from where he could keep in touch with and encourage Khalqi officers in the various cantonments.[7]

The second incident occurred after Taraki and Karmal had returned to the radio station and a public announcement was being prepared. Against Amin's insistence that the party leader himself should read the announce-ment, Karmal argued that at this stage the direct involvement of Taraki, a known communist, could rally the opposition, especially right-wing officers in the armed forces. He proposed that the announcement should be made in Dari (Persian) by Qadir, known for his nationalistic views, to which Taraki agreed, offering Amin a compromise in the form of a Pashtu version to be read by the Khalqi Watanjar. Such incidents must have brought home to Amin the urgent need to wean Taraki away from Karmal's influence through flattery and sycophancy, and to put him off his guard before taking a shot at the indecisive dreamer and drunkard, Taraki himself. Amin did not waste time. In less than 18 months he had achieved both objectives.

Within three months of the coup, Amin had deftly outmanoeuvred the Parchamis. At a meeting of the Central Committee on 27 June, it was decided that state policy would be decided exclusively by Khalq. Amin was inducted into the Politburo and appointed to the key post of general secretary. Karmal's idea of a united national front was abandoned in favour of a party-centred centralized authority on the Stalinist model. The powers of the provincial governors appointed in line with Parchami recommendations were transferred to provincial party secretaries, with party functionaries eventually assuming power down to district and sub-district levels. Khalqis were also appointed to organize and run movements of peasants, women and youth.

Karmal and other leading Parchamis were shunted off to live in glorified exile as ambassadors. The 27 June decisions had virtually ousted Karmal from the government. But as a party veteran he could not have given way so easily before the machinations of a relative newcomer like Amin. It appears that before leaving to take up his post in Prague, he had laid down plans to take power with the help of Parchamis who were still in place, notably Defence Minister Qadir and the Army Chief of Staff, General Shahpur Ahmedzai. The coup was planned for 4 September, on the day of the major religious festival of Eid, when soldiers and officers would be on leave and the atmosphere relaxed. A situation was to be created in which Qadir and Shahpur would intervene on the pretext of fighting in defence of the government, assume power, and form a 'United National Front' with Qadir at its head. As Anwar says, the plot was ill-considered in political terms: Qadir, who was to play the central role, was a non-Pashtun, and a Shi'ite from Herat, while the majority of the officer corps were Pashtun, Sunni and solidly pro-Khalqi.

As it turned out, the conspiracy was blown in August. The Afghan ambassador in New Delhi, a Daoud appointee who had been left in place as he had become a closet Khalqi supporter (unbeknown to Karmal who had trustingly confided his plans to him), tipped off Taraki and Amin. The 'Eid plot' played well into Amin's hands. Qadir, Shahpur and others were promptly arrested. It is said that Asadullah Sarwari, Amin's intelligence chief, made Qadir 'sing like a canary'. Amin went on a witch hunt for Parchamis, eliminating them and their sympathizers from key government and party posts and filling the jails with them.[8] Parchami ambassadors, including Karmal and Najibullah, were recalled but did not return, absconding, it was alleged, with their embassy funds. With the defence portfolio vacant after Qadir's imprisonment, Taraki and Amin fell out openly on the question of a replacement, the former favouring the appointment of Watanjar to counterbalance Amin's influence over the officer corps. Taraki compromised by taking over the portfolio himself with Amin as his deputy.

The Afghan communists were deeply aware of the fact that they were a minority striving to bring about a revolution in a country with a small working class concentrated in Kabul and a few other cities, and an apathetic peasantry. They had gained power through a military coup and felt they had

to strike swiftly and ruthlessly before a 'counter-revolution' was able to organize itself. They tried to achieve this by three means: repression, made possible
by the existence of a loyal and well-equipped army; agrarian reforms, which
they thought would win the support of rural people; and a mass literacy
campaign to wean the people away from the influence of the clergy and to
spread the communist ideology. The arbitrary manner in which this 'revolution from above' was carried out in a rural society whose inner workings they
were not aware of, or which they simply misunderstood or ignored, was a
prime cause of the spate of spontaneous uprisings that took place before the
Soviet invasion.

The triumphant PDPA ruled by decree, establishing Taraki as the supreme leader (Decree No. 1), setting up a government (No. 2), and abrogating
the Daoud constitution (No. 3). Subsequent decrees elevated the Uzbek,
Turcoman, Baluchi and Nuristani languages to the status of 'national languages' to be promoted by the media (No. 4), deprived members of the royal
family of their citizenship (No. 5), cancelled land mortgages (No. 6), gave
equal rights to women (No. 7), and ordered land reforms (No. 8).

Decree No. 6 was aimed at abolishing the mortgage system that went
hand in hand with rural debt. Peasants owning smaller plots of land had
been forced over the years, because of their lack of capital to buy seed, fertilizer and tools, to mortgage their sole asset to landlords or money lenders.
Debts and mortgages incurred by peasants owning five acres or less were
cancelled by the decree, and the land returned to its owners without further
encumbrance. It was assumed that 81 per cent of the rural population would
benefit from such a humane and equitable measure. The decree did not apply
to mortgaged lands above the five-acre ceiling. But the implementation of the
fiat from Kabul was doomed to failure.

In the first place, almost all land deals were contracted orally, with no
written or documented records to cover the bulk of the mortgages. Secondly,
the decree was implemented by inexperienced party officials, usually primary
school teachers, as the PDPA lacked the organizational resources at the
grassroots level to see the reforms through. Also the intruding presence of
district officials, perceived by the local qawm as representatives of the much-
resented central authority, precluded any meaningful cooperation with them.
Thirdly, in the absence of rural credit facilities backed by the government,
smallholders and landless peasants could only obtain financial help for the
purchase of seed, fertilizer and other capital inputs from money-lending
nomads, traders, landowners and tribal khans, often at exorbitant rates of
interest. Thus when the decree was published, money lenders stopped extending loans to their impoverished clients. The overall effect of the decree
was to short-circuit the traditional and informal system of rural credit that
enabled the peasants to survive. One result was that those few farmers who

had managed to repossess their holdings re-mortgaged them to their old creditors. Another was that those directly hit by the decree, the landlords and the money lenders, joined hands to resist the change. They found ready allies as usual among the mullahs and ulema, often landowners themselves, who gave their blessings to the unholy cause of defending the marriage of Islam and usury that was a mark of tribal economic relations in Afghanistan.

This paper decree was complemented by another (No. 8) that set an upper limit of 15 acres on landholdings. This meant in theory that 50 per cent of the agricultural land in the country would become available for distribution to landless peasants and others with holdings under five acres. At the same time all sources of irrigation were nationalized. The Ministry of Agriculture and the newly created Land Reform Commission were entrusted with the task, traditionally assumed by the qawm, of determining the allocation of water resources, leaving village cooperatives and water supply departments to handle the local arrangements. Financial help was in theory made available from the Kabul-based Agricultural Bank set up by Zahir Shah, whose main beneficiaries in the past had only been important landowners.

Another assumption made by the PDPA was that 40 per cent of the agricultural land was not cultivated due to lack of seed, fertilizer and water, and the prevalence of 'feudal' conditions in the countryside,[9] and that if the uncultivated land could be made productive, the country could achieve self-sufficiency in food. The land reform decrees were aimed at accomplishing this task. But the means employed were not only inadequate but showed the ignorance of the PDPA's activists of the complex rural realities.

Committees were set up in every district to implement the reforms. They were placed under the overall supervision of a provincial committee headed by the governor. Squads of city-bred youth, long on revolutionary zeal and pitifully short on knowledge and experience, would descend on villages, harangue the assembled peasants, and hand out title-deeds to the landless. Anwar cites an incident when a Party worker used derogatory language to describe a local landlord, whereupon one of the recipients reprimanded him for his lack of respect towards the khan and shot him dead. Such incidents took place across the country and attested to the PDPA's failure to appreciate the internal dynamics of the rural communities they were trying to change.[10]

Olivier Roy advances the hypothesis that the agrarian reforms were intended to break down the traditional socio-economic structures and not to create a system of modest individual landholdings backed up by an efficient system of rural credit that would have made them economically viable:

> Later on the government planned to set up cooperatives which would group small farmers who had benefited from the land reforms, and who would have now come to realise that it was impossible for them to make a living from their farms by themselves. In support of this view we might add that the official document which

published the article dealing with the establishment of agricultural cooperatives appeared in September 1978, that is to say before Decree 8. The agrarian reform may not have been a collectivist reform, but it seems that it was worked out with the clear intention that it should be the first stage on the route to a collectivist society of the future.[11]

The natural resistance of landlords to the agricultural reforms had a further dimension in that they counted among their ranks some of the country's most influential political, social and even religious leaders, such as the heads of the Mujaddidi and Gailani clans. Private property is considered sacrosanct in Islam, and the landlords found natural allies in the religious establishment of the mullahs and the ulema in a symbiotic relationship. As a Russian historian cited by Anwar states:

> It is important to note that Muslim theologians were the first to form into a privileged estate of the Pashtun society, and it was they who made the first breach in the system of agrarian relationships based on common ownership ... seri - a land benefice granted to the clergy can and must be regarded as the initial form of feudal land tenure.

This situation prevailed because seri lands once granted were never revoked. To cultivate them the mullah had recourse to members of other tribes who either sought refuge in the qawm or who had been vanquished in tribal conflicts, and as such were outsiders having no social status in the host tribe and easily exploitable as landless labourers.

These decrees, carried out without adequate preparation and with the hasty zeal of doctrinaire Marxist reformers, resulted in a disastrous drop in agricultural production. In an average year Afghanistan imported some 200,000 tonnes of wheat to offset the deficit in domestic production. The unrest in the countryside and the spreading civil strife soon caused a steep drop in domestic production. In 1979 some 350,000 tonnes of wheat had to be imported. In the spring of 1980, after the Soviet invasion, Babrak Karmal informed the country that out of a total cultivable area of 9.5 million acres, only 8.75 million acres had been cropped, reducing the average annual yield from 6.5 million tonnes to 5.9 million tonnes. There were similar falls in the production of other food crops, as well as cash crops like cotton, which registered a drop of 30 per cent.

Another source of tension was the implementation of the literacy campaign throughout the country: children and adults, young and old, had to learn to read and write within one year. The programme called for 18,500 teachers to be sent into the countryside, 16,000 of whom would be volunteers. The response of the rural people to the campaign was mixed. Previous regimes had spared no effort in bringing education to the countryside by establishing village schools, encouraging villagers to participate in the construction of the school buildings, with the government taking responsibility for the payment of teachers' salaries. The opportunity to learn was welcomed and teachers enjoyed a certain esteem as long as they did not overturn tradition. The PDPA's campaign came to be resented for a number of reasons: the teachers employed in the campaign were usually student volunteers supportive of the regime but who came from outside the qawm, often from Kabul and other cities, and who behaved in an authoritarian and arrogant manner; village elders and other old men who were forced to attend the courses were profoundly humiliated; the texts used had a Marxist slant that disturbed the devout, for one of the aims of the campaign was political indoctrination. But what sparked open resistance leading to revolt was the mixing of the sexes in the literacy classes, conducted mainly by adult males and adolescents from the cities because of the dearth of female teachers. Roy observes that there was a close correlation between the regions targeted in the literacy campaign and those where uprisings took place. By the winter of 1979–80, the literacy campaign had come to a halt in the countryside and now only affected the urban areas that were firmly in the grip of the regime.

Decree No. 7 related to the rights of women: child marriages were declared illegal, the minimum marriageable age for boys was set at 18 years, and for girls at 16, and the mutual consent of the bride and groom was declared essential. The aspect of the decree that provoked the most controversy was the upper limit of 300 afghanis placed on the *haq mehr*, or money payable to the wife in case of dissolution of the marriage. Generally, the bride-price payable by the groom's family was negotiated in advance by the two parties, the actual sum arrived at depending on the economic and social standing of the families. The provision of freedom of choice came up against other traditional practices such as the 'barter' arrangements whereby a daughter would be married to a brother's son, with a view not only to settling them but to keeping property within the extended family. Marriages were also used among the more influential classes to forge strategic alliances. It was also not unusual for marriage contracts to be negotiated when the prospective bride and groom were no more than infants. The decree was welcomed in more advanced urban circles where young people were able to marry the partners of their choice for the first time in Afghan history. But it was perceived as a frontal attack on tradition by the backward and unlettered people of rural Afghanistan.[12]

Repression during the Taraki–Amin period was at first selective, aimed at the complete elimination of certain social categories that were thought to be potential counter-revolutionaries. In the towns the victims were drawn from the higher ranks of the clergy, intellectuals, liberals and Maoists. In the countryside the targeted victims were drawn from among the clergy, leaders of the Sufi orders and people of influence in the local communities. Promi-

nent among those executed were the prestigious head of the Naqshbandiya
Sufi order, the Hazrat of Shor Bazar, and all male members of his Mujaddidi
family present in Kabul. Some 200 Islamic student militants, who had been
arrested by Daoud and had remained in the Pul-i-Charki prison without trial
since 1975, were executed in a single night in June 1979. In February 1980
the government put in place by the Soviets admitted that 12,000 people had
'officially' died, meaning that they had disappeared. The number of those
executed or missing in the countryside was uncountable: Roy estimates that
in all some 50,000 to 100,000 people disappeared.

Another kind of repression was in response to spontaneous uprisings that
began as local reactions to heavy-handed attempts by governmental authorities and their militant agents to impose their land reform and literacy
programmes, or to make arrests. The revolts typically took the form of an
attack led by religious leaders, village headmen and elders on a government
post, with heavy casualties on both sides. If the attack was successful, the
communist militants were executed, and non-communist soldiers and officials were allowed to leave. Then the revolt would spread to surrounding
areas where ethnic affiliation or tribal solidarity operated, and stop when the
frontier of the ethnic or tribal territory was reached. The earliest such revolt
took place in Nuristan in July 1978. Another successful revolt took place in
the Shi'ite Hazarajat in December 1978. Both these regions remained
autonomous for the duration of the civil war. Generally speaking the uprisings occurred in non-Pashtun or in detribalized Pashtun zones.

Those who remained passive or neutral during these uprisings or even
collaborated actively with the Khalqis were drawn from the urban lower
middle class of officials and employees dependent on the state, modern in
their outlook, and cut off from their roots in the countryside. Many high
officials retained their positions even as real power passed into the hands of
young and incompetent militants of the PDPA and their Soviet advisers. The
regime was even able to draw support and recruit militias from among those
peasants who had benefited from the land distribution programme at the
expense of rival tribes or clans. Roy states that 'as a general rule, zones which
had a strong mixture of uprooted tribal elements, migrants of all kinds, and a
hotch-potch of ethnic groups were more subject to government influence
(which was able to play upon the rivalries and frustrations plaguing subordi-
nate groups) than zones that were homogenous from an ethnic or a tribal
point of view.' Even in the latter zones, Ghilzai Pashtun tribal solidarity could
sometimes prevail over other factors as the Khalqi leadership was Ghilzai, the
first to take power in Afghanistan since the Durrani ascendancy began in the
second half of the eighteenth century.

It took only seven feverish months in 1978 for the PDPA's Khalqi faction
to get rid of Karmal and his Parchamis and initiate their reforms. But the

regime was vulnerable on many fronts. In addition to financial difficulties, the land reforms did not have the hoped-for result of an exploited and impoverished peasant population rallying gratefully and enthusiastically to the cause of revolution. The reforms, on the other hand, provoked unprece- dented tensions in the countryside. The pressure brought on them forced many tribal chiefs and their followers to move into Pakistan where they were received with open arms by the unpopular Zia ul-Haq regime, eager for an anti-communist cause to support and the means to consolidate its rule with international assistance. Every arriving Afghan was given a daily stipend of four rupees – more than the average income of an Afghan peasant. By the end of 1978 some 80,000 Afghans had reached Pakistan according to gov- ernment figures. Pakistan also claimed to have spent the equivalent of $145 million on 'humanitarian assistance' to the Afghan refugees. In the meantime the forces of opposition were rallying in Pakistan: eight training camps were established in the North West Frontier Province to turn simple Afghan refugees into guerrilla fighters.

In December 1978 Taraki and Amin flew to Moscow to conclude a Treaty of Friendship and Cooperation with the Soviet Union. To most observers it seemed a routine renewal of the 1921 treaty signed by King Amanullah. But there was a new provision that called for Soviet military assistance if needed, subject to two amendments introduced personally by Amin that augured his future independent stance vis-à-vis the Soviet Union, and which was to bring about his downfall: first, any Soviet troops sent for would serve under Afghan officers, and second, their eventual return would be decided by the host government. Large numbers of Soviet military and civilian advisers were already present in the country before the new treaty was concluded. Its signature was also a signal to the US and its Pakistani ally that their support of counter-revolutionary forces would bring in the Red Army.

But Pakistan's Zia ul-Haq, fired by his Islamic and anti-communist zeal, was not to be deterred. In January 1979 a first contingent of some 5000 insurrectionists under the banner of Gulbuddin Hekmatyar's Hizbi-i-Islami entered Kunar province, attacked Asadabad, its principal town, and captured a strategically located government fort. Most ominously its success was due to the defection of the local army brigade led by Abdur Rauf, who had previ- ously joined the Khalqis but now became a leading mujahideen commander. In February the abduction of the US ambassador by terrorists belonging to Badakhshi's Sitm-e-Melli group, who sought the release of their imprisoned leaders, provoked US hostility. Ambassador Dubs was killed when Amin's troops stormed the hotel room where he was being kept. On 15 March there was a major uprising in Herat involving Afghan Shi'ite seasonal workers who had returned in large numbers after the fall of the Shah. The 17th Army Division stationed there virtually collapsed. An artillery regiment and an infantry regiment defected to the rebels. One of their commanders, Ismail Khan, led a successful attack on what was left of the garrison, and was to emerge later, in alignment with the Jamiat, as one of the most effective commanders of the mujahideen. The rebellion was crushed by paratroopers from Kandahar, at a cost of 25,000 lives. In April major attacks were mounted in Jalalabad, in Paktia province, and in Gardez, by mujahideen organized from Pakistan by Sayyed Ahmad Gailani and Mujaddidi. Fighting raged on till June and was quelled when the government brought into play for the first time helicopter gunships supplied by the Soviets. On 23 June there were violent anti-government demonstrations staged in Kabul by Shi'ite Hazaras.

Between March and July 1979 disagreements between Taraki and Amin came to a head. A bone of contention was the unresolved issue of the defence portfolio held by Taraki, but effectively under the control of Amin, his deputy. Despite Amin's manoeuvring, Taraki's favourite, General Aslam Watanjar, was appointed to the post. Amin's position was weak, as the failed army commanders in Asadabad and Herat had been his appointees. But Amin succeeded in having his brother-in-law elevated to chief of staff, while the head of the army's powerful political department was also an Amin man. At a meeting of the Politburo on 28 July, Amin overtly held Taraki responsible for the government's failures through his proneness to unilateral decision making, and proposed 'a collective leadership and collective decisions'. With Amin's faction now commanding a majority, the Defence Ministry was once more returned to Taraki's charge, with Amin as his deputy. Watanjar was shunted back to the Interior Ministry; the Foreign Ministry and the Deputy Premiership was passed on to an Amin loyalist, Akbar Shah Wali; and the Tribal Affairs Ministry to Mazdooriyar, with Amin-leaning deputies appointed to the Foreign and Interior Ministries. Other key appointments reduced Taraki to a mere figurehead, with Amin controlling the levers of power in the government and in the army. An Amin loyalist, Major Daud Arun, was appointed to head the presidential guard. Amin was now poised for a final showdown with Taraki when the opportunity arose.

By August the Khalqi PDPA had polarized into Taraki and Amin factions, the former led by Watanjar, Ghulabzoi, Mazdooriyar and Asadullah Sarwari, formerly an assiduous Amin supporter who, as intelligence chief, had hounded the Parchamis and had now defected to the Taraki cause.[13] They came to be known as the 'gang of four'. In August, according to Mrs Taraki, Taraki chided Amin by saying: 'We are a Marxist Party, but people accuse us of nepotism. You have appointed Abdullah Amin [who was not even a member of the Party] Supervisory Governor of the four northern provinces, and your nephew has been made Deputy Foreign Minister.' Amin replied angrily: 'So, should I murder my family?'

On 4 September Taraki left for Havana by way of Moscow for a summit meeting of 'non-aligned nations' including Pakistan. Two days before Taraki's departure, Sarwari confided to the Soviet adviser attached to his Department of Intelligence that 'it is my information that Amin has decided to kill Taraki and take over power'. None of the 'gang of four' slept at his own house thereafter, out of fear that Amin might have them killed. On 7 September Sarwari telephoned Taraki in Havana to tell him that 'Amin is planning to either arrest us or have us all killed so that he can take over the government before your return'. This call may have prompted Taraki to arrange for a secret meeting with Brezhnev during a stop-over at Moscow airport on his return journey from Havana on 12 September. Babrak Karmal may also have been present. At the prompting of the Soviet foreign minister, Andrei Gromyko, it was decided that Amin should be sent into diplomatic exile and a 'national democratic' government be formed, with Karmal as prime minister and half the cabinet nominated from outside the PDPA.

The events of the next three days, as narrated by Anwar citing first-hand sources, can only be described as a bizarre combination of cloak-and-dagger politics taking place in a cowboys-and-Indians scenario, with ambushes planned by Sarwari, and with Amin keeping a step ahead, thanks to his spies at every level. In the end, as in a western, Taraki and his Indians lost out. The 'Great Leader' himself became a prisoner in his palace. On 15 September Amin announced to the Central Committee that Taraki had tendered his resignation on grounds of ill health. The chief conspirators against Amin – Sarwari, Watanjar and Ghulabzoi – sought refuge in the Soviet embassy. The precise circumstances of Taraki's death on 8 or 9 October – whether he was hanged in prison or suffocated with a pillow at the Arg palace – have not been elucidated.[14]

During Amin's 100 days in power, the dice were already cast against him. Three-quarters of the country was in a state of rebellion. In September 1979 the powerful Jadran tribe in Paktia province rose in revolt. The government launched a full-scale military operation that ended in a decisive defeat. Because of widespread desertions and defections, the effective army had already been reduced to a third or less of its full complement of 100,000 before the coup d'état. Sixty out of 62 generals had been relieved of their commands after the April 1978 communist putsch and replaced by PDPA supporters from the ranks of captains and majors. The morale of the Afghan armed forces, the mainstay of the regime, was low, as a contemporary Soviet Defence Ministry evaluation revealed.

In the autumn of 1979, after his overthrow of Taraki, Amin must have realized that his position was vulnerable: the country was in a ferment, his army in disarray, and he could not nurture the illusion that Pakistan would withdraw its support of the Peshawar-based Islamic opposition parties, although the material support was very minimal at this stage, compared to the levels that were to be reached after the Soviet invasion. Nevertheless, in addition to some conciliatory gestures on the domestic front, Amin began to make friendly overtures to Pakistan. He was considering a trade-off: Afghan acceptance of the Durand Line as an international frontier in return for an end to Pakistani support of the regime's enemies. He extended an invitation to Zia ul-Haq to send his foreign minister, Agha Shahi, to Kabul. He did receive a positive response from Zia but the scheduled visit in December was called off at the last moment.

At the same time, Amin initiated some overtures to the US with whom relations had soured since the Dubs episode and the suspension of US assistance programmes. In an interview given by Amin to correspondents from two leading US newspapers in October, he invited the US to study the Afghan situation 'in a realistic manner' and 'provide us with more assistance'. It was probably not material assistance that he meant as he was getting enough of that from the USSR. Washington was aware of the growing tensions between Amin and Moscow. As early as July 1979 the US chargé d'affaires was told by the East German ambassador in Kabul that Moscow considered 'the key ingredient' in a political solution to the regime's problems to be 'the departure of Prime Minister Hafizullah Amin'.[15] Some US diplomatic contacts with Amin had taken place in the autumn but nothing had come of them. Amin was in a Catch 22 situation: his complete dependence on Soviet support could not be reconciled with a manifest desire to follow an independent course in foreign policy. Moscow on its part may have come to perceive in Amin an independent-minded nationalist, a fledgling Tito who would not be Moscow's puppet. The murder of the less ambiguously pro-Soviet Taraki was the last straw.

CHAPTER 7

Prelude to the Soviet Invasion

S oviet foreign policy since the Bolshevik Revolution had been dominated by a deep fear of military encirclement. International
considerations therefore certainly played a part in the Soviet decision to
invade Afghanistan. The break with Mao Tse Tung's China, the successive
confrontations with China on border questions, and the ideological rivalry
with this country had made the USSR realize that it had a formidable and
hostile neighbour on its eastern frontiers. The rapidly improving relations
between China and the United States in the late 1970s, after President
Nixon's visit and the resumption of diplomatic ties, stirred up fears of an
eventual Beijing–Washington axis directed at the Soviet Union. Another
cause of concern was the regional instability brought about by the fall of the
Shah in Iran. In November 1979 US embassy staff in Tehran had been taken
hostage by militant students, and there were reports of an American naval
build-up in the Persian Gulf during the ongoing crisis and the creation of a
rapid deployment force to police south-west Asia after the US had lost all its
Iranian facilities. Was Washington planning to seek a more permanent
alternative to the military facilities that Iran had previously provided? As
Brezhnev told *Pravda* after the Soviet invasion, there had been 'a real threat
that Afghanistan would lose its independence and be turned into an imperialist military bridgehead on our southern border'.[1] A more immediate cause
for concern was the tacit US backing, through its Pakistani and Saudi allies,
of the Peshawar-based Afghan Islamist parties. The establishment in Iran of a
radically Islamic regime that was as stridently anti-communist as it was anti-
American, as well as the prospect of an Islamist Afghanistan, could have
serious repercussions in the contiguous Soviet republics of Central Asia
where Muslim revivalist movements were gaining influence.

In the 1970s the Cold War had turned into a worldwide struggle. After
the ill-fated Prague Spring of 1968 and the Soviet invasion of Czechoslovakia,
Brezhnev promulgated his doctrine that any state that had once 'turned'
socialist would never be permitted to revert to its original form of government or indeed to any other. This doctrine applied particularly to Eastern
Europe, which constituted the USSR's security shield in the west. But it
could also hold true by extension to countries in other regions where the

Soviet Union had come to acquire a dominant influence. There were many examples of this influence. In Yemen in 1970 the former British colony of Aden turned into a people's democratic republic with close ties to the USSR, and the Portuguese transfer of power in Angola and Mozambique in 1975 led to the constitution of the Marxist-style and Soviet-backed MPLA and Frelimo governments respectively. The Soviet Union's Cuban proxies intervened directly in the ensuing civil wars in both these countries. In Somalia the Siad Barre regime, in power since 1970, developed pretensions of effecting a socialist transformation with Soviet assistance. The strategic port of Berbera was handed over to the Soviets who turned it into a major warm-water naval base that gave them access to the Mediterranean and the Indian Ocean. In Ethiopia the ousting of Haile Selassie in 1974 led to the emergence in 1976–77, with Soviet support, of the Marxist-style Dergue regime of Colonel Mengistu Haile Mariam. In Indochina the final debacle of the South Vietnamese army and government that had been shored up for so many years by the United States at a massive cost in lives and material, and the spectacular entry of North Vietnamese troops into Saigon in April 1975, were closely followed by the seizure of Phnom Penh by the Khmer Rouge guerrillas, and the proclamation of the communist Lao People's Democratic Republic in Vientiane. Only in Egypt did the Soviets suffer a major reversal when Anwar Sadat repudiated them in favour of an alliance with the US, expelling Soviet advisers and technicians en masse, in return for massive doses of US economic and military aid.

The Brezhnev doctrine was to be countered by the Reagan doctrine that no communist de facto conquests should or would go unchallenged. It would insist on combating and rolling back the communist acquisitions and thrusts wherever they occurred, not only in America's own backyard, as in Nicaragua and El Salvador, but also in Africa and elsewhere. Reagan's appointee to head the CIA from 1981 to 1987, William J. Casey, became a most active 'Cold Warrior', using fair means or foul to counter Soviet advances. But this is to anticipate events.

At the height of the insurrection in Herat, a full meeting of the Soviet Politburo was convened on 17–19 March 1979 to discuss 'the deterioration of conditions in Afghanistan and possible response from our side'.[2] Foreign Minister Andrei Gromyko, in his introductory briefing, said that the Afghan army division stationed in Herat had 'essentially collapsed', with two entire regiments going over to the insurgents. Reportedly, bands of saboteurs and terrorists trained in Iran and Pakistan had joined forces with domestic counter-revolutionaries, especially fanatics linked to religious figures, and were committing atrocities. The situation was confused. He had had a telephone conversation with Hafizullah Amin who had not expressed 'the slightest alarm'; on the contrary, he had said 'with Olympian tranquillity' that 'the situation was not all that complicated, the army was in control, and so forth'. But later he had received news that Taraki had summoned the chief Soviet military adviser in Kabul, General Gorelov, and the chargé d'affaires, Alexeev, to request urgent help in the form of military equipment, ammunition and food rations, adding, 'almost in passing', that Soviet 'air and ground support' would be required. He understood this to mean the deployment of ground and air forces into Afghanistan.[3] But before the multiple implications of such a measure were discussed, the Politburo agreed with Gromyko: 'We must proceed from a fundamental proposition in considering aid to Afghanistan, namely: under no circumstances may we lose Afghanistan.'

Defence Minister Ustinov stated that his forces would be ready for deployment 'within three days': sending the 105th Airborne Division into Afghanistan 'in the course of a single day', dispatching an infantry motorized regiment into Kabul, and placing two motorized divisions on the border. But KGB chief Yuri Andropov came out strongly against the use of Soviet forces:

> We must consider very very seriously the question of whose cause we will be supporting if we deploy forces into Afghanistan. It's completely clear to us that Afghanistan is not ready at this time to resolve all of the issues it faces through socialism. The economy is backward, the Islamic religion predominates, and nearly all of the rural population is illiterate. We know about Lenin's teaching about a revolutionary situation. Whatever situation we are talking about in Afghanistan, it is not that type of situation. Therefore, I believe that we can suppress a revolution in Afghanistan only with the aid of our bayonets, and that is for us completely inadmissible.

Andropov's view was supported by Gromyko who, after spelling out the unacceptable international implications, emphasized that the sending of troops had no legal justification: 'According to the UN Charter a country can appeal for assistance, and we could send troops, in case it is subject to external aggression. Afghanistan has not been subject to any aggression. This is its internal affair, a revolutionary internal conflict, a battle of one group of the population against another. Incidentally, the Afghans haven't officially addressed us on bringing troops.' The Politburo also agreed to Prime Minister Alexei Kosygin's proposal to invite Taraki to Tashkent or Moscow and inform him that the USSR would support him 'with all means and measures' but would 'not deploy troops'.

Chairman Leonid Brezhnev, attending the 19 March session in person, stated that 'the Politburo had correctly determined that the time is not right for us to become entangled' in the war in Afghanistan. He had, however, authorized all the measures proposed by the Politburo at its two previous sessions. These were:

- the immediate delivery of military equipment and supplies, including the waiver of the usual charge of 25 per cent of cost, payable on the basis of a ten-year loan at 2 per cent interest, as imposed on such deliveries since January 1979
- a gift of 100,000 tonnes of wheat
- a rise in the price of gas purchased by the USSR from 15 to 25 roubles per thousand cubic centimetres, to defray the Kabul government's increased expenditure
- the redeployment of two Soviet divisions to the Afghan border
- the sending of some 500 more Soviet military and civilian advisers and specialists, in addition to the 550 who were already present in Afghanistan; according to previous arrangements, the advisers were sent at Soviet expense, but the provision of living quarters, transport and medical services was the responsibility of the Afghan side
- the invitation for Taraki to meet at Tashkent or Moscow.

The Soviet position was conveyed personally to Taraki by Kosygin, Gromyko, Ustinov and Boris Ponomarev at a meeting in Moscow on 20 March. According to their written report to the Politburo, Kosygin made clear to Taraki that the friendship between the USSR and Afghanistan was 'not conditional. ... We will continue to give assistance in the fight against all enemies now and against those who may clash in the future.' Referring to the Vietnamese example, Kosygin said: 'No one can accuse the Vietnamese of using foreign troops to deal with their problem.' They had received word that day that mutinous sections of the 17th Division in Herat had been subdued by paratroopers and tanks sent from Kandahar. In Herat 'it seemed that all would fall apart, but when you really took charge of the matter, you were able to seize control of the situation'. Kosygin reiterated that the USSR would render every type of assistance 'short of deploying Soviet troops on Afghan soil which will invite all sorts of international complications', engendering 'conflict not only with imperialist countries but one's own people'. He added that the most effective support would be through exercising Soviet political influence on neighbouring countries. Letters had been sent that day to Iran and Pakistan requesting them 'not to meddle in the affairs of Afghanistan'.

Taraki replied in a somewhat rambling way that emerging problems should be dealt with through political means and that military actions should be 'auxiliary in nature'. Regarding the events in Herat, he put the blame on 'aristocrats and feudalists' who were 'class enemies'. He said that the PDPA's land reforms had secured the authority of the government among the Afghan people, and that anti-Khomeini demonstrations in Herat and elsewhere protesting against the Iranian role in Herat had convinced him that the regime's internal enemies 'were not so numerous'. He referred vaguely to

Pakistani and Iranian infiltrators 'dressed in Afghan army uniforms'. In reply to a question from Kosygin, referring to news from Iran that all foreign experts and workers had to leave the country in June–July, Taraki mentioned a figure of 'no less than 200,000' Afghans who had moved to work in Iran under Daoud or even earlier; some of them, he said, may come back as guerrillas.

The Soviet side reiterated its promise of maximum political support and extensive assistance in the line of military and other shipments. In response to Taraki's further request for armoured helicopters, Ustinov undertook to deliver six MI-24s in June–July and six others in the last quarter of 1979. The Soviets would also send maintenance specialists 'but not battle crews'. Taraki retorted, 'Why not pilots and tank operators from socialist countries?' He also requested a 1000-watt transmitter for Radio Kabul.

At the Politburo session of 22 March, Brezhnev reported on his private meeting with Taraki. He had made it clear that 'the ideo-political cohesion of the PDPA was of primary significance in pursuing political work among the masses', and that 'primarily political and economic means' should be employed to broaden its base of support, 'not repression'. He had also made it clear to Taraki that the introduction of Soviet military forces would be 'inexpedient ... in the current situation. This could only play into the hands of our common enemy.' Two months later the Soviet position remained unchanged. A Politburo meeting on 24 May confirmed the dispatch of military equipment costing 53 million roubles;[4] it had also been explained to Taraki again that there was no question of providing helicopters and transport planes with Soviet crews, or of sending paratroopers to Kabul.

Contrary to what was bruited about in the international media at the time, and later in the extensive literature that has grown up around the subject, the Soviet leadership was not at all eager to send their armed forces into Afghanistan. The Politburo's decisions were guided by the recommendations of a task force, or Special Commission (comprising Gromyko, Andropov, Ustinov and Ponomarev), appointed to monitor developments in Afghanistan. Decisions were also taken on a collegial basis and endorsed by Brezhnev. The archival records reveal the leadership's extreme circumspection and reserve in the face of persistent demands by Taraki and Amin for an active Soviet role. There is a report from Gorelov on a meeting on 14 April when Amin requested the dispatch to Kabul of 15 to 20 helicopters with ammunition and 'Soviet crews ... to be used eventually against bands of terrorists and infiltrators from Pakistan'. The transcript ends with a terse instruction from the Soviet Chief of Staff, Marshal N.V. Ogarkov: 'This shall not be done'. Again in July, Taraki and Amin returned to the issue, demanding in particular the introduction of two Soviet divisions 'in the event of emergency circumstances ... at the request of the legal government of Afghanistan'. Again they were told, 'the USSR cannot do this'. On 21 July, when Amin requested eight to ten helicopters 'with Soviet crews', Ambassador Puzanov clearly repeated the Soviet policy line: 'the Soviet side cannot embark on the participation of Soviet personnel in combat operations'.

But the policy of non-intervention did not preclude some contingency planning in line with Brezhnev's 19 March directives, notably the positioning of two Soviet divisions on the Afghan border. On 28 June a joint report to the Central Committee of the CPSU by the Politburo's four-member Special Commission referred to the 'objective' and 'subjective' weaknesses in the situation of the Democratic Republic of Afghanistan (DRA), concluding that 'the main support of the Afghan government in the struggle with the counter-revolution continues to be the army'. It was therefore considered expedient to send to Afghanistan an experienced general and a group of officers to work directly among the troops, in the divisions and regiments, and to:

> provide for the security and defence for the Soviet air squadrons at the Bagram field, send to the DRA, with the agreement of the Afghan side, a parachute battalion disguised in the uniform (overalls) of an aviation technical maintenance team. For the defence of the Soviet Embassy, send to Kabul a special detachment of the KGB USSR (125–150 men), disguised as Embassy service personnel. At the beginning of August, ... send to the DRA (to the Bagram airfield) a special detachment of the GRU of the General Staff to be used in the event of a sharp aggravation of the situation for the security and defence of particularly important installations.[5]

A transcript of 5 November reports on the mission led by Deputy Defence Minister General I.G. Pavlovsky (17 August to 22 October) to review the state of the Afghan armed forces and the organization and methods of their combat operations against the rebels, to provide for on-site assistance to the Afghan commanders, and to prepare recommendations for the further strengthening of their combat capabilities. The mission was able to render some practical short-term assistance 'so that the Afghan armed forces, instead of relying on passive defence and faltering operations by small units, were able to launch coordinated and active operations against the rebels'. This, according to the mission's report, enabled them 'to gain the initiative and to destroy the most dangerous forces of counter-revolution in the provinces of Paktia, Ghazni, Parvan, Bamian and several other areas'. But the mission concluded that the army's combat morale, discipline and willingness to act were still low. Military regulations that were codified with Soviet help had had no impact on the practical life of the soldiers. 'The commanders, staffs, political organs, and party organizations do not always coordinate their work in resolving tasks among the troops. Staffs at all levels, including the General Staff, have still not become a central directing organ in the daily life of large and small units and in the troops' combat activity.' The report's conclusions were communicated to Amin who expressed the hope that Soviet military advisers would be assigned to every battalion.

It is clear that the subsequent murder of Taraki, the Pavlovsky report, and Amin's attempts to reorient Afghan foreign policy during his 100 days in power caused a gradual shift in Soviet thinking and strategy that was compatible with the bottom-line decision adopted at the March 1979 sessions of the Politburo: 'under no circumstances may we lose Afghanistan'.

In the meantime there were some last-ditch attempts to save the situation. Before Taraki's deposition and murder, a Politburo directive of 13 September instructed the Soviet ambassador in Kabul to meet Taraki and Amin and express the hope that 'they must come together and act in concord from a position of unanimity in the name of saving the revolution'. But, as Puzanov was advised, 'we cannot take it upon ourselves to arrest Amin with our own battalion force, since this would be a direct interference in the internal affairs of Afghanistan (and) would have far-reaching consequences. Indeed, this is practically unfeasible.' After Amin's coup, Gromyko communicated to the Soviet representatives in Kabul a Politburo decision of 15 September to continue to deal with Amin but to restrain him from repressing Taraki and his followers.

As Brezhnev commented in a transcript dated 20 September: 'Events developed so swiftly in Afghanistan that essentially there was little opportunity to somehow interfere in them. Right now our mission is to determine our further actions, so as to preserve our position in Afghanistan and to secure our influence there.' What these 'further actions' amounted to, as we know, was a full-scale armed intervention in Afghanistan.

A transcript of 3 November refers to a conversation that Puzanov had with Amin, informing him of the Soviet leadership's readiness to receive him in Moscow and expressing their satisfaction over the measures he was taking in the area of party and state building. On 6 December a new ambassador to Kabul, F.A. Tabeev, renewed Moscow's invitation to Amin. On the same day, there was a Politburo decision to send to the DRA a special detachment, 'in response to Amin's request for a motorized rifle battalion to defend his residence'. It was to be drawn from 'the GRV of the General Staff which has been prepared for these goals, with a complement of some 500 men in uniforms that do not reveal their belonging to the armed forces of the USSR and to be airdropped by military transport aircraft'.

But a personal memorandum from Andropov to Brezhnev in early December (undated) speaks of 'the undesirable turn of events' for the USSR after the murder of Taraki: the ongoing destruction of the army and government apparatus as a result of mass repressions carried out by Amin, and 'alarming information' about Amin's 'secret activities forewarning of a possible political shift to the West'. It speaks further of contacts made by the émigrés Karmal and Sarwari 'informing us that they have worked out a plan for opposing Amin and creating new party and state organs, and raising the question of possible assistance, including military assistance, in case of need'. And Andropov ends:

> We have two battalions stationed in Kabul and there is the capability of rendering this assistance. It appears that this is entirely sufficient for a successful operation. But, as a precautionary measure in the event of unforeseen complications, it would be wise to have a military group close to the border. In case of the deployment of military forces we could at the same time decide various questions pertaining to the liquidation of gangs. The implementation of the given operation would allow us to decide the question of defending the gains of the April revolution, establishing Leninist principles in the party and state leadership of Afghanistan, and securing our positions in this country.

The groundwork for a Soviet military intervention and the positioning of a compliant post-Amin regime had thus been prepared. But the decision relating to the military intervention came very late in the day and recorded in a handwritten note dated 12 December.

The transcript of a document dated 31 December 1979, signed by the four members of the Special Commission and addressed to the Central Committee of the CPSU, is a sort of apology for the invasion that began on 27–28 December. It refers to 'the regime of personal dictatorship' that Amin had been trying to establish since September with the objective of liquidating the party: 'more than 600 members of the PDPA, military personnel and other persons suspected of anti-Amin sentiments were executed without trial or investigation'. It speaks of Amin's smear campaigns against the Soviet Union, his hampering of the activities of Soviet personnel in the country and of his efforts to mend relations with the United States, as part of 'a more balanced foreign policy strategy'.

> Expressing alarm over the fate of the revolution and the independence of the country, and reacting keenly to the rise of anti-Amin sentiments in Afghanistan, Karmal Babrak and Asadullah Sarwari, both living abroad as émigrés, have undertaken to unite all anti-Amin groups in the country and abroad, in order to save the motherland and the revolution. In addition the currently underground group "Parcham", under the leadership of an illegal CC, has carried out significant work to rally all progressive forces, including Taraki supporters from the former "Khalq" group. ...

> In this extremely difficult situation, which has threatened the gains of the April revolution and the interests of maintaining our national security, it has become necessary to render additional military assistance to Afghanistan, specially since such requests had been made by previous administrations in DRA. In accordance

with the provisions of the Soviet–Afghan treaty of 1978, a decision has been made to send the necessary contingent of the Soviet Army to Afghanistan.

It appears from Rajah Anwar's account of his conversations with Amin's widow in the Pul-i-Charki prison that the initial Soviet plan was to physically incapacitate Amin by having his food doctored by his Russian cook, and have him transferred in an unconscious state to a Soviet medical facility before he was tried for Taraki's murder or exiled. There are also other versions of the story. But somehow the plans went awry, and KGB commandos, or the Spetznaz, or both, went into action against Amin's residence and killed him in the operation.[6]

As was to be expected, the condemnation of the Soviet invasion was worldwide. The United Nations General Assembly, convened in a special session in January 1980, tabled a resolution adopted by 104 votes, with 48 negative votes and abstentions, that called for an immediate withdrawal of (unnamed) 'foreign troops' from Afghanistan. President Carter characterized the aggression as 'the greatest threat to peace since World War II' – something of a hyperbole if one takes into consideration the Cuban missile crisis of 1962. Carter also announced a package of sanctions, including the non-ratification of the SALT II non-proliferation treaty, a ban of exports of wheat and high technology to the USSR, and a boycott of the 1980 Moscow Olympics. It was the end of a long period of détente that had incidentally proved very profitable for East–West trade, particularly the exports of wheat from countries like Canada and Argentina or of high technology from West Germany and France: hence the somewhat lukewarm response of some members of the Western alliance on the issue of sweeping sanctions.

A meeting of the Politburo called on 27 January 1980 discussed 'the further measures to be taken to provide for the national interests of the USSR in relation to the events in Afghanistan'. These were international damage control measures, to mobilize support where possible for Soviet actions, or at least to blunt the effects of hostile acts and propaganda inspired or directed by the United States. Soviet diplomacy was to operate on a wide variety of fronts: calling on the support of the Non-Aligned Movement (using Cuba and Vietnam) and working-class and progressive parties everywhere; exploiting the latent differences within NATO on the question of sanctions (the Federal Republic of Germany, France, Turkey); putting spokes in the wheel of the ongoing rapprochement between Washington and Beijing; preserving the anti-imperialist, primarily anti-American, elements in the foreign policy of Iran, 'insofar as the continuation of the crisis in Iran–American relations limits the possibilities of the Khomeini regime to inspire anti-government uprisings on Moslem grounds in Afghanistan'; and actively blocking Washington's 'policy of knocking together a united front of the

West and certain Moslem countries, and of reorienting Islamic fanaticism on an anti-Soviet course'.

There are two interesting lines of approach in this document. First, it expressed caution as regards relations with the United States: 'Despite the fact that Washington will in the future continue to initiate an anti-Soviet campaign and will strive to impart a coordinated character to the actions of its allies, to realize our countermeasures proceeding from the inexpedience of complicating the entire complex of multi-level relations between the Soviet Union and the USA.' Second, the Politburo set out to contradict the correlation that British Prime Minister Margaret Thatcher was trying to draw between the change in the Afghan leadership and the deployment of Soviet contingents in Afghanistan: 'There is no relationship here; it is purely coincidental. ... [It is important that] while conducting foreign policy and propagandistic measures, to use even more widely the thesis that the Soviet Union's provision of military assistance to Afghanistan cannot be viewed in isolation from the USA's provocative efforts, which have already been undertaken over the course of a long time, to achieve unilateral military advantages in regions which are strategically important to the USSR.'

This was also the substance of the briefing given by Gromyko in Moscow to the new Afghan foreign minister, Shah Mohamed Dost, on 4 January 1980. In the guise of 'sharing his thoughts about the current situation in the Security Council' as well as 'the character of your appearance at the forthcoming session', Gromyko was in fact giving instructions to Dost, who was advised: 'You have every reason to be the accuser – not the accused.' He was also informed that a senior Soviet official, V.S Safronchyuk, was being sent to New York 'to assist you as you have requested earlier'. But officially he was going there in the capacity of a member of the Soviet delegation to the United Nations. Dost was cautioned to exercise discretion in his meetings with Safronchyuk, to be held preferably in Soviet premises such as the consulate-general. And so the regime in Kabul became the creature of a foreign power for the first time since Amir Abdur Rahman had begun laying the foundations of a neutral and independent Afghan state 100 years earlier.

Foreign minister Dost had told Gromyko that at meetings of the Afghan Politburo, 'Babrak continuously stressed the necessity to pay attention carefully to the friendly and timely advice and wishes coming from the Soviet leaders'. In his conversations with President Karmal and other members of the new Afghan leadership during his visit to Kabul at the beginning of February, Andropov laid down the broad lines of the domestic policies they were to follow. He emphasized the need for developing genuine party unity within a broad-based PDPA consisting of both Parcham and Khalqi elements; strengthening relations between the PDPA and government with the masses, including the tribes and moderate religious leaders; instituting normal economic life in the country; and heightening the military readiness of the armed forces.

Andropov reported on his conversations with Afghan leaders at a Soviet Politburo meeting of 7 February presided over by Brezhnev. A time-frame for an eventual withdrawal of Soviet forces was also discussed, with Ustinov proposing a period of one to one and a half years to allow for the internal situation to stabilize. Gromyko, after posing a rhetorical question ('Can we speak of a full withdrawal without getting anything in return?') went on to stress the need to think about agreed obligations to set between the sides before a withdrawal could be contemplated. He said that as the USSR would not be able to secure a full guarantee against attacks by hostile forces, they would have to provide for the full security of Afghanistan. Thus he left open the issue of a time-frame for a Soviet withdrawal as well as the question of the size of the forces that would be required to secure Afghanistan. The Soviet forces were to grow to more than 100,000 in the course of the occupation, allowing for periodic fluctuations in the figure, of which some 15,000 were to die and countless others be disabled or injured. Afghanistan was thus to become the Soviet Union's Vietnam, but with consequences far beyond any that could have been contemplated at the time, not least the revelation that the USSR was a giant with feet of clay.

CHAPTER 8

The Sovietization of Afghanistan (1979–89)

Babrak Karmal announced his own accession to power as the 'new phase' of the 'Saur Revolution'. He began his first broadcast to the nation on the night of 27–28 December 1979 by intoning the traditional Koranic invocation, embracing all elements of the Afghan nation, and paying lip-service to Taraki, 'our dear leader and noble founder of our party' murdered by 'that rogue' Amin. He went on to throw open the gates of the Pul-i-Charki prison, and decided to induct non-Party individuals into his administration in fulfilment of his old strategy of setting up a 'national democratic government' that would mobilize all sectors of society before a socialist transformation could be effected. By May 1980, of the 191 important appointments that were made, 78 were from outside the ranks of the PDPA.[1]

Karmal also declared a general amnesty, promising exiles that they would be given back their houses, lands and properties if they came back to Afghanistan, making his promise doubly attractive by announcing that even if the real owners did not return, their close relatives would be treated as the owners if they came back.[2] Karmal also announced a provisional constitution under the heading of Basic Principles, one of these being the formation of a broad-based National Fatherland Front, another the acknowledgement of the supremacy of Islam. In pursuit of the latter policy, a separate Department of Islamic Affairs was set up, later turned into a full ministry, for the first time in Afghan history, and under communist patronage. But this was also a device to bring the clergy under close government supervision. The department was given control over the private finances and endowments of mosques throughout the country. The funds served not only to pay the stipends of the clergy, thus making them state employees, but also to finance the building and renovation of mosques. New mosques, 34 in Kabul alone, were eventually built, and 523 others renovated throughout the country. But such measures to win Muslim hearts and minds were ineffective. Before the Soviet invasion traditional fundamentalists had, in the name of Islam, railed against the modernizing decrees of Kabul, which they saw as intrusions by the state into the sacrosanct way of life of the qawm. After the Soviet action, their rallying cry became that of jihad, a holy war for the liberation of Muslim Afghanistan from the infidel invaders and the overthrow of their local pup-pets.

Some two months after the arrival of the Soviet forces, a nationwide movement called Allah-u-Akbar (God is Great) was mobilized against the Karmal regime. Processions were organized during which slogans were chanted against the regime and its Soviet backers. At night-time the entire population would gather on the rooftops to intone the *azan*, the Muslim call to prayer, a novel form of non-violent protest that had been used in Pakistan to overthrow Zulfikar Ali Bhutto in 1977. Anti-government pamphlets were distributed, terrorist activities multiplied in the towns as well as in rural areas, and Party members and activists were murdered.

So desperate had Karmal become in the face of widespread and growing resistance that in the summer of 1981 he announced a set of exemptions to the agricultural reforms that had been a major plank in the PDPA pro-gramme to eliminate landlordism and 'feudal' practices. The land reform decrees were no longer applicable to landowners in the following categories: officers of the armed forces, tribal leaders who supported the government, large landowners who were willing to undertake mechanized farming and sell the excess produce to the government, and smallholders and landless peas-ants who voluntarily offered to send their sons for national service in the Afghan armed forces – the last category being given special preference in the allotment of redistributed lands. Karmal's concessions did have an apprecia-ble effect in areas where the military presence of the government was substantive. However, in areas where rebels were in control and where lan-dless peasants continued to work for absentee landlords in Pakistan enjoying income from their lands, the concessions had little effect in gathering sup-port for the regime.

The Karmal regime was further weakened by the resurgence of the old Parcham–Khalqi struggle within the ranks of the PDPA. The nationalist Khalqis led by Asadullah Sarwari, who had cooperated with Karmal in bring-ing in the Red Army to oust Amin, remained loyal to the memory of Taraki. The Khalqis were dominant in the officer corps of the Afghan armed forces and expected that Karmal's position would become weak when the Red Army withdrew after it had fulfilled its mission. But the Red Army did not with-draw. The Soviet leadership, as we have seen, had its own mission to fulfil.

One of the main points that Andropov had stressed during his talks with the Afghan leadership was the need to develop genuine party unity. In the very month of Andropov's lecture, Parchamis and Khalqis came to odds over what seemed to be the trivial issue of the national flag. Karmal wanted a new tricolour to replace the red banner favoured by the Khalqis. It was noted that at the march-past held to mark the second anniversary of the Saur Revolution, very few of the motorized units taking part flew the tricolour. Many of the tank commanders defiantly displayed the old red banner of the Khalqis. Karmal had to watch in embarrassed silence. There was nothing he could do. He was well aware that the Khalqis' chief source of support was the army which he could not afford to alienate. He attempted, however, to make changes in the army's top leadership by transferring, as a first step, seven commanders of important provincial garrisons to other duties. But when Parchami officers arrived to take charge, the Khalqi officers refused to honour their orders. No disciplinary action was taken against them for fear of a general revolt. The old political battles were now being fought within the military establishment.

The defence minister was a Parchami, as were the political commissars attached to army units; but no pro-Khalqi officers were inclined to obey them. Instead Khalqi officers, officials and party cadres rallied round Sarwari, an uncompromising nationalist who began to openly advocate the departure of the Red Army. Sarwari believed that the Afghan masses would turn against the revolution because of the Soviet military presence.[3] In June 1980 Karmal, with the Kremlin's help, had Sarwari leave for Moscow for 'medical treatment', before reassigning him to Mongolia as ambassador.

Pul-i-Charki prison began to fill up once again, this time with Khalqi officials, cadres and officers, and 13 of them, including three ministers, were executed in June 1980. Some officers fled to join the resistance. In order to exploit the internal dissensions within the regime to their advantage, rebel leaders began to maintain lists of known pro-Khalqi officers who were not necessarily anti-Parcham activists. When a rebel was arrested by police or intelligence agents, and such lists were found on his person, the officers whose names figured on the lists were inculpated. According to an estimate cited by Rajah Anwar, some 600 such officers were imprisoned on conspiracy charges in the month of January 1981 alone, though many of them were later released for lack of evidence. Such futile vendettas undermined morale and weakened the motivation of the armed forces in fighting for a regime that could not command their loyalty.

The inter-factional rivalry became institutionalized within the power structure. The Interior Ministry was headed by a prominent Khalqi, Syed Ghulabzoi, the junior Air Force officer who had played a key role in the 1978 military putsch. Karmal could not easily dislodge him because of the power that his position gave him. Instead he separated the Intelligence Department from the Ministry's jurisdiction and set it up as an independent entity responsible for all matters relating to intelligence-gathering, arrests and the interrogation of prisoners and political detainees and so on, leaving Ghulabzoi's police to deal only with common criminals. The department, known by its notorious acronym KhaD, was placed under a loyal Karmal supporter,

Dr Najibullah, who was accorded military rank as a brigadier. He was promoted to lieutenant-general when the KHaD came to be equipped with an army division complete with helicopters, tanks and armoured cars. KHaD's cadres and agents were taken under the wing of the KGB and the East German Stasi and trained by their experts. KHaD became a dreaded instrument of state control. It had many responsibilities, ranging from internal intelligence, arrests and interrogations to the subversion of border tribes, assassinations, counter-intelligence operations, the infiltration of refugee organizations and sabotage in Pakistan. The tactics of terror and intimidation employed by KHaD became a staple of the stories narrated by Afghan refugees in Iran and Pakistan.

Ghulabzoi, for his part, expanded the police force under his control by drawing recruits from among Khalqi supporters and sympathizers until it became numerically superior to the army itself. Many of its units were converted into a light infantry force called Sarandoy. Armed clashes between KHaD and Sarandoy were not infrequent, and the sabotage of each others' efforts in their struggle against the Afghan resistance and mujahideen fighters was fairly common.

With a resentful and divided officer corps, and defections and desertions among the ranks, the armed forces dwindled to some 30,000 men, a third of its former size, within the first year of the Soviet invasion. So bad had the situation become that Karmal had difficulty in replenishing the emptying army cantonments. He was not even in a position to demobilize soldiers who had completed their year of compulsory military service. In December 1980 some 600 such soldiers threw down their weapons in front of the main police building in Kabul, formed themselves into a procession, and marched through the city demanding their immediate discharge. Karmal had to beat a hasty retreat. In 1981 an emergency programme of recruitment was ordered involving also the recall of men who had already performed their military service. Such forced recruitment only served to swell the numbers of those in the ranks who could be expected to desert at the earliest opportunity.

To supplement the crumbling armed forces a wide variety of militias was set up. The earliest, known as Soldiers of the Revolution, drew on city-bred party activists who soon proved no match for guerrilla fighters. Later, ordinary government employees were obliged to perform night-time guard duties. Additional civil defence units were set up to defend farms, factories and government buildings. There were women's militias, youth militias, ethnic militias and frontier militias. Some, as in tribal areas, were entirely mercenary; others had a hard core of committed party members and supporters. In 1987 Najibullah was to claim that the regime had half a million people under arms.

It is estimated that on the eve of the Soviet invasion, hard-core members of the PDPA, i.e. those fulfilling the stringent requirements for party membership according to Soviet-inspired norms, did not number more than 2500. First-hand observers like Rajah Anwar would allow a maximum of 5000, taking into account the purges of Parchamis by Taraki and Amin, the purges of Khalqis by Karmal, and the inevitable growth of a party that held the reins of power, attracting teachers, government employees, officers of the armed forces and others who acted out of self-interest rather than ideological conviction. In mid-1982 Karmal claimed that the PDPA had 70,000 members, a wildly exaggerated figure according to Western observers who put the figure closer to 20,000.[4]

As the Kremlin became more and more aware of the unpopularity and unreliability of the Karmal regime, it adopted a longer-term strategy to achieve its objective of 'securing' the future of Afghanistan in line with its 'national interests'. This involved the building of a youthful new elite that would loyally run a communist administration and stay committed to a pro-Soviet future for Afghanistan. Indoctrination began early. School children were encouraged or forced to enrol in the 'Young Pioneers' at the age of ten, and trained, among other things, to spy on their classmates or even on their families. A nationwide membership of 40,000 for the Young Pioneers was claimed in 1982. In Kabul there was a Palace of Pioneers, with a cinema, library and workshops, where propagandistic education was imparted twice weekly. According to George Arney:

> At the age of fifteen, Young Pioneers were expected to join the Democratic Youth Organization of Afghanistan (DYOA), where they were split into small groups and assigned responsibilities such as surveillance and propaganda work, or guarding schools and government buildings. Membership of the DYOA led straight on to enrolment in the party, and, in 1987, Dr. Najibullah claimed that thirty percent of all students belonged either to the DYOA or the PDPA. Orphans, and children kidnapped from bombed villages, had the least chance of escaping indoctrination. They were educated in 'Fatherland Training Centres', or 'Watan Nurseries', where there was no check on communist propaganda. Mrs. Karmal was the official patron of the nurseries, but they were under the supervision of KHaD, and were designed to turn out highly committed agents. Children as young as ten years old were occasionally discovered infiltrating mujahedin groups.[5]

Even students who avoided enrolment in these organizations did not escape the process of Sovietization. The school curriculum was changed to include compulsory political science and Russian language courses. New textbooks were prepared under the supervision of Soviet advisers, and teachers were directed to lecture their students regularly on Afghan–Soviet friendship.

At Kabul University, student numbers dropped from 15,000 at the time of the Russian invasion to less than 5000 in 1983. All remaining students, many of them women, were required to attend courses in Marxist-Leninist political theory, 'scientific' sociology and dialectical materialism. Independent-minded professors were purged or imprisoned and replaced by young party activists recruited for their loyalty rather than their qualifications. Soviet influences percolated throughout the whole system.

Tens of thousands of young Afghans were sent to study in the Soviet Union to further separate them from their roots. By 1984, 4000 students a year were being sent for 'advanced political indoctrination', according to US State Department estimates quoted by Arney. That same year, it was scheduled to send 2000 children between seven and ten years old annually for at least ten years' schooling in the USSR. Some were taken from the Watan Nurseries, but it was evident when the first batch of children was sent out to Central Asia in November 1984 that others had parents and relatives who had come to see them off at the airport.

Adults did not escape the programme of indoctrination, as may well be imagined in a Soviet-style state where the entire media was state-controlled. The radio, television, press and cinema provided an unrelieved diet of Marxist propaganda and 'socialist realism', to project an image of the Soviet Union as a workers' paradise, in contrast to Afghanistan's 'feudal' past. Soviet advisers controlled the news programmes, and Russian films were screened regularly on television and in the cinemas.

Another aspect of Sovietization was the introduction into Afghanistan – in a modified form – of the 'nationalities policy' that had been implemented in Soviet Central Asia by Stalin. In that case, the Russian Turkestan of the czars had been broken up into five 'autonomous' Soviet republics based on ethnic and linguistic lines. As we have seen, the PDPA's Decree No. 4 had elevated the Uzbek, Turcoman, Baluchi and Nuristani languages to the status of national languages, as in the case of Pashtun and the Afghan variant of Persian known as Dari. Dari, spoken by the Pashtun elite and by the Tajiks, was the lingua franca of Afghanistan and the usual medium of instruction in state schools. The PDPA had begun to promote the language and culture of the different ethnic groups through the media. The Karmal regime went even further: provincial schools began teaching children in their respective mother tongues for the first time. Newspapers, magazines and books were imported from the Central Asian Republics, and the historical and cultural affinities between the ethnic groups in the north and their cousins across the Amu Darya were highlighted by Afghan and Soviet propaganda. Nationalist-minded Afghans saw these policies as an attempt to isolate ethnic groups from each other and from the wider Muslim world, as the Soviets had done in Central Asia, and to drive a wedge between these groups and the Pashtuns who had traditionally dominated Afghan politics. The intensive exploitation by the Soviets of the natural resources of the north, especially its gas deposits, was also seen as evidence of a plan to economically integrate that region with the rest of Central Asia.[6]

In the Pashtun regions of the south and east, the game of divide and rule was played out in a different way. The strategy was to establish contact with an influential tribal malik who was known to be the rival of a neighbouring malik who supported the resistance. The bargaining might, it was argued, lead to a mutual non-aggression pact in which the malik would receive weapons and cash subsidies in return for turning his kin group into a pro-government militia. It was a risky business though, as Arney points out. In one incident in September 1980 Karmal's minister for tribal affairs, Faiz Mohammad Faiz, set off from Kabul with a bagful of afghanis and several fattened sheep to celebrate the conclusion of lengthy peace negotiations with his own Zadran tribe. The tribal elders feasted themselves on the lamb and then shot him dead.

Despite the opposition of doctrinaire Marxists in the PDPA, Karmal adopted a more flexible and conciliatory policy towards the Pashtun tribes, particularly those straddling the south-eastern borders, in an effort to choke off the mujahideen supply lines from Pakistan. Some, like the Mohmands, were won over by offers of food, fuel, weapons and cash subsidies. A policy of non-interference in the customs and traditions of the tribes was also announced. In September 1985 a 'High Jirga of the Tribes' was held, with 4000 delegates attending – of whom a third were from Pakistan.

Attempts to make the regime more palatable to the population were half-hearted until a radical change in direction occurred in the Kremlin itself. In the spring of 1985 Mikhail Gorbachev became general secretary of the CPSU after a long period of inertia at the Kremlin during the short-lived tenures of Andropov and Chernenko following the death of Brezhnev in November 1982. Nationwide elections to the long-promised loya jirga was announced by Karmal in April 1985. In the course of the year, the National Fatherland Front was given a non-PDPA chairman and efforts were made to 'broaden the social pillars of the revolution': the Revolutionary Council was doubled in size to include members of the clergy, the intelligentsia and the business community; dozens of non-Marxists were appointed to government posts; and tax breaks were accorded to the private economic sector.

But to restore the credibility of the regime, Karmal himself had to go. He could never live down the opprobrium of having been installed by Soviet tanks. Within the PDPA he had exacerbated rather than healed party divisions. Rumours circulated in Kabul about his mistresses and his drunken bouts; he had been truly reduced to a puppet, being increasingly sidelined at every turn by his Soviet advisers who took their cues from the Soviet ambassador. If it was already Gorbachev's intention at this stage to prepare for the withdrawal of Soviet troops, no Afghan government led by Karmal could be expected to survive that eventuality.

CHAPTER 9

Pakistan, the United States and
the Afghan Resistance

E xactly 100 years after the British contrived to set up Afghanistan as a
buffer state between the expanding Russian empire in Central Asia
and their empire in India, the Soviet occupation of Afghanistan
blurred the frontiers between the successor states of the czars and the British.
Pakistan also acquired the status of a 'front line state' in the Cold War. This
at least was the perception of certain circles in Washington.

Pakistan's military dictator, Zia ul-Haq, was more than willing to lead a
crusade against the Soviets in Afghanistan. After he had ousted the elected
government of Zulfikar Ali Bhutto in July 1977, he had considerably tar-
nished his image both at home and abroad. He had promised elections 'in six
months' for the re-establishment of civilian rule. Instead he had set up a
military dictatorship and martial law. His ignominious hanging of Bhutto,
despite worldwide appeals for clemency, had been condemned by all sides,
and he felt isolated. As a zealous Muslim and anti-communist his natural
sympathies lay with the Afghan resistance which he had been covertly assisting. After the Soviet invasion, his trusted director-general of Inter-Services
Intelligence (ISI), the Pashtun General Akhtar Abdur Rehman Khan, advised
him that there would be a convergence of religious, political and strategic
gains if Pakistan were to assume the role of an Islamic champion against
communist aggression.[1]

Zia also had ready-made instruments to hand in order to accomplish such
a role covertly, without provoking possible retaliation under the terms of the
Afghan–Soviet Treaty of 1978. These were the various Afghan political
parties that had set up their headquarters in Peshawar after their failed
uprisings against Daoud. Some of them had become active in supporting the
internal resistance against the communists. The tribal insurrections in Afghanistan's south-eastern provinces in the summer of 1979, the Kabul
regime's murderous counter-attacks and repression, and the Soviet invasion,
had turned the refugee influx into a flood. From an estimated 80,000 refugees in Pakistan at the end of 1978, their numbers reached 400,000 by 1980.
The Pakistani authorities were overwhelmed, and turned to the exiled Afghan leaders in Peshawar to manage the situation. Since the refugees had to

be recommended by one of the parties in order to be eligible for food rations, the small, unrepresentative Peshawar-based parties became mass organizations. When entire tribal clans and villages fled across the border, a plethora of new parties appeared under tribal leaders who were too proud to surrender their autonomy to the Peshawar parties. In an effort to simplify matters in terms of distribution of relief supplies to the refugees, as well as financial and military support to the mujahideen, the Pakistani authorities eventually obliged all such parties and groups to align themselves with one of seven Islamist parties to become eligible for assistance.

The Jamiat-i-Islami of Burhanuddin Rabbani, the Tajik from Badakhshan who had succeeded Nyazi, the founder of the party executed by Daoud, had a Sufi background, and attended a state madrasa before going on to study in Ankara and graduate at Al-Azhar in Cairo. He enjoyed great personal prestige as a versatile Islamic intellectual, but his cautious and conciliatory approach resulted in an early split with the younger and more radical elements within the Jamiat, led by the autocratic and unscrupulous Gulbuddin Hekmatyar. The latter formed the Hizbi-i-Islami (Party of Islam), tightly organized according to a Stalinist model, with a cell structure and a pyramidal chain of authority with himself at the apex. Hekmatyar was a detribalized Ghilzai Pashtun from Kunduz with a rather narrow base of support, and an Islamic purist seeking to eradicate traditional Pashtun customs and practices, including consensual decision-making. Although he was chosen eventually by Pakistan as her protégé during the jihad, he was never very popular with the mainstream, tribally organized Pashtuns.

Another splinter group had emerged in 1979, this time from within the Hizbi-i-Islami. It was led by Maulana Younis Khalis, a tribal leader from Paktia province with a radical Islamic agenda inspired by the Deoband school near Delhi where he had been trained, as had several generations of Afghan ulema before him. He had a following of traditional religious leaders and village mullahs in the south-east. Mullah Omar, the future leader of the Taliban, fought in the ranks of Khalis's mujahideen later in the jihad. A fourth Islamist party, the Ittehad-e-Islami, was formed by Abdul Rasul Sayyaf, a lecturer in theology at Kabul University who had been released from prison by the communist government and had fled to Pakistan in 1979. His party had no territorial base but had strong financial support from Saudi Arabia, whose extreme Wahhabi and anti-Shi'a ideology he shared. Another party that emerged was the Harakat-e-Inquilab-Islami of Maulana Mohammad Nabi Mohammedi, an Islamic scholar with a strong following among the ulema and mullahs who had led the early uprisings against the communist regime. But lacking a territorial base or organizational capacity, the party's adherents later drifted into the ranks of other mujahideen parties. The last two of the seven Afghan parties recognized by the Pakistani government in 1980 as eligible for material support in the war in Afghanistan were associated with the two most important Sufi orders in Afghanistan: Sighbatullah Mujaddedi of the Naqhshbandi, and Pir Sayyed Ahmad Gailani of the Qadiriya. They drew their followers from among those who venerated their ancient Sufi lineage. Their parties were not strictly Islamist, as defined by Olivier Roy. The two leaders also had family ties to the former royal establishment and professional classes. They, along with Nabi, were usually described as 'moderates', as opposed to the 'radicals' leading the four other Islamic parties.

As we have seen in previous chapters, both Kabul and Moscow were convinced, not without reason, that the spreading insurrections in Afghanistan were encouraged, armed and directed by Pakistan. Whenever such charges were publicly levelled at Pakistan, they were flatly denied. Pakistan was able to maintain the fiction for at least three reasons. In the first place, the Afghan resistance was a spontaneous affair and did not depend on external moral or material support for its élan. Secondly, the material support hitherto provided by Pakistan to the mujahideen through the Peshawar parties was modest, consisting mainly of outdated equipment from its own armouries that were replenished with more modern Chinese weapons bought with funds donated by Saudi Arabia and the Gulf States. Thirdly, the whole support programme was a very covert operation from beginning to end, conducted in paranoid secrecy by the ISI, whose chief, General Akhtar, reported directly to Zia. The rest of the administration, including the Foreign Ministry and the regular armed forces, were kept in the dark. The fiction was maintained even when the level of support reached massive proportions after the United States became involved.

United States policy in west Asia had been in the doldrums after the fall of the Shah of Iran and the ongoing hostage crisis. President Carter had clearly stated that the US had 'a moral obligation' to help the Afghan resistance. There were hawks in his administration - such as the National Security Adviser, Zbigniew Brzezinski, and some members of Congress - who advocated a more pro-active role. But the initial US reaction to the Soviet invasion was more a concern that Pakistan's territorial integrity might be jeopardized with Soviet troops on its frontiers. The invasion coincided with Mrs Indira Gandhi's sweeping victory in the Indian elections. When Gromyko publicly declared shortly afterwards in New Delhi that 'if Pakistan continues to serve as a puppet of imperialism in the future, it will jeopardize its existence and its integrity as an independent state', Pakistan's worst fears of a Moscow-Kabul-New Delhi axis seemed to be confirmed.

On 4 January 1980 President Carter announced that 'along with other countries, we will provide military equipment, food and other assistance to help Pakistan defend its independence'. But when in March he offered $400 million in economic and military aid spread over two years, General Zia felt emboldened to reject the offer as 'peanuts'. What he wanted was massive US military assistance to secure his borders with India and to make the armed forces that were his regime's only prop happy. This he obtained when Ronald Reagan was elected US president later that year. In September 1981 the United States agreed to a $3.2 billion economic and military aid package spread over six years, plus an option to sell 40 advanced F-16 fighter jets. Zia was thus in a position to serve as Washington's link with the Afghan resistance in a covert operation to 'roll back' what Reagan called 'the evil empire'.

Both Washington and Islamabad went to extraordinary lengths to cover up their assistance to the Afghan mujahideen. For this reason it was decided that only Warsaw Pact weaponry would be delivered, as such weapons could not be traced back to the US. Also, in the early stages of the resistance, many of the weapons used by the mujahideen were Soviet-made, captured from government forces or taken from, or sold by, deserters. Another reason was that Soviet weaponry such as AK47 assault rifles (Kalashnikovs), heavy machine guns (Dashikas) and pistols (Makarovs) were considered 'peasant proof': a Kalashnikov broke down into four components that could be reassembled easily and worked, even if wet, grimy or dirty, unlike American weapons.[2]

Bill Casey's CIA procurers scoured the globe in search of Soviet-style weapons. Egypt, which had large stockpiles of automatic weapons, land mines, grenade launchers and anti-aircraft missiles delivered by the Soviets, was the first source.[3] In return Washington offered to replenish her stocks with new US weapons. Other sources were Israel, which had a supply of Soviet-made weapons – captured during the Six Day War and from Syrian troops and Palestinians in Lebanon – and China. Using Pakistan's Inter-Services Intelligence (ISI) as a go-between, the CIA contracted with the Chinese government to manufacture rocket launchers, AK47s and heavy machine guns in return for hard currency and new equipment. China became a major source of supply. As the requirements grew, the CIA arranged for copies of Soviet weapons to be manufactured in factories in Cairo and in the US, where one leading firm was given a classified contract to upgrade SAM-7 anti-aircraft missiles.

Between 1981 and 1985 annual US military aid to the mujahideen channelled through Pakistan's ISI grew from $30 million to $280 million, making it the biggest single CIA covert operation anywhere in the world. The US Congress, in a rare show of bi-partisanship, and prompted by friends of the Afghan resistance such as Charles Wilson, Gordon Humphrey, Orrin Hatch and Bill Bradley, also took the lead in voting more money for the mujahideen than the Reagan administration requested, sometimes by diverting funds from the defence budget to the CIA. Its director, Bill Casey, was also able to persuade sympathetic Arab governments to contribute to a reserve fund that could be kept secret from Congress and the State Department. In late 1981 Saudi Arabia, in exchange for permission to buy five AWAC surveillance planes in spite of Congressional opposition, began to match the CIA dollar for dollar in the financing of purchases of weapons for the Afghan resistance. According to Arney, Saudi Arabia funnelled more than half a billion dollars to CIA accounts in Switzerland and the Cayman Islands. This was in addition to its substantial direct contributions of cash and weapons to its own favourites among the mujahideen parties.

As word spread that the CIA had a blank cheque to purchase Soviet-style weaponry and ammunition, a bizarre combination of arms dealers, bankers, smugglers and gun-runners emerged from the woodwork to claim a 'part of the action'. One of the biggest operators was the Saudi businessman, Adnan Kashoggi, who openly fronted for his government in procuring and distributing weapons and munitions to the mujahideen through the ISI. He was an agent of the head of the Saudi intelligence agency, Prince Turki, and also acted as a watchdog on the expenditure of Saudi funds.

The CIA's payments, as well as Saudi payments for the arms supplied by the various dealers, were made out of special 'Afghan War' accounts managed by the Geneva-based Bank of Credit and Commerce International (BCCI).[4] Its head was a Pakistani banker from Karachi, Agha Hasan Abedi. BCCI's major owners were Saudi and Arab Emirate political and banking figures. Abedi had close ties with President Zia and the ISI's General Akhtar who handled the whole supply network to the Afghan resistance on the ground.

Casey meanwhile undertook a variety of operations described as 'off-the-books', i.e. not accounted for in detail by the CIA's record-keeping apparatus. As the CIA was a federal government agency answerable to Congress and thus to the US public, Casey considered his 'off-the-books' operations as jobs undertaken in his role as adviser to the president, through his membership of the National Security Council, which was accountable only to the president.[5]

Thus the CIA's accounts with BCCI, where Saudi funds were similarly deposited, also served to secretly finance an altogether different kind of clandestine operation that had no Congressional approval or endorsement. The Boland Amendment had specifically excluded the supply by the US of lethal weapons to the right-wing Contras fighting the Sandinistas in Nicaragua. The CIA circumvented this obstacle by simply asking the Saudis to pay for the arms supplied to the Contras which they did through the BCCI accounts. Kurt Lohbeck asserts that at least one CIA contract with Kashoggi called for NATO-type weaponry to be sent to Honduras for the Contras, and Warsaw Pact weapons to the ISI for the Afghans – paid out of a single BCCI account. Kashoggi could later argue during the US Senate's investigation into BCCI that the account was actually divided in two, with the Nicaraguan portion of the contract paid out of Saudi funds in the account and the

Afghan portion from the US funds. But the American greenback has only one colour. And why the Saudis, who were traditionally given to supporting only Islamic causes, should take any special interest in the Contras is beyond understanding unless it was part of a deal with the CIA. Kashoggi's role, as the CIA's contractual partner and paymaster through BCCI for the various arms supplies, was central.[6]

On the Pakistan side the chain of command under martial law was more straightforward. The chief martial law administrator was the president, General Zia ul-Haq. The armed forces governed the country and Zia, as Chief of Army Staff, controlled the armed forces. Zia's right-hand man was the powerful director-general of the ISI, General Akhtar Abdur Rehman. Within the ISI, the Afghan Bureau was the command post for the war in Afghanistan and operated in the greatest secrecy, with its military staff wearing civilian clothes. Its head reported to Akhtar, who also devoted some 50 per cent of his time to the affairs of the Bureau and reported directly to Zia. The respective roles of the CIA and the ISI's Afghan Bureau are best summed up by the army officer personally selected by Akhtar in October 1983 to head the Bureau, Brigadier Mohammad Yousaf:

> To sum up: the CIA's tasks in Afghanistan were to purchase arms and equipment and their transportation to Pakistan; provide funds for the purchase of vehicles and transportation inside Pakistan and Afghanistan; train Pakistani instructors on new weapons or equipment; provide satellite photographs and maps for our operational planning; provide radio equipment and training, and advise on technical matters when requested. The entire planning of the war, all types of training for the mujahideen, and the allocation and distribution of arms and supplies were the sole responsibility of the ISI, and my office in particular.[7]

The operational base of the ISI's Afghan Bureau was the Ojhri Camp, located on the northern outskirts of Rawalpindi, and 12 kilometres from the capital, Islamabad. The 70 to 80-acre complex contained warehouses through which 70 per cent of all arms and ammunition for the mujahideen passed – garages for some 300 civilian vehicles, training areas, barracks and mess halls. At the height of operations the Bureau included 50 officers, 100 warrant officers and 300 NCOs.

The Bureau had three branches. First, an operations branch under a full colonel was responsible for coordinating intelligence from various sources and controlling day-to-day planning and operations; selecting targets in accordance with the overall strategy; allocating tasks to the mujahideen and organizing training courses for them. From 1984 to 1987, during Brigadier Yousaf's stewardship, some 80,000 mujahideen were trained at the camps. The second, a logistics branch with another colonel in charge, was responsible for collecting the weaponry delivered by the CIA from the port of Karachi and airforce bases around the country and for allocating, dispatching and delivering it to the warehouses belonging to the Peshawar parties for distribution to their mujahideen commanders. Inland transportation was carried out in the hundreds of trucks purchased with CIA funds and operated by the National Logistics Cell (NLC). The NLC also carried the food and relief supplies for Afghan refugees in Pakistan procured by international humanitarian aid agencies such as UNHCR and WFP. The third branch dealt with psychological warfare: the operation of border radio stations, the distribution of pamphlets, the conduct of interviews, and so on.

With many billions of dollars spent by the CIA on the arms pipeline as well as on large cash transfers to Pakistan, it was inevitable that unequalled opportunities were created all down the line for the operation of human greed and avarice. On the supply side, Yousaf cites some interesting examples. When the boxes of weapons arriving from Egypt were opened, rifles were found to be 'rusted together, barrels were solid with dirt and corrosion, some boxes were empty, while in others the contents were deficient'. The ammunition was 'rarely packed, but came in heaps of loose rounds'. And, '30,000 82mm mortar bombs were found unusable on the battlefield as the cartridges had swollen in the damp and would not fit the bombs. The Egyptians had cobbled together arms that had been lying exposed to the atmosphere for years in order to make a substantial sum of money.'[8] Another example concerned an offer of weapons by Turkey that Brigadier Yousaf was sent to inspect before shipment. He found that they had been manufactured in 1940-42 and had been withdrawn from the Turkish army 30 years before. His refusal to accept them was overruled by his superiors for political reasons. 'In the end 60,000 rifles, 8,000 light machine guns, 10,000 pistols and over 100 million rounds of ammunition duly arrived. Most were badly corroded or faulty and could not be given to the mujahideen.'[9]

In 1984 a shipment of 100,000 .303 rifles arrived in Karachi. When the Afghan Bureau protested that they had not requested this enormous quantity and had no storage space, they were advised by the CIA that the delivery included an advance on the 1985 shipment and that it had been bought at rock-bottom prices in India. It did not escape the ISI's notice that the Indians knew that the weapons would be used against their friends, the Soviets. The ammunition for the Indian rifles was sold to the CIA by a Pakistani dealer through his overseas office without revealing the true source of the 30 million rounds, sold at 50 cents a round. When the CIA notified the Afghan Bureau of the arrival of the shipment in Karachi and the crates were opened, it was found that every round had POF (Pakistan Ordnance Factory) stamped on it. The ammunition had come from old stocks of the Pakistan army which no longer used the weapon. Obviously the ship had been loaded in Karachi, sailed out and doubled back to the port for discharge. According to Yousaf, it took three years and much money to have the rounds defaced at the factory to conceal their provenance before they could be used in Afghanistan. The main losers in this sorry game were Uncle Sam and his taxpayers and the end-users of the weapons, the mujahideen themselves.

A high proportion of the CIA aid was in the form of cash that was additional to and separate from that used for buying arms. These funds were transferred to special accounts in Pakistan controlled by the ISI and were critical to the war effort. As Yousaf states: 'As it was continually brought home to me, without money nothing moves - particularly in Pakistan.' The logistics requirements alone 'soaked up cash as a sponge does water'. In addition to the purchase of the trucks for ferrying the weaponry to the border, the recurrent bills for fuel and maintenance were huge. Furthermore the parties representing the mujahideen themselves needed funds to buy or hire vehicles, mules, horses and camels for transporting the arms and supplies inside Afghanistan. Tribal khans and maliks in the autonomous Frontier Agencies imposed tolls and had to be paid off. In addition, there was a need to purchase building materials, tools and equipment for the construction of warehouses and bases, and tents, clothing, winter equipment and rations. Medical expenses incurred by the parties sponsoring the mujahideen also had to be covered.

As the British in earlier wars had found out to their cost, the Afghan warrior is a formidable fighter. If he knows fear, it is not the fear of death. His physical courage is such that he can bear pain unflinchingly. One of the features of the war that boggled the imagination of outsiders was the journey made by badly injured mujahideen to ICRC hospitals in Peshawar and Quetta. They were brought into Pakistan through rugged and mountainous territory, on makeshift stretchers strapped to the backs of horses or mules. As the journey could take days, mangled feet or legs were amputated in advance to prevent infection, with an axe or a knife, and without anaesthetics. Some mercifully died of the shock. But those who survived made the journey that would have proved daunting to lesser men, stoically, silently, as it is deemed unmanly for an Afghan to scream or cry out in pain. Their courage was reinforced by their literal belief that if they fell in a jihad against infidels, they would go straight to paradise as a *shaheed* (martyr). They also believed that there was a special place in paradise for the *gazi*, that is, for those who fought in a jihad and lived.

An Afghan who has survived childhood has a physique, a resilience and an uncommon ability to endure privation that has been developed in a harsh and arid physical environment with extremes of heat and cold. He has learned to live off the land and can subsist on very little. All he needs is *nan*, a fatty, flat bread, and tea, that can keep him going for days until he reaches a hospitable village or his base camp where he can then down huge quantities of food. It also takes very little to equip an Afghan warrior, his indispensable accoutrements being his rifle – the vintage models having now been replaced by Kalashnikovs – and his all-purpose blanket, usually of a dirty greyish-brown colour that blends well with the rocks beside which he can take shelter or lie in ambush.

On the downside, however, the mujahideen's tactics in battle during the Afghan war left much to be desired. Theirs was typically tribal fighting, localized in area, and pursued for immediate tangible gains such as loot, or the prestige of their commander, with no higher strategic objective. In one typical example described by Yousaf, two large groups of mujahideen attacked the neighbouring garrison towns of Khost and Urgun in 1983. When the government troops in Khost successfully counter-attacked and opened up the road, the mujahideen around Khost moved to Urgun in case it would fall without their help, which would make them ineligible for a share of the spoils. When the mujahideen were armed with more sophisticated weapons later in the war, they would bombard by night a government post at long range, move closer to fire mortars, and then get 30 to 40 men to surround the post and open up with machine guns and rocket launchers at short range. If the garrison withdrew or the post was captured, the mujahideen secured the loot in the form of rations, arms and ammunition that could be used or sold. Another weakness was the Afghan fighter's reluctance to dig in when he gained an advantage, construct overhead cover, and remain in a static defensive position, or crawl unseen on his belly to get close to an enemy position or to sabotage an installation. Such standard fieldcraft taught at the ISI's training courses was below the mujahideen's dignity and lacked the noise and excitement of openly assaulting an enemy post to cries of *Allah-u-Akbar* ('God is Great'), firing, inflicting casualties, and gaining personal glory, booty or the ineffable joys of martyrdom.

Another major weakness was the endless bickering among groups of mujahideen over real or imagined slights and the refusal of their commanders to cooperate with one another in order to coordinate their separate actions in pursuit of a common objective or strategy. This was particularly true if commanders belonged to rival political parties. As we have seen, one of the first tasks of the ISI was to cajole the Peshawar-based parties to agree to form a Seven Party Alliance, and to establish the principle that every mujahideen commander in the field belong to one of the seven parties. If he failed to do so, the commander obtained nothing from the ISI – no arms, no ammunition, no training for his troops, without which he could not exist. So he joined a party, provided he could find one to accept him. But rivalries and petty jealousies did not simply disappear because of the Alliance. As Yousaf states, in some ways the rivalry, even enmity, between the members of the Alliance exacerbated the problems:

Different commanders from the same area would join different Parties, thus widening existing gaps between them. A Commander considered himself king in his area; he felt entitled to the support of the villages and to local taxes. He wanted the loot from attacking any nearby government post, and he wanted the heavy weapons to do it with, as they increased his chances of success and prestige, which in turn facilitated his recruiting a larger force. Such men often reacted violently to other commanders entering, passing through, or 'poaching' on their territory. I could foresee serious difficulties in coordinating joint operations. No Party had a monopoly of power within specific areas or provinces in Afghanistan, although some might predominate. For example, in Paktia Province Hikmetyar, Khalis, Sayyaf and Gailani all had Commanders operating, but only if they combined could any large-scale operations be effective.[10]

Besides, each commander had his own base, usually in the remoter mountain valleys, within or near small village communities, from which he could receive reinforcements, food, shelter and sometimes money. As many of the 325 districts of Afghanistan were likely to have several local bases with commanders affiliated to different parties, the total number would have been considerable at the height of the war. But these did not add up to a network of bases that could be mobilized for coordinated large-scale operations because of the fractious nature of the resistance.[11] Another weakness was that the mujahideen, however strong their motivation, were unpaid volunteers who did not make up a permanent fighting force. They would spend three or four months in the field serving this or that commander according to their local or tribal ties, and spend the rest of the year as farmers, shopkeepers or contract workers in Iran or Pakistan, or caring for the women and children of several families in the refugee camps when their other menfolk were away fighting or working. When such a volunteer felt he had had enough, he went home or to a refugee camp and was temporarily replaced by a relative. Thus, as Yousaf states, a commander might boast that he had 10,000 men under his control, but he would be able in practice to muster no more than 2000 at a time, unless there was a major offensive planned or under way that could attract more fighters.

The Afghan refugee concentrations in Iran and Pakistan, the largest in the world, provided an inexhaustible supply of manpower for the resistance. In Pakistan the number of refugees had risen from 400,000 in 1980 to 2.7 million in 1983, 2.878 million in 1987, 3.156 million in 1988, 3.255 million in 1989, and peaked at 3.272 million in 1990. The numbers in Iran in the corresponding years were 200,000 in 1980, 1.2 million in 1983, 2.221 million in 1987, 2.7 million in 1988, 2.9 million in 1989, and 2.94 million in 1990.[12] After the initial dramatic increase in the exodus following the Soviet invasion, periodic increases in subsequent years can be correlated with the intensification of Soviet offensive actions, such as the 'scorched earth' tactics adopted by the Soviets in the mid-1980s in populated rural areas, particularly in the eastern parts of the country.

But the greatest advantage that the mujahideen as a guerrilla force had were the safe havens in Pakistan to which they could withdraw from time to time to rest and refit, gather the supplies that they needed, receive training in the use of the increasingly sophisticated weapons that the United States was delivering, and be briefed on the superior intelligence concerning Soviet military deployments that the CIA was providing through the ISI.

The arms 'pipeline' to the mujahideen consisted of three distinct parts, the first being the responsibility of the CIA who bought the weapons and paid for their delivery to Pakistan. The second stretch involved their transport across Pakistan and their allocation and delivery to the parties. This was the responsibility of the ISI. The final leg of the journey belonged to the parties and to their commanders in the field. There were six main routes used in the supply line into Afghanistan. The shortest, cheapest and safest passage was from Chitral in the north into Badakhshan and the northern provinces, and into the Panjshir Valley, the principal base of operations of 'the Lion of Panjshir', Commander Ahmad Shah Massoud. But this route was closed by the snows for eight months of the year. The busiest route, through which 40 per cent of the supplies passed, was from Parachinar, the 'Parrot's Beak' that abutted into the province of Logar and was the shortest way to Kabul. A third was from Miranshah, also south-west of Peshawar into Logar and beyond. Another important route was from Quetta to Kandahar through more open country, therefore making the convoys more vulnerable to attack. The most vulnerable route, unpopular among the private trucking contractors, lay through Baluchistan and was used to supply the southern provinces and Herat. A sixth route passed through Iran and crossed into Afghanistan at a point leading to Herat. This was only a three-day journey but it took up to six months for special permits to be obtained for each shipment from the Iranian authorities who allowed in only small arms and subjected the trucks to inspection and escort by their Revolutionary Guards.

The large-scale satellite maps and photographs, and the intelligence made freely available to the ISI's Afghan Bureau by the CIA, made it fairly clear that the Soviet military strategy was limited to protecting the Kabul regime from its internal and external enemies. The numbers, composition and deployment of their forces were revealing factors. From the beginning the Soviets had concentrated their forces in and around Kabul, and in the critical eastern parts of the country where the major infiltrations of the mujahideen from Pakistan were taking place. Thus some 50 per cent of the troops, comprising two motor rifle divisions (MRDs) and the major components of their artillery, transport, signals and engineering formations, as well as their support and headquarters staff, were quartered in the Kabul region. In the eastern sector, motor rifle and air assault brigades of paratroopers (MRBs and AABs) were stationed in Jalalabad, Asadabad, Gardez and Ghazni. There were major deployments of ground and air forces at the Bagram air base, to guard the approaches to the Salang Tunnel and to provide air support for the ground forces defending the Soviet supply routes, and for offensive actions against the mujahideen when required. Other significant forces were based in Mazar-i-Sharif, Kunduz and Faizabad in the north, to protect the main land supply routes from the USSR. Outside these main areas of deployment, coverage in the west was confined only to Kandahar, the Shindand air base and Herat.

The ISI estimated that the highest troop strength reached by the Soviets inside Afghanistan did not exceed 85,000, a number reached within a year of the invasion and maintained at that level until the withdrawal began in 1988. This number comprised 60,000 motorized troops and paratroopers, and 25,000 others, made up of artillery, engineering, signals, construction, border and security units, and airforce personnel. The 85,000 were complemented by a further 30,000 troops deployed in Uzbekistan and Turkmenistan, mainly with administrative and training responsibilities, but with battalion-sized units sent across the river when required for operational duties within Afghanistan.

The overall Soviet strategy appeared to be static and defensive – to try and hold a series of major military bases and key towns, and the routes that linked them, with no attempts to retain large tracts of intervening countryside. Thus great importance was attached to the Kabul–Bagram complex and all approaches to it, and the areas north of the Hindu Kush that were important to the Soviets not only for strategic but also for economic reasons.[13] The Soviets were also sensitive to the potentially subversive implications of the ethnic and religious affiliations of the populations on both sides of the border. The main thrust of the Soviet strategy after the initial deployment of their forces was to improve their tactics, rationalize their forces, develop the use of air power, introduce more suitable weapons and bolster the capacity of the Afghan armed forces. But the greatest Soviet blunders were to underestimate the mujahideen capacity to wage a war of attrition and to overestimate the potential of the Afghan army.

As mentioned in Chapter 7, the Pavlovsky report had showed up the weaknesses of the Afghan armed forces. The Soviet invasion intensified the 'revolving door' phase of the Afghan army: as fast as the Kabul government could round up recruits, the number of deserters swelled. The invasion gave the resistance its greatest recruitment boost of the war as thousands of civilians and soldiers joined what had now become a jihad. On the other hand, the pool of manpower from which army recruits were drawn became more restricted. Kabul found it more and more difficult to tap the rural areas outside their control, leaving only the larger cities to provide conscripts. The situation by the end of 1980 had become so desperate that severe penalties were imposed to keep the men in:

> For ignoring call-up papers up to four years jail, for absence without leave up to five years and for desertion, conspiracy against the revolution and a long list of other offences, fifteen years or execution. Later the period of service was extended to four years, which sparked off several mutinies. I heard of men conscripted twice, even three times. Once conscripted a private had to exist on 200 afghanis ($2) a month, whereas if he had volunteered he would have got 3000–6000 afghanis. Everywhere he went he was watched, an escort accompanied him to the toilet, and sometimes it was two months before he was allowed a weapon at night, or ammunition for his rifle.[14]

Commanders confined their men to their bases, or within defensive posts, since taking them out on an operation was tantamount to sending them over to the mujahideen. The Afghan army shrivelled from a force of 100,000 to a mere 25,000 unreliable men.

Such was the force that the Soviets expected to go out and fight the guerrillas. Yousaf adds that 1980 was the year in which the mujahideen could have won the war, for four reasons: the Afghan army was almost useless as a military force; the Soviets themselves were ill-equipped, ill-trained and disinclined to mount counter-insurgency operations; the Soviets were under intense international pressure as aggressors; and finally, the mujahideen received that year the highest number of recruits from a population of which nine-tenths were opposed to communism. The resistance did not take advantage of the enemy's weakness because it did not attempt to combine its disparate forces. Furthermore it was not supplied at the time with sufficient weapons designed to engage tanks, armoured personnel carriers and aircraft.

According to Yousaf, it took about three years to make the Afghan army function as a viable force. Total strength climbed to between 35,000 and 40,000 by 1983, but divisional strength did not exceed 5000 men, and battalions of no more than 500 men were not uncommon. But the Afghans were overseen at every level and at every post by their Soviet counterparts who treated them as second-rate, even expendable, allies. They were ordered to undertake dangerous missions while the Soviets remained secure in their bases. All strategic and most tactical decisions were made by their Soviet masters. A Soviet military adviser was attached to every Afghan unit, from headquarters down to every isolated company post. All the minor posts and garrisons in the vulnerable eastern sector along the Pakistan border were manned by Afghans, so that Afghan was fighting Afghan when it came to close combat operations against the mujahideen.

But the Soviets could not come up with a credible strategy to effectively confront guerrilla irregulars operating in mountainous territory except by using conventional methods such as heavy armour supported by helicopter gunships and jet fighters. Arney quotes from an eyewitness account of a French doctor working for Medecins sans frontières in the mountains and valleys of the Hazarajat in central Afghanistan at an earlier stage of the war:

> Several hundred armoured vehicles would leave Kabul or Jaghori and occupy a valley that could easily be entered. The population, which had warning either by rumour or because they had seen the helicopter movement, fled into the mountains. The Soviet troops, therefore, entered empty villages where they would remain for a few days, harassed by the Muslim resistance groups – the mujahidin – who also barred access to the upper villages. During these few days, the soldiers pillaged and burned homes, set fire to crops and dragged off with them the few inhabitants left behind – mostly old people whom they interrogated or executed.[15]

The frustrations of waging what appeared to be an 'unwinnable war' against unconventional guerrilla forces denied the Soviets the prospect of ever hoping to permanently pacify the countryside or to expand the areas under their control. The mujahideen were like Mao Tse Tung's fish in the sea, and the Soviets in the mid-1980s began to adopt a policy aimed at draining the sea itself. Civilians were driven out of their homes as Soviet forces indiscriminately bombed villages and destroyed crops, orchards and irrigation systems, and scattered anti-personnel mines over large tracts of the countryside where a guerrilla presence was suspected. These tactics were combined with smaller, more surgical counter-insurgency operations, replacing the large-scale sweeps by armour and infantry. Helicopter-borne troops were dropped on the high ground behind guerrilla positions to seal off strategic passes, while Afghan government troops advanced from the front. Special airborne troops were also used to carry out raids deep into guerrilla-held territory – either bases or large villages known to be cooperating with the mujahideen. Massive Soviet firepower – artillery, tanks, aircraft – penned the guerrillas into 'hunting zones'. Small groups of Spetznaz commandos carried out night-time raids and ambushes against mujahideen caravans.[16]

The worst period of the war for the mujahideen and the Afghan population in general coincided with the Kremlin leadership of the hardliner, Konstantin Chernenko, who succeeded Yuri Andropov in February 1984. In the spring of that year the Soviets mounted large-scale offensives against mujahideen strongholds, systematically spread their scorched-earth tactics, and also began bombing and shelling raids in border zones in Pakistan, which they accused of direct military involvement. This accusation was not far from the mark, as we have seen.

Internationally the Cold War reached new heights after the shooting down in September 1983 of a South Korean civilian airliner that had strayed into Soviet airspace. The deployment by the United States of Cruise and Pershing missiles in Europe caused the Soviets to walk out of the arms reduction talks in Geneva. In April 1984 President Reagan signed a National Security Council directive calling for efforts to drive out the Soviet forces from Afghanistan 'by all means available'. In the autumn of 1984 the US Congress started voting huge increases in funds for the covert CIA operations in support of the Afghan resistance. President Reagan raised the stakes for the Soviets still higher by authorizing the delivery of Stinger surface-to-air missiles to the mujahideen, thus making the Soviet forces dangerously vulnerable in the air for the first time since the war began. All pretences that the United States was not directly involved in the Afghan war were thus dissipated at a stroke.

CHAPTER 10

The Geneva Accords and the Soviet Withdrawal

D uring the eventful years of the Soviet occupation of Afghanistan, when the vicissitudes of the war were the subject of the world's newspaper headlines and almost continuously brought to the public's attention, quieter and far less dramatic processes were going on in the corridors of the United Nations. In February 1981, in response to a request by Pakistan that the United Nations secretary-general appoint a mediator to initiate talks between the parties concerned, Kurt Waldheim named the Peruvian diplomat, Xavier Perez de Cuellar, as his personal representative.

At the XXVIth Congress of the Communist Party of the Soviet Union (CPSU) that year, however, President Brezhnev reiterated the 'fundamental condition' consistent with previous Soviet declarations: since the USSR's 'limited contingent' of troops had been invited in by a legitimate Afghan government, they would be withdrawn 'only with the agreement of the Afghan government'; moreover, troops would only be withdrawn after 'counter-revolutionary' activities against the PDPA were 'completely stopped' and on the basis of 'accords between Afghanistan and its neighbours' who would be required to give 'dependable guarantees' that they would no longer support the 'counter-revolutionary gangs'. But Pakistan refused to talk to Kabul except through the UN mediator, with the withdrawal of Soviet troops and Afghan self-determination at the top of her demands. For its part Kabul demanded direct bilateral talks with Islamabad, with minimal UN involvement, stressing that there should be an end to all aid to the mujahideen; there was no mention of Soviet troop withdrawals. And Iran refused to deal unless the Afghan resistance was involved in the talks. The negotiating positions of the various parties thus seemed unbridgeable.

When Yuri Andropov succeeded to the Kremlin leadership after Brezhnev's death in November 1982, the prospect of a settlement appeared momentarily to brighten. As long-time head of the KGB and a member of the Politburo's Special Commission on Afghanistan, Andropov had a hands-on knowledge of Afghan affairs. He had eloquently advised against a Soviet invasion at the famous Politburo meeting of March 1979 described in Chapter 7. As a gesture of détente, he personally received General Zia at

117

Brezhnev's funeral. That same year, Perez de Cuellar, now UN secretary-general, nominated Diego Cordovez, a persuasive and tenacious diplomat from Ecuador, as his special representative. In March 1983 de Cuellar and Cordovez held discussions with Andropov in Moscow. As Cordovez later recalled, Andropov ended the hour-long meeting 'by holding up his hand and pulling down his fingers, one by one, as he listed the reasons why the Soviet Union felt a solution had to be found soon to the Afghan problem: the situation was harmful to relations, not only with the West, but also with socialist states, the Muslim world, and other Third World states. Finally he said, pointing his thumb down, it was harmful for the Soviet Union internally, for its economy and its society.'[1]

The diplomatic deadlock between Islamabad and Kabul was broken by Diego Cordovez who proposed a single package as a basis for 'indirect talks', with Kabul accepting the UN as 'honest broker', and Pakistan dropping temporarily its demand for Afghan self-determination. The central issue of a Soviet troop withdrawal was relegated to the back-burner. The 'indirect talks' involved some awkward and cumbersome procedures. Initially Cordovez held alternate talks with the Pakistan and Afghan delegations in separate morning and afternoon sessions at Geneva's Palais des Nations. By 1984 he had progressed to simultaneous sessions by shuttling between the two delegations sitting in separate rooms – adding a new meaning to the concept and practice of shuttle diplomacy. In the process the Kabul regime was winning for itself tacit, de facto UN acceptance of its legitimacy, and Pakistan was gaining recognition of its claim to represent the interests of the Afghan resistance and the refugees.[2]

But progress was painfully slow. Andropov died in February 1984, and his successor, the hardliner Konstantin Chernenko, was not inclined to make any concessions. But when Mikhail Gorbachev, a protégé of Andropov, arrived on the scene in March 1985, there was a distinct improvement in the climate. Gorbachev's subsequent words and actions reveal that he had set his mind early on to extricating the USSR from the Afghan morass as soon as it was politically feasible to do so. Soon after his assumption of power, he is believed to have authorized his generals to break the back of the Afghan resistance, but within a specified time-frame. In a speech to the XXVIIth Congress of the CPSU in February 1986, Gorbachev stated that 'counter-revolution and imperialism have transformed Afghanistan into a bleeding wound'. He announced that a withdrawal schedule had been worked out with Kabul and would be implemented as soon as a political settlement had been reached.

Gorbachev's problem was how to ensure that a friendly pro-Soviet government remained in power in Kabul after Soviet troops had left. The stability of the government depended on broadening the regime's base so as to make it more acceptable. To this end, pressure was brought to bear on Babrak Karmal, who announced in April 1985 that nationwide elections to the long-promised loya jirga would be held. But to restore the credibility of the regime, Karmal himself had to go. At the end of 1985 an article in *Pravda* admitted that Karmal's government was not universally popular. In April 1986, on the eve of the eighth anniversary of the Saur Revolution, Karmal was called to Moscow, and Dr Najibullah, who had resigned his post as head of KHaD, the Afghan secret police, took the salute at the celebratory military parade.

By the end of the month, Najibullah was unanimously elected general secretary of the PDPA's Central Committee. As head of KHaD, Najibullah had acquired a reputation for ruthlessness as the strong man of the regime. But he was intelligent and shrewd, and had come to understand his countrymen very well. He had begun his political life as a high school student and continued as an early associate of Parcham after he completed his medical degree. The fact that he was a Ghilzai Pashtun improved his chances of working closely with the Ghilzai-dominated Khalqis and the officer corps in the armed forces as well as with the tribes on both sides of the border. He also had some advantages that marked him for leadership status among the Afghans: he had an imposing physique, acquired as a wrestler and weight-lifter since youth, that had earned him his nickname of 'The Ox'; he was related to the royal family through his wife, and had connections across the border in Peshawar where his father had been trade commissioner during Daoud's presidency. His private life was beyond reproach, unlike Karmal's, living in a modest house with his wife and three daughters. Above all, he could be trusted to be loyal to Moscow.

Najibullah was Gorbachev's chosen instrument to carry out his game plan. On 1 January 1987 Najibullah announced his programme of 'national reconciliation' comprising three key elements: a six-month unilateral cease-fire, the formation of a government of 'national unity' and the return of over 5 million refugees from Pakistan and Iran.

An 'Extraordinary Supreme Commission for National Reconciliation' was set up and branches were opened all over the country. Their job was to make contact with relatives and friends in exile or fighting with resistance groups, pass on the message of peace, and distribute essential relief items for the use of returning refugees.[3] Other inducements offered were tax concessions, the return of confiscated property and the deferment of military service. Radio Kabul started calling the mujahideen fighters 'angry brothers' rather than 'bandits'. Some 4000 political prisoners were released. Six months later, just before the expiry of the six-month ceasefire, Najibullah was able to claim that 59,000 refugees had returned; tens of thousands of armed men were negotiating with the government; 4000 representatives of the opposition had been included in the reconciliation committees; and coalition governments had already been formed in several villages, sub-districts, districts and provinces.

Even if these claims were considered dubious by many observers at the time, Najibullah, with Gorbachev determined to pull out Soviet troops as soon as possible behind him, had seized the initiative. In the days following the announcement of the reconciliation programme, refugees in Pakistan rushed to exchange their rupees for afghanis, and vehicles were sold off in an effort to beat an anticipated rush to dispose of property in Pakistan. Arney quotes an Afghan refugee official in Peshawar as saying: 'You get the impression in the camps these days, that if anything happens, ninety percent of the refugees are ready to move.'⁴ But Najibullah's proposals were turned down with disbelief and contempt by members of the seven-party alliance in Peshawar.

The Islamist parties, forced together into an 'alliance' by the ISI at the behest of General Zia to fight the jihad, were a squabbling, bickering lot who could 'not even agree where to put the ashtrays', as one insider confided to Arney. It was clear that these parties claiming to represent the mujahideen resistance had developed into vested interests that were not receptive to power-sharing arrangements. They and their Pakistani sponsors, replete with funds and weapons generously contributed by 'the international community', developed their own agendas for a post-Soviet Afghanistan. But an opportunity had been missed by the self-appointed representatives of the Afghan people. In fact the Islamic parties in Peshawar represented only themselves. A survey among Afghan refugees conducted in 1987 by one of Afghanistan's outstanding academics and intellectuals, Professor S.B. Majrooh, found that less than half a per cent of those polled would choose one of the seven Peshawar leaders to rule a free Afghanistan. Majrooh was later shot dead outside his own home in Peshawar. It was rumoured that Hekmatyar was behind the assassination. According to the Pakistani Commissioner for Afghan Refugees, 'these seven leaders have been built up and have their tentacles, their small organizations, in virtually every refugee camp. They have great influence now, but their status in tomorrow's Afghanistan could be anything.'⁵ The parties owed their 'influence' to the fact that they served as somewhat porous conduits for the US and Saudi funds and weapons channelled to the resistance fighters inside Afghanistan by Pakistan's ISI.

Najibullah for his part pressed on with a programme of reconciliation that amounted in effect to the dissolution of the monolithic communist state that the Soviet Union itself had come in to protect. In June 1987 the ceasefire was extended for a further six months. In July a draft constitution was published and the opposition invited to suggest changes. In October Najibullah named the Peshawar parties in his appeal for a coalition government and announced that they would be allowed to open offices in Kabul and publish newspapers if they ended their resistance.

The new constitution was formally adopted by a loya jirga in November 1987. It established Islam as the state religion and converted Afghanistan in theory into a multi-party parliamentary democracy. Five months later, elections were held under the new constitution, in a move to coincide with the conclusion in April 1988 of the Geneva Accords negotiated by the UN mediator, Diego Cordovez. A quarter of the seats in the Wolesi Jirga – or lower house of the Afghan parliament – were left vacant for the opposition, while others were contested by the non-PDPA National Fatherland Front (NFF) or by newly formed parties. As a result, which Arney describes as 'rigging in reverse', the Marxist PDPA ended up with only 22 per cent of the seats.

The Geneva Accords were the fruit of the tireless efforts deployed by Diego Cordovez. The agreement concluded on 14 April 1988 by the foreign ministers of Afghanistan, Pakistan, the Soviet Union and the United States at the European headquarters of the United Nations, the Palais des Nations in Geneva, called for the withdrawal of all Soviet troops within nine months, non-interference in each other's affairs by Pakistan and Afghanistan, and the voluntary repatriation of Afghan refugees. The United States and the Soviet Union pledged to 'guarantee' the settlement in a separate document. The Accords were universally acclaimed by the international community – and many exaggerated claims were made regarding their significance – but they guaranteed the continuation of the Afghan civil war.

The Afghan academic Amin Saikal has observed that Cordovez conducted his mediation in narrow conformity with the UN resolutions concerning the troop withdrawal and with the politics of Cold War superpower rivalry:

> He seemed to view the Afghan crisis more as a proxy conflict between the superpowers than as one with political and social origins within Afghanistan itself. He felt that if he could find common ground between Moscow and Washington, and enable these two powers to climb down from their maximalist positions, then he had a good chance of persuading them as well as the PDPA government and the Government of Pakistan not to insist on any linkage between the need for a Soviet troop withdrawal and an overall settlement of the Afghanistan problem.[6]

Implicit in Cordovez's approach, Saikal adds, was that the fewer the actors he involved in the negotiating process, the more chance he had to achieve the task he had set himself. He concludes that Cordovez did not therefore make any serious effort to involve the leaders of the Afghan resistance in his mediation. Nor to some extent were the interests of Iran considered relevant to the problem.

Two crucial developments came to Cordovez's assistance in the achievement of the primary task that he had set for himself – that of securing the agreement of the two superpowers and of their proxies in the Afghan war. The first was the arrival of Mikhail Gorbachev on the scene and a Politburo decision in November 1986 to cut the USSR's losses and end its involvement in an unwinnable war. Although there was no reference to UN mediation in the Politburo document, it was clear to Gorbachev that the Cordovez mediation offered him the best option to achieve a troop withdrawal with honour. The problem for him assumed greater urgency when the Reagan administration decided to supply the mujahideen with Stinger missiles, thus increasing the cost of the war to Moscow. The second development was a softening on the part of the US administration in its position concerning the Afghan war. Secretary of State George Shultz could argue that it was in the interests of the United States to be helpful to Gorbachev by refraining from activities that could undermine his position and thwart his domestic and foreign policy reforms.

But it must be stated in fairness to Cordovez that he did make the effort to involve the other parties to the conflict by working on a 'second track' – parallel negotiations to secure a coalition or caretaker government in Kabul acceptable to all sides. In September 1987 Cordovez circulated a memorandum to Moscow, Kabul, Islamabad and Washington that suggested that a dialogue be started under UN auspices between the PDPA, the Peshawar Seven-Party Alliance and Afghan nationalists in exile. The proposal was not adopted formally. But Cordovez's efforts did not fail for lack of seriousness on his part. He and Perez de Cuellar had had ample opportunities to become familiar with the internal dynamics of Afghan politics during their long involvement as special representatives. His failure was due, first, to the total intransigence of the Peshawar parties, and second, to the ambivalent attitude of General Zia who had his own agenda to fulfil – to establish in Kabul a government amenable to Pakistani interests and dominated by his fundamentalist Pashtun clients in Peshawar.

Zia at various times sent conflicting signals that were confusing to the peacemakers. In November 1987 he appeared to concede, according to a British newspaper report quoted by Arney, that any caretaker government would have to have the confidence of 'the three main elements in the Afghanistan conflict: the freedom fighters, the refugees and the present Kabul government'.[7] Gorbachev, fearing a bloodbath after the Soviet troop withdrawal, had encouraged Cordovez to sound out Zahir Shah in Rome about heading a neutral caretaker government. Notwithstanding the stridently expressed hostility of the Islamic fundamentalists, the ex-king was regarded with a favourable, somewhat nostalgic eye, by a substantial number of the refugees. For a brief period it seemed that all roads were leading to Rome. But Zia ruled out the option when India sent an envoy to meet the ex-king.

Zia confidently expected the Najibullah regime to fall soon after the departure of Soviet troops. He was therefore in no hurry to promote an intra-Afghan dialogue that would include Najibullah. The chronic disunity of the so-called Seven-Party Alliance, which could only agree on the withdrawal of 'infidel' troops and the unconditional surrender of an 'infidel' regime, played into Zia's hands. The Alliance's decision-making procedures, which required unanimity, meant that the more moderate and flexible parties, such as Gailani's National Islamic Front of Afghanistan (NIFA), were outvoted at every turn. Their appeals to Zia, for the holding of a referendum among the refugees that could result in a united leadership confidently capable of conducting negotiations with Kabul without betraying the cause, were refused. Cordovez was denied access to Peshawar where he wished to meet with Alliance and refugee leaders.

On 8 February 1988 Gorbachev publicly announced that Soviet troops would start pulling out on 15 May and complete their withdrawal within ten months. When a Soviet envoy, Yuri Vorontsov, delivered the message in Islamabad, Zia stated categorically that he would never sign an agreement with the Najibullah government, thus completely blunting the principal thrust of the Cordovez mediation. Vorontsov countered by saying that the formation of a coalition government in Kabul was 'nobody's business but the business of the Afghans themselves'.[8]

Zia's response, through his ISI handlers, was to bully the Peshawar parties to make proposals to counter Najibullah's offer of a government of national reconciliation. After weeks of bitter argument, and ten days before the scheduled commencement of the final round of the Geneva talks, the Alliance announced the formation of an interim government to replace the Najibullah regime. The role of this government was to oversee the Soviet withdrawal and hold elections within six months for a constituent assembly, with a quarter of the seats reserved for 'Muslims presently living in Afghanistan' – meaning non-communist members of the PDPA government. The Alliance also reserved for itself the dominant position by forming a 'grand council' to oversee the government – an Afghan equivalent of Iran's Council of Guardians, an unelected, coopted body of conservative clerics formed to ensure that the elected representatives of the people did not stray from the tenets of the Khomeini revolution as interpreted by them. These proposals required the virtual capitulation of the Kabul government. A member of one of the moderate parties in the Alliance quoted by Arney described them as 'Pakistan's brainchild ... Zia wants to close all other doors, torpedo all other efforts, by erecting this government'.[9]

Zia was also under pressure on the domestic front. In 1985 elections had been held with a view to setting up a civilian administration with a prime minister, Mohammad Khan Junejo, handpicked by Zia from among the

politicians of the dominant Muslim League. What was known as 'Zia's Afghan war' had become increasingly unpopular in Pakistan. The country's
growing ills – the spread of a culture of drugs and weapons, bombings in the
cities believed to be KHaD-sponsored that began in 1987, including a blast
that killed 70 people in Karachi – were all blamed on the presence of over 3
million Afghan refugees and their activities. The rift between the civilian and
military members of the ruling establishment came to a head at the end of
1987, when Prime Minister Junejo asserted his own authority over the conduct of foreign policy by taking over the portfolio himself. On his
instructions, the Foreign Ministry stopped its practice of automatically clearing all decisions with Zia. Junejo strengthened his hand by convening an
unprecedented all-party conference to reach a national consensus on Afghanistan and to use 'the opportunity of a lifetime' afforded by Moscow's
determination to conclude a settlement.

It may well be that the crucial factor that persuaded Zia to back down
from his refusal to sign an agreement with Najibullah was the US State
Department's last-minute decision, made under pressure from right-wing
elements in Washington that accused it of a' sell-out', not to honour its
previous commitment to halt military supplies to the mujahideen on the day
that Soviet troops began to pull out. The department announced that aid
would not be stopped without 'a symmetrical cessation of military supplies to
the regime in Kabul'. Confronted with the US volte-face, Moscow had no
choice but to refuse to halt its own military supplies to Kabul, arguing with
some plausibility that its own obligations dated back to the Soviet Union's
Treaty of Peace and Friendship with Afghanistan concluded in 1920. Thus
emerged the formula of 'positive symmetry' in continuing arms deliveries to
all sides in the civil war. On 14 April 1988, just before the signing ceremony
at the Palais de Nations in Geneva, the UN secretary-general received a
formal notification that the United States reserved the right to continue
supplying the mujahideen, although 'it would meet Soviet restraint with
restraint'.

When Secretary of State George Shultz signed the Geneva Accords a few
hours later, he knew that his country's formal guarantee of the settlement
had become meaningless. Pakistan's signature bound it to specific undertakings, to 'prevent within its territory the presence, harbouring, in camps and
bases or otherwise, organizing, training, financing, equipping and arming of
individuals, and political, ethnic or other groups'. How these formal treaty
obligations could be squared with Washington continuing to supply the
mujahideen with weapons that could only be delivered through Pakistani
territory would boggle even the legal imagination. Yaqub Khan, the foreign
minister re-instated by the 'the grinning general' after he sacked the civilian
administration in May 1988, used cricketing jargon to describe a game that

was not quite cricket: 'the Geneva Accords were just an inconvenient episode which interrupted play'.[10] And so the war continued, becoming even more murderous this time around, with Afghans fighting Afghans, battling not only against Najibullah's forces but with one another.

On 17 August 1988 the Pakistani presidential aircraft crashed, killing all on board: President Zia, the former head of the ISI, General Akhtar Rehman Khan, promoted to the post of Chairman of the Joint Chiefs of Staff Committee, US Ambassador Arnold Raphel and a number of top Pakistani generals. Autopsies were not carried out on the badly charred bodies of the victims – one reason for an abundance of conspiracy theories later. The long-postponed parliamentary elections were scheduled to be held in November that year, pending which the civilian head of the Senate, Ghulam Ishaq Khan, took over as interim president. The vice-chief of army staff, General Mirza Aslam Beg, was appointed chief, a post that General Zia had always retained during his years as president. The November elections resulted in a victory for the People's Action Party led by the daughter of Zulfikar Ali Bhutto, Benazir, who now became prime minister in a civilian, democratically elected government. In the United States, President Reagan's vice-president, George Bush, won the presidential elections in November 1988, and his administration was installed on 1 January 1989. But new actors did not bring about any radical changes in US and Pakistani policies where Afghanistan was concerned. Benazir Bhutto had been an implacable foe of General Zia, whom she consistently accused of murdering her revered father. However, she retained the services of Zia's appointee as head of the ISI, General Hamid Gul, who drew Pakistan into a more flagrantly interventionist role in Afghan affairs.

By mid-February 1989 all Soviet troops had left Afghanistan in an orderly retreat, the Soviet commander, General Boris Gromov, being the last to leave, walking across a bridge on the Amu Darya on the 15th of the month. Many in the US and Pakistani political and military establishments expected the Najibullah regime to collapse within a matter of weeks, with triumphant mujahideen swarming across the country to claim victory for the jihad in Kabul. Nothing of the kind happened. What was seen as a desperately hasty evacuation of garrisons in areas bordering Pakistan was in fact a planned redeployment of government forces in towns and cities, and in major bases and strongholds formerly held by Soviet forces to secure vital lines of communications, in order to wage a defensive war. The mujahideen were ill-prepared to transform their hit-and-run methods of waging 'ten years of pinpricks' on the regime's forces, as described in the last chapter, into a conventional war against conventional forces. They had no armour and no air force; most of all, they lacked a unified military command capable of mounting coordinated offensives, and of following up rocket and artillery bombardments with ground assaults. Their weaknesses were best shown up in their disorderly and disastrous attempt to capture the city of Jalalabad in March 1989.

When it seemed that the Soviet troop pull-out was in fact taking place, all kinds of deals were worked out to fill the power vacuum, in the event of the Najibullah regime falling – which was generally expected. The horse-trading involved the Peshawar parties, tribal groups, pro-government militias, mujahideen commanders and Pakistan's ISI. In Kandahar, for example, Pir Gailani's NIFA attempted to reactivate the Durrani Pashtun tribal networks in favour of a Zahir Shah return, and to establish contacts with the governor and senior officers of the local garrison for a bloodless transfer of power. NIFA's efforts were sabotaged by the ISI which channelled arms and money to rival tribes and commanders in partisan arrangements with their favourite son, Hekmatyar, who wanted to use his military muscle and tightly controlled party organization for a swift and decisive victory over Najibullah's forces.

When the Russian troop pull-out was nearing its end, the establishment of a mujahideen government, preferably inside Afghanistan, became an imperative both for the Peshawar parties and for their Pakistani sponsors. If the Kabul regime fell quickly, such a government would be needed to forestall a bloody struggle between the various resistance factions for the spoils of war. If Najibullah survived, it was feared that his regime could secure international recognition by default, win the Afghan seat in international organizations, and benefit from the disbursements of the projected US$1.6 billion in international aid sought by the UN's 'Operation Salaam' – set up after the Geneva Accords for the post-war relief and reconstruction of Afghanistan and headed by Prince Sadruddin Aga Khan. The proposals formulated in April 1988 by the Seven-Party Alliance had lacked credibility. The feuding political parties, safely ensconced in their comfortable, indeed luxurious quarters in Peshawar, had failed to win the allegiance of the more militarily effective commanders in the field who had no political voice. The Pashtun-dominated parties had also failed to establish any meaningful links with the second largest population group in Afghanistan, the Hazaras and their Shi'ite parties. The Shi'ites had become a political force to be reckoned with during the long years of virtual autonomy they had enjoyed during communist rule. With the end of the war with Iraq, Iran had begun to play a more pro-active role in Afghan affairs. Tehran had exerted pressure on the Shi'ites to put an end to their internal feuds and to form an eight-party alliance called the Hizb-i-Wahdat. Iran now claimed a major share for the Shi'ites in any post-PDPA government in Kabul.

Just five days before the Soviet troops were to complete their withdrawal, Pakistan hastily organized a shura, or consultative assembly, in Islamabad, bringing together some 500 Afghans claiming to represent the entire resistance: mujahideen political leaders from Peshawar and Tehran, field commanders, religious leaders, nationalist exiles and refugee elders. With the shura packed with delegates from the Peshawar parties, the proceedings turned out to be a sham. After bitter debates in public and private deals worked out behind the scenes, a vote was taken, and an Afghan Interim Government (AIG) was elected with all 35 ministries shared out among the seven Peshawar parties. As the local BBC correspondent who had succeeded Arney said: 'it's taken thirteen days for the shura to select the seven leaders they've already had'.[11]

At his inaugural press conference, the provisional 'president' of the AIG, Sibghatullah Mujaddedi, declared that the AIG would establish its 'provisional' capital inside Afghanistan 'within a month'. This would remove the stain of foreign sponsorship, and secure its claims to legitimacy, international recognition and the funds it craved. The city chosen for this purpose was the country's third largest, Jalalabad, close enough to Pakistan for re-supply purposes, and closer to Kabul than Kandahar, a power-broking Pashtun stronghold that had stronger political credentials. The ISI drew up the battleplans and arranged the logistics, the intelligence and the communications. But there was more bravado in the venture, pushed by the most radical of the Islamic fundamentalists, Hekmatyar and Younis Khalis, who were both well represented and commanded local support in the area, than sound military strategy. A former Afghan army officer, General Yahya Nauroz, appointed the AIG 'chief of staff', pointed out the folly of engaging a government stronghold where the defenders outnumbered the attackers by an estimated ratio of three to one.[12]

The attack at first seemed to go well, when Gailani's NIFA guerrillas captured the government base of Samarkhel, 12 miles south-east of Jalalabad, on 7 March 1989. Several thousand government troops surrendered without a fight, probably on account of arrangements made in advance with NIFA, while the rest fled to Jalalabad. The guerrillas then advanced to the airport where they ran into heavy resistance. Despite human wave assaults and a heavy bombardment of the city that cost over 2000, mostly civilian lives, the mujahideen could not advance any further. Then in July, when many of them returned to Peshawar to observe the month of Ramadan, armoured columns broke out of the city and swept into Samarkhel, recapturing the base with minimal resistance.

The ISI's original battle plans were ignored in the fighting which was directed by two rival shuras of commanders acting independently of each other. Even the blockade of the city was uncoordinated and ineffective. It was carried out by two ideologically opposed parties, NIFA and the extremely fundamentalist Hizb of Younis Khalis, which took turns to guard the only road leading through the mountains into Jalalabad from Kabul. Large government re-supply convoys were able to slip through into the city when the guard was being changed!

The mujahideen leaders had badly underestimated the resolve of the government forces, putting their faith in the expected mass defections that did not take place. Some 20,000 troop reinforcements had been brought into the city from outside Pashtun regions, and the local pro-government militias were recruited from among the tribal rivals of the mujahideen resistance forces of the province. There was therefore less likelihood of fraternizing and defections, particularly after the murder in cold blood of 70 Afghan army officers by a fanatical Khalis commander after the capture of Samarkhel. In the summer of 1989 the government forces, after months of static defence, began active operations that cleared the road up to the Pakistani border. They beat off another major attack on Khost in the autumn, inflicting heavy casualties. The Afghan army had successfully defended Jalalabad against the most massive attack ever undertaken by the mujahideen during the whole war. It had demonstrated its superiority in waging conventional warfare without Soviet help against undisciplined, guerrilla irregulars. Its air force, operating over a broad plain without ground cover, was particularly effective. New weapons that brought terror to the mujahideen were the freshly ac-quired long-range Scud-B missiles fired from Kabul.

With his regime's morale having received a strong boost after the Jalala-bad victory, Najibullah could confidently set about pursuing his declared policy of national reconciliation in the face of the uncompromising, die-hard attitude of the fundamentalist parties in Peshawar. As these had foreign sponsors, Najibullah could appeal to the nationalistic impulse in his attempts to forge a broad coalition, bringing together the Marxist left of both factions of the PDPA, now inclined to be more conciliatory and less doctrinaire, with other segments of Afghan society: the educated middle classes and secular nationalists, religious and ethnic minorities, as well as the traditional, tribally organized strata of the Pashtuns from which the jihad had drawn its strength and its legitimacy. After the Soviet withdrawal, the spirit of jihad was also draining away, now that Afghans were being called upon to fight Afghans. There were many reasons for this change, the greatest perhaps being the claims of the qawm. It was observed, for instance, that in areas vacated by government troops for strategic reasons, the first priority of the local com-manders was to consolidate the authority of their clan, lay claim to land, and settle local disputes, rather than to move on to attack the nearest government garrison. Rank-and-file mujahideen were also increasingly loth to attack urban centres where relatives and friends would be in as much danger as those in military targets.

PART III: THE DISINTEGRATION OF THE STATE

CHAPTER 11

The Fragmentation of Afghanistan

What Najibullah had to offer, and that which contributed to the survival of his regime, was what the qawm, the rural-based communities of Afghanistan, had always wanted: strong local autonomy, with generous subsidies of money and arms to go with it. Some of Najibullah's initiatives formed part of an overall strategy; other autonomous or semi-autonomous centres of community-based power arose spontaneously by default, during and after the Soviet occupation.

The development of largely qawm-based, locally autonomous regions, was partly the result of a deliberate strategy adopted by Najibullah to build up forces to combat the mujahideen that could operate independently of the command structures of the Ministry of Defence, dominated by Khalqi officers. One of these, the militia led by the tribal leader Juma Khan in Andarab, had initially aligned itself with Hekmatyar who used it to block supplies to his arch-rival, Ahmad Shah Massoud, in the adjacent Panjshir Valley. Juma Khan later rallied to the Kabul regime on account of tribal rivalry with the Panjshiris. A more typical pro-government militia leader was Ismatullah Muslim, a Soviet-trained army officer from the Achazkai tribe that occupied the area between Kandahar and the Pakistani border and was notorious for its age-old traditions of raiding and smuggling. In 1979 Muslim had led his tribe into the resistance, but in 1984, following disputes with the ISI over his smuggling activities and his refusal to join any of the Peshawar-based parties, he defected to the regime, was made a general and a member of the Revolutionary Council, and acquired a house in Kabul where he gave parties at which alcohol, drugs, female dancers, and more besides, were present. Ismat Muslim's profile was typical of the warlords who flourished after the Soviet withdrawal, some of them serving the purposes of the Kabul regime, others aligning themselves with one or other of the Peshawar parties. Their fickle loyalties were bought with cash, arms and equipment, and the freedom to enrich themselves by smuggling, drug-trafficking and the imposition of road tolls.

A major problem faced by Najibullah after the departure of the Soviets was the defence of the vital supply routes from the north, through the Salang Tunnel and into Kabul. As we have seen in Chapter 9, most of the Soviet forces had been concentrated in these areas, and Najibullah lacked adequate conventional forces to defend them. One militia that was of great strategic value had come into being spontaneously at the start of the war in the area north of the Salang Tunnel. It was inhabited by the Ismailis, a Shi'ite sect that was considered heretical by both the Sunnis and the mainstream Imami Shi'ites who were the Hazaras. When most of the Tajiks and Pashtuns in the area aligned themselves either with the Jamiat or with the fanatical Hizbi-i-Islami, Sayyed Mansur Naderi of Kaihan, the brother of the *pir* (spiritual head) of the Ismailis,[1] organized his community to arm and defend themselves. Najibullah patronized the Ismailis. Sayyed Mansur was eventually made a general, the governor of Baghlan province and a member of the Revolutionary Council. This represented a great social advance for a highly stigmatized group. By 1989 Naderi had 13,000 troops organized in the 80th Division under the command of his son, Jaffar. He acted as an intermediary in distributing Soviet aid and as an informal channel of communications between Kabul and the mujahideen.

The largest and most effective of the pro-government militias was led by an Uzbek, General Abdul Rashid Dostum, who began his career organizing self-defence units for the state natural gas company's installations in the north. His earliest recruits were Uzbeks from Jauzjan province who had long been oppressed and exploited by Durrani Pashtun landlords supported by the Afghan monarchy. Although the militia were initially known as Jauzjanis, Dostum recruited from all ethnic groups. His political grouping came to be known as the Jumbesh. By 1991 his forces numbered 40,000 men. Their main task was to replace the Soviet troops protecting the gas fields and the supply routes from the Soviet border and southwards through Mazar-i-Sharif. They were a well-equipped mobile force capable of conducting combat operations outside these areas. In 1989 units of the force were dispatched to Kandahar, to replace the departing Soviet garrison and to thwart any coup plans by Pashtun mujahideen and disaffected army officers. They also played a key role in the defence of Jalalabad in March–June 1990.

Other autonomous regions came into being by default, as a direct consequence of the internal resistance to the Soviet invasion. The first of these was in Nuristan in the north-east of Afghanistan. The most important came about through the empowerment of the Hazaras, descendants of the Turco-Mongol armies of Chingiz Khan and his successors, who had settled in the central highlands of Afghanistan, converted to Shi'ism, spoke a form of Persian, and formed self-governing communities led by their khans and *mirs*.

Their religious leaders were called *shaykhs*, clerics who were trained at Shi'ite theological schools such as Qum in Iran or Najaf in Iraq.

The Hazaras lost their relative autonomy in the late nineteenth century when Amir Abdur Rahman waged a ruthless war to bring them under his direct authority. In the course of five years, the Hazara population was reduced through massacres, serfdom, expulsion and resettlement to a fifth of its former size. Much of their pasture and arable land was redistributed among Ghilzai Pashtun nomads, the *kuchi*. Hazara exile communities emerged in secluded settlements in northern Afghanistan, around the city of Mashad in north-eastern Iran, and in Quetta in British Baluchistan.

The Hazaras in Afghanistan became a grossly deprived community. Economic reasons forced thousands of them to seek poorly paid employment in the cities, particularly in Kabul, where thousands before them had been relocated by force by the Iron Amir to serve as indentured serfs or household servants. They were treated as inferiors on racial and religious grounds. Until the 1960s they were generally denied access to higher education or the higher ranks of the military and bureaucracy. Thereafter, when young Hazara from privileged khan families were increasingly accepted at high schools and the university, they inclined to left-wing politics. As mentioned in Chapter 4, Hazara workers figured prominently in the labour associations organized by the Marxist Mahmoodi brothers in the 1960s. During the Daoud dictatorship, Hazara activists fled to Pakistan where they combined with the exiled Hazara community in Quetta to form a Hazara national association. The Hazara exiles had done well in their Pakistani surroundings, where an awareness of their distinct history and culture had taken root and was given expression in numerous publications and journals. One Pakistani Hazara had even risen to the rank of an army general during the presidency of Ayub Khan in the 1950s. In the 1960s and 1970s, tens of thousands of impoverished Hazaras also went to Iraq and Iran as migrant workers employed in the construction boom of those oil-rich economies, to be joined later by greater numbers of refugees fleeing the Soviet invasion.

The rural Hazaras of the Hazarajat were the first to stage a large-scale rebellion against the PDPA regime. By 1979 their home regions, with the exception of the capital, Bamiyan, were liberated from communist rule and were to remain autonomous for the best part of the next 20 years. The resistance was led by the khans of the villages in the mountains and valleys, while the sayyeds and leaders of the religious schools or madrasas, trained in the Shi'ite centres of Iraq and Iran, also mobilized their followers. In mid-1979 the leaders of the Hazara resistance formed an alliance called the Council of Harmony (Shura-ye-Ittefaq) led by the sayyeds who, unlike the khans whose influence was limited to their local fiefs, developed a network of followers throughout the Hazarajat. But the khans, through their family and political links with the exiled community in Quetta, were able to provide the shura with weapons and other services.

Hazara autonomy during the communist years led not to peace but to a bloody war that produced more victims and refugees than the struggles against the communists and the Soviet army. The sayyeds had been permitted to use the religious offerings (khum) destined for the needs of the Shi'ite religious centres in Iraq and Iran to wage a holy war both against the com-munists and the leftist Hazara parties. Proponents of a Khomeini-style Islamic state, led by Shaykh Ali Akbari of the Sepah-e-Pasdaran, fought against the shura of the sayyeds while the khans fought efforts aimed at their expulsion from their fiefs. There were eight different political parties involved at the height of the internecine conflict, which came to an end only under Iranian pressure.[2] The Shi'ite parties formed an alliance called the Hizb-i-Wahdat. Shaykh Abdolali Mazari of the Hazara nationalist Nasr Party won control of the alliance after defeating Akbari's Sepah. Another important Shi'ite party, the Harakat-e-Islami, which was formed by a Sayyed religious scholar, the Ayatollah Asif Mohseni, and included urban and non-Hazara Shi'ites, held aloof from the alliance, but eventually lost its Hazara members to the Wahdat.

During the years of communist rule, the Hazaras in Kabul had become a major population group. Benefiting also from the regime's liberal nationali-ties policy, they had been transformed by a political, economic and cultural emancipation to become a force to be reckoned with in the capital. One of them, Sultan Ali Keshtmand, was appointed prime minister by Karmal Karmal and continued in that function under Najibullah. Hazara entrepre-neurs were engaged in lucrative commercial activities, particularly in the transport sector, and they were also well armed, since the government dis-tributed weapons to the population of Kabul to defend themselves against mujahideen attacks and acts of sabotage.[3]

In the west, Captain Ismail Khan, who was one of the leaders of the mutiny of March 1979 of the Afghan army's 17th Division based in Herat, had built up a conventional type of military organization. In 1988 his Hamza Division had five regiments, each with six to nine battalions of about 200 men made up of combat units of 25 men. These military units were organized directly under his command by Ismail Khan himself, rather than by mobiliz-ing mujahideen forces based on social groups with their own commanders. After the suppression of the 1979 insurrection in Herat, Ismail Khan had taken refuge with his followers in the mountainous province of Ghor which became the base of his resistance forces. His top-down approach provoked complaints from other commanders operating in Farah, Badghis and Herat. To assuage these complaints, he convened in Ghor a shura of commanders from nine western provinces which led to improved military cooperation among resistance groups in the west.

Although Ismail Khan gave priority to military organization, he also directed an embryonic regional administration with a system of committees supervising local administration in mujahideen-controlled areas, in matters of finance, health, education, agriculture and the judiciary. Herat and its hinterland had been for centuries an economic and cultural centre of the vast Iranian province of Khorasan. It contained an ethnically heterogeneous mix of populations who spoke Farsi-based dialects and practised religious tolerance in relations between Sunnis and Shi'ites.

In the north-east, the earliest resistance to the communist regime in Kabul and to the Soviets was led by ulema allied to the loosely structured Harakat of Mohammad Nabi Mohammedi. By 1982 many Tajik and Uzbek ulema, as well as commanders nominally allied to the NIFA, switched their allegiance to the Jamiat and to its most effective commander, Ahmad Shah Massoud. The latter was able to build up an autonomous power-base in his native Panjshir Valley which, after years of effort, grew into a regional cooperative of Jamiat commanders called the Supervisory Council of the North (SCN).

Massoud had to contend not only with the regime's forces and the Russians, who had set up a string of bases along the supply routes from Soviet Uzbekistan and Tajikistan to Kabul and the south, but also with the hostility of Hekmatyar's Hizbi-i-Islami, which drew its support from detribalized Pashtuns relocated to the north by the 'Iron Amir'. While the Hizbi encouraged civilians in their areas of control to emigrate so that they could be freer in their armed operations, Massoud adopted from the beginning a strategy for integrating the military, political and economic components of the resistance at the grassroots level. In this he was assisted by the relative absence of rivalries among the Tajiks and other non-tribal ethnic groups and by the greater freedom he enjoyed from ISI interference and control. His independence in this respect, as in the case of Ismail Khan's in the west, was not only due to his own personality and non-Pashtun ethnic identity but also to his region's geographical distance from Pakistan. His aloofness did not endear him to the Pakistanis from whom he received the bare minimum of support in their distribution of US largesse.

In Panjshir Massoud used his superior organizational skills to build up village militias and mujahideen bases (one for every six or seven villages) that could be used to stage defensive and offensive operations. There were 20 such bases in the Panjshir Valley. At another level, Massoud organized a more mobile striking force under his personal command. It was composed of young volunteers who were required to be literate, were highly trained and wore uniforms. Massoud used his commandos to ambush Soviet supply convoys.

In 1983, after the Soviets failed in their sixth consecutive offensive against Panjshir, a truce was called. This occurred in the briefly conciliatory Andropov era. Massoud used the truce to implement a broader regional strategy. His commandos effected a bloodless take-over of the neighbouring Andarab Valley, where a Hizbi-allied tribal militia had been blocking his supply lines from Pakistan. He also sent emissaries to other Jamiat commanders in the north to propose a plan of cooperation. When the Soviets launched their seventh attack on the Panjshir Valley in April 1984, Massoud had already evacuated the valley and established his forces in the Warsaj Valley of Takhan province, which remained his main base until 1988.

In January 1985 Massoud convened a shura of Jamiat commanders from five north-eastern provinces to coordinate their activities, reorganize and train their forces, and contribute volunteers to the formation of central fighting units under his direct control. Supervision of the implementation of the decisions made at the shura was entrusted to a permanent council of commanders presided over by Massoud himself. Commando units on the lines of those initially created by Massoud in Panjshir were subsequently formed in areas outside Panjshir and together constituted the Central Forces under his personal command and control. As before, they were composed of literate volunteers who trained and fought together without regard to qawm, local origins or party, and used Persian as their language of command. As Massoud's reputation as the 'Lion of Panjshir' spread nationally (and internationally, thanks to BBC coverage and interviews conducted by French journalists[4]), young Afghan volunteers, particularly from non-Pashtun areas, flocked to his standard.

As in the Panjshir, Massoud also built up a political and administrative infrastructure under the SCN umbrella to support his military goals. The SCN included sub-councils consisting of commanders, religious leaders and village elders. There were six functional committees in addition to the military committee that planned and conducted armed operations. They dealt with finance, health, education and culture, political affairs (including Kabuli affairs) and information. Each of the sub-committees employed hundreds of people. Massoud demonstrated an ability to recruit skilled and motivated cadres, particularly from among Panjshiris with educational and professional experience acquired as émigrés in Kabul. His sources of income were three-fold: a third consisted of booty from Soviet supply convoys and army garrisons and posts; a third from taxes on the lapis lazuli and emerald mines famous in the region since antiquity; and the remainder from a 5 per cent tax levied on government employees, private donations from businessmen, and what he could obtain from Jamiat headquarters in Peshawar. Massoud imposed no *zakat* (religious tax) nor *ushr* (land tax) on the impoverished peasant populations in the SCN's areas of control. On the contrary, he ran a welfare system to provide basic foodstuffs and necessities.

Pakistan's Afghan policy, as formulated by President Zia and his adviser, General Akhtar, whose ISI, as described in Chapter 9, played an exclusive role in its implementation, also had far-reaching effects on the fragmentation of Afghanistan after the Soviet withdrawal. Zia and the ISI shared a home-grown military tradition that placed politics below considerations of national security. The generals, in marked contrast to those in a democratic India, conceded no legitimate role to civilian politicians on security matters.

Zia's policy had a sub-text consistent with longer-term Pakistani interests. Because of the cultural affinities of the Sunni Muslim Pashtuns on either side of the border, and through the influence of Pashtuns in the upper echelons of the army and bureaucracy, the policy in practice tilted in favour of the Pashtun mujahideen parties. A friendly and amenable Pashtun-led post-communist regime in Kabul would pre-empt, it was hoped, the revival of the calls for a 'Greater Pashtunistan' that had so bedevilled Pakistan's relations with its neighbour since independence, assuming crisis proportions when the irredentist Daoud was in power. It was for the same reasons that early attempts by Afghan nationalists in exile to convene a loya jirga in Pakistan and form a unified command through which weapons could be channelled to fight the jihad were discouraged by Zia.[5] Instead, as we have seen, he chose to distribute the weapons and cash separately to the seven mutually hostile parties of the so-called Alliance in Peshawar. This mode of distribution had far-reaching political and social consequences.

The seven Peshawar-based parties had operated independently in the long years of the Afghan resistance, but had never been able to agree on a common political platform for the exercise of power in a post-communist Islamic republic. No single group or leader had managed to develop a national profile with a country-wide following. Each functioned as a sponsor of fighting militias within the specific regions or localities from which they drew their support, substantially on the basis of ethno-linguistic or tribal identification, although Rabbani's Jamiat attempted to transcend such limits. A complementary and important role was played by their respective capacities to dispense the funds and arms channelled from external sources to their field commanders and resistance fighters within Afghanistan.

The ISI's distribution system in turn had the effect of empowering mujahideen commanders inside Afghanistan with the potential to become local warlords once the Soviet troops had left, and Kabul's capacity to exert its direct authority over the whole country had weakened, had been diluted through deals with local militias, or had become non-existent in some regions. The retreat of the state to urban strongholds also had the general effect of strengthening local and regional leaderships, both personal and collective, since the qawm by tradition liked to be left alone to manage its own affairs and resented the intrusions of the central authority represented by Kabul.

It is instructive to review at this stage the extent of the assistance provided to the Afghan resistance over the years by the United States through Pakistan's ISI and the Peshawar-based parties. The Carter administration had initially pledged $30 million in 1980, followed up by another $50 million in 1981. The Reagan administration increased the amount to $80 million for the fiscal year 1984 (plus an additional $40 million from the Defence Department's budget for the purchase of the Swiss-made Oerlikon anti-aircraft cannon – a sophisticated and bulky weapon that proved useless in the guerrilla warfare waged in mountainous Afghanistan). The administration's request for a similar amount for the fiscal year 1985 was tripled by Congress to $250 million. In 1985 President Reagan signed National Security Directive 166, which authorized a harsh new policy of driving out the Soviets from Afghanistan 'by all means available'.[6] A further $470 million was pledged for 1986, including the delivery to the mujahideen of the shoulder-held, laser-guided, anti-aircraft Stinger missile, the first to be provided outside NATO arsenals in Europe. The US contribution was increased once again to $630 million in 1987. These contributions, in addition to those of Saudi Arabia and other Arab states, represented extraordinary infusions of cash and arms that empowered the feuding rival parties in Afghanistan to pursue their factional fighting.

Freed from the constraints of a Soviet presence, many of the local commanders were also able to achieve financial autonomy by levying tolls on road transport by traders, smugglers and government suppliers. The opium trade also became an increasingly lucrative source of revenue. Impoverished peasants turned more and more to poppy production in regions where the cultivation of food crops, especially where irrigation systems had been damaged or destroyed, hardly provided them with the means of subsistence.

The major poppy-growing region was the Helmand Valley, the fiefdom of Mullah Nasim Akhunzada, a resistance leader allied to the Harakat party who had been appointed deputy minister of defence in the AIG. Poppies for opium production had been grown traditionally in the mountainous areas of North Helmand, but under Mullah Nasim's entrepreneurship it spread to South Helmand as well. Mullah Nasim paid cash for the crop at the time of sowing, at low prices relative to the yield at harvest, and also set production quotas of 50 per cent of the land to be sown with poppy, inflicting harsh penalties on farmers who did not meet their quotas. The raw opium was sold to refineries mainly controlled by Hekmatyar's Hizbi-i-Islami which then hired smugglers to transport the finished product to Pakistan, or to Zahedan in Iran where Mullah Nasim maintained an office to handle his portion of the trade.

When the ISI came under US pressure in 1989 to cease arms shipments to drug traffickers, Mullah Nasim turned up at the US embassy in Islamabad to discuss a settlement. Ambassador Robert Oakley offered him $2 million in return for a ban on poppy cultivation. Early in 1990 Mullah Nasim ordered drastic cutbacks in poppy cultivation in areas under his control. In March that year he and five of his lieutenants were gunned down, mafia-style, in Peshawar – murders that were attributed to Pakistani drug cartels acting in collusion with Hekmatyar's Hizbi-i-Islami, which had counted on high levels of opium production in Helmand to supply what was becoming a highly profitable business. The drug trade, with its high margins of profit for middlemen, became not only a major source of income for erstwhile mujahideen commanders but also a new cause of conflict between them. The Peshawar murders led to a war between the Hizbi-i-Islami and other parties in Helmand. Eventually Mullah Nasim's brother, Ghulam Rasul, regained control of the province and ordered the resumption of poppy cultivation when Ambassador Oakley reneged on the agreement with his brother. The ambassador had been informed by the State Department that his deal with Mullah Nasim violated US policy against negotiating with drug traffickers.

Other important centres of poppy cultivation, and the related trade and traffic, grew up around Kandahar and Jalalabad, where mujahideen commanders were able to turn themselves into powerful local warlords. They came to depend less on the hand-outs from the ISI through their respective parties than on their increasingly lucrative business activities which included the smuggling and sale of cheap Russian goods in the bazaars of Pakistan. The Jalalabad commanders' shura was even able to import by air duty-free goods from Dubai which were then smuggled into Pakistan and sold in bazaars close to Peshawar. These were located in Tribal Agencies that lay outside the reach of Pakistani laws.

In 1989 and thereafter, following the Soviet withdrawal, Afghan policy under the Bush administration began to vacillate. On the one hand, there was the commitment made at the time of the Geneva Accords to match Soviet military aid to the Najibullah regime by continuing US support to the mujahideen ('positive symmetry'). The US pledged $600 million in 1989, matched by another $600 million from Saudi Arabia, with the US increasing its contribution by another $100 million later that year. The increase in the US contribution was to meet the additional cost involved in providing more Stinger missiles as well as heavy artillery and other weapons that would enable the mujahideen to shift from guerrilla to conventional warfare. As mentioned in the last chapter, it was believed at the time that it would require only one final concerted effort before the Kabul regime fell to the resistance. A further $280 million was pledged by the United States for 1990, supplemented by contributions of $435 million from Saudi Arabia and $100 million of private funds from Saudi, Kuwaiti and UAE sources.

On the other hand, other factors began to erode the consensus that had existed between the administration and Congress during the Soviet occupation, and thus intrude on the formulation of clearer US policies. The mujahideen were far from winning; the siege of Jalalabad in March–June 1989 had turned into a fiasco; indeed, it represented a victory for Najibullah.

The beginnings of an active Iranian role in Afghan affairs after the end of the Iraqi war in 1989 was a new source of worry for US policy makers. As we have seen, Iran had applied pressure on the feuding Shi'ite Hazara parties to form the Wahdat alliance to which it was now providing assistance. At the same time, Tehran encouraged the Wahdat to seek a rapprochement with Kabul, and signalled to Moscow and the United Nations its support of a political settlement. The combined US and Saudi contributions in support of the mujahideen in 1989, which reached an unprecedented annual figure of $1.3 billion, was prompted in part by their common anti-Iranian stance. Iran on her part made no attempt to disguise her dislike of the dominant Sunni Pashtun composition of the Afghan Interim Government (AIG) and its fanatically anti-Shi'ite elements, such as Hekmatyar and Sayyaf, backed by the Saudis, and began to initiate contacts with both her fellow Persian-speakers in the Jamiat and the moderate Afghan parties. The United States thus found itself on the side of the Islamic fundamentalists actively promoted by its Pakistani ally and confronted by a pragmatic and conciliatory Iran.

Another factor was the evolution of the situation in Eastern Europe and the evaporation of the Soviet threat as a result of Gorbachev's policies of *glasnost* and *perestroika*. Their full implications had not begun to sink in, and their results were impossible to predict. When the Berlin Wall was dismantled in November 1989, no one could have foreseen the coming dissolution of the Soviet empire, indeed of the Soviet Union itself.

In Afghanistan, the United States had allowed the ISI to distribute arms and funds to the mujahideen parties with little or no supervision, but now challenged the large share that went to Hekmatyar and Sayyaf and the exclusive use of the Peshawar-based parties as conduits for assistance. Supporters of the mujahideen in Congress charged the CIA with incompetence and of complete acquiescence in ISI policies. The head of the CIA's Afghan Task Force was dismissed in September 1989. Officially the United States now favoured self-determination for Afghanistan as before but began a diplomatic dialogue with the USSR for a UN-sponsored political settlement. The policy included the exclusion of anti-American extremists like Hekmatyar who opposed such a settlement, and the strengthening of the capacity of local military shuras inside Afghanistan. In practice the new approach made little difference on the ground: Saudi and other Arab funds took up the slack in aid to the extremists; the maintenance of the US arms pipeline through the ISI strengthened the very Afghan groups that the policy aimed at weakening.

When the US-Soviet dialogue began in the fall of 1989, a Pakistani military mission went to Washington with an action plan for a new mujahideen political and military offensive. The political component was the convening by the AIG of a shura, with representation from around the country, and elections to provide its supervisory council with greater legitimacy. The heart of the military strategy was the creation of a conventional mujahideen army that would consist of eight battalions based in Pakistan.

In practice the majority of the battalions called the Lashkar-i-Isar (the Army of Sacrifice) came under the control of Hekmatyar who recruited his officers and men from the refugee camps and from the madrasas in Pakistan – the future recruiting grounds of the Taliban. The first attempt to use this force came in March 1990. In Kabul Najibullah's Khalqi minister of defence, General Shahnawaz Tanai, launched a coup by bombing the presidential palace and opening the security cordon south of Kabul to let Hekmatyar's battalions into the city. According to Rubin,[7] the ISI and the Saudis pressured the other mujahideen parties to support the coup, reportedly paying their commanders as much as $15,000 each. With US backing, the other leaders resisted. The coup failed, and Tanai fled to Pakistan, where Hekmatyar appointed him commander of his Army of Sacrifice.

On 6 August 1990, four days after Saddam Hussein's invasion of Kuwait, Pakistani President Ghulam Ishaq Khan dismissed the elected government of Prime Minister Benazir Bhutto at the behest of the military. The military had now a free hand. The ISI tried to coordinate a massive assault on Kabul by Hekmatyar to whom they reportedly transferred 40,000 rockets and 700 truckloads of ammunition. The plan was stopped by the forceful intervention of the US State Department which favoured the initiative of some mujahideen commanders inside Afghanistan who wished to pursue a political and military strategy independent of the ISI and Hekmatyar. Soon after the failure of the Tanai coup, these commanders formed a National Commanders' Shura (NCS) which convened a meeting in October 1990 in Kunar. The meeting was boycotted by Hekmatyar and Sayyaf, but included a broader representation of regions and ethnic groups than any previous gatherings of mujahideen commanders. Instead of making direct attacks on Kabul, the NCS planned to capture provincial outposts of the Najibullah regime and set up regional administrations (base areas) in nine zones, according to the model pioneered by Massoud in the north-east.

International Islamist opposition to the US-led coalition operating from Saudi Arabia against Iraq was reflected in a polarization of the forces involved in the Afghan war: the new civilian government of Nawaz Sharif in Pakistan

and the nationalist and moderate mujahideen parties supported the US–
Saudi operation; Hekmatyar and other radical elements and their supporters
in the ISI and the Pakistan military took a pro-Saddam stance. Saudi funding
of Hekmatyar ceased (temporarily), while most US funding, now confined to
the support of AIG ministries, ceased altogether.

Another development that affected the Afghan situation was the ascen-
dance of communist hardliners in the USSR that led to the resignation of
Soviet Foreign Minister Eduard Shevardnadze, who had been conducting a
dialogue with US Secretary of State James Baker on an Afghan settlement.
Soviet armed intervention in Lithuania, to prevent by force the movements
towards independence by the Baltic states, encouraged the CIA and ISI to
insist that further military action was required in Afghanistan. Immediately
after the end of the Gulf War, they threw their resources into a mujahideen
campaign to capture the Afghan army garrison town of Khost in Paktia
province. This move was consistent with the NCS strategy, and the garrison
finally fell to the tribal forces led by a prominent figure in the NCS, commander Jalaluddin Haqqani. The coalition put together by the ISI before the
assault, including arrangements for the sharing of booty, fell apart when
Hekmatyar's Hizbi-i-Islami, which had played only a minor role in the fighting, seized the radio station and most of the garrison's heavy weapons, in
violation of the pre-campaign agreements. Instead of establishing an administration in Khost, the mujahideen pillaged it. The military option lost
credibility, and both Pakistan and the Saudis agreed that it was time for a
political settlement.

But developments in the USSR in the summer of 1991 were to bring
about the extinction of the Najibullah regime. Gorbachev was negotiating a
new Union Treaty that would have devolved powers to the remaining constituent republics of the Soviet Union. The three Baltic republics had
declared their independence earlier that year, and Georgia stood aloof. On
the eve of the signature came the communist hardliner coup in Moscow that
attempted to scuttle the treaty and preserve Russian hegemony. After the
failure of the coup, thwarted by Boris Yeltsin who was able to successfully
rally the pro-reformist and democratic forces (in a dramatic stand in front of
the White House, the Russian Parliament building), Gorbachev banned the
Communist Party of the Soviet Union (CPSU) and had the decision endorsed by the Supreme Soviet. But Gorbachev failed to obtain the support of
the republics for the new Union Treaty. The deadlock prompted the leaders
of the three Slav republics of Russia, the Belarus and Ukraine to formally
dissolve the Soviet Union and set up the Commonwealth of Independent
States (CIS) at a meeting held in Minsk on 8 December 1991. It is noteworthy that none of the Central Asian Republics had been invited to the Minsk

meeting, nor had they been consulted. The Muslim republics of Central Asia had literally been dumped by their erstwhile Slav masters.[8]

In Afghanistan Najibullah was likewise orphaned, as he could not survive without Russian aid. Commander Massoud of the Jamiat was best positioned to seize Kabul because of his better organized and disciplined forces, and the defection of Najibullah's ally, the Uzbek General Dostum, a development that was the immediate cause of Najibullah's precipitate abandonment of power. But their control of the city was not complete, as they were not able to prevent their main rivals, Hekmatyar's Hizbi-i-Islam and the Hazara Shi'ite Wahdat, from occupying the southern and western districts of the capital.

Massoud was acutely aware, however, that no single group, still less a largely non-Pashtun group like his own Jamiat, could govern the fragmented country on its own. There was therefore an urgent need for a power-sharing arrangement among the Peshawar-based leaders, whereby they, acting not only on behalf of their respective parties but also on behalf of the various ethno-linguistic groups, could construct a power structure: its durability and effectiveness would depend on the goodwill of the participants to respect each other's sides of the bargain and on their respective capacities to control their armed forces inside Afghanistan. Massoud called on the Peshawar-based parties to conclude such a deal.

The Peshawar Agreement of 24 April 1992, brokered by the Pakistani Prime Minister Nawaz Sharif, was the result. It provided the framework for an interim government to be implemented in stages: the dispatch to Kabul of Mujaddedi, the leader of a small Pashtun party, as a compromise choice to head a two-month transitional government, to be followed by a four-month interim government to be headed by Rabbani, the leader of the Jamiat, as a prelude to the formation of a council that would act as an interim government for 18 months before the holding of nationwide elections.

CHAPTER 12

Afghan Buzkashi[1]: The Players
and the Stakes (1989–98)

The Peshawar Agreement soon became inoperative because of the intransigence of Hekmatyar who refused to sign it. He argued that the position of prime minister reserved for his party should not be subordinated to that of the president, and that the position of defence minister (to which Massoud had been appointed by Mujaddedi) should fall under the control of the prime minister. He also objected to the inclusion in the coalition of General Dostum, the leader of the Uzbek militias of the north, previously associated with the communists. He conveniently overlooked in this regard his own opportunistic alliance with Najibullah's former Khalqi communist ministers, Shahnawaz Tanai and Aslam Watanjar.

In August 1992 Hekmatyar launched a barrage of rockets against Kabul from his bases south and east of the city that killed over a thousand civilians. Even after he was named prime minister in another agreement signed in Islamabad in March 1993, he did not take up his post but remained outside Kabul. In January 1994, in alliance with Dostum who had defected from the Kabul coalition, and Mujaddedi, who had been frustrated in his efforts to have his two-month interim presidency extended to two years – a shura convened in late 1992 had endorsed the continuation of the Rabbani presidency for another 18 months – Hekmatyar unleashed the most ferocious artillery and rocket attacks that Kabul had ever experienced. These attacks destroyed half the city, took some 25,000 civilian lives, and caused tens of thousands of Kabulis to seek safety in Pakistan or in the north.

Hekmatyar's objectives, according to Amin Saikal,[2] were to ensure that the Rabbani government did not consolidate its power by building a credible administration and expanding its territorial control, and that it did not acquire the capacity, with lavish international support, for the reconstruction of the country,[3] and to dispense patronage, and thus attract the loyalty of the population. Hekmatyar succeeded only too well. In the process, he exacerbated the anarchic conditions that paved the way for the success of the Taliban, discrediting also the Islamist parties, most of all his own. By his failure to take Kabul, he also lost his own credibility in the eyes of his Pakistani sponsors as a vehicle for their regional ambitions of achieving 'strategic depth' by installing an amenable client government in Kabul. Hekmatyar was disliked and even hated by other mujahideen, who alleged that his forces had killed more mujahideen during the jihad than communists.

The Taliban, mysterious new actors, burst on to the chaotic Afghan political scene in November 1994, by 'rescuing' a 30-truck Pakistani commercial convoy on its way from Quetta to Turkmenistan. The phenomenal rise to power of a movement of purely religious inspiration that was able to transform itself into a motivated and effective military force and impose its will on a country that had been torn apart by 20 years of civil war, armed foreign intervention and anarchy, became the subject of much speculation in the media of the time and in specialist journals, and also of some myths fostered by Taliban spokesmen and their foreign supporters.

The heavy Pakistani involvement in arming, training and even providing logistical support in Taliban field operations was no secret to informed observers as early as 1995. The generous Saudi funding was also well known. The United States, while not directly implicated, was not an uninterested party. An eventual take-over of Afghanistan by the Taliban, with their Pakistani allies playing the role of midwife, would have served both the US political strategy of 'containing' an Iran perceived as irremediably hostile and as a launching pad for anti-American terrorist activities, as well as its economic interests in fostering, inter alia, an alternative land route through Afghanistan and Pakistan for the exploitation by US-led companies of the seemingly inexhaustible oil and gas reserves of Central Asia.

Taliban is the Persian (and Pashtu) plural of the Arabic *talib* or religious student, of humble social status and receiving a religious training based on the Koran and the hadith, learned by rote in the predominantly rural-based and privately run madrasas in Afghanistan and in the Muslim regions of the sub-continent. The zealous and disciplined talib, a seeker of religious knowledge, was part of the Muslim landscape of west Asia for centuries after the Arab conquest. But the young men of the Afghan Taliban movement were, as Ahmed Rashid states, literally 'children of the jihad' who had known nothing but war: most of them were born in Pakistani refugee camps, some were war orphans. They received their basic education in the network of madrasas run for their benefit in Pakistan's North West Frontier Province and in Baluchistan. If they spoke a second language, it was Urdu and not Persian, the lingua franca of their homeland. They were therefore basically rootless and receptive to the ideological influences to which they were exposed in the madrasas of Pakistan.[4]

The chief influence on the ideological make-up of the Taliban was the Jamiat-i-Ulema-i-Islami (JUI) which ran the network of madrasas, including two major ones in Baluchistan and in Karachi that some of the Taliban leaders had attended. The JUI was ideologically linked to the Muslim theological school in Deoband in central India, which had also trained genera-tions of the Afghan ulema. It was characterized by its fundamentalist interpretations of Islam, its opposition to *ijtihad* (innovation in adapting to new conditions), its injunctions against any meaningful role for women outside their homes, and its opposition to feudal and tribal structures.

The JUI as a political party had won a few seats in elections to the Na-tional and Baluchistan Assemblies but had remained in opposition to governments. In 1993 the situation changed when it supported the victorious Pakistan People's Party (PPP) of Benazir Bhutto. Its leader, Maulana Fazlur Rehman, was made chairman of the National Assembly's Committee for Foreign Affairs, a position that enabled him to influence Pakistan's Afghan policy. He established close links with the army, the ISI and with Bhutto's Pashtun minister of the interior, the retired General Naseerullah Babar. Babar had been the adviser to Benazir's father on Afghan affairs during the Daoud presidency, and now became the *éminence grise* of Pakistan's Afghan policy, relegating the Foreign Ministry and the ISI to a back-seat role. Fazlur Rehman in his turn was to become the most vocal advocate of the Taliban in Pakistan after their appearance on the Afghan scene, lobbying Washington and European capitals on their behalf, and successfully mobilizing financial and other assistance from Saudi Arabia and the Gulf states.

The end of the Cold War had opened up new perspectives for Pakistan's regional ambitions. With the independence of the Central Asian states, Afghanistan's northern frontier was no longer a barrier to legitimate trade with the south. Islamabad had become enamoured since 1991 of the idea of winning a privileged place for Pakistan in Central Asian markets. But a fresh outbreak of fighting between Hekmatyar and the Kabul coalition forces in January 1994 made the traditional northern route from Peshawar via Kabul and the Salang Tunnel impracticable. Also the increasing hostility of the Kabul government, provoked by Pakistan's continuing support for Hekmat-yar, forced Islamabad to consider the feasibility of a southern route from Baluchistan to Turkmenistan via Kandahar and Herat. The stakes for Paki-stani ambitions were raised even higher with the beginnings of intense international competition for the exploitation of the oil and gas reserves of Central Asia and the Caspian Basin.

The opening of the southern route became Minister Babar's obsession. In September 1994 he visited Chaman, the last Pakistani way-station before Kandahar, surveyed the highway inside Afghanistan, and announced the experimental use of the road by Pakistani traders – the convoy that was to propel the Taliban on to the Afghan scene. That same month, he took a party of six Islamabad-based ambassadors from potential donor countries to Kandahar and Herat, in the hope of raising $300 million to rebuild the highway between Kandahar and Herat, and additional funds for a railway track and a satellite communication system. The party was accompanied by senior Pakistani officials from technical ministries and corporations. So brazen had Pakistan's interventions become that this trip was undertaken without the prior authorization of the Kabul government that held Afghanistan's seat at the United Nations. After the Taliban capture of Kandahar, which surprised the Pakistanis as well as the Taliban (as they themselves admitted), and their mounting successes thereafter, Babar set up an Afghan Trade Development Cell within his Ministry to coordinate with other ministries and corporations on the road project. The Cell became a source of considerable logistics and infrastructure support for the Taliban: a microwave telephone network for Kandahar linked to the Pakistani grid, an internal wireless network for Taliban field operations, repairs to the airport in Kandahar and to captured aircraft by PIA technicians, and so on. Ministries were encouraged to finance such projects from their own budgets, thus 'civilianizing' Pakistani assistance to the Taliban.

The small group led by a modest and poor village mullah, Mohammad Omar, had the limited objectives of putting an end to the activities of the petty ex-mujahideen warlords who were preying on the local population, and of establishing order and security by disarming their militias. The group's first breakthrough was the seizure in October 1994 of the major trucking stopover at Spin Boldak and the huge Pasha arms depot near the Pakistan border. These were controlled by Hekmatyar's forces. Some 200 Taliban took part in these operations. The famous 30-truck Pakistani convoy was accompanied by ISI officers with the Taliban riding shotgun. It was halted before it could reach Kandahar by warlord militias demanding what amounted to political ransom. On 3 November Taliban reinforcements from Pakistan freed the convoy and swept on into Kandahar, capturing the city after two days of fighting.

The Taliban Offensive (1994–96)

Within three weeks, the Taliban forces had grown to some 2500 fighters, many of them armed with brand-new weapons that could only have come from ISI warehouses in Pakistan. In Kandahar they acquired for the first time the hardware (planes, helicopters, tanks and armoured vehicles) needed for more conventional warfare. Kandahar-based units then moved to Uruzgan, north of the Helmand River, and to Zabul, to the east of Kandahar, which they took without a shot being fired. Where the Taliban's moral and religious credentials failed to win over the local warlords, generous disbursements of cash helped to win the day. In Helmand the Taliban took sides in a vicious feud between local warlords and became involved for the first time in a major military engagement, with hundreds of casualties on both sides.

Meanwhile in Ghazni, Hekmatyar precipitated hostilities by attacking the Kabul-appointed governor, Qari Baba, who called on the Taliban for assistance. Hekmatyar's forces were driven out and the governor was persuaded to give up his weapons. Ghazni was a watershed.[5] It is interesting to note that the Rabbani government was not at first hostile to the Taliban who had earlier sent a delegation to Kabul requesting assistance against the Kandahari warlords. In fact the leader of the most important of the Kandahari militias, who was their corps commander, had received instructions from Kabul not to oppose the Taliban and to surrender his weaponry.

In Ghazni it appeared that the Taliban had intervened on behalf of a government appointee. Reports to this effect were immediately denied by a Taliban spokesman: 'We are neutral in the power struggle between Rabbani and Hekmatyar.' After Ghazni the movement's initial objectives were expanded into a crusade to disarm what they called the mujahideen 'criminals' across the country. The Taliban advanced victoriously against Hekmatyar's bases ranged in a wide arc south of Kabul. With his position in Charasyab between government and Taliban forces proving untenable, Hekmatyar beat an ignominious retreat to Sarobi in February 1995.

During this advance, the Taliban came into possession of vast quantities of heavy artillery, tanks and ammunition. Their ranks had also mushroomed into an army of some 12,000 fighters, not only from madrasas in Pakistan and the Pashtun 'Koran Belt', but through defections from the more radical Islamist parties, including Hekmatyar's. An important aspect of the Taliban's military operations was that, in several respects, they displayed features that were hitherto unknown on the battlefields of Afghanistan, where the jihad-era warfare consisted of hit-and-run raids, organizationally fragmented and seldom, if ever, fought to a conclusion. Instead the Taliban displayed great mobility and flexibility, a readiness to undertake night operations and persistence in attacking an enemy position until it was overrun, the whole supported by an efficient communications and command-and-control network. Noticeable also was the impressive accuracy of Taliban mortar and artillery fire.

The professional know-how could not have been acquired in JUI madrasas nor in a few weeks of ISI training, but attest to the truth of contemporary reports that the technical functions required for mobile warfare in artillery and armour were directed by Pashtun ex-army officers of the communist PDPA. The former defence minister under Najibullah, General Shahnawaz Tanai, who had fled to Pakistan in March 1990 after his abortive coup, may have reactivated his Khalqi networks in support of the Taliban. These trained officers and technicians, now receiving regular salaries from the Taliban, supplied the expertise, the madrasa students provided the discipline and motivation and the infrastructure came from Pakistan.

According to the Pakistani journalist, Ejaz Haider, who interviewed Babar in April 1998, the advent of the Bhutto government in October 1993 had made Hekmatyar expendable. One reason was domestic: his close links with Pakistan's Jamiat, now in opposition and a fierce rival of the JUI and its chief, Fazlur Rehman, now allied with the government. Hekmatyar had also become a diplomatic embarrassment to Pakistan because of the enormous sufferings he was inflicting on the Kabul population in his heavy-handed efforts to dislodge the Rabbani–Massoud duo. Another consideration may have been Tehran's annoyance at Islamabad's 'interference' in Afghanistan, aimed at sabotaging Iran's genuine interest in its neighbour, including the welfare of its Shi'ite population. This was clearly expressed during Bhutto's visit to Iran in November 1993. The Iranian President Rafsanjani warned her that if Islamabad were to pursue its policy of installing a client government in Kabul, Tehran might be forced to exercise a military option to resolve the issue. The warning was taken seriously, and discussed by Benazir Bhutto at a closed meeting with a few select members of her cabinet. Babar requested that he be put in charge of Afghan policy: 'I'll see to it that Iran is neutralized in Afghanistan.'[6]

Babar's southern route project required the cooperation of the Herati administration of governor Ismail Khan. The circumstances appeared to be propitious to detach him from his Jamiat allies in Kabul. Tensions with the Kabul government had developed as a result of the governor's independent stance on the running of his administration of a region that was becoming prosperous, and where order and stability prevailed. Ismail Khan's having declared himself 'amir' of western Afghanistan was not to Kabul's taste. The object of Babar's visit to Herat with the six ambassadors in September 1994 was to secure Ismail Khan's assistance in return for the economic and political gains he could obtain through the opening of the southern route. Ismail Khan indicated his willingness to cooperate provided that the security of the road to Herat, controlled by the warlords and bandits of southern Afghanistan, could be assured. This was followed up by Bhutto's visit on 28 October to Ashkabad, Turkmenistan, where she met with Ismail Khan and Dostum.

The advent of the Taliban, their seizure of Kandahar and subsequent conquest of Helmand, opened golden new windows of opportunity for Pakistan, not only with respect to the security of the southern route. By getting on board Ismail Khan in the west, and eventually Dostum, the Uzbek warlord of the north, Pakistan hoped to work them into a strategic alliance with the Taliban that would not only isolate and weaken the Kabul regime, but also facilitate the recognition of the Pashtun Taliban heading a broad-based government: a friendly Kabul regime would, in the longer term, serve Pakistan's broader strategic interests. In the case of Dostum, Islamabad tried to woo him by various means, including assistance in operating the Shibergan gas fields and telephone connections to Mazar-i-Sharif.

It transpired, however, that the Taliban had developed their own agenda and refused to dance to the Pakistani tune. The first major expression of Taliban independence was their decision to take Herat in March 1995, pointedly ignoring Pakistani advice to the contrary. After the unfortunate choice of Hekmatyar as Pakistan's instrument, which was the first mistake in her Afghan policy, switching her support to the Taliban as a means of realizing her regional ambitions was Pakistan's second biggest failure, an even more costly one in international terms, as it led to her isolation in the region as a whole.

After Hekmatyar's hasty abandonment of Charasyab before Taliban forces in February 1995, the base was swiftly occupied by government troops. But at the demand of the Taliban, the base was handed over to them. Government mechanics even assisted in repairs to an MI-17 helicopter that had fallen into Taliban hands, according to eyewitness reports by Western journalists. Massoud had other fish to fry, and had no intention of confronting madrasa students whose fighting capacities and intentions he may have misjudged at the time. Massoud had twice met leading Taliban commanders, once in Maidanshahr and once in Kabul. His concern was to play for enough time to deal with his remaining enemies inside Kabul: the Shi'ite Wahdat led by Shaykh Abdolali Mazari, who were allied with Dostum, the remnants of whose Kabul contingent were dug into the south-west of the city.

On 6 March 1995 Massoud opened a full-scale offensive against the Wahdat. After two days of fighting involving heavy casualties, Mazari turned in desperation to the Taliban: he agreed to surrender his heavy weapons to the Taliban who would take positions along the front line in western Kabul as a buffer force. When the Taliban began moving into the Shi'ite quarter, government forces opened fire. The Taliban suffered a further reversal when Mazari's troops refused to surrender their weapons and joined the pro-government forces of the Wahdat's pro-Iranian splinter faction led by Shaykh Ali Akbari. The defection of his forces to Akbari was not part of Mazari's calculation, but the Taliban regarded it as a betrayal. Mazari paid for his miscalculations with his life. Taken bound to Charasyab, he was killed – after an attempt to seize a guard's weapon on a helicopter flight to Kandahar, according to the Taliban version.

Massoud continued his offensive in Kabul and its outskirts, with his troops allegedly looting and pillaging the Shi'ite quarters,[7] and striking at Taliban bases taken from Hekmatyar to the south and south-west of the city. By 19 March Massoud had taken Charasyab, and for the first time had won complete control of the capital, with the Taliban pushed beyond rocket range. Karim Khalili, Mazari's successor as leader of the Wahdat, withdrew with his troops to the Hazarajat, where he had to reconquer the towns of Bamyan and Yakaolang from governments troops allied with Akbari. The large influx of armed urban Hazara refugees from Kabul brought new tensions into the area.

In the west, the Taliban offensive aimed at capturing Herat against Pakistani advice was initially successful. By mid-March they had swept up much of Nimroz and Farah, part of Ismail Khan's western fiefdom, and were poised to attack the Shindand air base, 75 miles south of Herat. Meanwhile Dostum's forces arrayed in the north-west in Badghis province moved to the attack. Massoud came to Ismail Khan's assistance in this precarious situation by airlifting 2000 of his central forces to Herat. They succeeded in holding a line within sight of Shindand. Unchallenged government air power played a decisive role in forcing the Taliban to abandon their ill-planned offensive by the end of April. They had taken heavy casualties under relentless air strikes, and were hindered by poor logistics and ammunition shortages. The summer of 1995 brought a lull in the Taliban's military operations. But rather than being a prelude to collapse after their set-backs outside Kabul and Shindand, the lull provided a breathing space for the Taliban to consolidate and improve their capacity to wage war with Pakistani help.

During this period the ISI stepped up training for the Taliban, placing a greater emphasis on mobility, while the serious deficiencies in their logistics, shown up in the western campaign, were made up by the acquisition of large numbers of pick-up trucks donated by the Saudis. Pakistan also brokered arrangements with Dostum whereby his technicians, arriving in Kandahar from Mazar-i-Sharif via Peshawar and Quetta, set about restoring captured aircraft to air-worthiness. On 3 August a Taliban-controlled MiG-21 fighter forced down a chartered Russian aircraft carrying ammunition from Albania to Kabul, and captured its Russian crew; likewise in September an Ariana Afghan aircraft carrying duty-free goods from Dubai for the smuggling operations of the Jalalabad shura led by Abdul Qadir was also forced down. Recruitment was also stepped up, with volunteers arriving from the madrasas of Baluchistan and the NWFP, as well as from mujahideen groups from the eastern border provinces. Khost, the only sizeable town that had been captured from Najibullah by the mujahideen, contributed a contingent of 2000 seasoned fighters supplied by the veteran mujahideen commander, Jalaluddin Haqqani, who had rallied to the Taliban cause. By the end of 1995 Taliban forces had reached a total of some 25,000 men.

In August 1995 the government ordered an offensive in the west in order to relieve the pressure around Kabul. Ismail Khan's troops, backed by exiled Helmandi and Kandahari militia and by Massoud's central forces, pushed south along the highway and scored a series of successes against unprepared Taliban positions that threatened their stronghold of Kandahar itself. What went wrong after this can be attributed to several factors. Ismail Khan had shored up his forces with reluctant Herati recruits dragooned into his regular units without an adequate logistics infrastructure to support them. His forces had become severely overstretched logistically. As Davis states: 'Raw hunger and indifferent motivation made for a disastrous combination.'

As government columns advanced along the main road and along two flanks, the road force blundered into a well-prepared Taliban ambush in which scores were killed. Ismail Khan, from his position in the vanguard, ordered a general retreat, but his retreating forces were thrown into disarray when Taliban units mounted on pick-ups began cutting the road behind them. Also Ismail Khan's prior failure to establish defensive positions around Shindand was disastrous. Troop morale was low, and the logistics required to keep his troops fed had collapsed. According to Davis:

> The Taliban exploited these weaknesses with an adroitness and a speed that was impressive – maintaining the momentum of the offensive in company-sized units of one or two hundred men, moving fast off the main and anticipated axes of advance in pick-ups with truck-mounted ZU-2 anti-aircraft cannon and BM-21 multiple-barrelled rocket launchers. These Blitzkrieg tactics proved strikingly successful and again, it bears emphasizing, marked a sudden shift to mobile warfare that caught the government completely off balance.[8]

The rout was complete, and the end came quickly. On 3 September Ismail Khan made the inexplicable decision to abandon Shindand without a fight, much to the consternation of his commanders. It was too late for Massoud to bail him out once again, and on 5 September Ismail Khan and his commanders abandoned the city of Herat and fled to the Iranian border.

The loss of Herat was an immense blow to the morale of the Rabbani government. It accused Pakistani military personnel of participating in the Taliban offensive. The embassy in Kabul was sacked the next day by angry protesters. But while there was no evidence of direct Pakistani participation in the actual operations, there is no doubt that Pakistan through its ISI had played a key role in reinforcing the Taliban's capacity to wage war.

In the autumn of 1995, with Herat and the west in their hands, the Taliban moved swiftly to exploit their advantage by moving against Kabul before the onset of the winter. With the exception of Charasyab, which they recaptured, their temporary gains were negated by Massoud's counter-offensives launched from his well-entrenched defensive positions. By January 1996 the Taliban had to content themselves with daily rocket attacks on the city – the terror tactics against civilians, habitually employed by the unscrupulous Hekmatyar, that they had publicly eschewed earlier on high moral grounds.

It has been argued that had Massoud launched a major winter offensive against the Taliban, he might have avoided the impending debacle. His central forces, now numbering between 20,000 to 30,000 men, were in better shape than when they entered Kabul after the ousting of Najibullah. Re-supply from both Russia and Iran in 1995 had boosted their reserves of ammunition. At the core of his army were his battle-hardened Panjshiri veterans who had played a decisive role in the Herati campaign of March–April 1995. The Taliban, on the other hand, were exhausted by their failed autumn offensives and were sitting out a bitter winter in a wide arc around southern Kabul.

It may well be that the debacle also came about through political compli-cations that circumscribed the cautious Massoud's freedom of action. Hekmatyar had been abandoned by Pakistan. His eventual assumption in June 1996 of his reserved place as prime minister in the Kabul coalition, after the humiliating defeats suffered by his forces at the hands of the Taliban, caused great resentment in the Jamiat ranks that had been his main victims. Hekmatyar was also a liability for the Kabul coalition, in that his forces had been the first to retreat, surrender or defect in large numbers to the Taliban. His recruits were drawn from backgrounds similar to, if not identical with, those from which the Taliban drew theirs. They also shared a similar radical Islamic ideology. Submitting to Hekmatyar's pressure, Massoud was now forced into over-extending his forces by engaging the Taliban in the defence of Hekmatyar's bases in the east.

At the beginning of September 1996 the Taliban had defeated Hekmat-yar's forces in Paktia province and captured his main base at Spin Shigar near the Pakistan border. Under pressure from Hekmatyar, government rein-forcements sent from Kabul and Sarobi were unable to stem the Taliban advance. In Nangarhar the fractious provincial shura split into anti- and pro-Taliban groups. Its leader, Haji Qadir, who had belatedly thrown in his lot with the Kabul government, was forced to flee Jalalabad for Pakistan. With-out pausing for breath, Taliban flying columns then drove on into Laghman and Kunar provinces north of Nangarhar, their real target being Sarobi, which lay midway between Jalalabad and Kabul. Massoud had chosen the easily defensible town, a Hekmatyar stronghold, as the new linchpin of Kabul's defences on the eastern front. But the sheer speed of the Taliban advance caught his commanders by surprise.

Taliban columns pushed towards Sarobi, not only along the main highway as Massoud had expected but also in a pincer movement from the south and the north. On the night of 24 September the Taliban carried out a three-pronged attack on the town and routed the defenders. Again without paus-ing, Taliban columns advanced along the highway to Kabul, as well as northwards, threatening the airbase at Bagram and the highway from Kabul to the north. On 25 September Massoud attempted a last-ditch stand at Pul-i-Charki at the eastern edge of the Kabul plain. But airstrikes and helicopter gunships could not compensate for the confusion and despair on the ground where government troops faced multi-pronged attacks. On the afternoon of 26 September Massoud met his senior commanders and gave the order for a general withdrawal from the capital. In a brilliantly organized retreat, Massoud's forces were able to escape to the north, taking with them the bulk of their armour and artillery.

It is clear from the interviews carried out on the ground at the time by Anthony Davis that the victorious Taliban campaign that led to the capture of Kabul was the result of a carefully planned and integrated strategy. It was undertaken by up to 10,000 Taliban troops, and was preceded by some political groundwork that sought to win over to their side both pro-government and uncommitted militia. Generous disbursements of cash may also have played a role in softening up the potential opposition. Osama bin Laden reportedly contributed $3 million to the Taliban's war chest in the summer of 1996. It was also alleged that in Jalalabad, the powerful warlord, Haji Qadir, was induced to abandon the city with a bribe of $2 million and the promise of asylum in Pakistan. The massive explosion of an ammunition dump in Sarobi, prior to the Taliban advance, was apparently the work of their sympathizers. Government defences were thrown into confusion by the desertion or defection to the Taliban of Hekmatyar's Hizbi-i-Islami forces to their rear. Zardad, their commander in Sarobi who blocked the advance up the narrow mountain defile from Jalalabad, was allegedly paid off by the Taliban.

The period after the Taliban occupation of Kabul, which brought over 70 per cent of the country under its armed control, until its final occupation of Mazar-i-Sharif and most of the north in September 1998, was the most vicious and murderous in the game of Afghan *buzkashi*. In their efforts to extend their control over the whole country, the Taliban revealed their intransigence in refusing to transform their tactical alliances with non-Pashtun factions, in a scenario of 'changing equations', into credible power-sharing arrangements.[9] In opting for a purely military solution, the Taliban suffered serious reverses that deflated the aura of invincibility acquired during the virtual blitzkrieg preceding their seizure of Kabul. Their visceral sectarian prejudices, as shown up by their impositions on the urban populations and their treatment of Shi'ites in Kabul, in the Hazarajat, and during their aborted attempt to take Mazar-i-Sharif in May 1997, eroded their claims to legitimacy as a serious political force that could bring about order, stability and national reconciliation in a unified Afghanistan. Taliban policies also accentuated the process of polarization of the country, already nascent, along ethno-linguistic lines.

One of the Taliban's first acts after entering Kabul was to violate the United Nations diplomatic premises where Najibullah had found refuge since April 1992, to torture and execute him and two companions in a particularly gruesome manner, and expose their mutilated bodies in a Kabul square.

Changing equations: The final showdown (1996–98)

On 10 October 1996 Massoud, Dostum and Karim Khalili formed a Supreme Council for the Defence of the Motherland with Mazar-i-Sharif as their capital. By the end of the month, Massoud recaptured key positions along the Salang highway – Jabul Seraj, Bagram and Charikar – which brought the fighting within 20 kilometres of Kabul and caused hundreds of casualties. While some 50,000 people were forced to abandon their villages to seek the relative safety of Kabul, tens of thousands of Kabulis, mostly Tajiks and Hazara, fled to Pakistan or to Mazar to escape Taliban arrests and reprisals.

In heavy fighting with Dostum's forces, the Taliban captured Badghis province in the north. Ismail Khan and 2000 of his followers who had trained and been re-equipped during their Iranian exile were flown to Maimana in Dostum's aircraft to reinforce his defences in Faryab province. As heavy fighting took place in November and December 1996, over 50,000 displaced persons sought refuge in Herat, causing a humanitarian crisis. Meanwhile the Taliban recaptured the territory they had lost previously along the Salang highway, forcing Massoud to retreat to his stronghold in Panjshir.

In May 1997, exploiting a bitter feud that had developed between Dostum and his deputy, General Malik Pahlawan, whose brother had been killed with his bodyguard in an ambush the previous June (an assassination attributed to Dostum), the Taliban turned their attention to the capture of Mazar-i-Sharif. In this somewhat murky episode, Malik appears to have cut a deal, brokered by Pakistan, that in exchange for Uzbek autonomy in the north, he would switch his support to the Taliban. Malik's power-base lay in Faryab province west of Mazar, near the front-line with Taliban forces in Badghis. As a token of his new alliance, Malik handed over Ismail Khan and his followers to the Taliban. Active Pakistani involvement in this deal-making was made abundantly clear in the subsequent developments. On 23 May their consular staff in Mazar were evacuated on a UN flight to Islamabad in anticipation of battles in the city, and on 25 May the Pakistani foreign minister and other senior officials flew into Mazar. At a hastily organized press conference, Pakistan recognized the Taliban as constituting the government of Afghanistan, persuading Saudi Arabia and the United Arab Emirates to follow suit. Dostum found refuge in Uzbekistan and then went to Turkey.

As some 2500 Taliban fighters swarmed into Mazar from the north-west, a number of senior Taliban leaders flew into Mazar to claim victory. Another

Taliban expeditionary force, with reinforcements from Pakistani madrasas and led by senior figures, headed north from Kabul and were able to cross the Salang Tunnel because of the unexpected defection of a senior Massoud commander, Bashir Salangi.

It then appeared that the Taliban were not prepared for any power-sharing arrangements with Malik, to whom they offered the inconsequential post of deputy foreign minister. When the uncouth Taliban fighters arrogantly began disarming Uzbek and Hazara militias, took over the mosques, imposed their version of the shari'a, shut down schools and the only functioning university in the country, and drove the women off the streets of a city that had remained the most open and liberal in Afghanistan, they invited disaster.

Alone among the major urban centres, Mazar had been spared the disastrous physical and psychological effects of the civil war and had become a haven of peace and prosperity under Dostum, who had also provided security to the waves of non-Pashtun refugees from Kabul. He had run functioning health and education systems. Some 1800 girls emancipated in their dress and behaviour attended Balkh University The shops and bazaars were well stocked. Imported goods trucked from across the border with Central Asia, only 70 miles from Mazar, provided Dostum with a steady income in transit taxes and customs duties. His own Balkh Airlines brought in goods from duty-free Dubai. The northern provinces in general were a mainstay of Afghan agriculture and industry, with the cultivation and export of cotton from the Kunduz region being practised since the 1930s.

On 25 May 1997, when groups of Hazaras and Malik's Uzbek forces resisted being disarmed, the Hazaras and the rest of the population rose in revolt. The Taliban, untrained in street fighting and trapped in the maze of the city's narrow alleyways, could not escape the withering fire from houses and rooftops. Some 600 of them were massacred in the streets, and a thousand others, including their foreign minister and other senior leaders, were captured at the airport when they tried to flee. Malik's Uzbek militia looted the city and swiftly retook the four provinces that had been captured by the Taliban only five days earlier. Heavy fighting continued for the control of three other provinces. In what was certainly a pre-arranged manoeuvre, Bashir Salangi, the Massoud commander who had previously 'defected', closed off the Salang Tunnel, thereby trapping the Taliban forces in the north. With their escape routes blocked, thousands of Taliban, and hundreds of Pakistani madrasa students in their ranks, were captured or subsequently shot dead and buried in mass graves.[10]

Taking advantage of the Taliban disarray in the north, Massoud's forces surged out of the Panjshir Valley and headed south along the fertile Shomali Valley, recapturing Charikar and the Bagram air base. Spurred on by their victory in Mazar, the Hazaras led by Khalili also counter-attacked from their homeland in the Hazarajat, pushing back Taliban forces at the entrance to the Bamiyan Valley, moving south and forcing Pashtun settlers and nomads protected by the Taliban to flee to Kabul.

Following Dostum's departure from the scene, Massoud, Khalili and Malik formed a new alliance on 13 June 1997 called the United National and Islamic Front for the Salvation of the Homeland. Rabbani was re-elected president, with Massoud as defence minister. The alliance promised to form a new government that would include tribal and Islamic leaders as well as technocrats, and declared Mazar their capital. The alliance forces were now in a position to take Kabul, with Massoud's forces to the west and north of the city, and Khalili's Hazaras to the east and south.

After the Taliban reversals in the north and their acute losses in manpower, Mullah Omar called on his supporters in the Pakistani Jamiat-i-Islami for help. Pakistani madrasas were closed down and thousands of new recruits – Afghan and Pakistani – arrived to enlist with the Taliban. The reclusive Mullah Omar himself chose to leave his Kandahar sanctuary for the first time and visit Kabul to meet his commanders and raise morale.

In the meantime the remaining Taliban forces in the north broke out of their refuge in Kunduz and, with the help of Pashtun sympathizers in the area, launched another attack on Mazar. On 7 September they captured the town of Tashkurgan, creating panic in Mazar. As the Taliban advanced, heavy fighting broke out between Uzbek troops loyal to Malik and others to Dostum. Malik fled to his base in Faryab, and then escaped to Iran via Turkmenistan. Dostum returned from his exile in Turkey and rallied his men to defeat Malik's supporters and push the Taliban out of the Mazar region. With the Taliban retreating to Kunduz, Dostum tried to consolidate his position but was forced to abandon the city and return to his home-base in Shibergan in the face of Hazara hostility. Mazar was now virtually in the hands of Hazara forces.

The Taliban response was to close all the roads leading into the Hazarajat from the south, west and east, and enforce a food blockade to compel the Hazaras to surrender. It was the first time in 20 years of conflict that food was used as a weapon of war. Food convoys organized by the World Food Programme (WFP) and the ICRC into food-deficient areas like Kabul were always let through by besieging forces, but subjected sometimes to road tolls or payment of a portion of the food. In the winter of 1997 300,000 Hazaras in Bamyan and 700,000 others in the neighbouring provinces of Ghor, Wardak and Ghazni were starving. Permission to allow relief convoys through was refused by the Taliban after tortuous negotiations by the United Nations and the WFP. Nor could the UN count on Pakistani help: Pakistan had contracted to provide the Taliban with 600,000 tonnes of wheat but apparently made no demands on the Taliban to lift the blockade on humanitarian grounds. The Taliban's fanatically ferocious treatment of the Shi'ite Hazaras, whom they qualified as *munafiqun*, or 'Hypocrites' masquerading as Muslims, was shown up in this tragic episode as well as after their defeat of Hazara forces in Mazar in September 1998. But the Hazaras were not without friends: Iran was flying in military supplies to a newly constructed airstrip outside Bamyan, and their leader, Khalili, visited Tehran, Moscow, Ankara and New Delhi in quest of more military aid.

The Taliban were also annoyed by the prominent role women had come to play in Hazara affairs during the years of autonomy. Despite the frequent outbursts of fighting and other great odds, the Wahdat had organized basic literacy, health care and family programmes in which women played a prominent part. UN programmes were also staffed by women. Female professors who had fled Kabul had even set up a primitively housed university centre. The 80-member Wahdat Central Council included eight women, mostly educated professionals. Women had fought alongside their men in Mazar the previous May.

But the anti-Taliban alliance in the north was a shambles. The alliance was dealt an unexpected blow when the prime minister designate of a new national government, Abdul Rahim Ghaffurzai, an experienced Pashtun from the royal clan, was killed with 40 other leaders in a plane crash in August 1997. Unlike the Taliban, all anti-Taliban groups maintained their own separate political and military command structures. Factions among the Wahdat fought each other for territory, influence and foreign aid, and against the Uzbeks. The Russians tried to mediate between the Hazaras and Dostum, and the Iranians between the Wahdat factions. In February 1998, as heavy fighting erupted between the Hazaras and the Uzbeks, Massoud paid his first visit to Tehran to seek Iranian help in saving the Northern Alliance. Meanwhile the Taliban sat out the winter watching their enemies tear themselves apart, while tightening their siege around Bamyan and preparing an attack on Mazar. But fighting continued in Faryab province against the Uzbeks, where the Taliban carried out a massacre in cold blood of 600 Uzbek villagers, as confirmed later after investigations by Western aid workers in the area.

By mid-1998 foreign intervention had become quite overt in military support for the two opposing sides in anticipation of the coming showdown: Iran flew in plane-loads of weapons directly from its eastern city of Mashad to Bamyan to assist the beleaguered Hazaras; the Russians and Iranians provided weapons that were stockpiled at the Kulyab airbase in southern Tajikistan whence they were ferried to Afghanistan by Massoud; in response to Taliban requests, the head of Saudi intelligence, Prince Turki al-Faisal, visited Kandahar in mid-June, after which 400 pick-up trucks and financial aid were provided; Pakistan prepared a budget of 2 billion rupees ($5 million) for logistical support; ISI officers visited Kandahar frequently to prepare the attack on Mazar and thousands of new recruits were bussed into Afghanistan from refugee camps and madrasas in Pakistan.

In July 1998 the Taliban swept northwards from Herat, capturing Maimana in Dostum's base of Faryab province, and routing his forces, capturing 100 tanks and 800 Uzbek fighters, most of whom they massacred. On 1 August they captured Dostum's headquarters at Shibergan after several of his commanders received cash inducements to switch sides. Dostum fled to Uzbekistan and then to Turkey. Demoralized by their leader's desertion, Uzbek commanders guarding the western approaches to Mazar were likewise induced to yield, exposing the 1500-strong Hazara forces outside the city to a surprise attack. On 4 August the Hazaras found themselves surrounded, but fought until their ammunition ran out and only some 100 of them were left.

What followed was a massacre of Hazara civilians in Mazar that was genocidal in its frenzy and intensity. In revenge for their losses in the city the previous year, the Taliban drove their pick-ups through the narrow streets shooting at everything that moved: men, women, children, even goats and donkeys. According to a UNHCR report cited by Ahmed Rashid,[11] as people ran for shelter to their houses, armed Taliban barged in and massacred whole Hazara households. Women were raped. After a full day of indiscriminate killings the Taliban targeted the Hazaras, enlisting local Pashtuns who knew the city well in their search parties. Thousands of Hazaras were taken to the main jail, and when it was full they were dumped in locked containers and suffocated. Some containers were taken to the desert outside Mazar and their piteous human contents, if still alive, were massacred – following the horrific example set by Malik's Uzbek militia a year before in their treatment of Taliban prisoners. As tens of thousands of Hazara civilians tried to escape the city, they were subjected to aerial bombardments. A Taliban commander cited by Rashid said that their leader, Mullah Omar, had authorized his followers to kill for two hours, but that they had killed for two days. Their aim was to clear the north of the Shi'ite Hazaras who had settled there over the years.

Mullah Niazi, who was instrumental in murdering Najibullah, was appointed governor of Mazar, and within hours of the taking of the city, Taliban mullahs were proclaiming from the mosques that the Shia had three choices: convert to Sunni Islam, leave for Iran or face death. As Mullah Niazi declared from Mazar's central mosque: 'Last year you rebelled against us and killed us. From all your homes you shot at us. Now we are here to deal with you. The Hazaras are not Muslims and now we have to kill Hazaras. You either accept to be Muslims or leave Afghanistan. Wherever you go we will catch you.'[12]

Another incident that was to draw an international outcry and almost provoke a war with Iran was the murder in cold blood of 11 Iranian diplomats in their consulate in Mazar by a Taliban unit, led by a mullah called Dost Mohammad, that included Pakistanis from the fanatical anti-Shi'ite Sepah-e-Sahaba Party. Tehran had earlier contacted the Pakistani government to ensure the diplomatic inviolability of its premises and the security of its personnel, as it knew that ISI officers had driven into Mazar with the Taliban. Rashid states that Mullah Omar himself had given the go-ahead for the murders when contacted by Dost on his wireless.[13]

Side show: Pipeline politics

There were other actors who played roles, but not decisive ones, in the Taliban drive for power. The stakes for them were high, nothing less than the inestimable riches of the oil and gas reserves of Central Asia. Except for the oil reserves of the Caspian Basin, centring on Azerbaijan, these had been left largely untapped by the Soviets who had exploited instead their Siberian fields.

The pipeline politics in which the Central Asian Republics (CARs) and Afghanistan were caught up have to be seen in the larger context of the quest for alternative energy sources by the industrial countries of the Organization for Economic Cooperation and Development (OECD) after the major disruption in oil supplies that occurred twice in the last quarter of the twentieth century: the Arab oil embargo of 1973 and the Iranian upheaval in 1979. The risks of overdependence on energy resources from an unstable and politically volatile region were driven home once again by Saddam Hussein's invasion of Kuwait in 1990. In addition, the oil reserves of the Persian Gulf countries are not inexhaustible: at current levels of production they are estimated to last up to the end of the twenty-first century at best.[14]

The dismantlement of the Soviet Union and the independence of the CARs opened up entirely new perspectives. But there were major though not insurmountable problems in exporting oil and gas from these landlocked countries, two of which, Kazakhstan and Turkmenistan, had considerable proven reserves. There were three possible outlets to the sea: the first was through Russia and the network of Soviet-era pipelines. This overland system was extensive, could deliver oil and gas to Western Europe, and was already linked to the rich Tenghiz oilfield in Kazakhstan and to the Daulatabad gas field in Turkmenistan and to the gas fields in northern Afghanistan developed by the Soviets. But the internal situation in Russia was chaotic, and the transit taxes payable to the Russian state monopolies made the route expensive. The most feasible and economical outlet was through Iran, as the oil and gas could be delivered through existing pipelines to the Persian Gulf. But

Iran was closed to US oil companies because of the US-imposed sanctions. The third possible outlet was to Pakistan overland through Afghanistan, but called for a major investment.[15]

Into this scene stepped an unlikely but far-sighted investor, Carlos Bulgheroni, chairman of Bridas, an Argentinian oil company that had become the third largest independent oil company in Latin America. Bridas had no experience in Asia but had extensive experience in discovering, developing and transporting gas through cross-border pipelines to multiple markets in Latin America. In 1991 Bridas took a huge risk by becoming the first Western oil company to bid for leases in Turkmenistan, shunned by other oil companies because it was land-locked, had no legislation to protect investors, and no outlets except through the Russian system. These companies had problems in obtaining contracts to develop Soviet-era oil and gas fields in Siberia. Russia could not object, however, to the development of new fields if discovered in an independent Turkmenistan. But Russia's use of its built-in advantages and political clout in keeping the CARs economically dependent was a source of friction. Turkmenistan was virtually bankrupt: it had accumulated over $1 billion in unpaid bills for its gas exports to Russia, the Ukraine and Georgia.

Thus the old-style former communist apparatchik, President Saparmurad Niyazov of Turkmenistan, who had recycled himself, like most of the other CAR presidents, into a new-style autocrat with a thriving personality cult, was more than receptive to the overtures of the first and only Western oil company with an interest in investing in his impoverished country. In January 1994 Bridas was awarded the Yashlar block in the eastern part of the Karakum desert, with a 50–50 share of the profits, with even more favourable terms of 75 to 25 when it was awarded the Keimur block near the Caspian. Bridas spent the large sum of $400 million in exploring its leases, and began exporting oil from its Keimur field in 1994. The next year it struck gold in Yashlar, with estimated reserves of 27 trillion cubic feet of gas, or more than double Pakistan's total reserves. Unlike oil, gas needs an immediate and accessible market, and Bridas set about devising one with aplomb.

In November 1994 Bulgheroni persuaded Niyazov to set up a working group to study the feasibility of a gas pipeline to Pakistan through Afghanistan. In March 1995 Niyazov signed a memorandum with Prime Minister Benazir Bhutto of Pakistan commissioning Bridas to prepare a pre-feasibility study of the proposed pipeline. The indefatigable Bulgheroni spent nine months in 1995 and 1996 flying in his executive jet from warlord to warlord in Afghanistan, and to Islamabad, Ashkabad, Moscow and Washington to persuade leaders of the feasibility of his project. As we have seen earlier in this chapter, Pakistan's policy makers like General Babar were ecstatic about a pipeline that would not only open up export markets for Turkmenistan gas through its ports on the Arabian Sea and bring financial benefits such as transit fees, but also provide strategic and commercial links with the Central Asian states. The project was also attractive to the United States as the pipeline would bypass Iran which was subject to sanctions. In February 1996 Bulgheroni signed a 30-year agreement with the Rabbani government in Kabul for the construction and operation of a gas pipeline by Bridas and an international consortium that it would create. That same month, he reported to Niyazov and Bhutto that he had signed agreements with the warlords, and now with the Taliban, giving right of way through the territories they controlled.

For Pakistan, the Bridas project offered the greatest opportunities: an 875-mile gas pipeline from the Yashlar field, crossing Afghanistan to Sui in its Baluchistan province where its gas reserves and pipeline network originates, could be extended to the even bigger market of India via Multan in Sind province. Bridas proposed an open-access pipeline so that other companies and countries could eventually feed their own gas into it. This was of particular interest to whoever controlled northern Afghanistan, where the gas fields developed by the Soviets, now inoperative, had once supplied Uzbekistan.

But Bridas fell victim to the vicious international competition that his pioneering efforts had engendered. It had opened negotiations with other oil companies such as UNOCAL, the 12th largest in the US with experience in Pakistan. Under Bridas sponsorship, Turkmen officials visited Houston in April 1995, and a UNOCAL delegation visited Ashkabad and Islamabad to discuss the Bridas proposals. But Bridas was running into problems with Niyazov who, having been advised by his aides that they were being exploited under the Bridas contracts, blocked oil exports from Keimar. After the Yashlar discovery, Niyazov insisted on re-negotiating both the Keimar and Yashlar contracts. But Bridas would not budge. When UNOCAL expressed an interest in building its own pipeline from the existing Daulatabad gas fields, the profits from which would accrue to Turkmenistan, Niyazov, ignoring his contractual obligations with Bridas, saw both the financial and political advantage of engaging a major US company, and with it the US government, in his impoverished country's development.

Niyazov needed the US, and the US was supportive if this was a way to prevent him from being dependent on Iran. During a visit to New York, Niyazov summoned both Bridas and UNOCAL executives, and on 21 October 1995 signed an agreement with UNOCAL and its partner, the Saudi-owned Delta oil company, to build a gas pipeline through Afghanistan. 'We were shocked', said a Bridas executive quoted by Ahmed Rashid, 'and when we spoke to Niyazov, he just turned around and said, "why don't you build a second pipeline".' Henry Kissinger, one of many former US officials whom

UNOCAL had engaged as a consultant, quipped at the signing ceremony that the deal was 'a triumph of hope over experience'.[16]

With the Taliban in control of both Kabul and the provinces through which the gas pipeline would pass, Bridas and UNOCAL wooed them as-siduously. Bridas sponsored a visit by a Taliban delegation to Buenos Aires in February 1997, and a Bridas office was set up in Kabul soon afterwards. Bridas envisaged a partnership with a Saudi company for the funding of the Afghan portion of the pipeline, and set up a separate consortium with West-ern companies to build the Turkmen and Pakistani ends of the pipeline. It offered to start work immediately, without preconditions. On the other hand, UNOCAL, which handled public relations for the Taliban and spon-sored visits to Washington and Houston, had its hands tied by US policy on Afghanistan. No pipeline could be built, nor commercial terms discussed with the Taliban by US companies, until there was a functioning government in Kabul that was internationally recognized. The Taliban themselves were non-committal. While they favoured Bridas as a politically neutral company, the UNOCAL project carried the possibility of US recognition for which they were desperate. The competition also made them more demanding: they were not merely interested in receiving a rent for the pipeline route, esti-mated at US$100 million a year, but wanted the oil companies to build the infrastructure along the route, such as roads, water supplies, telephone and power lines.

In the end the pipeline projects through Afghanistan remained what they had always been: pipedreams. As one analyst cited by Rashid stated, 'The players in the game of pipeline politics must remind themselves that peace can bring a pipeline, but a pipeline cannot bring peace.' In September 1997 Bridas sold 60 per cent of its company's stake in Latin America to the US oil giant Amoco, in the hope that a US company could influence Niyazov to ease off on its frozen assets in Turkmenistan. UNOCAL had meanwhile become the target of attacks from its shareholders and from feminist groups in the US because of its relations with the Taliban. By 1998 both the Bridas and UNOCAL projects had become dead letters.

CHAPTER 13

Regional and International Reactions and Repercussions

Historically it was the issue of security between imperial Britain and czarist Russia that determined the status of Afghanistan as a buffer state rather than the issue of its sovereignty. Its spatial location and paucity of natural resources denied it the possibility of becoming a viable state on its own. Before Ahmad Shah Durrani in the mid-eighteenth century, Afghanistan was a part of other empires; after him, Afghan rulers depended largely on resources generated from raids, loot, plunder, and taxes from neighbouring regions over which they had nominal suzerainty through Ahmad Shah's conquests. With Abdur Rahman in the late nineteenth century, Afghanistan was useful for the British and the Russians as a buffer state for the maintenance of the balance of power in the region; the amir in return received subsidies from the British chiefly to enable him to maintain internal order and stability.[1] Britain continued to pay these annual subsidies to his successors. But when in their modernizing efforts these successors embarked on programmes of development, they became almost entirely dependent on foreign aid to build up an economic and social infrastructure. This dependence made Afghanistan a 'rentier state', as defined in Chapter 4, to an extent without parallel elsewhere in the world.

The civil war that erupted after the communist coup d'état of April 1978 escalated primarily due to the massive military aid and support extended to the opposing sides: the Soviet Union to its client regime in Kabul, and Pakistan serving as a covert conduit for military aid from the United States to the Afghan resistance. In Afghanistan the two major global powers fought the Cold War by proxy. The Geneva Accords of 1988, brokered by the United Nations, paved the way for the withdrawal of Soviet troops. The treaty postulated the need for international cooperation for peace in Afghanistan rather than war, and provided for the cessation of arms deliveries to both sides. But the civil war continued, fuelled by continuing external interference and by the huge arsenal that had come into the hands of the warring factions. As the Kabul regime weakened, the power vacuum was filled by armed peripheral forces and factions pursuing their own separate agendas. When a coalition of the resistance parties replaced the Najibullah regime in 1992, it was not able to exercise the monopoly of the use of force that is one of the chief attributes of a functioning state. One result of the Soviet withdrawal was the diffusion of the use of force by armed warlords throughout the country. It was in this situation of generalized anarchy that the Taliban movement was able to impose control over a territory and a population made weary by 20 years of a ruinous civil war. With their occupation of Mazar-i-Sharif and most of the north in 1998, the Taliban extended their armed control to over 90 per cent of the territory.

Russia and Central Asia

The fall of Kabul to the Taliban in September 1996 rang alarm bells across the region. The old issue of security of the southern borders was revived, not only by Russia but also by the successor states of the former Soviet Union. It was mistakenly assumed by these states that the ongoing civil war in Tajikistan originated in Afghanistan. The exodus of some 80,000 Tajik refugees into the contiguous northern provinces of Afghanistan and the presence there of elements of the defeated Tajik Islamist opposition was a source of concern. The possible break-up of Afghanistan along ethnic lines was also feared by the Central Asian Republics (CARs), as that could call into question their own borders, arbitrarily drawn up by Stalin in the 1920s, and open up a Pandora's box of conflicting irredentist nationalist demands. There were more Tajiks in Afghanistan than in Tajikistan itself.

At an emergency session called in Almaty, Kazakhstan, on 4 October 1996, Russia's prime minister, Victor Chernomyrdin, met four of the five Central Asian presidents. Their final communiqué, while ruling out any form of military intervention in Afghanistan's internal affairs, called on the Security Council of the 11-nation Commonwealth of Independent States (CIS) to 'examine urgently the situation which was developing on the southern borders of the CIS and to take necessary measures to strengthen the security of the CIS's external borders'. While any military aid to anti-Taliban forces inside Afghanistan was specifically denied, provision was made for 'humanitarian assistance', including food and electricity for the population of the northern regions and for refugees. One concrete effect of these regional concerns was that when the Taliban made their bid to capture Mazar-i-Sharif in the spring of 1997, it forced the Tajik government to come to a peace settlement in June 1997 with the Islamist and democratic opposition parties. The settlement was brokered by Russia and the United Nations.[2] It permitted tens of thousands of Tajik refugees in northern Afghanistan to return to their homes and provided for the stationing of 25,000 CIS troops under Russian command along the southern Tajik border.

If Afghanistan had become marginalized internationally at the end of the Cold War, the evolution of its internal situation had become a major security concern for the countries of the region. In the case of the successor states of the former Soviet Union in Central Asia, their own internal situations made them vulnerable. Before the 1920s, Russian Turkestan was simply a vast geographical region consisting of the settled areas of cities that had grown up around fertile oases, like historic Bukhara and Samarkand, boundless steppes inhabited by nomads, and vast deserts. Josef Stalin had arbitrarily carved out of this map five 'ethnic homelands' that had no relation to the complex political, social and cultural realities on the ground. Uzbeks and Kyrgyz, for example, belong to the same ethnic stock, the difference being that the former were steppe dwellers and the latter mountain dwellers. They were made into two nations by Stalin's territorial dictat. The fertile and densely populated Ferghana Valley, home to the famous horses, was divided up between Kyrgyzstan, Tajikistan and Uzbekistan. On the territorial framework of five 'autonomous Soviet socialist republics' was superimposed a uniform political and economic system based on the communist, collectivist ethic.

But far from destroying the old tribal and clan politics of Central Asia, the Bolsheviks had coopted the clans into the power structures of the local communist parties.[3] In societies without a conception of nationhood or still less of statehood, as in nineteenth-century Afghanistan, the system contributed to stability when it worked. The former secretary-general of the Kazakh Communist Party, Nursultan Nazarbayev, who became the first elected president of Kazakhstan, and the non-communist president of Kyrgyzstan, Askar Asayev, both came from traditional elite families from within their respective clan systems to which they owed their support and popularity. But no autonomous nation-building or state-building processes had taken place in the 70 years of communist rule. Elite power structures built on existing feudal or clan allegiances were created. As with other communist parties in the former Soviet Union, there was no popular participation in decision making. The aims of the successor regimes in the CARs were to survive. Except in Kyrgyzstan, there were no attempts to democratize power, or to involve the common people in the political process. Hence the majority of the people were alienated from the political structure, leaving many of them only a private place in Sufi Islam.

The potentially explosive consequences of Stalin's artificial territorial arrangements were driven home in the case of Tajikistan and Uzbekistan when these CARs became independent states. Of Tajikistan's total population of 5.4 million, only 58 per cent were ethnic Tajiks, 23 per cent were Uzbeks, 11 per cent were settlers of Russian or Slav origin who had immigrated there since czarist times,[4] and 388,000 belonged to various other ethnic or linguistic groups. There were also some 4 million ethnic Tajiks across Tajikistan's 1030-kilometre border with Afghanistan, over a million Tajiks in Uzbekistan, and tens of thousand of others in Kyrgyzstan and in China's Xinjiang province. The historic cities of Bukhara and Samarkand, which were the cultural centres of the Persian-speaking Tajiks, had been incorporated by Stalin into Uzbekistan.

Uzbekistan itself has a population of 22 million that makes it the most populous of the CARs. While ethnic Uzbeks make up 71 per cent of the population, there are over a million Tajiks and 7 million others of various ethnic and linguistic groups. Tashkent, the capital, had been the local centre of government of czarist Turkestan. Tens of thousands of Russians and other Slavs were imported there to man the czarist army and bureaucracy, and create the largest industrial centre in Central Asia. Russian-speakers make up a majority of Tashkent's population of over 2 million. The fact that some 5 million Uzbeks live in the other four CARs means that their presence is part of a political reality that the rulers of those states cannot ignore. Uzbekistan's president, the former communist Islam Karimov, became the principal political actor on the Central Asian stage. This role not only reflects the demographic and economic importance of his state but has historical antece-dents. Since Shaybani Khan united the Uzbeks at the end of the fifteenth century, replaced the rule of the Timurids, and imposed Uzbek hegemony over much of Central Asia, Uzbeks have been the chief political force in the region. They ruled through their emirate of Bukhara and the khanates of Khiva and Kokand until these were annexed by the Russians. There are also some 2 million Uzbeks in northern Afghanistan, most of them settled there since the time of the Shaybani Uzbek invasion and ruled by their own khans and begs until Abdur Rahman put an end to their autonomy. Tens of thou-sands of others came there as refugees after Stalin suppressed the Basmachi rebellion in the 1920s and 1930s.

Another important problem that the new CARs had to cope with was that they could not guarantee their own security. With no armed forces of their own, they were forced to depend on the security forces of the former imperial power. At the end of the civil war, the triumphant Red Army had established the Turkestan Military District (TMD) with its headquarters in Tashkent. Stalin had built up an enormous military infrastructure to keep the peace in Central Asia: roads, railways, telecommunications, depots, work-shops and factories helped control one of the most volatile regions of the USSR. The TMD came to be of great strategic value to the USSR when it was invaded by Nazi Germany in the Second World War. Later the TMD was used as a counterweight to the military encirclement of the USSR from the south when the US gained access to military bases in Turkey, Iran and Paki-stan in the context of CENTO. When China became the enemy, the TMD was turned around to face the Chinese border. It was the TMD that organ-

ized the invasion of Afghanistan and kept the Soviet forces there manned
and supplied for a decade.

When the USSR ceased to exist, the TMD was also dismantled, much to
the dismay of the CARs. There were only token forces remaining under the
joint command of Russia and the respective republics: Tajikistan had 6000
soldiers, Kyrgyzstan 8000, Uzbekistan 16,000, Turkmenistan 34,000, and
Kazakhstan 63,000. The majority of the conscripts were drawn from within
each republic, but many of the officers were Russians who had volunteered to
stay on. But this was a loose ad hoc arrangement without a coordinating
mechanism: each republic negotiated for itself rather than following a common strategy.

When Russia announced in March 1992 that it would create its own army
and Defence Ministry rather than rely on a united CIS force, the CARs were
forced to think about creating their own national forces: Nazarbayev announced the setting up of a Kazakh National Guard; Karimov said that he
would create an Uzbek national army of 25,000 men; Turkmenistan wanted
no more than 2000 men, relying entirely on CIS forces; Kyrgyzstan renounced the idea of a national army altogether. But the CARs were in such
straitened economic circumstances after the break-up of the Soviet system
that they were all strapped for the necessary cash. No agreement could be
reached by the CARs' leaders on coordination or a common defence strategy.
Common systems of collective security, when proposed by some leaders,
proved to be unworkable in practice because of the divergent security interests of each CAR, and a fear by some leaders, notably Karimov, that CIS
forces under Russian command would play a neo-colonial role in their republics. Thus the CARs' attitude towards Russia remained ambivalent. While
recognizing the need for Russia as a senior partner to guarantee their security,
they also feared a reassertion of Russian hegemony. Russia played on their
fears of the spread of Islamic fundamentalism to keep the CARs in a state of
dependency.

The Tajik civil war that erupted in 1993 forced Russia to review its military commitments to the CARs by providing assistance to the neo-communist
government against the Islamic and democratic opposition. It was commonly
feared by Russia and the CARs that the Tajik example of civil war, economic
breakdown, and Muslim revivalism would spread to the other republics. It
was also commonly perceived that the Tajik Islamic Renaissance Party (IRP)
was a fundamentalist party inspired and sustained by their Afghan counterparts.[5] The leader of the Tajik IRP, Mohammad Sharif Himatzade, had
fought with other IRP leaders in the Afghan mujahideen. The IRP received
support from Hekmatyar's Hizbi-i-Islami and from Massoud, who had become a national hero to the Tajiks.

The Tajik civil war, however, was more a manifestation of clan politics gone wrong. Under communist rule in Tajikistan, clan divisions had become so enshrined in the communist party that leadership positions were openly fought over among the clans. Localism and patronage flourished, creating one of the most corrupt and inefficient regimes in the former USSR. Power was fought over between north and south, between the industrial regions of Khojent in the north and Kuliab in the south-east where clan-based support for the communists was strongest, and between Kuliab and Turgan Tube in the south-east which supported the Islamists. These divisions were exacerbated by widespread social unrest brought about by rapid industrial decline, disastrous falls in income, land hunger and an unemployment rate of over 25 per cent in a republic that had registered the highest population growth in the whole of the former USSR.

Tajikistan, like the Ferghana Valley, had been a centre of the Basmachi movement in the early years of Soviet rule. The Basmachis were local guerrilla groups led by mullahs, tribal chiefs and landlords who had resisted Soviet rule across the whole of Central Asia and continued their unequal struggle until the 1930s. After the ruthless suppression of the Basmachis, who, like the Afghan mujahideen, were inspired by Islam, the Soviets tried to extirpate all the outward symbols of Islam through the wholesale destruction of mosques and madrasas. An official Muslim hierarchy was created that was subservient to the communist state.

But Islam was kept alive in Central Asia by Sufism, the mystical trend in Islam that has always been a reaction against authority, the sterile dogmatism of the Muslim ulema and the mullahs, and could sustain ordinary Muslims in the most trying circumstances. Through prayer, meditation and rituals practised in the various Sufi orders, pious Muslims could create for themselves an inner space that was impervious to religious repression by the state. Sufism also made Islam in Central Asia a tolerant creed; the different ways to God preached by Sufi mystics are seen by them as 'paths leading to the summit of the same mountain'. The Sufis also practised the art of isolating themselves from their oppressors without trying to confront or overthrow them. Thus when there was a significant Islamic revival after *perestroika*, it did not emerge from a religious vacuum. It was a re-traditionalization of Central Asian societies that was taken by the region's ex-communist and secularist leaders, and by Russia, as a sign of the spread of Afghan-style Islamic fundamentalism.

Iran and Saudi Arabia

It is pertinent to review briefly the history of Saudi and Iranian interests in Afghanistan and in Central Asia against the backdrop of their rivalry for leadership of the Muslim world that became pronounced after the Khomeini revolution and the Soviet invasion. In order to counter the threat of Nasser's Arab nationalism to the legitimacy of its rulers, Saudi Arabia had offered pan-Islamism as an ideological alternative. To this end the Saudis sponsored the creation of the Organization of the Islamic Conference (OIC), to coordinate the foreign policies of Muslim countries, and the Muslim World League, to institutionalize Saudi influence in cultural and religious activities in the Muslim world. The eclipse of Nasserism after the Arab defeat by the Israelis in the Six Day War of 1967 and its own financial power gave Saudi Arabia the leverage to position itself as leader of the Muslim world. As we have seen, the Saudis were generous in their funding of the more radical of the Afghan mujahideen parties. They also sponsored Wahhabism, their own brand of Islamic fundamentalism, in Afghanistan and later in Central Asia.[6]

Saudi pretensions were challenged by revolutionary Iran, which posed an even greater threat than Nasserism by asserting that monarchy was incompatible with Islam, and that the kingdom's close links with the US were against the interests of Muslims and made it an unworthy guardian of Islam's holy places. The Saudis were genuinely alarmed when a group of zealots challenging the legitimacy of the royal family occupied the Great Mosque in Mecca during the hajj pilgrimage of 1979.

Because of the war with Iraq, Tehran had maintained a low profile during the Afghan conflict, shying away from any confrontation with the Soviets despite the potential threat to Iran's security and the presence of nearly 2 million Afghan refugees on her soil. After the ousting of the democratically inclined Iranian nationalists (Bazargan, Bani-Sadr, Qotbzadeh), the radical clerics who succeeded them focused more narrowly on the interests of their Afghan Shi'ite brethren, supporting in particular the pro-Iranian Shi'ite political groups, Nasr and Sepah. This policy antagonized both the other Hazara Shi'ite parties and the Peshawar-based parties. The latter denied any political role for the Shi'ites in a post-communist Afghanistan. As in Pakistan, the Iranian Foreign Ministry had great difficulty in keeping its foreign policy on an even keel, steering between the vested interests of multiple government departments and private lobbies: the Shi'ite clergy, themselves ideologically divided, the Revolutionary Guards identified with hardline clergy, the military, and the Bunyads or charitable foundations that ran much of the state-sector economy and financed foreign adventures with their unaccounted funds, much to the embarrassment of the Rafsanjani government.

Iranian policy underwent a sea-change at the end of the Cold War. Largely ideological considerations during the Khomeini period gave way to the pursuit of state and Persian national interests. Iran became very active in Afghanistan, cultivating contacts with the non-Pashtun parties - the Jamiat, the Wahdat, Dostum's Uzbeks and the Ismailis - to counter the Peshawar-based Pashtun parties, particularly those with a pro-Saudi bias. The coalition of largely non-Pashtun parties that took power from Najibullah in April 1992, pre-empting a scheduled transfer of power to a UN-selected neutral team of Afghans, represented a major diplomatic triumph for Iran. She provided substantial material support for the Kabul coalition to counter Pakistani and Saudi support for Hekmatyar.[7] When the coalition fragmented during the opportunistic shifts in alliances in 1993–94, Iranian support for the Shi'ite Wahdat, now allied to Dostum and Hekmatyar, was used to counter Saudi financial support for the Rabbani–Massoud regime.

The 1989 visit of Russian Foreign Minister Eduard Shevardnadze to Tehran and his call on Ayatollah Khomeini had given legitimacy in Iranian eyes to the development of Russo-Iranian relations. Between 1989 and 1993, Russia sold $10 billion in arms to Iran to help rebuild her depleted arsenal after the war with Iraq. Iran also developed links with non-Muslim states across her borders, such as Georgia, Ukraine and Armenia, and declined to support Muslim Azerbaijan in her war with Christian Armenia, despite her own considerable Azeri population in the north-west. Iran also developed links with the CARs. In November 1991 the Iranian foreign minister, Ali Akbar Velayati, visited Central Asia. Iran signed an agreement with Turkmenistan to build a railway link between the two countries at her own expense. Iran also had a special interest in developing cultural contacts with Persian-speaking Tajikistan, where it maintained the largest foreign embassy in Dushanbe and actively supported UN and Russian efforts to end the Tajik civil war.

During the Taliban drive to power, Iranian hostility to the anti-Shi'ia movement was overt and consistent. The fall of Herat to the Taliban in 1995 was perceived by Iran as a direct threat to her national security. It developed an airlift from Mashad in its Khorasan province to the Bagram airbase where it flew in arms supplies for Massoud's forces: Pakistani intelligence once reported that 13 Iranian flights landed on a single day at Bagram. Iran established five training camps near Mashad for 5000 fighters led by the exiled governor of Herat, Ismail Khan. As mentioned in Chapter 12, 2000 of these men were airlifted by Dostum to reinforce his defences in the north. Iran's high-profile involvement continued after the fall of Kabul to the Taliban, in her consistent support of the anti-Taliban forces. The equally consistent support to the Taliban by Pakistan and Saudi Arabia was seen by Iran as a US-inspired conspiracy to isolate her in the region.

When US Secretary of State James Baker toured Central Asia in 1991, he warned its leaders of the dangers of Islamic fundamentalism and urged them to emulate Turkey's secular model as an antidote to Iranian-style fundamentalism. In official US eyes Islamic fundamentalism meant the Khomeini brand, which, as serious students of the subject are aware, is a homegrown

Shi'ite variety closely associated with a genuine revolution indigenous to Iran that is not suitable for export to the mainstream Sunni Muslim world.[8] Uzbek, Kazakh and Kyrgyz leaders came to see, however, that Wahhabism, actively propagated by a US ally, Saudi Arabia, was the biggest political threat to stability in Central Asia. Also the United States, through its long support of the Afghan mujahideen, had empowered Islamist extremists whose major political manifestation was the indigenous Taliban movement. The Taliban in turn provided a refuge for the so-called 'Arab Afghans' directed by the sinister Saudi rebel, Osama bin Laden, who established his *état majeur* and his training camps for Islamic terrorists in Afghanistan. This was one of the 'blowback' effects of past US policies.

James Baker, who was a frequent visitor to Central Asian capitals, declared again in 1992 that Washington would do everything in its power to block Iranian influence in Central Asia.[9] If there was any consistency in US policy in the region, it was this policy of 'containing' Iran. In practical terms this meant that Iran, because of US-imposed sanctions, was off limits to US traders and investors, leaving non-US firms to exploit the field. It also had repercussions on the pipeline politics to which Central Asia, including Afghanistan, fell prey in the mid-1990s. US companies were discouraged from participating in pipeline projects that would develop routes through Iran. These were in fact more viable and far less expensive than alternative routes from gas and oil fields in Turkmenistan, such as the US-supported project to carry Turkmen and Caspian oil via Azerbaijan and Georgia to the Turkish port of Ceyhan on the Mediterranean.[10] Turkmenistan, however, concluded a swap arrangement whereby it would supply oil to Iran, which would then export the equivalent from its southern fields to Europe on behalf of Turkmenistan. In May 1996 a railway line linking Ashkabad with Mashad was opened. When extended to the Iranian port of Bandar Abbas on the Persian Gulf, the line would provide the Central Asian states with their first access to the sea in history. In December 1996 Iran also signed agreements with Turkmenistan and Turkey for the construction of a pipeline that would carry Turkmen gas via Iran to the Turkish cities of Erzerum, Ankara and Istanbul.[11]

United States policies

Behind the somewhat passive US acquiescence in an eventual Taliban takeover, engineered by its Pakistan and Saudi allies, lay the UNOCAL game plan. UNOCAL was a consortium of US oil companies formed to exploit the hydrocarbon reserves of Central Asia. UNOCAL and its Saudi partner, Delta, had hired every available American involved in Afghan operations during the jihad years, including Robert Oakley, a former ambassador to

Pakistan, and worked hand-in-glove with US officials. UNOCAL staff acted for a time as an unofficial lobby for the Taliban and were regularly briefed by the CIA and Pakistan's ISI.[12] In US eyes, the most important function of the Taliban would have been to provide security for the roads, and potentially for the gas and oil pipelines that would link the Central Asian states to the international markets through Afghanistan rather than Iran. According to a US diplomat quoted by Ahmed Rashid, 'the Taliban will probably develop like the Saudis did. There will be Aramco, pipelines, an emir, no parliament and lots of shari'a law. We can live with that.'[13] The US assistant secretary of state for South Asian Affairs, Robin Raphael, went so far as to state that the Taliban capture of Kabul was 'a positive step'. US policy on Afghanistan had become so aligned with that of Pakistan that it no longer represented an independent policy. It was another case of the tail wagging the dog.

US policy took a fresh direction with the appointment of Madeleine Albright as secretary of state in early 1997, and the replacement of the entire chain of command responsible for Afghan affairs at the State Department by experienced staff, who brought with them a less blinkered and more nuanced grasp of Afghan realities. The new assistant secretary for South Asian Affairs, Karl Inderfurth, made a clearer policy statement to the US Senate in October 1997. He said that Washington's objective was 'an Afghan government that is multi-ethnic, broad-based, and that observes international norms of behaviour'. During a visit to an Afghan refugee camp in Peshawar a month later, Albright, herself a former refugee, when asked by a local reporter why the US did not recognize the Taliban replied, to the consternation of her Pakistani hosts: 'I think it is clear why we are opposed to the Taliban. Because of their approach to human rights, their despicable treatment of women and children, and their general lack of respect for human dignity ... that is more reminiscent of the past than of the future.' The Clinton administration was no doubt also beginning to feel the pressure in an election year of American feminist groups that condemned the Taliban for their treatment of women.

US policy towards Iran also began to soften after the election as president of Mohammad Khatami on a platform of political liberalization, and a thaw in Iranian relations with the West. In July 1998 Madeleine Albright acknowledged the critical role that Iran played in the region that makes, 'the question of USA–Iran relations a topic of great interest and importance to this Secretary of State'.[14] There was also the fear that by being too inflexible on its sanctions policy, US companies would be upstaged in the lucrative Iranian market by their European and Asian rivals: three European companies were participating in a gas pipeline project linking Turkmenistan and Turkey via Iran; an Australian company had announced its sponsorship of a pipeline costing $2.7 billion that could deliver 2 billion cubic feet per day of gas from southern Iran to Karachi, and later to India (see map). In July 1997 the

United States quietly announced that she would not object to the participation of US companies in the Turkmenistan-Iran-Turkey pipeline project.

A senior State Department official, Strobe Talbott, set what it was hoped would be the benchmark for future US policy in the region, particularly with regard to Russia, in a July 1997 speech in Washington:

> It has been fashionable to proclaim, or at least to predict, a replay of the "Great Game" in the Caucasus and Central Asia. The implication, of course, is that the driving dynamic of the region, fuelled and lubricated by oil, will be the competition of the great powers. Our goal is to avoid, and actively to discourage, that atavistic outcome. Let's leave Rudyard Kipling and George McDonald Fraser where they belong - on the shelves of history. The Great Game which starred Kipling's Kim and Fraser's Flashman was very much of the zero-sum variety.[15]

The current danger does not lie in the replay of some archaic and arcane Great Game but in the geo-political fact that Central Asia is where all of Eurasia's backyards meet. Backyards, particularly those that are unfenced and untended, are also where neighbours, their children and their dogs come to poke, prod and rummage. Zbigniew Brzezinski called Central Asia a 'black hole' containing a concentration of socio-political combustible material.

Russian policies

Ten years after the dissolution of the Soviet Union, all five of the former Soviet republics, where no autonomous nation-building or state-building processes took place in the 70 years of Soviet-style communism, have become weak and vulnerable. The economic contraction together with the simultaneous collapse of the socialist life-support systems - guaranteed jobs, subsidized food, health and other social infrastructure - produced hardships that were even worse than in the rest of the former Soviet Union. In the first post-independence decade, Tajikistan lost two-thirds of its GDP; Turkmenistan, just under one half; and Kazakhstan and Kyrgyzstan, two fifths. Uzbekistan fared a little better, with a loss of around a tenth, according to the official statistics. But the bulk of the working people in Uzbekistan earn the equivalent of between US$2.5 and $9 per month, with $15 considered a good salary, and $25–30 very good indeed. But as large families are the norm in Muslim Central Asia, taking into account the number of dependants and the informal safety net, these bleak statistics mask a devastating drop in living standards in comparison with the late Soviet era. Dmitri Trenin sums it up:

> The abject poverty of the majority of Central Asia's population is part of a pattern that includes ruthless authoritarian clan rule, the opulent wealth of the 'first families', pervasive official corruption, and government incompetence. With Tajikistan's 1990-97 civil war serving as a demonstration case, the ruling elites (particularly in Uzbekistan and Turkmenistan) have concluded that political free-

dom is destabilising, and that political Islam represents mortal danger. Thus, they have made sure that their political opponents are either in jail or in exile. Even the purportedly democratic Kyrgyzstan has resorted to political hardball in an effort to eliminate all credible opposition to President Askar Akayev in the run-up to his 2000 re-election. Moreover there have been attempts, as in Uzbekistan in 1998, to clamp down on religion by closing mosques and medressahs. All this makes one draw uneasy – and not too far-fetched – parallels with the Shah's Iran.[16]

The situation is exacerbated by the ethnic strife and the difficult inter-state relations engendered by Stalin's erratic boundary making, as we have seen, and by the precipitate removal of the security apparatus and economic arrangements of the former Soviet Union. Instead of assisting the former Soviet republics to address the real internal issues at stake, which are socio-economic and political, Russia's policy in the region was an incoherent mix. Under Vladimir Putin the policy has been consolidated into two tracks, according to Trenin: the pursuit of economic opportunities and shoring up stability by the military means of buffer-building. 'Common to both tracks is the desire to keep the CARs within Moscow's orbit, and to minimize outside influence in the region.'[17]

The first track is being followed by seeking to direct as much as possible the oil and gas exports of Kazakhstan and Turkmenistan through Soviet pipeline routes and to re-establish economic links through cooperation projects. The Russian routes, although requiring upgrading, are well established. The importance Russia attaches to this policy is the projected pipeline that would carry oil from the rich Tenghiz fields in Kazakhstan to its Black Sea port of Novorossysk. Turkmenistan has sought to bolster its independence by seeking alternative routes, as we have noted, through Iran and Turkey and through Afghanistan and Pakistan for its gas exports, and through the US-supported pipeline through Azerbaijan, Georgia and Turkey for its oil exports (see map). Economic cooperation is being pushed through the Customs Union of Russia, Belarus and Russia's three Central Asian allies, Kazakhstan, Kyrgyzstan and Tajikistan, which was upgraded in October 2000 to a Eurasian Economic Community (EAEC).

The development of the second track is coloured, or distorted, by the Russian equivalent of America's 'Vietnam Syndrome'. This is the 'Afghan Syndrome'. For the past 20 years Russian soldiers have been fighting only one sort of enemy, the Muslim resistance fighter/rebel/terrorist. The interventions in Afghanistan in 1979 and in Chechnya in 1994 were conceded subsequently to have been major blunders by Russia's own leaders and political analysts. Their result, according to the official statistics, was that 13,500 Russian servicemen died in Afghanistan between 1979 and 1989, about 4000 in the first Chechen war (1994–96), and about 3000 in the first 15 months of the second Chechen war. They continue to die in Chechnya even after the end of the 'war phase' of the operation. But the lessons do not appear to have been learned.

Drawing their conclusions from their bitter experiences, Russian policy makers have invented a whole new scenario dominated by the spectre of 'Islamism'. In this apocalyptic and dangerous vision, they see developments in Chechnya, Central Asia, Afghanistan and south Asia as being part of a plot hatched by a secretive network of Islamic activists and terrorists whose main goal, according to Russia's Federal Security Service (FSS), is

> the creation of several quasi-state units (in Chechnya, Dagestan and Kokand, for example) and their subsequent inclusion in a Great Islamic caliphate. This caliphate would not only include the North Caucasus and Central Asia: Astrakhan, Ufa and Kazan are believed to be likely candidates for subversion and eventual take-over. Thus Russia will suffer not only at the edges; the territorial unity of the federation will be irrevocably compromised. ... Reinforcing this perception is the revival of Islam inside Russia itself, where some 13% of the population is Muslim, and where the so-called Islamic enclaves (such as Tatarstan and Bashkortostan) almost form a contiguous territory with the broader Islamic world via Kazakhstan.

The plot is seen as aimed at 'rolling back secularism along a wide arc (or front) stretching from Kosovo across the Caucasus and Central Asia all the way to the Philippines. This would make Russia the last barrier between civilization and barbarity, the would-be saviour of Europe.'[18]

At the heart of this scenario is Osama bin Laden and his secretive terrorist networks that are alleged to be the masterminds and financiers of the plot, with the Taliban's Afghanistan as their supply base, training area and geographic abode: 'the nest of all rogues'.[19] Beyond lies a politically unstable Pakistan, increasingly 'talibanized', with a nuclear capability that produced the first 'Islamic Bomb', to the great delight of large sections of the Muslim world.

One of the first diplomatic initiatives of the Bolsheviks was to secure their southern borders by concluding treaties with Turkey, Iran and Afghanistan and by crushing the Basmachi. The independence of the CARs eliminated Afghanistan as a buffer zone along one large segment of its southern flank. It was feared that the destabilization of Tajikistan by Islamic rebels would pose a direct threat to Uzbekistan, whose fall, according to the scenario, would initiate a domino reaction across the region, eventually precipitate the collapse of Kazakhstan with its 6 million Slavs and lead to a 7500-kilometre virtually indefensible border with Russia. All this has a familiar ring to students of the Cold War, except that the 'strategic thinking' emanates this time from Moscow.

As is often the case, there are elements of truth that could shore up such scenarios. No doubt external factors are involved. The Russian government estimated the outside funding of extremist Islamic activities at $1.3 billion in the first nine months of 2000.[20] It is not clear what the external sources of funding are, or what they finance specifically. As noted earlier in this chapter, the Saudis have financed Wahhabi movements in Central Asia, and have been important sources of support for the Taliban and the Deobandi madrasas in Pakistan that produce extremist Islamic militants. Bin Laden himself has provided large infusions of cash. It is now thought that he relied on drug trafficking after his bank accounts were blocked by the UN-imposed sanctions.

The possible link between drugs and terrorism is specially evident in Tajikistan. The collapse of the Soviet-era economies and the elimination of Soviet-policed borders stimulated the production and trafficking of drugs via Central Asia to Russia and Europe. Between 1992 and 2000, Russian border guards in Tajikistan seized about ten tonnes of drugs including a tonne of heroin. These seizures are believed to be a fraction of what actually gets through, given the multitude of river crossing points and other factors, for instance the openness to corruption of underpaid Tajik and Russian soldiers and border guards, the extreme poverty of the population on both sides of the long border where unemployed young men are prepared to take risks as smugglers, and the existence in northern Afghanistan of a flourishing drugs industry.

Before the Taliban occupation of Kunduz in May 1997, laboratories operated by factions allied to Hekmatyar's Hizbi-i-Islami produced heroin of a high quality. These factions continued their operations after rallying to the Taliban. According to evidence gathered at first hand in the area by the Paris-based Observatoire géopolitique des drogues (OGD), opium is purchased from farmers at $50 per kilo and resold by the buyers at $110 per kilo to traders at border villages who recruit the smugglers. In the town of Khorog in south Tajikistan, heroin is available to buyers at $7000 per kilo. The drugs can then be carried by road to Dushanbe, or through the mountains to Ost in Kyrgyzstan, which is a centre of Islamic activism, and then on commercial and military flights from Tajikistan to Moscow.[21]

Since the 1997 peace agreement, Tajikistan is run by local clans who are themselves engaged in the highly profitable drugs trade. It is the demand that fuels the supply, and given the enormous spread between the street prices of heroin in Europe and North America and the prices paid to the farmers for the raw opium, the enormous profits accruing to the middlemen and the cartels can only be guessed at. If some of these profits are used in the cause of terrorism, it can be plausibly argued that Western drug addicts finance terrorists.

Geo-political considerations, imagined or real, dominate Russia's policy of buffer-building – the second track – to preserve Central Asia as a buffer zone between Russia and the forces of militant Islam. It keeps its forces in Tajikistan in a state of high combat readiness and holds regular joint exercises with CAR armies: 10,000 troops participated in the Southern Shield exercise in April 2000. Bilateral security and defence arrangements are strengthened, with arms and equipment supplied to her three nominal allies. Russia is also seeking to keep alive the 1992 Collective Security Treaty that was activated during the Tajik war but has subsequently been undermined by divergent perceptions as to the nature of the external threat. Uzbekistan in particular has distanced herself from the anti-Taliban forces of Massoud, actively supported by Russia and Tajikistan, after the eclipse of General Dostum, her former protégé.

By putting security in Central Asia before democracy and human rights, and with the Defence Ministry taking the lead in policy making, Russia has given too little thought to the non-military means of promoting stability: influencing the domestic policies of the autocratic regimes in place, engaging the constructive opposition in the CARs including moderate Islamic circles, and coming to grips with the drug trafficking originating in Central Asia.

In these endeavours, the United States could be mobilized as a powerful ally. Before Putin, Russian officials have generally been suspicious of US intentions in Central Asia and Afghanistan. Washington has declared that it only sought to make Kazakhstan a nuclear free country and assist the CARs generally to follow the path to free markets and democratization. Here there could be a convergence of interests and a fertile field for Russo-American cooperation. The United States has a stake in the region's stability, if only because of the huge energy resources of the Caspian Basin and the heavy financial involvement of US companies in the development of the oil and gas fields of Kazakhstan and Turkmenistan and the construction of new pipeline routes.

CHAPTER 14

Pakistan and the Taliban

The ulema and village mullahs of Afghanistan were at the heart of the Taliban movement. These religious leaders were marginalized during the years of state building, although attempts were made at various times to coopt them into the state structure by putting them on government payrolls. These attempts were manipulative – as under Amir Abdur Rahman, Daoud, and later, the communists – and intended to curb or control their traditional influence over the rural populations of Afghanistan; King Nadir Shah used the ulema on the other hand to legitimize and reinforce his own seizure of power.

The Taliban were not therefore, as is widely believed, an upstart movement. One writer calls them 'a sort of religious proletariat', an inseparable part of the Afghan social fabric, associated with religious schools, mosques, shrines and all kinds of Islamic activities. They could be rapidly mobilized by the ulema as mujahideen, or holy warriors (jihadis) when the cause of Islam was felt to be threatened. The earliest resistance to the Soviets arose through the loosely structured Harakat-i-Inquilab-Islami Party headed by Maulvi Mohammad Nabi Mohammedi. Olivier Roy personally observed the 'Tolaba fronts' of fighting madrasa students in the provinces of Uruzgan, Zabul and Kandahar in 1984. He described madrasas functioning as military camps where dozens, even hundreds, of youths studied and fought together under religious leaders of fighting age. Russian attacks sometimes forced them to more defensible mountain redoubts – like the Moroccan *ribat*. These 'fighting monks' were drawn from different Pashtun tribes and clans and organized without regard to their tribal affiliations. It is Roy's thesis that the Taliban movement grew out of the network of military madrasas.[1]

That would also explain their rapid mobilization and successes in 1994–95. The rural madrasas in the Pashtun tribal areas of Afghanistan, and the network of madrasas organized by the Jamiat-i-Ulema-i-Islami (JUI) in Pakistan, where millions of Afghans took refuge after the communist coup d'état in 1978, provided almost the only education available to a generation of Pashtun boys reaching school age. The minimal education in the rural madrasas was imparted by semi-educated mullahs and confined to reading, or rather the decipherment and memorizing of religious texts. The talib, or more advanced religious student, sat at the feet of *maulvis* (or *maulanas*), scholars trained at schools like Deoband in northern India, who were versed in subjects such as Islamic jurisprudence, Arabic grammar and rhetoric.[2]

The founders of the Islamic theological school in Deoband were inspired by an eighteenth-century Indian Muslim reformer, Shah Waliullah, who in turn revived the reformist tradition of Shaykh Ahmad Sirhindi Faruqi, born in Sirhind, India, in 1564. Sirhindi was the pir or spiritual head of the Naqshbandiya Sufi order.[3] Sirhindi was an *alim* (plural *ulema*) who opposed the syncretist religion incorporating Hindu influences promulgated by the Moghul Emperor Akbar (1556-1605).[4] Akbar was seen as a heretic by the ulema. Sirhindi's objective was two-fold: to purify Islam in India of all Hindu influences and to ensure that the spiritual dimension of Sufism was freed from the legalistic formalism that was the orthodoxy of the ulema of the time. The Emperor Jahangir (1605-27) continued his father's tolerant religious policy but gave Sirhindi's Muslim revivalist movement great support. Sirhindi himself was given the title of Mujaddid Alf-e-Thani ('Reformer of the Second Millennium').[5] The descendant of the hereditary spiritual head of the order, or pir, Qayum Jehan, moved with his family to Afghanistan at the invitation of Ahmad Shah in the late eighteenth century. He settled in the Shor Bazar district of Kabul, where the successive pirs came to be known as the Hazrat of Shor Bazar. In 1979 the Hazrat and 79 members of his family were executed by the communists.

Shah Waliullah (1703-62) broke with the rigidities imposed by Muslim orthodoxy since the eleventh century by re-introducing the practice of *ijtihad*, or personal interpretation of the Koran and the Sunnah to confront new situations. He also preached Islam in social and political terms, advocating greater social justice among Muslims. He did not recognize the religious authority of the Moghul emperors.[6]

Shah Waliullah's reformist legacy was taken up by the militant Muslim revivalist movement of Sayyed Ahmad Barelvi (1786-1831), who established networks throughout Muslim India to collect funds and enlist volunteers for a jihad against infidel rulers. His first target was Ranjit Singh and his Sikhs who had crossed the Indus in 1823 and occupied the Muslim Pashtun lands. Barelvi urged the Pashtuns to oust their khans wherever possible, and replace their leadership with the ulema, renounce their tribal customs and adopt the *shariat*. He put in place a system of tax collection for the war effort against the Sikhs. Barelvi also laid the groundwork for a Muslim political organization that did not depend on Muslim rulers and tribal khans, but tried to establish an alternative, village-based power structure, with a network of preachers, judges and tax collectors. But his anti-Sikh campaign was a failure. He himself was captured and executed by the Sikhs as a result of the treachery of a local khan.

After his death, there were numerous Muslim uprisings led by charismatic religious leaders – a precursor of subsequent notions of jihad against non-Muslim rulers. Indeed the so-called Indian Mutiny of 1857 against the British was actively supported by the survivors of the Barelvi movement and by the majority of the ulema. Their participation in the Mutiny, which was, however, as much a Hindu as a Muslim affair, represented perhaps the last attempt by Indian Muslims to reassert their political power. Two widely differing strategies were henceforth adopted by the Muslims of British India.

Educated Muslims, acutely aware of the social and economic backwardness of the Muslim masses and the obscurantism of the Indian ulema, and inspired also by the contemporary Salaffiya movement of the Egyptian Mohamad Abduh and the Persian-Afghan Jamal al-Din al-Afghani, chose to adapt Muslim mores to modern needs through a Western-type education.[7] The anglophile Sir Sayyad Ahmed founded the Anglo-Oriental College in Aligarh and was supported in his efforts by the wealthy patrician Muslim families of the old Moghul provincial administrations. He also received the financial backing of the fabulously wealthy Nizam of Hyderabad. The modernists were also generally loyal to the British who, in keeping with their usual imperial tradition of divide-and-rule by favouring minorities, were seen by Hindu nationalists as being partial to the Muslims.[8]

In stark contrast to the response of enlightened Indian Muslims,[9] others, led by the ulema, founded the Deoband school in 1867. It adhered to a strict orthodoxy, with a traditional curriculum focused on the study of Islamic law (the shari'a) and jurisprudence (fiqh) that took ten years to complete. The school, while hostile to innovative interpretations in religious matters (ijtihad), accepted Sufism – many of the teachers belonged to the Naqshbandiya or Qadiriya Sufi orders – while rejecting the cult of saints associated with Sufism.[10] The Deobandis were anti-British and pan-Islamist. A leading figure, Mohamad al-Hassan (1850-1921), did not hide his political aim of subverting British rule. The Deobandis sought to train a new generation of Indian Muslim scholars in the interpretation of the classical texts of the shari'a so that they might better understand how Islam could cope with the current realities of colonial rule. Their graduates set up madrasas, of which there were 12 in British India in 1879. When the school celebrated its centenary in 1967, there were 9000 across south Asia.

Many Afghan ulema received their theological training at Deoband. In 1933 Zahir Shah invited leading teachers from Deoband to his coronation. They said that their school 'would prepare such ulema in the changed circumstances of the period that they may cooperate fully with the aim and purpose of the free governments in the world of Islam and prove sincere workers for the state'.[11] However, the few state-sponsored madrasas did not prove very popular in Afghanistan.

Deobandi madrasas developed much faster in Pakistan after the creation of this state in 1947. The Deobandis set up the Jamiat-i-Ulema-i-Islami (JUI) as a purely religious movement. In 1962 its leader in the North West Frontier Province (NWFP), Maulana Ghulam Ghaus Hazarvi, turned the JUI into a political party which then split into factions. The Pashtun faction of the JUI in the NWFP was taken over by Maulana Mufti Mehmood who campaigned against military rule in the 1970 elections, with an Islamic agenda consisting of a progressive social programme and a strong anti-American stance. The JUI campaign led to a bitter feud with the Jamiat-i-Islami that persists to this day.

As described in Chapter 9, President Zia ul-Haq conducted his Afghan policy with the help of the mainstream Pakistani Jamiat-i-Islami (with which Hekmatyar's Hizbi-i-Islami was associated) and not with the JUI, and his policy instrument in the distribution of US and Saudi aid to the mujahideen was the ISI. The JUI, led during this period by Mufti Mehmood's son, Maulana Fazlur Rehman, had no political role. However, he set up hundreds of madrasas in the Pashtun belt of the NWFP and in Baluchistan, at which young Pakistanis and Afghan refugees were offered the chance of a free education, food, shelter and sometimes military training.

Most of these madrasas were in rural areas and in Afghan refugee camps; they were run by semi-educated mullahs whose reading of the shari'a texts was heavily influenced by the tribal code of the Pashtuns, the Pashtunwali. What was taught, and what the young rootless Afghans who were to become the future cadres of the Taliban imbibed, was often far removed from the original reformist ideology of the Deobandi school. This is reflected both in Mullah Omar's 'decrees' and in the aberrant behaviour of the religious police in enforcing the strictures imposed on women, especially in the cities.

The JUI itself remained in political opposition to the governments elected after President Zia's death in 1988. After the 1993 elections, however, it became part of the coalition government of Benazir Bhutto, and its leader, Fazlur Rehman, played a pivotal role in his advocacy of the Taliban, as described in Chapter 12. The Deobandi tradition, of which the JUI was an offshoot, did not provide the discipline of a centralized hierarchy, and many breakaway factions emerged. Some, like the virulently anti-Shia Sepah-i-Sebah and the Laskar-i-Jangvi, were extremist groups that specialized in terrorism and came under Osama bin Laden's sponsorship.

The most influential of the JUI factions was led by Maulana Samiul Haq, a religious and political leader who presided over the Dar-ul-Uloom Haqqania in Akhora Khattak in the NWFP. This theological school was founded in 1947 by his father, who was a student and teacher in Deoband. The Haqqania has a boarding school for 1500 students and a high school for

1000 students, and offers an eight-year master's course in Islamic studies and a doctorate after two additional years of study.

Many in the Taliban leadership studied at the Haqqania.[12] It was privately funded and charged its students nothing. Samiul Haq was an important mentor and adviser to the semi-educated Mullah Omar, who sought his advice on international relations and on important decisions. In response to a telephone call for help from Mullah Omar after the Taliban debacle in Mazar-i-Sharif in 1997, Haq closed down his school and sent his entire student body to fight alongside the Taliban. After their success in Mazar in 1998, Haq organized the dispatch of reinforcements for the Taliban militia by also closing down his 12 affiliated madrasas in the NWFP for a month. Another JUI faction ran the Jamiat-ul-Uloomi Islamiya in Binori near Karachi which had 8000 students including hundreds of Afghans, and was also well funded through donations from foreign Muslim benefactors. Several Taliban leaders also studied in Binori, which sent 600 students to join Taliban fighters in 1997.

The Taliban thus had social and ideological links to institutional elements within Pakistani society that provided much material support during their rise to power. They also had sources of support in Pakistan that lay outside the official structures of the government and the military, and from agencies such as the ISI. Unlike the mujahideen of the Afghan resistance during the 1980s, whose links with Pakistan were exclusively with the ISI and the Peshawar-based Afghan parties, the Taliban developed access to influential lobbies and vested interests that made them less beholden to the government of Pakistan and less amenable to official Pakistani pressures. This made them both autonomous and politically independent. The Taliban became their own masters.

Important sources of support for the Taliban movement were the private commercial truckers and transporters in the two border provinces who had developed a thriving business after the departure of Soviet troops, moving food and other commodities to needy Afghan cities and smuggling contraband on their return trips. They were exasperated by the civil war and the anarchy. For the Peshawar-based truckers, trading goods between Pakistan, Afghanistan and Uzbekistan, the Salang route had become dangerous, and the Quetta-based transporters had to contend with the rapacity of the Kandahari warlords who had set up dozens of toll-chains along their route from Pakistan to Herat. The Taliban occupation of Kandahar was a boon to the Quetta traders and they were the first to provide financial support to the Taliban movement.

The Taliban at first received a monthly retainer; but as they advanced westwards they demanded more funds. According to Ahmed Rashid, the Taliban received a 'donation' of 6 million rupees ($130,000) in a single day, and twice that amount the next day, from the Quetta transport mafia, as they prepared their attack on Herat in 1995. This attack had been encouraged by the transporters, contrary to ISI advice, as Ismail Khan had begun charging exorbitant transit fees. After this offensive, the route was made secure by the Taliban, with truck convoys going into Iran, Turkmenistan, the other CARs, and even Russia. After the Taliban occupation of Kabul in 1996, they levied a straight fee of 6000 rupees ($150) on a truck travelling from Peshawar to Kabul; truckers previously had to pay five to eight times as much to the warlords on this route. These levies became the principal source of revenue for the Taliban. They became more important when the Taliban imposed taxes both on poppy production and on the transport of opium and heroin, processed in laboratories located in the Tribal Agencies straddling the Durand Line.[13]

During the Afghan war, and under cover of the clandestine CIA–ISI operations in support of the mujahideen, an extensive trade in narcotics had developed in Pakistan. Producing around 800 tonnes of opium in the 1980s, Pakistan supplied some 70 per cent of the world's heroin in 1989. A 1992 study cited by Ahmed Rashid concluded: 'During the 1980s, corruption, covert operations and narcotics became intertwined in a manner which made it difficult to separate Pakistan's narcotics from more complex questions of regional security and insurgent warfare.'[14]

The extent of official collusion was brought to light when President Zia's newly appointed ISI chief, General Akhtar Abdur Rehman, had to remove his entire ISI staff in Quetta in 1983 because of their involvement in the drugs trade and the sale of CIA-supplied weapons. The largest drug seizures in Pakistan's history were carried out in 1986: an army officer was intercepted when driving from Peshawar to Karachi with 220 kilograms of high-grade heroin; two months later, an Air Force officer was caught on the same route with 220 kilograms of heroin, confessing that it was his fifth such mission. The US street value of just these two seizures was estimated at US$600 million, or the equivalent of the total value of US aid to Pakistan that year. Pakistan had limited jurisdiction over the Tribal Agencies where the raw opium was processed. The US Drug Enforcement Agency (DEA) had a large staff in Pakistan who identified 40 major narcotics syndicates during the 1980s, but none of them were broken up during that decade. The priority was to defeat the Soviet Union in the Afghan war.

It was only after the Soviet withdrawal, and in response to Western pressures, that official efforts were made to curtail the traffic. In 1992 the new army chief, General Asif Nawaz, led a concerted effort to root out the narcotics mafia that had developed in the armed forces. From 1989 to 1999 the United States made some US$100 million available to Pakistan for crop substitution projects in opium-growing areas. Poppy cultivation was reduced to 27 tonnes in 1997 and to two tonnes by 1999. But the drug dealers and the transportation mafia associated with them did not disappear. Drug money had so penetrated Pakistan's economy, politics and society that drug lords were even elected to parliament when democracy was restored after President Zia's death in 1988. Drug lords funded candidates who attained office in the first governments of Benazir Bhutto (1988-1990) and Nawaz Sharif (1990-93).

The production of the poppy, as well as the production of its derivatives, had been outlawed by Afghan governments before 1978. But the situation changed after the withdrawal of the Soviet forces from Afghanistan. In the ensuing civil war, the drugs trade served to finance the warlords. It became a major activity when the Taliban extended their control over the country.

The Taliban occupation of the southern provinces in 1994-95 gave a clear boost to the agricultural economy in the region because of the stability and security they provided; hence the initial reports of the beneficial effects of Taliban rule. Opium production in Helmand, which had expanded due to the entrepreneurial efforts of the clerical Akhunzada clan after the Soviet withdrawal, also received a boost. The other major opium-producing areas were also brought into the Taliban domain after their occupation of Jalalabad in 1996.

US estimates of poppy production based on satellite photographs were believed to give only half the picture. In 1994 field studies sponsored by the European Union and conducted by the UN's Drug Control Programme (UNDCP) revealed that 80,000 hectares of the best agricultural land was given over to the lucrative production of the poppy, yielding a harvest of over 3000 tonnes of raw opium. This made Afghanistan the world's largest producer after Burma. The provinces of Helmand and Nangarhar produced 1500 tonnes each, followed by Uruzgan with 150 tonnes and smaller quantities elsewhere. The country-wide production in 1994 represented an annual sale of the equivalent of $220 million.[15]

According to UNDCP statistics, opium production in Afghanistan reached 4600 tonnes in 1999, which was double the 1998 crop; 97 per cent of the crop was produced in Taliban-controlled areas. The 1999 opium harvest had an estimated value of some $183 million. Farmers paid ushr, an Islamic agricultural tax of 10 per cent to local Taliban commanders and mullahs. The Taliban also imposed a separate tax of 20 per cent on drug dealers, transporters and refining laboratories in the name of zakat, but this went directly into the Taliban war chest. These taxes were an essential source of income for the Taliban.[16]

The opium and heroin, processed in laboratories also located in Afghanistan, were smuggled by Pakistani and Afghan truckers across Pakistan, Iran, the CARs and Russia, with Chechnya becoming a major transit point for

Afghan heroin on its way to markets in Europe. The street value of the processed product in Europe and North America was inestimable, making it most lucrative for the buyers, the transporters, the dealers and the numerous other middlemen engaged in the illicit trade.

However, the largest source of income for the Taliban was derived from the smuggling of consumer and other durable goods. The traffic, which was highly profitable for the Afghan and Pakistani transporters and for the Taliban who imposed their transit taxes, was also highly damaging to Pakistan. It was made easier by two peculiar historical arrangements over which Pakistan had little control. The first was the special status of the autonomous Tribal Agencies on Pakistan's side of the Durand Line, the second was the Afghan Transit Trade (ATT).

While the Taliban made the roads secure for the traffic inside Afghanistan, the special status of the so-called Federal Administered Tribal Areas (FATA) – the five autonomous Tribal Agencies that straddle the Durand Line over which Pakistan technically has no jurisdiction – facilitated the traffic to and from Pakistan. Independent Pakistan had continued the British practice of paying stipends to the tribal maliks, and this system of patronage became much more extensive after 1979. The maliks received payments and weapons from the ISI and the Peshawar-based Afghan mujahideen parties for granting access across their territory for the ferrying of supplies and weapons for those fighting inside Afghanistan. The maliks also received payments for hiring out their pack animals, guides and manpower for transportation purposes. The chief ministers of the provincial governments of the NWFP and Baluchistan were also authorized to issue permits to the maliks to buy food in Pakistani markets to supply the mujahideen.

After the Soviet withdrawal, while the payments for rights of passage became less important, the permit system boomed, as tens of thousands of Afghan refugees returned, and there was a need for food imports in an agriculturally devastated country. When the repatriation surged, after the Najibullah regime was replaced by a mujahideen government and Russian commodity assistance dried up, there was a dramatic increase in the demand for food supplies from Pakistan. The permit system became a major source of patronage for the chief ministers to retain the loyalty of politicians and tribal chiefs in the two frontier provinces. As the provincial governors also had the power to issue export permits, there was considerable infighting going on when the Taliban arrived on the scene.

The Taliban's strong links with the JUI, now associated with the Benazir Bhutto government, enabled them to develop links with Pakistani business interests close to Benazir's husband, Asif Ali Zardari, who were given permits to export fuel to Afghanistan. As the Taliban's war machine expanded, permits for their fuel supplies from Pakistan, including considerable donations of fuel by Saudi Arabia, became a major source of patronage for the government and a lucrative source of income for Pakistani politicians and middlemen. Thus there were entrenched lobbies interested in promoting the Taliban drive for power. These vested interests also played a role in blocking the Bhutto government's efforts between 1994 and 1996 to persuade the Taliban to expand their political base.

A major loophole in the smuggling trade was the Afghan Transit Trade (ATT). In terms of an agreement concluded in 1950 between the Pakistani and Afghan governments, goods imported by the Afghan side that entered the port of Karachi were exempt from customs duties. As they were now carried in sealed containers, these were transported by truck across the border, de-stuffed on the Afghan side, and goods that had a ready market in Pakistan, such as electrical appliances, were smuggled back using mules through the porous borders of the frontier agencies. In one example cited by Rashid, Pakistan, which manufactured its own air-conditioners, imported just 30 million rupees' worth of foreign-made air-conditioners in 1994. A country almost bereft of electricity like Afghanistan imported through the ATT a billion dollars' worth of air-conditioners, which were sold in the informal bazaars (baras) in Pakistan. Local manufactures could not compete with the duty-free foreign products available at these baras, which were upgraded to include specialized shops selling brand-name products. 'The ATT has destroyed economic activity in the province and people have given up the idea of honest earnings and consider smuggling as their right', the chief minister of the NWFP is quoted as saying in December 1998.

In 1997 the World Bank estimated that the ATT between Afghanistan and Pakistan was worth $2.5 billion. This was equivalent to half of Afghanistan's estimated gross domestic product and 15 per cent of Pakistan's total trade. This trade had expanded to Dubai, Iran, the five CARs and the Caucasus. The total smuggling trade across the region, including ATT, was estimated at between $4.5 and $5 billion in 1999. Taliban taxes on this smuggling trade raised some $70 million towards their total war budget of $100 million. Their taxes on the drugs trade were supplemented by direct financial aid from Pakistan and, until 1998, from Saudi Arabia. Pakistan had been paying the Taliban some $10 million a year for the salaries of Taliban administrators. Osama bin Laden funded a brigade of Islamic militants that fought alongside the Taliban and financed offensives against Massoud's forces. Pakistan, and later Turkmenistan, provided indirect aid, such as fuel, technical help in maintaining airports and aircraft, electrical supply in the cities, road construction and other assistance that kept the Taliban war machine functioning.[17]

The long-term damage to Pakistan's economy was extensive and profound, and the social effects deleterious and insidious. According to officials of the

Central Board of Revenue interviewed by Rashid, it was estimated that the country lost 3.5 billion rupees in customs revenue in the financial year 1992–93, 11 billion rupees in 1993-94, 20 billion rupees in 1994-95, and 30 billion rupees ($600 million) in 1997-98 – a staggering escalation that coincided with the expansion of the Taliban hold on Afghanistan. The transport mafia also smuggled duty-free goods from the Persian Gulf on Ariana, the Afghan national airline now controlled by the Taliban, and exported heroin concealed in Afghan dried fruit consignments. The ATT fed the black economy in Pakistan, according to a study concluded in 1998 by the Pakistan Institute of Development Economics. The smuggling trade, which contributed some 100 billion rupees to the underground economy in 1993, escalated to over 300 billion rupees in 1998, or the equivalent of 30 per cent of the country's total import bill of $10 billion, or equal to the entire revenue collection target of 300 billion rupees for the fiscal year 1998-99. In addition the Afghan–Pakistan trade in drugs was estimated at 50 billion rupees annually. The black economy in Pakistan snowballed from 15 billion rupees in 1973 to 1115 billion rupees in 1996, with its share of GDP increasing from 20 per cent to 51 per cent. During the same period, tax evasion, including the non-payment of customs duties, increased from 1.5 billion to 152 billion rupees, accelerating at a rate of 88 billion rupees per year.

As the transport mafia expanded their trade, Pakistani entrepreneurs associated with them stripped Afghanistan's eastern forests of their timber, carried away scrap metal from disused factories, and destroyed tanks and vehicles, to be sold to steel mills in Pakistan. The theft of cars also became big business in Pakistan: in Karachi alone 65,000 vehicles were stolen in 1992–93, with the majority moved to Afghanistan to reappear later in Pakistan with all identification removed.

Corruption, tax evasion and other social evils have been endemic in Pakistan. But the opportunities for corruption increased by leaps and bounds during the Afghan war as unprecedented amounts of cash were injected into the economy through US largesse in bankrolling the mujahideen through their Pakistani ally. President Zia himself could not be accused of corruption (as his successors were), but he seemingly turned a blind eye to those in the civil and military establishment who had greedy eyes and few scruples to go with them.

What Ahmed Rashid calls 'an enormous nexus of corruption' emerged in Pakistan due to the ATT and the immensely lucrative smuggling trade:

> All the Pakistani agencies involved were taking bribes – Customs, Customs Intelligence, CBR, the Frontier Constabulary and the administrators in the tribal belt. Lucrative customs jobs on the Afghan border were 'bought' by applicants who paid bribes to senior bureaucrats to get the posting. These bribes, considered an investment, were then made up by the appointed officials who extracted bribes

from the ATT. ... This nexus extended to politicians and cabinet ministers in Baluchistan and the NWFP. The chief ministers and governors of the two provinces issued route permits for trucks to operate and wheat and sugar permits for the export of these commodities to Afghanistan. Senior army officers complained to me in 1995 and again in 1996, that the competition between the chief ministers and governors of the two provinces in issuing route permits was a major source of corruption paralyzing the entire administrative machinery, interfering and often at odds with the ISI's policy on Afghanistan and creating widespread Taliban 'control' over Pakistani politicians.[18]

Paul Kennedy, the US historian, has stated: 'Ten years of active involvement in the Afghan war has changed the social profile of Pakistan to such an extent that any government faces serious problems in effective governance. Pakistan's society is now more fractured, inundated with sophisticated weapons, brutalized due to growing civic violence and overwhelmed by the spread of narcotics.'

When General Pervez Musharraf overthrew the elected government of Nawaz Sharif and installed a military regime in October 1999, Pakistan was on the verge of economic and social collapse. It owed over $30 billion in debts to its international creditors, incurring a crippling debt-service burden. The economic sanctions imposed as a result of Pakistan's nuclear tests caused further hardships, including the drying up of international investments.

In his first television address to the nation to justify his coup, the general referred to the failure of Pakistan's elites. He proceeded to name them one by one: the political elite, the civil service, the armed forces, the industrial and commercial classes, the universities, and so on. He then spelled out his immediate agenda – rooting out corruption and tax evasion, and the establishment of an accountable administration and a civil society – before restoring the country to constitutional rule after a two-year period.

What he failed to mention were the social and political realities that had emerged in Pakistani society, including the armed forces, that would impose major constraints on his government's freedom of action both domestically and internationally. These were related to what came to be called the 'talibanization' of Pakistan.

The same Deobandi madrasas in Pakistan that had spawned the Taliban's fighting cadres continue to churn out tens of thousands of young Pakistanis who have nothing but rage and hatred in their hearts towards those whom they consider the enemies of Islam. The madrasas are run by semi-literate mullahs who, like the Taliban, have distorted views of Islamic history and civilization, indeed, if they have any knowledge of history at all. These semi-educated teachers inculcate a singularly perverse interpretation of the shari'a that has little to do with the original teachings of the Deobandi school in India. Because of the Saudi influence that followed Saudi funding, their ideology, as in the case of the Taliban, moved closer to Wahhabism, the official ideology of Saudi Arabia whose major exponent was Osama bin Laden. Their increasing influence spawned the sectarian violence targeting Shi'ias that have become an almost daily source of tension in Pakistani cities.

The Pakistani neo-Taliban movements came to wield considerable political influence not only in the Pashtun areas of the North West Frontier Province and in Baluchistan but also in the Punjab and in Sind. Indeed most of the 8000 Pakistani militants who joined the Taliban's successful military offensive against Massoud's forces in Taloqan in September 1999 were not Pashtuns but Punjabis and Sindhis. They could not have entered Afghanistan in such large numbers without the knowledge and even support of Pakistan. But there were no Western protests. Generally speaking, Pakistan was given a free hand in Afghanistan, in return for exercising restraint in Kashmir, for fear of destabilizing what had now become a nuclear state.

Although the Pakistan government was forced to withdraw its troops from the Line of Control in Kashmir after the Kargil crisis in the spring of 1999, General Musharraf's military government had little influence over the Deobandi groups and their sympathizers who provide unstinting support for the Muslim cause in Kashmir. As this cause is highly popular in Pakistan, including the armed forces, any efforts to rein in the armed Pakistani militants who infiltrated Kashmir, along with the Afghan and Arab militants of the bin Laden terrorist network who received their training in Afghan camps, would be perceived as a betrayal of the Kashmiri cause that Pakistan officially upholds.

The concept and practice of jihad, or holy war in the cause of Islam, which had disappeared in the Muslim world after the tenth century, was revived in a big way during the Afghan resistance against the Soviet invaders. The Soviet withdrawal was popularly seen in the Muslim world as a victory for jihad, for Islam. Islamic militants, such as the Arab volunteers mobilized by bin Laden who fought alongside the Afghan mujahideen, have since misapplied jihad by turning it into a weapon against any group or state that is perceived as an 'enemy of Islam'. The Taliban who first presented themselves as a reform movement, then sought to derive their legitimacy from jihad, waged this time against their Muslim opponents.[19]

The militants of the bin Laden terrorist networks were drawn from an arc of Arab states from north Africa to west Asia, whose governments had lost legitimacy in their eyes. Although allowing varying degrees of democratic expression, these states remain, in the last analysis, unaccountable to their largely Sunni Muslim populations. They are either autocratic monarchies (Morocco, Jordan, Saudi Arabia, the United Arab Emirates), or outright dictatorships (Algeria, Libya, Iraq), or dominated by wealthy political and economic elites (Tunisia, Egypt, Lebanon). These are admittedly broad generalizations that mask the more complex profiles of the individual states. But they are all ruled by political elites sustained by the military and by industrial and commercial classes who own most of the economic assets. Their ostentatious wealth is in stark contrast to the poverty of the general population, as any visitor to the most populous of the Arab countries, Egypt, can see at first hand.

A substantial proportion of the population of these Arab states occupy the lowest quarter of the age pyramid. The educated youth face bleak prospects of gainful employment and even bleaker prospects of upward social mobility in these countries. Where the future offers no hope, the psychological pressures to escape – to seek freedom and economic opportunity in liberal democracies – are overwhelming. Where legal means to emigrate do not exist, uncounted numbers take the risk of placing themselves in the hands of unscrupulous 'people smugglers'. The grim sight of drowned bodies washed up on the shores of the Mediterranean in recent years bears silent testimony to the desperation of these young men and women. Those who remain are politically radicalized, turning their frustrations and despair into rage directed at their own governments and the foreign states that support them. The rage is often articulated in the language of Islamic discourse, which attacks the corruption of the ruling classes and the failure of their governments to establish social justice. Some turn to Islamic militancy.

In Algeria the frustrations of the population found expression in the widespread support given to the 'political Islam' of the Islamic Salvation Front (FIS), which won the first round of voting in the 1991 elections. The FIS was subsequently severely repressed by the military and forced to disband. But its more radical elements formed the Groupe islamique armée (GIA) that resorted to guerrilla warfare. Their unbridled ferocity has been unleashed not only against the symbols of the state, such as the police and the military, but has also been directed against innocent civilians in the form of wholesale massacres.

Similar sentiments of frustration and rage inform those segments of Pakistani society that have been 'talibanized' and are most responsive to the kind of radical Islamic discourse that is articulated by those such as Osama bin Laden. The functioning institutions that the British colonial administration left behind – the rule of law, the independence of the judiciary, an upright and dedicated civil service – were undermined over the years by the corruption of the political process. General Musharraf spoke of the failure of the elites. As in the Arab states, those who have been able to enrich themselves in a society where loyalty to one's family and class counts more than loyalty to the state, in a situation of generalized corruption, there are real risks of an implosion. It has been estimated that in Pakistan 10 per cent of the population own 80 per cent of the economic assets. The social resentments that are provoked by the contrast between the opulence of the few and the poverty of the many are fertile grounds for the radicalization of the many and do not augur well for the future.

If one sits in the lavishly furnished drawing rooms of the elite in Islamabad or Lahore, sips the premium Scotch served by one's most hospitable hosts, and listens to the worldly conversation, one is transported to a different world, far from the madding crowd. The talk usually turns to the progress of sons and daughters studying in the United States, or of brothers and cousins who have prospered in the West. If one is tactful, bringing politics and religion into the conversation is best avoided. To talk of India would invite diatribes. And it is impolite to abuse the hospitality of one's hosts, to enjoy the rich food, and to talk of the impoverished, illiterate and uneducated millions in a land that is otherwise rich in natural and human resources and reasonably well endowed with a modern infrastructure. Such a subject amounts to implicit criticism by a foreigner of the failure of this same educated and Westernized elite to construct a civil society. It is also the failure of a ethnically divided state whose sole basis for existence was religion. Internationally there is also talk of 'a failed state'.

Portraits of the 'Founder of the Nation' hang in every government office, but Jinnah's vision of a secular Pakistan has become as alien to the Muslim masses as Gandhian ideals have become irrelevant to the elected rulers of a secular India. But there are more Muslims in multi-ethnic, multi-cultural and democratic India. And Indian Muslims have reached the highest offices of state, as presidents, supreme court judges, cabinet ministers at the federal and state levels, even generals, not to mention national heroes in the country's touring cricket teams. Pakistan's religious minorities, such as the nation's 2 million indigenous Christians, have no such luck.[20]

CHAPTER 15

The Withered State (1996–2001)

In the territory of the blind the one-eyed man is king – Erasmus

T he leader of the Taliban, Mullah Mohammad Omar, was born in 1959 into a family of poor landless peasants belonging to the Hotak clan of the Ghilzai Pashtuns. The family had no status, tribally or socially. As a young man of 21, Omar had to fend for his fatherless family and, needing a job, moved to the village of Singesar in the Maiwand district of Kandahar province, where he became the village mullah and opened a madrasa. Between 1989 and 1992, after the Soviet withdrawal, he joined the fighting ranks of the Khalis faction of the Hizbi-i-Islami against the Najibullah regime. He lost an eye in combat. The installation of a mujahideen government in Kabul had not brought peace, and groups of madrasa students and disillusioned mujahideen gathered round Omar to discuss what they could do to end the depredations of the Kandahari warlords. Their concerns were immediate. In early 1994 Omar enlisted the help of 30 madrasa students to free two teenage girls who had been abducted and raped by a warlord. He also intervened, or so the story goes, when two warlords fought over a young boy they wanted as a catamite. The victims were rescued and summary justice meted out to the perpetrators. Omar's reputation spread, and other appeals for his intervention began to pour in. The rest is history.

The Taliban militants chose Omar as their leader for his piety and not for any special qualities, charismatic or other. In March 1996, in anticipation of the projected Taliban attack on Kabul to topple the Rabbani government, some 1200 ulema and mullahs from around the country gathered in a shura in Kandahar and nominated Omar as Amir al-Muminin (Commander of the Believers), a military title first assumed by the second Islamic caliph, Omar, in Medina. Mullah Omar wrapped the Cloak of the Prophet around him to give him Islamic legitimacy as amir of Afghanistan. No Afghan ruler had adopted the Islamic title since Dost Mohammad in 1834; the use of the Prophet's cloak, preserved in Kandahar, was even more symbolic. The council that nominated him was not the traditional Afghan loya jirga but the Arab shura, an Islamic council convened to achieve community consensus (*ijma*).

The method of selection was a throwback to the shura convened by the third of the first four 'Rightly Guided Caliphs', 'Uthman, to elect his successor. The legitimacy that this act conferred was Islamic, thereby making it both religious and political. As Olivier Roy says, 'one need only skim the literature of the ulemas, or the Islamists, or listen to the sermons in the mosques, to admit that there is an Islamic political imagination dominated by a single paradigm: that of the first community of believers at the time of the Prophet and of the first four caliphs.'[1]

In Afghanistan the ulema directly and collectively assumed power, electing Mullah Omar, who was neither charismatic nor a dynamic tribal leader, as their amir. Although of undeniably Deobandi inspiration, they applied a 'legal system' based exclusively on their particular interpretation of the shari'a that incorporated elements of the Pashtun tribal code, the Pashtunwali. But when the two were in conflict or in contradiction, the primacy of the shari'a was re-affirmed, as in Mullah Omar's 1998 decree restoring certain property rights of women that the code violated. Despite their anti-Shi'a stance and bloodily repressive actions against the Hazaras, which is Deobandi and Wahhabi in inspiration, the Taliban formed an alliance subsequently with the Hazara Shi'ite religious hierarchy led by Shaykh Akbari. This alliance was founded on their common relationship to the categories of the ulema and would be incomprehensible in a narrowly tribal or ethnically oriented system.[2]

The shura left unanswered the question of how the Taliban would govern Afghanistan, nor did it lay out any plans for the country's economic and social development. Ruling structures did, however, emerge after the ousting of the Rabbani government in September 1996. These consisted of a ten-member Supreme Shura in Kandahar presided over by Omar and two committees that reported to him and took directives from him – a military shura and a Kabul shura. The Kabul shura was in fact a sort of cabinet with each of its 14 members assuming nominal ministerial functions.

Although members of the Kabul shura, the 'ministers', were more pragmatic and flexible – as in their dealings with the United Nations and NGOs – their 'decisions' were often overruled by Mullah Omar and his dogmatic Kandahar shura. There was thus a confusing dichotomy of power that did not make life easy for those who had to deal with them. The Taliban had a unified but not a monolithic power structure.

When the mujahideen entered Kabul in April 1992, there still remained a government infrastructure of ministries and municipalities functioning chiefly at the lower administrative levels. This infrastructure collapsed after the arrival in 1996 of the Taliban in the city, which they considered a nest of corruption. Their subsequent pruning of the government bureaucracy was part of their explicit policy of rooting out corruption. The Taliban replaced all senior Hazara, Tajik and Uzbek bureaucrats with inexperienced Pashtuns so that ministries effectively ceased to function. Their exclusion of women from employment also meant that schools ceased to operate, the majority of teachers being women. Their gender policies likewise sorely affected the health services.

There were no native Kabulis in the Kabul shura that dealt with the day-to-day problems of government. It referred important decisions to the Supreme Shura in Kandahar, which was dominated by Mullah Omar's original friends and colleagues, mainly Durrani Pashtuns. They were called 'the Kandaharis'. Although the core membership appeared permanent, provincial governors, military commanders, tribal elders and ulema took part in the Kandahar shura when important questions were debated or when strategy was being planned. It was thus in practice a loose and amorphous body.

Senior Taliban officials in Kabul, Herat and Mazar, such as the governors, mayors and police chiefs, were invariably Kandahari Pashtuns who did not speak Dari, the lingua franca of these cities, or did not speak it well. There were some non-Kandaharis among the provincial governors, but they were all from outside the region they administered, and were prevented from building up a local power-base by Omar, who shifted them around, or sent them as commanders to the battle fronts. Their power was even further reduced by the lack of funds at their disposal to carry out any serious economic rehabilitation or development. Thus political power was centralized at the level of the Kandaharis under Omar, to whom all revenues were also remitted. He reportedly made payments in cash, for such items as the salaries of administrators and military officers, from tin trunks kept under his bed.

Mullah Omar also headed the military shura which had a chief of general staff and chiefs of staff for the army and air force. But there was no clearly discernible hierarchical structure of officers and commanders. The Taliban movement began and largely remained a military organization, composed initially of madrasa student volunteers and defectors from the mujahideen and warlord militias, and later enlarged by conscription. Individual Pashtun commanders from specific Pashtun regions were responsible for recruiting men, paying them and looking after their needs in the field, acquiring the resources to do so – money, food, fuel, transport, weapons and ammunition – from the military shura. The majority of Taliban fighters were not paid salaries and it was their commander who was responsible for paying his men an adequate sum of money when they returned to their families on leave. Those who were paid regular salaries were those from the former communist armed forces, such as those commanded by Najibullah's defence minister, General Tanai, who defected to Pakistan after his failed coup in 1990 and was later mobilized by the ISI to assist the Taliban in their drive to power. These Pashtun mercenaries – tank drivers, gunners, pilots and mechanics –

perhaps made all the difference in making the Taliban an effective fighting machine.

According to Ahmed Rashid, the Taliban's standing army had never numbered more than 25,000 to 30,000 fighters, although this would have been increased before new offensives, such as those that led to the capture of Kabul in 1996 and Mazar in 1998. Madrasa students from Pakistan, who by 1999 had made up some 30 per cent of the Taliban's military manpower, also served for short periods before returning home and sending back fresh recruits. Eight thousand Pakistani militants are reported to have participated in the capture of Massoud's urban stronghold of Taloqan in September 1999.[3] The Taliban's haphazard styles of recruitment and remuneration more resembled the traditional *lashkar* (local militia) that could be quickly mobilized by a tribal leader to defend tribal territory or to fight a local feud. The lashkar were unpaid volunteers who shared in any loot captured from the enemy. Taliban fighters were, however, prohibited from looting, but their discipline could sometimes break down, as when they took Mazar in 1998.

Any potential that the country might have had for the re-constitution of the viable administrative structures necessary for a functioning state was compromised by the almost total depletion of the educated professional classes. Their exodus began in the 1980s, accelerated after the installation of the Rabbani government in 1992, when anti-communists were joined in their exile by trained communist cadres, and continued after the Taliban axed the remaining bureaucracy and closed the university. But the educated classes represented a minority who were unlikely to end their exile, particularly in Western countries.[4]

Far larger numbers of farmers and other ordinary Afghans made up the world's largest groups of refugees in the two neighbouring countries. Twenty years of foreign invasion, civil war and anarchy in one of the poorest countries in the world produced the largest single refugee exodus in the last half of the twentieth century.[5] The numbers peaked on the eve of the Soviet withdrawal at 3,722,000 Afghan refugees in Pakistan and 2,940,000 in Iran. From then onwards, repatriation movements began to take place, some 'spontaneously' (that is without assistance), but the majority with UNHCR assistance. The return movements took on dramatic proportions after the fall of the Najibullah regime in April 1992: a total of 1,568,000 from Pakistan and Iran in 1992, and a further 964,000 in 1993.[6]

The core of the UNHCR's repatriation package in Pakistan was a cash grant to defray transportation and other expenses, and an adequate stock of wheat distributed by the World Food Programme (WFP) to cover the basic food needs of each returning family until they could harvest their first crops in their home villages. This package was available only to refugees registered in the camps who had received passbooks with which they could draw their periodic food rations. Prior to repatriation, the passbooks were surrendered in return for the grants of cash and wheat. The system was liable to abuse. When swamped by the sheer numbers of new arrivals, the UNHCR and the government had distributed ration books collectively to their group leaders and maliks who drew rations on their behalf. For one thing, the size of families as claimed could not be verified; sometimes cleverly forged passbooks were produced. The abuses, particularly prevalent in Baluchistan, were tolerated for many years because of the trickle-down effect on the large population of unregistered refugees inside and outside the established camps. Afghan group solidarity would not allow any of their members to be short of food. In 1990–91, however, the registration system was re-validated by the wholesale replacement of the old passbooks with new fool-proof documents including photographs of family members.

When the encashment of passbooks began on a large scale during the massive repatriation movements of 1992–93, the passbooks acquired a market value of their own: it became clear that some were being sold by group leaders and refugees who had no intention of repatriating. Partly as a result of the application of stricter controls, tying encashment to actual repatriation, or because of the intensification of the civil war, the repatriation process lost momentum after 1993, but picked up again after 1995 when the Taliban extended their control and brought security to those provinces in the south and east where most of the refugees in Pakistan originated.

Following recommendations from its Executive Committee that the UNHCR 'intensify its activities in the safe areas of Afghanistan for the return of refugees and displaced persons to their places of origin', greater rehabilitation efforts were deployed within Afghanistan. In Pakistan the total assisted caseload fell below the 1 million mark by mid-1995. The WFP brought its food distribution in the camps to an end, and the UNHCR reoriented its activities from the provision of care and maintenance to the encouragement of refugee self-reliance. Repatriation assistance was directly linked to rehabilitation assistance by transferring the encashment process to Afghanistan proper, and by increasing the cash grant, with UNHCR/WFP strengthening their presence in safe areas and involving the local shuras in the work of rehabilitation.[7]

The extraordinary conditions under which agencies of the United Nations system had to operate during the protracted Afghan civil war revealed their statutory and operational limitations; they also demonstrated that these agencies would need to come up with novel and imaginative solutions if they were to carry out their mandates in a meaningful way.

The agencies of the UN system are non-partisan. In the polarized world before Gorbachev, however, international relief efforts for Afghan refugees led by an apolitical UNHCR essentially funded a rear base for mujahideen fighters backed militarily by the United States through its Pakistani surrogate. These efforts were complemented by USAID-funded cross-border projects to build the grassroots capacity of resistance forces within Afghanistan. Between 1986 and 1990, $60.6 million was committed for health projects, $30.2 million for education and $60 million for agriculture. These projects were implemented by NGOs who saw themselves as front-line operators in the war against the Soviets, or, more innocently, as humanitarian workers braving great dangers and hardships to bring essential services to embattled poverty-stricken communities.

After the Geneva Accords of 1988 a single UN entity was established to coordinate all humanitarian efforts inside and outside Afghanistan. This was the UN Office of the Coordinator for Afghanistan (UNOCA), headed by a distinguished former High Commissioner for Refugees, Prince Sadruddin Aga Khan. UNOCA's ambitious plans for the relief and rehabilitation of the stricken populations and for reconstruction of the country, code-named Operation Salaam, were aborted by the continuing civil war and the anarchic conditions. But numerous NGOs that had also mobilized for the effort continued to carry out rehabilitation work wherever possible. Their work received far less publicity in the media than the civil war and carnage. Some of them, like the Swedish Committee for Afghanistan (SCA), or the Danish Committee for Aid to Afghan Refugees (DACAAR), were generously funded by their national governments, and served also as implementing agencies for the UNHCR, UNDP and USAID projects in Afghanistan as well as in Pakistan. NGO coordination and the sharing of information was ensured by an umbrella organization based in Peshawar, the Agency Coordination Bureau for Afghan Relief (ACBAR). In the 1990s there were some 70 NGOs and contractors participating in this voluntary body, with a combined budget of US$80 million.[8]

UNOCA was replaced by the UN Office of the Coordinator for Humanitarian Affairs in Afghanistan (UNOCHA). But a purely humanitarian response in the face of the complex political realities on the ground proved inadequate; negotiating agreements between the warring parties to enable humanitarian assistance to be delivered across political and military lines was no substitute for serious diplomatic efforts aimed at bringing peace through an overall political settlement. At the end of 1993 a UN Special Mission in Afghanistan (UNSMA) was authorized by the General Assembly and a former Tunisian foreign minister, Mehmoud Mestiri, was appointed to mediate between the parties in the conflict.

There are aspects to Mestiri's handling of his mediation that could have laid him open to the charge of having been an inept outsider (like his successors during their even more brief tenures) with little understanding of the internal dynamics and complexities of the Afghan conflicts. UN peacemaking efforts were confined to a narrow and fruitless world of ceasefires, exchanges of prisoners and talks about talks. But a far more serious reason for the failure of the mediation was the UN's reluctance to condemn outright those of its member states that continued to interfere by supporting the warring factions for their own ends. In his 1997 Report on Afghanistan, UN Secretary-General Kofi Annan candidly suggested: 'It could be argued that the role of the United Nations in Afghanistan is little more than an alibi to provide cover for the inaction – or worse – of the international community at large.'[9]

In July 1997 Kofi Annan appointed a special envoy, Lakhdar Brahimi, a former Algerian foreign minister, to take in hand the diplomatic efforts to bring the warring factions to the negotiating table. But by this time the situation on the ground had so evolved that there was a polarization of the parties in the conflict: a tenuous and weakened Northern Alliance opposing the Taliban but in virtual retreat before their advance. With their capture of Mazar-i-Sharif in September 1998, the Taliban effectively imposed the military solution that they had wanted all along, by refusing any power-sharing arrangements proposed during the UN mediation. With over 90 per cent of the country under Taliban control, there was now a virtual *pax talibana* that brought new problems and raised new issues and dilemmas for the international community.

International agencies providing relief and basic services to the stricken populations in Kabul and elsewhere had to operate under the most difficult conditions. As Lakhdar Brahimi stated bluntly: 'In the north we have complete insecurity for our aid operations and in the south we have a hell of a horrible time working with the Taliban.' The UN withdrew from all northern areas when its offices were sacked and goods looted during fighting in Mazar-i-Sharif in 1997. The UN also had to withdraw from Kandahar and southern Afghanistan for three months in 1998 because of a dispute with the Taliban over an issue affecting its Muslim female expatriate staff. In the course of a shouting match, the peg-legged Taliban governor threw a teapot at a senior UN official. The head of UNOCHA, Alfredo Witschi-Cestari, was eventually constrained to leave the country because of his forceful advocacy of international norms and principles.[10]

The first of the dilemmas was a practical one: how could the aid agencies deal with a group that claimed to be the government but could assume no governmental functions, had no administrative capacity, and appeared to have abdicated responsibility for the ordinary welfare of Afghan communities. As summed up by Witschi-Cestari: 'Although the Taliban technically control most of Afghanistan, they do not have the means to administer and run public services in a centralized fashion: each region is administered by local authorities who appear to act quite autonomously.'[11]

A second major dilemma raised some important questions of principle. After their occupation of Herat and Kabul, the Taliban closed all schools for girls, forbade female employment (which meant in effect that boys' schools could also not function as the majority of their teachers were women), confined women to their homes, imposed the *burqa* – a tight head covering that allowed only the eyes to be seen – on women venturing outside their homes, and prohibited male doctors from attending to their women patients in the few functioning hospitals and clinics. These injunctions were carried out by an ever-vigilant religious police on the Saudi Arabian model called the Ministry for the Promotion of Virtue and the Suppression of Vice. It was perhaps the only well-manned and well-funded institution to function under the Taliban.

Taliban strictures came to a head in 1998: new edicts, inspired by their own bizarre version of the shari'a, were issued, stipulating the exact lengths of beard to be mandatorily worn by adult males, prescribing a list of Muslim names to be given to newborn children, abolishing the celebration of the traditional spring festival of Nawroz (considered an un-Islamic relic of ancient pagan rites), enforcing the previous ban on all music and dancing and the possession of music tapes and video cassettes, and the flying of kites. But it was the gender issue that raised the greatest international outcry. In Kabul the Taliban shut down the few makeshift schools for girls organized in private homes by volunteer female teachers; the religious police forced women off the streets and insisted that householders blacken their windows to render their women invisible from the street.[12]

Taliban hardliners also seemed intent on forcing UN agencies and NGOs that employed large numbers of educated Afghan women in their programmes to leave the country by provoking a number of incidents that tested their patience to the limit. In February 1998 the UN halted all its aid operations in Kandahar and pulled out its staff after the Taliban had beaten up some of them. In June the Taliban barred all women from attending general hospitals, and ordered all Muslim female expatriate staff visiting or working in the country to be chaperoned by a male blood relative (*mehram*) – an impossible demand to meet, as agencies had increased the number of female aid-workers to satisfy previous Taliban pressures and to gain access to Afghan women needing help. The Taliban then insisted that all NGOs working in Kabul move out of their offices and relocate to a single disused and decrepit building, the former Kabul Polytechnic. Twenty out of 30 NGOs voted to pull out of the country if the Taliban demand was not retracted, but the Taliban insisted that the issue was not negotiable. The European Union (EU), a major funding source for NGOs, suspended all humanitarian aid to areas under Taliban control. Lakhdar Brahimi went public regarding the UN's frustrations by saying that the Taliban was 'an organization that hands out edicts that prevent us from doing our job'. But the Taliban did not relent. On 20 July they closed down all NGO offices by force, and an exodus of foreign staff began. On the same day the bodies of two staff members from the UNHCR and WFP who had previously been kidnapped were found in Jalalabad, but no explanations for their deaths were offered by the Taliban.

No one questions the need for humanitarian assistance in Afghanistan – a country that has long been near the bottom of the world's list in terms of human development.[13] Over 20 years of war, during which over a million people are estimated to have died and 700,000 women been made widows, added new records to the grim list: the number of refugees and internally displaced people, the increasingly large numbers dependent on food support, the proportion of physically and mentally disabled people, the widespread lethal presence of land mines and unexploded ordnance, the collapse of industrial activities and of the opportunities for gainful employment outside a precarious indigenous agriculture. The UNDP dropped Afghanistan from its rankings in the 1997 edition of its *UN Development Report* when the gathering of relevant data became unmanageable.

Three successive years of drought made the situation infinitely worse. According to the UN some 3.8 million people were close to famine conditions. A three-member USAID technical team that surveyed affected areas of western and northern Afghanistan in June 2001 confirmed the possibility of starvation unless urgent measures were taken. At the time, the WFP was feeding 3 million Afghans a day, in the cities, in camps for internally displaced persons and in rural areas, with food mainly donated by the United States. Were the efforts of the UN system and of the NGOs to be disrupted for any reason, there would have been a colossal humanitarian disaster.

The moral case for international assistance to reconstruct a country that was a surrogate for the selfish and callous geo-politics of foreign powers also could not be in doubt. Furthermore, in a country where the authorities had abdicated their responsibility for governance except in matters of security, and priority was accorded to implementing the shari'a and to fighting their enemies, foreign assistance became the only source of life-giving support outside agriculture.[14]

Quite rightly the provision of aid was not factored in as a bargaining counter in the diplomatic negotiations of the UN mediators to force the warring parties to the conference table. The ICRC's position had always been clear: political considerations should in no way be an obstacle to carrying out its mandate or compromise its provision of humanitarian assistance to those in need. But UNICEF was led to suspend its operations on the grounds that the Taliban strictures on women violated international norms and human rights covenants. Thus the issue of conditionality, that lurks among the numerous dilemmas that agencies have to face when delivering humanitarian assistance to needy populations in war regions, was brought to the fore in Afghanistan. Sergio Vieira de Mello, the UN's then under-secretary-general for humanitarian affairs, stated the problem succinctly: 'how to balance the need to provide humanitarian assistance, while promoting international human rights standards in an inconducive environment'. As Michael Keating observes:

> Afghanistan is thus currently the crucible for many dilemmas facing the global assistance community, including how to operationalise UN human rights and gender equity principles, how to reconcile these principles with the dictates of International Humanitarian Law, how to reorder the way in which the assistance actors work with each other in complex emergency situations and how to reenergise and reform the UN.[15]

In the spring of every year, the heads of specialized agencies of the UN system, the World Bank and the IMF, meet in closed session in Geneva, in the little-known Administrative Committee on Coordination (ACC). It is presided over by the UN secretary-general. At its April 1997 session the members agreed to strengthen efforts in crisis countries where the UN operated social and economic programmes tied to peace-building political programmes mandated by the Security Council or the General Assembly. It chose two countries as test cases, one of which was Afghanistan. In January that year, leading actors in the aid community had also got together in an international forum in Ashkabad, Turkmenistan, to address the dilemmas and to reach consensus on the objectives, principles and content of international assistance to Afghanistan.

The ACC's own decision resulted in the drafting in November 1997 of a Strategic Framework for Afghanistan, which attempted to spell out explicitly the responsibilities for the prolongation of the social, economic and humanitarian crisis in Afghanistan, and to place the work of the international assistance community in a realistic geo-political and economic context.

A parallel and related UN initiative was the adoption of a Common Assistance Strategy for the formulation of a Common Programme for Afghanistan, to be developed in coordination with donors and NGOs. Sergio Vieira de Mello surveyed the prospects after a mission to Afghanistan in February 1998. While he found support for this innovative approach among donors and local actors, there was less enthusiasm at the headquarters of UN agencies. This is not surprising, since agencies have different mandates, management structures, procedures and control mechanisms. There was also the traditional penchant for jealously guarding their respective territories. Among the points highlighted by de Mello in the Afghan context was a lack of clarity between relief and rehabilitation programmes, and the lack of common policies with regard to education, health and employment. Agencies also had difficulties reconciling their priorities: for example, nearly all agencies were involved in income-generating projects, but there was no clear policy nor a clear division of labour. At a more prosaic level, de Mello was surprised to find that in Faizabad, the chief town in Commander Massoud's Badakhshan, there were four agencies operating four separate offices, duplicating administrations, communications systems and other facilities, equipment and guards. Usually in foreign aid programmes, priorities are set and projects integrated at the national level by governments. But in Afghanistan the lack of a proper government threw the burden of integration on the UN and its agencies. The idea of a Common Fund for the Common Programme was temporarily shelved owing to the resistance of the agencies. However, an initiative called the Poverty Eradication and Community Empowerment Programme (PEACE) was found to be having some success.

PEACE was launched in 1997 by the UNDP with a US$33 million budget to address humanitarian and developmental needs, and to build up social and economic infrastructures in the context of the breakdown at all levels of governance in Afghanistan. A number of UN agencies and NGOs participate in this programme according to their areas of expertise and in selected locations. UN staff sit down with the local community at each location and work out what needs to done. In the words of the then UN Coordinator for Afghanistan:

> The community elects a development committee, following the traditional Afghan shura principle, which is responsible for representing local points of view, for working out how activities are carried out, and finding people to take part in them. In this way, the programme hopes to create a sense of community ownership for rehabilitation and reconstruction initiatives and enhance people's ability to rebuild over the longer term without external assistance.[16]

This grassroots approach offers some interesting perspectives. On the one hand it relates to an alternative model of economic and social development which might be made viable and sustainable by empowering the target community or social group.[17] On the other hand, such an approach recognizes and validates the central fact of Afghan political culture, namely the qawm. Essentially the qawm is a community of interests, local and traditional, cemented by kinship, tribal or other ties. Another way of characterizing the qawm is to describe it as a solidarity group (encompassing family lineages, clans, tribes or sectarian, linguistic or ethnic groups) that is politically self-governing and economically self-sustaining. This traditional mode of community governance has proved remarkably resilient. It has survived despite the efforts of successive rulers and bureaucracies in Kabul to bring it within the strait-jacket of a modern nation-state, on the questionable assumption that the European construct of the nation-state was a *summum bonum*, a kind of political form of organization that is self-evident, a 'natural' culmination of all societies.[18]

In discussions in the literature on Afghanistan after the arrival of the Taliban, it became customary to refer to the 'fragmentation' of the country, or of its being a 'failed state'. The ethnic, linguistic, tribal and other fault lines of Afghanistan, obscured at times, have always existed below the surface and explain the country's complex politics. In an interesting essay, the anthropologist Bernt Glatzer outlines the basic organizing principles of the major ethno-linguistic groups, defining ethnicity not as an innate quality of a social group, but as a relation between groups, with each group affirming its identity in contrast to other groups. He makes the point that ethnicity in Afghanistan is concerned with social boundary-making, not the break-up of the country. In fact none of the warring factions, however bitter and bloody their conflicts, had ever envisaged such a contingency. Glatzer's second major insight is that tribal and clan systems of solidarity made for resilience and stability in times of turmoil; indeed, where they were functioning well, presumably in their own Pashtun regions, the Taliban had not dared interfere with them.[19]

We might add that the Taliban owed their success in disarming the Pashtun warlords to the fact that they were perceived as outsiders, motivated by religion, and not identified with any particular tribal affiliation. This was in marked contrast to the fierce resistance they encountered when they attempted to disarm the Uzbek and Hazara militias in Mazar-i-Sharif in September 1997.

As regards the failure of the state, what failed in Afghanistan was the effort by successive rulers in Kabul since Abdur Rahman to build and impose a strong, centralized nation-state with foreign assistance. This failure was not a bad thing in itself. In the name of national unity, the 'Iron Amir' brought under his direct rule (as we have seen in Chapter 1) all autonomous local communities, Pashtun and non-Pashtun, by brutally decimating their leadership through executions, confiscations of property, exile or imprisonment, or by relocating entire populations. His state-building was accomplished by coopting members of his family and of their Mohammadzai clan into the centralized state structures, thus establishing paternalism, nepotism, favouritism and tribalism as the constitutive principles of the Afghan state until the communist seizure of power. Twenty years of civil war dismantled the old state and tribal networks of power and authority, leaving the field open to the Taliban.

Curiously enough, in the five years after they occupied Kabul, the heart and symbol of past state authority, the Taliban did not appear to have given any priority to state-building, nor to the development of the economic and social infrastructure that is essential for the functioning of a viable state and for the welfare of its citizens. According to Ahmed Rashid: 'the limited reconstruction which the Taliban has undertaken is entirely limited to improving the efficiency of smuggling and drugs trafficking, such as repairing roads, setting up petrol pumps, and inviting US businessmen to set up a mobile telephone network which will qualitatively speed up the movement of drugs and illicit trade'.[20]

In fact traders found a new social status in Afghanistan. Kandahar, the Taliban 'capital' from where the reclusive Mullah Omar issued his decrees, is located on a principal axis of trade and developed into a busy commercial centre, with trading networks established between Pakistan and Central Asia, and with the United Arab Emirates where large numbers of Afghans and Pakistanis lived. This was all part of a decentralized laissez-faire economy that was in keeping with the centuries-old traditions of Islam, where the right to hold private property is held sacred, and trading is considered a legitimate source of wealth.

While the Taliban did not seem to be interested in assuming the responsibilities of government, they were remarkably effective in exercising the monopoly on the use of force that is an essential attribute of a state. This is not surprising since the Taliban movement began as a military organization. It explained their success in routing their opponents. Given their unwillingness to participate in any power-sharing arrangements, they seemed to be bent on pursuing the military option until the last pockets of resistance, held by the remnants of the Northern Alliance led by the indomitable Commander Massoud and supported by his foreign allies, notably Iran and Russia, submitted to their terms.

A striking demonstration of their effectiveness in enforcement and repression was provided by their application of Mullah Omar's July 2000 decree prohibiting opium production. The UNDCP vouched for its success despite the hardships incurred by farmers in the production zones where opium proved to be a life-saving crop after three successive years of drought. As a result of the enforcement of the decree, farmers who were indebted to the drug traffickers (who paid in advance for the crop) were sometimes forced to sell their under-age daughters in marriage. The decree may have also been a partial response to the UN sanctions, to obtain the international diplomatic recognition that they craved.[21]

Pakistan, as we have noted, had prematurely recognized the Taliban as the government of Afghanistan during their temporary occupation of Mazar-i-Sharif in September 1997, persuading Saudi Arabia and the United Arab Emirates to follow suit. In October 1999, with 90 per cent of the country and 27 of its 31 provinces under its virtual control, the Taliban laid formal claim to the Afghan seat at the United Nations. Their bid was not only rebuffed, but the UN's Security Council voted that same month to impose economic sanctions, including a ban on international flights to and from Afghanistan.

The sanctions were to take effect in 30 days if the Taliban did not extradite, for trial in a US court, the Saudi businessman, Osama bin Laden.

Bin Laden, or at least members of a terrorist network traceable to him known as al-Qaeda, had been implicated in the simultaneous bombings of the US embassies in Dar es Salaam, Tanzania, and Nairobi, Kenya, on 7 August 1998. The suicide bombings had killed 235 people including 13 Americans, and injured 5500 others. The majority of the victims were African civilians. The US retaliated on 28 August by firing 67 cruise missiles from aircraft carriers in the Indian Ocean at bin Laden's alleged terrorist bases in Zhawar in Paktia province. Bin Laden himself had drawn attention to his anti-American crusade in a 28 May interview given to an ABC News reporter, John Miller, describing a so-called *fatwa* he had issued calling for the killing of Americans: 'We do not differentiate between those dressed in military uniforms and civilians; they are all targets in the fatwa.' But the retaliatory (and ineffective) missile attacks in Afghanistan, and on a pharmaceutical factory in Khartoum, Sudan, made bin Laden an instant hero of many in the Muslim world.

The United States took the lead in keeping the bin Laden issue at the top of the agenda in their efforts to combat international terrorism. Bin Laden was again implicated in the suicide bombing attack on the USS *Cole* in the harbour of Aden, Yemen, in September 1999, and headed the FBI's list of most wanted men. An initial reward of US$5 million offered for his capture was raised to $10 million. On 19 December 2000 the UN Security Council imposed new sanctions on Afghanistan, expanding the list to include the closure of terrorist training camps, the freezing of Taliban assets abroad, and an embargo on the import of arms and of the chemicals required for the production of heroin. The Taliban response was to reject the sanctions, and their leader, Mullah Omar, was provoked to state unequivocally: 'We will never hand Osama over to anyone and [will] protect him with our blood at any cost.'[22]

While the Taliban pursued their diplomatic campaign for recognition of their regime as the government of Afghanistan, their refusal to remove one of the chief obstacles to international recognition – the extradition of bin Laden – was a contradiction which could be explained only by their espousal of a pan-Islamist ideology that pursued its own inner logic, and was remarkably consistent in practice.

Mullah Omar was neither a head of state nor a head of government. He was proclaimed 'Commander of the Believers' by an assembly of ulema and he covered himself symbolically with the Cloak of the Prophet. He was amir of an Islamic emirate that was more religious than statist in its connotations, and Kandahar, not Kabul, was the 'capital' of Taliban Afghanistan. Theirs was a 'theocratic' regime, legitimized by religion and not by a nationalist ideology nor by tribal genealogies, which had no equivalent in the contemporary Muslim world.

Theocracy historically means government by the church. It could be argued that there can be no theocracy in Islam, since there is no church nor a priesthood in the Christian sense. But to cite the authoritative voice of Bernard Lewis, the ulema is a class of professional men of religion whose status is acquired by learning and who function in most respects as a priesthood 'in the sociological sense'. By interpreting 'God's law' (the shari'a), they exercise a real authority which has, however, never been directly political. Muslim political rulers may choose to heed, or ignore (at their peril), the religious authority of the ulema. In Afghanistan, as mentioned previously, Abdur Rahman appropriated for himself the role of imam, with the dubious right to interpret the shari'a. Daoud during his dictatorship took care to consult a panel of theological experts to give Islamic legitimacy to his liberal decrees concerning women.

In Iran, the ayatollahs took over political power directly, with Khomeini as their imam. By doing so, as Lewis states, they created something entirely new in Islamic doctrine and history. It was considered an aberration by the most learned of the Shi'ite ayatollahs, like Montazeri in Qom, and in their other great theological centre of Najaf in Iraq. The current contest of wills, between the reformist government of President Khatami, directly elected by the people, and the unelected Islamic Guardians who control the judiciary, the army and the security apparatus hinges on no less an issue, revolutionary in Islam, than the separation of church and state. The issue has not been articulated as such except by the more courageous of the reformists. It may explain why President Khatami, despite his overwhelming mandate from the people, has been proceeding so cautiously, being a member of the clergy himself. To state the issue in a different way, it is a question of political legitimacy based on the sovereignty of the people versus legitimacy based on the sovereignty of God. To paraphrase Lewis, theocracy literally means the rule of God, and in this sense Islam has, in principle or theory, if not in practice, always been a theocracy. In Imperial Rome Caesar was God, in Christendom God and Caesar co-exist. In Islam God is Caesar, in that he alone is the supreme head of state, the source of sovereignty, and hence also of authority and of law. The state is God's state, the law is God's law, the army is God's army – and of course, the enemy is God's enemy.[23]

The avowed pan-Islamic mission of the Taliban was manifest in ways that were incompatible with normal inter-state relations. For instance, rebel Islamic movements in Central Asia received ready sanctuary on Taliban territory. In May 1999 Tahir Yuldashev, the leader of the Islamic Movement of Uzbekistan (IMU), who was wanted on charges in connection with an assassination attempt on President Karimov in Tashkent on 16 February

1999 that killed 16 people and injured 128 others, was authorized to set up a military training camp near Mazar. The Taliban refused his extradition. Yuldashev trained Islamic militants from Uzbekistan, Tajikistan and Kyrgyzstan, as well as Uighur independence fighters from Chinese Xinjiang. The Taliban denied involvement when the Chinese authorities claimed that arms and explosives used by Uighur rebels originated in Afghanistan. The Taliban also maintained close links with Shamil Basayev, the leader of the Chechen independence movement, and with the Jordanian 'ex-Afghan', Khabib Abdel Rahman Khattab who led the invasion of Dagestan that resulted in the second round of fighting in Chechnya which is still continuing. On 16 February 2000 the Taliban recognized the Chechen rebel government and authorized the opening of a mission in Kabul. A Chechen mission that came shopping for arms received gifts of Stinger missiles and substantial cash grants from the Taliban and from Osama bin Laden. Chechen fighters are said to have participated in Taliban offensives against Commander Massoud of the Northern Alliance.

The year 1998 marked a watershed in the international dimensions of the Taliban phenomenon. As noted in Chapter 12, when the Taliban were preparing their final drive to capture Mazar-i-Sharif, there was a line-up of forces in the region in open support of the opposing sides: the Russians and Iranians rushed in weapons and supplies for the anti-Taliban alliance; Pakistan made available the equivalent of $5 million for logistical support to the Taliban and thousands of new recruits were bussed into Afghanistan from refugee camps and madrasas; and Saudi Arabia provided additional financial aid and 400 pick-up trucks. After their capture of Mazar in the summer of 1998, only Commander Massoud stood between the Taliban and final victory. By this time, Afghanistan had become the general headquarters for the implementation of a pan-Islamic strategy devised by Osama bin Laden and his shadowy network of Islamic terrorists known as al-Qaeda. The interaction between these groups, both regionally and internationally, is best illustrated in the case of the Islamic parties of Central Asia, one of which branched out into the Wahhabi-inspired fundamentalist IMU.

When the Soviet Union was collapsing, a group of young men with close ties to Saudi foundations, and supported by some 5000 followers, attempted to set up a Wahhabi mosque and madrasa in the Uzbek town of Namangan. The local mayor refused to give them land for the mosque, whereupon the Islamic militants attacked the local communist party headquarters and seized it. This was in late 1991. The Islamists belonged to the Islamic Renaissance Party (IRP), formed the previous year with branches in all the Central Asian Republics (CARs). The Uzbek branch, however, was not able to register as a legal party in Uzbekistan. The militants of Namangan, perceiving that the mainstream IRP was slow in their demands for the immediate transformation of the newly independent CARs into Islamic states, formed the Adolat (Justice) Party and set about imposing the strict observance of the shari'a in Namangan. Its leaders were Tahir Yuldashev, a young self-appointed mullah, and Jumabhoi Ahmadjonovich Khodhjiyev. The latter had served as a para-trooper with the Soviet forces in Afghanistan – an experience that transformed him into a born-again Muslim. In March 1992 Islam Karimov, the Uzbek president, cracked down on Adolat and arrested 27 of its members.

Yuldashev fled to Tajikistan, but when the civil war broke out there in 1993 he was given sanctuary, ISI support and funds in Pakistan. He travelled to Saudi Arabia, Iran, the UAE and Turkey, making contact with other Islamist parties, and establishing himself as the spiritual guide and spokes-man for an Islamic revolution in his native Uzbekistan. From 1995 to 1998 Yuldashev was based mostly in Peshawar, which had by now become the rallying-point of pan-Islamic jihadi groups. Pakistan's Jamiat Ulema-Islami (JUI) which, along with the ISI, had done so much to assist the Taliban in their drive for power, raised funds for Yuldashev and enrolled young Uzbek activists in its madrasas. Yuldashev also travelled to the Caucasus where he met Chechen insurgents.[24]

Meanwhile Khodjiyev had fled to the Islamic stronghold of Kurgan Tube in southern Tajikistan, accompanied by some 30 Uzbek militants as well as Arabs who had been liaising with Saudi Wahhabi foundations and Adolat. There he became involved in the Tajik civil war. His first-hand knowledge of the Soviet army was useful to the Tajik IRP, which was fighting the Soviet-trained Tajik armed forces. Because of his effectiveness as a military leader, Tajiks joined his fighting group, which was moved to a base in the Tavildara Valley in the mountains between Dushanbe and Kyrgyzstan. Khodjiyev adopted the nom de guerre of Juma Namangani. More militants fleeing Kari-mov's crackdown in the Uzbek part of the Ferghana Valley arrived to join him, as well as 'Arab-Afghans' who found a new Islamic cause to fight for. He received money from the Saudis and maintained contacts with the Afghan mujahideen parties. When the Tajik IRP ended its insurgency in June 1997 and became part of a coalition government, Namangani had to disband his fighters. He settled down as a farmer and transporter in a village on the main road from Dushanbe to the Kyrgyz border.

Here, in the village of Hoit close to the border, Yuldashev used to visit him to discuss future plans. There were visitors from all over Uzbekistan with stories of the atrocities committed by Karimov's police against ordinary Muslims. The reprisals were particularly harsh after incidents involving the killing of Uzbek officials and policemen. In 1998 Yuldashev moved from Peshawar to Kabul, where the Taliban gave him a house in the diplomatic quarter and another house in Kandahar. That same year, he and Namangani formed the IMU. The car-bomb explosion in February 1999 outside the building that housed the offices of the Uzbek council of ministers in the capital, in an apparent attempt to assassinate President Karimov, was allegedly planned by Yuldashev while on a visit to Dubai. In response to Uzbek complaints that Tajikistan was harbouring the terrorist Namangani, the Tajik president, Emomali Rakhmanov, put pressure on the IRP leaders in the coalition government to get rid of him.

In Hoit, Namangani had supplemented his farming by acquiring trucks in which he transported local produce to Dushanbe. As more Uzbeks joined him as a result of Karimov's repression, Namangani had to raise funds to feed and supply his entourage. He had promised the Tajik government that he would not intervene in Tajik politics. He only wanted transit rights so that he could cross the Tajik–Kyrgyz border into the Ferghana Valley. He would use trucks, taxis, and horse and donkey caravans for the four or five-day journey across the mountains into the foothills at the southern edge of the Valley. The imposition of border controls since the independence of the CARs had led to a thriving business in smuggling, and smugglers gave the IMU help with the logistics of carrying supplies for their fighters.

According to Rashid: 'Some say that to keep his organization going and feed his ever-growing entourage at Hoit, Namangani became heavily involved in the transport of heroin from Afghanistan to Tajikistan and on through Kyrgyzstan to Russia and Europe.' An Interpol official quoted by Rashid stated: 'IMU may be responsible for seventy per cent of the total amount of heroin and opium transiting through the area.' Rashid adds, 'Wherever the IMU appeared, it was clear that its fighters were never short of funds, and they were careful to pay for all the supplies they took from local villagers. Namangani reportedly paid his guerrillas monthly salaries of between a hundred and five hundred dollars – in US dollar bills. This rumour alone was enough to ensure that more recruits would join him from the poverty-stricken Ferghana Valley.'[25]

IMU guerrillas were very active in Kyrgyzstan in the summer of 1999, kidnapping Kyrgyz officials for ransom and safe passage into Tajikistan. One incident widely reported in the international press involved the kidnapping of a Kyrgyz general and four Japanese geologists, and caused a major flurry among the states in the region. Kyrgyz troops were mobilized to attack the guerrillas; Russian military units were sent to locate the hostages; Japanese secret service agents and diplomats arrived to negotiate with all concerned; and Uzbek planes attacked IMU-held villages around Batken and Osh. The Japanese hostages were released in late October 1999, reportedly after Japan had secretly given between 2 and 5 million dollars to Kyrgyz officials for delivery to the IMU. Islamic terrorism proved to be a highly profitable business.

With the approach of winter, the IMU guerrillas moved back to their almost impregnable base in the Tavildara Valley in Tajikistan. IRI government ministers arrived there to persuade Namangani to go to Afghanistan. In November 1999 some 300 militants and their families were escorted across the border by Russian soldiers. They were received with great ceremony by Yuldashev and the Taliban and housed in a former UN refugee camp in Mazar-i-Sharif. The Taliban allowed them to set up a training camp for fresh recruits trickling down from the Ferghana Valley. The IMU was free to carry out its attacks in Uzbekistan in return for its participation in Taliban attacks on Massoud.

Yuldashev and Namangani travelled frequently to Kandahar where they met with Mullah Omar and Bin Laden. According to Russian intelligence sources cited by Rashid, bin Laden paid for three MI-8 transport helicopters for the IMU and contributed $20 million in cash in the spring of 2000. The IMU's Saudi backers paid another $15 million for the purchase of high-tech equipment such as sniper rifles, communications devices and night-vision goggles. Bin Laden now had a new base of operations in Central Asia.

In July 2000 Namangani moved back to his Tavildara base with several hundred armed guerrillas to begin new offensives in Uzbekistan. He infiltrated his fighters into the mountains of the Uzbek province of Surkhandarya where they established a highly fortified base manned by some 170 guerrillas. The Uzbeks were taken by surprise when the IMU offensives began, and it took a month of heavy fighting, including aerial bombardments, before their army could storm the camp. Rashid refers to the plight of some 2000 poor and innocent herdsmen from five ethnic Tajik villages who were forcibly removed to a military camp where they were given nothing to eat. One man, who had been interviewed by the BBC and had described their misery, was tortured and killed by the Uzbek army. In August, ten foreign mountain climbers, including four Americans, were kidnapped by the guerrillas in Kyrgyzstan. The publicity this incident received led the US shortly thereafter to declare the IMU a terrorist group.

At the end of October 2000 Namangani withdrew his forces to Afghanistan. The IMU, now established in Mazar and Kunduz, was becoming a pan-Islamic force, with some 2000 militants from the CARs, the Caucasus and Chinese Xinjiang, trained in the integrated use of artillery and airpower. Yuldashev and Namangani had been tried in absentia in Tashkent and sentenced to death. In December 2000 Namangani returned to Tajikistan with a multinational force of 300 militants with a view to establishing an Islamic emirate in the Ferghana Valley. This led to accusations by Karimov that Tajikistan and Kyrgyzstan were harbouring the IMU. He took retaliatory measures – the cutting of gas supplies to the two countries, the mining of the borders, and the expulsion of ethnic Uzbek refugees who had fled to Uzbekistan during the Tajik civil war – that caused great misery to those affected. An urgent meeting of CAR heads of state took place on 5 January 2001 in Almaty, Kazakhstan, to consider the situation. What followed was a curious development: the transportation back to Afghanistan in February 2001 of Namangani and 250 of his fighters in Russian and Tajik helicopters.

This action lent credence to Uzbekistan's accusations that the Russian Federation, with Tajikistan's collusion, was justifying its continued military presence in Central Asia – the extension in April 1999 of the stationing in Tajikistan of Russia's 201st Division had provoked President Karimov's anger – on the pretext of an Islamic menace emanating from Afghanistan, while simultaneously keeping that menace alive by aiding and abetting the anti-Uzbek IMU. Namangani and his group were able to enter Tajikistan despite the presence of Russian troops and through territory held by Tajik Islamists who were part of the Tajik coalition government. In October 1999 Tajikistan had played host to a high-level meeting involving Russia, Iran and India that decided to strengthen Commander Massoud's capacity to resist the Taliban with gifts of Russian helicopters to transport his troops, a small Indian hospital in Dushanbe to treat his wounded, and a floating bridge across the Amu Darya constructed by the Iranians. This was in addition to the camp facilities that had previously been made available to him and the use of the Kulyab airfield in south Tajikistan. On 27 October Massoud met with the Russian and Iranian defence ministers in Dushanbe who promised to continue their military aid.

While Turkmenistan maintained relations with the Taliban after their taking of Herat in 1996, in the ever-present hope of a pipeline through Afghanistan that would increase exports of their abundant gas reserves, Kazakhstan contracted with the Taliban in August 1999 for the supply of 60,000 tonnes of wheat to be exported through Turkmenistan and destined for the Herat region. Uzbekistan appeared to develop a more flexible attitude towards the Taliban in the course of the year 2000. President Karimov refused to be associated with the Dushanbe meeting and announced in November 2000 that his country was prepared to deal with the Taliban: there was a project to supply Uzbek electricity to northern Afghanistan. These CARs appeared to have accepted that the Taliban had come to stay and that it would be in their interests to have a strong and stable government in Afghanistan with which they could deal.[26]

But stability was what the Taliban least contributed to the region. They polarized the whole area, creating unstable alliances brought together by fear of Islamic fundamentalism, and driving Pakistan, the steadfast supporter whose advice they heeded less and less, into diplomatic isolation. They provided an ideological focus and an inspiration for thousands of disaffected young Muslims around the world whose militants found fallback positions in

Afghanistan. The Taliban not only provided them with a sanctuary but also logistics and military resources for terrorist campaigns paid for by drug trafficking.[27]

However perverse the Taliban ideology, which made mainstream Muslims flinch, it was applied to their actions with a consistency bordering on the irrational. To the Taliban the monumental Buddhas of the Bamyan Valley that had awed travellers and visitors for centuries were only symbols of idolatry, susceptible to worship – contemptible vestiges of the pre-Islamic past. Their wanton destruction in February 2001 was carried out despite worldwide appeals at the highest levels, by leading religious authorities in the Muslim world such as the Rector of Al-Azhar, or even by their ideological mentor, Maulana Samiul Haq of the leading Deobandi theological school near Peshawar. To the Taliban, the Bamyan statues (and the pre-Islamic tombs, shrines and priceless images in the Kabul museum that were also destroyed) were symbols of the non-Muslim 'Other', like the Hindu merchants of Kabul's bazaars who were required to wear shameful badges of identity (such as the Jews of medieval Europe or, as people recalled with a shudder, the Jews who went to their slaughter in Nazi death camps.)

Taliban fanaticism and intolerance went against the grain of traditional Afghan attitudes influenced by Sufism, the mystical side of Islam that is tolerant of diversity. The arrest in August 2001 of eight Western humanitarian workers who had been accused of Christian proselytism was also a result of their peculiar mind-set, their pseudo-religious paranoia. As some observers had noted at the time, and revelations since September 11 have now confirmed, the fanatical intolerance that drove the Taliban to actions that were uncharacteristic from an Afghan point of view were actually signs of the increased ideological hold on the simple Mullah Omar of the radical Wahhabi militant, Osama bin Laden, and his foreign al-Qaeda entourage that had their headquarters in Afghanistan.

With regard to their policies towards women, when time-honoured tribal practices of the Pashtuns were seen to be in contradiction with the shari'a, the primacy of the shari'a was upheld under threat of punishment, as in Mullah Omar's seven-point decree in the autumn of 1998 with regard to women's rights in matters of inheritance and marriage. The sixth point declared notably that a woman's marriage was her personal affair, and that no one in the family, including her father or a brother, had the right to interfere.[28]

As Olivier Roy has demonstrated, the movements he describes and analyses as manifestations of 'political Islam' with their learned and sophisticated agendas for transforming Muslim societies in accordance with the shari'a, have failed to achieve anything of practical value within the limits of their narrow Islamic discourse. He determines the reasons for this in relation to such movements in various Muslim countries. Such a discourse assumes the 'sovereignty of God' and 'God's law' (the shari'a) without any reference to the sovereignty of the people, a concept that lies outside the parameters of the Islamic discourse, dominated as it is by a single paradigm, as mentioned earlier in this chapter. After a long evolution, secular democracies have firmly separated the sacred (religion) and the profane (human politics), to the mutual advantage of both. But for Khomeini, 'Islam is politics or it is nothing'[29] and Islam's beginnings as a military religion were associated with the exercise of power. But in Iran the political action of the Islamists has fallen in with the logic of the state; in Egypt the Muslim Brotherhood had to compromise with the state; in Algeria, the Front islamique du salut (FIS) was repressed by the state; in Pakistan, the Jamiat-i-Islami has worked within the legal framework of the state but its electoral record has been dismal.[30] The Koranic schools of its radical offshoot, the JUI, produced the Taliban and their ideology – a strange mix of the Deobandi, the Wahhabi and Pashtun tribal codes.

In Afghanistan the Taliban showed themselves unwilling, or unable, to build the institutions of a state, or to assume any responsibilities for the social and economic welfare of their fellow countrymen. These tasks they left to the international community of UN agencies and NGOs funded by foreign donors. However, far from encouraging them in their humanitarian endeavours, or assisting them, they kept creating difficulties for them. Their priorities lay elsewhere: fighting their opponents and engaging in a militant but woolly-minded pan-Islamic campaign inspired by dangerous foreign terrorist groups that could create only mischief for their neighbours.[31]

PART IV: THE RUDE AWAKENING

CHAPTER 16

Holy War, Unholy Terror

> ... any man's death
> diminishes me, because I am involved in Mankind,
> And therefore do not send to know for whom the bell tolls,
> It tolls for thee.
>
> John Donne[1]

On a sunny September morning in New York, a passenger aircraft crashed into the north tower of the World Trade Center in Lower Manhattan. Eighteen minutes later, thousands of rescue workers and bystanders in New York, and millions across the world on their television screens, watched with horror and disbelief as a second aircraft flew into the south tower. These were surely not accidents, but concerted, coordinated attacks on the towering outward symbols of American economic power, calculated to cause maximum destruction and loss of life: both aircraft had taken off from the same airport in Boston within a minute of each other, on the long flight to Los Angeles. When, at 0945 hours that morning, a third aircraft, on another scheduled flight to Los Angeles, crashed into the Pentagon, and a fourth, bound for San Francisco, but surely destined for a target in Washington DC, crashed into a field in Pennsylvania shortly afterwards, the circle of terror was complete. The targets now encompassed the seats and symbols of American military and political power.

As Stephen King, the prolific American writer of horror fiction, said, reacting to the traumatizing events of September 11, 2001, these scenes were not computer-generated images in a Hollywood disaster film: 'This is what it really looks like when an actual plane filled with actual human beings and loaded with jet fuel hits a skyscraper. ... Cost of weaponry? Based on what we know, less than $100.'

When millions watched in anguish as the 110-storey WTC towers collapsed, one after the other, in enormous clouds of smoke, dust and debris – the apocalyptic climax of what was surely a defining event in contemporary

history – one question immediately sprang to mind. Who could have mas-
terminded this deed? No commercial airline pilot, even with a hijacker's gun
at his head, would deliberately direct his plane into a skyscraper and take the
lives of his passengers with him. Or four crazed pilots? Most improbable.

This meant that the hijackers were suicidal terrorists, some of whom were
either qualified pilots or had acquired the skills required to operate the
controls of large passenger aircraft. The answer was soon provided when the
identities of the 19 hijackers were traced from the passenger lists, and their
personal histories and movements investigated and revealed by US intelligence agencies: of the 19, 15 were nationals of Saudi Arabia, two were
Yemenis, and the two others Lebanese and Egyptian.

Even before the accumulating evidence became public knowledge, the
attacks bore the unmistakable signature of Osama bin Laden and the nebulous al-Qaeda network of international terrorists that he headed and inspired:
the American targets, the absence of warning or of political demands in
advance, the careful long-term planning, the simultaneity of the attacks for
maximum effect and clarity of message, the use of suicidal fanatics, the total
disregard for the number and identity of civilian casualties. Had not bin
Laden himself referred to a so-called fatwa he had issued for the killing of
Americans, in an interview given to a US journalist on 28 May 1998: 'We do
not differentiate between those dressed in military uniforms and civilians;
they are all targets in the fatwa.'[2]

Shortly after the United States began its military campaign against al-
Qaeda targets in Afghanistan on 7 October, Osama bin Laden issued a
statement to the effect that the Americans 'have divided the entire world into
two regions – one of faith where there is no hypocrisy, and another of infidel-
ity, from which we hope God will protect us'. He went on, more obscurely,
'Hypocrisy stood behind the leader of global idolatry, behind the Hubal of
the age – namely America and its supporters.'

The symbolism of the words and images he uses would be intelligible to
some Muslims. But the conceptual world that lies behind the statement
requires some elucidation. When the Prophet Mohammad began to preach
his strictly monotheistic faith to the pagan tribes in Mecca early in the seventh century, Hubal was a stone idol that stood in the Kaabah – the structure
that Ibrahim (Abraham) had originally built on orders from Allah (God) as a
sanctuary of Islam, according to the Muslim tradition.[3] In the centuries
between Ibrahim and Mohammad, the Arabs had fallen away from the
worship of the one God and had begun to worship idols, of whom Hubal was
the most powerful. The chief of a tribe that had dwelt in Mecca before the
arrival of Mohammad's tribe of the Quraysh had brought the idol, symboliz-
ing the god of the moon, from Syria. It was set up in the Kaabah and became

the principal idol of the pagan Meccans. This pre-Islamic age in Arabia was called the Age of Ignorance (jahiliyya).[4]

When bin Laden called America 'the Hubal of the Age', he was implying that America was a symbol of idol-worship, and that through the presence of its troops on Saudi soil, it was polluting the Kaabah, a symbol of Islamic purity. Bin Laden, it must be noted, began his stridently anti-American campaign just before the Gulf War, when the United States began stationing troops in Saudi Arabia – the holy land of Islam barred to 'infidels' since the second Caliph Umar expelled or relocated its communities of Jews and Christians, an early example of 'ethnic cleansing'.

The references to 'hypocrisy' require some further forays into early Islamic history. The uncompromising monotheism that the Prophet preached in Mecca threatened the interests of the ruling mercantile oligarchy of the Quraysh and provoked their enmity. Mecca was not only a flourishing commercial centre, lying on the trade route between Yemen and the cities of Greater Syria, but also a focus of pilgrimage. Pagan Arabs from the far-flung corners of the peninsula came to worship Hubal as well as their own tribal deities who had shrines in the precincts of the Kaabah. Commerce and pagan religion were a profitable combination for the Meccan merchants.

Mohammad had made a few converts from among the traders and pilgrims of Yathrib, an oasis to the north of Mecca. When these converts or helpers (ansar) invited the persecuted Muslims to settle in Yathrib, Mohammad and his followers undertook the migration (hijrah) in CE622 that marks the starting date of the Islamic calendar. Yathrib was riven at the time by constant feuding and warring between two Arab tribes, involving also Jewish communities that had settled there. Mohammad was not only an enlightened religious reformer but an astute political leader. As a neutral mediator he brought peace, made more converts among the Arabs of Yathrib and others who came to seek his help as his reputation spread, and directed his energies to the practical tasks of organizing the believers into a close-knit and disciplined community that was at once religious and political.

Mohammad's ambition as he fought his Meccan enemies for survival was to unite all Arabs under Islam. Two years after the hijrah, the greatly outnumbered Muslims won an unexpected victory over Meccan troops who had been sent to protect a 1000-camel trade caravan that Mohammad had planned to ambush. The fledgling Muslim community was not only enriched by valuable booty but received a great psychological boost, their victory at Badr being interpreted as divine sanction for their new faith. However, a year later, outnumbered Muslims were defeated by the Quraysh at the Battle of Uhud, a defeat that was attributed to the treachery of the Hypocrites (munafiqun). Their leader, an important figure in Yathrib before the arrival of the Prophet, whose growing power he resented, withdrew his 300 horsemen

just before the battle. The Hypocrites were believed to be secret supporters of
the Quraysh while openly professing Islam. The Koran refers to them as
'propped up pieces of wood' and 'those in whose heart is a disease'.⁵ In
Osama bin Laden's mental universe, the Hypocrites are the treacherous
leaders of the Arab and Muslim worlds sheltering behind America, the Hubal
of the Age.

Muslim fundamentalist movements that seek to establish an ideal Muslim
state based on the shari'a are generally known as Salaffiya – derived from al-
Salaf al-Salih (venerable forefathers), which refers to the generation of the
Prophet and his Companions. When Mohammad died in CE632, Mecca had
submitted, and he had brought the remaining pagan tribes of Arabia under
his religious and political authority. He was not only the founder of a religion
but had become the political and military leader, lawgiver, judge and arbiter
in every aspect of the social and economic life of the Community of the
Faithful (umma). Yathrib, renamed Medinat al Nabi (City of the Prophet), or
Medina, had become the nucleus of the Arab nation, and its government the
ideal prototype of the Muslim state. Mohammad had declared himself the
Seal of the Prophets. Thus there was to be no more Revelation. He could
have no successor in the religious role. But he had not designated a political
successor.

The Revelation may have been written down in part, but it was largely
committed to memory – as was the custom in pre-literate cultures – by the
Prophet's Companions during his lifetime. Collections in writing of the
Prophet's utterances and prescriptions may have also been made after his
death. But a definitive or canonical text of the Koran was commissioned by
the third caliph, Uthman (CE644–56). It was during his caliphate that the
first civil wars between Muslims broke out, mainly in relation to questions
concerning the political succession. By this time the Arabs had begun con-
quering vast swathes of the Byzantine and Persian empires, and much was at
stake. In these civil wars doctrinal issues were invoked by the warring parties
to give legitimacy to their own claims to the political succession. In this
context the first major schism in Islam occurred between orthodox believers,
who came to be known as the Sunni, and the followers of the Prophet's son-
in-law, the fourth caliph, Ali, who claimed that the caliphate was reserved for
the descendants of the Prophet. The Party of Ali (shi'at Ali) came to be
known as Shi'ites.

The earliest of Muslim fundamentalist movements that is of contemporary relevance is Wahhabism. The eighteenth-century founder of the sect,
Mohammad ibn Abd al-Wahhab (1703–92), held that all changes and accre-
tions to Islam since the ninth century, including Sufism, were illegitimate and
should be expunged. Al-Wahhab branded all who disagreed with him as
heretics and apostates and even declared jihad (illegally according to the

Islamic canon) against Muslims. He preached in the Nejd, inhabited by the Saudi tribe. After the tribe's espousal of Wahhabism, their attempts to conquer the rest of Arabia were rebuffed by the Turkish sultan, nominally caliph of the Muslim world and guardian of the holy places.

It was only in the first quarter of the twentieth century, after the dismemberment of the Ottoman Empire, that the founder of the current dynasty, King Abd al-Aziz al-Saud, conquered the territories that now make up Saudi Arabia.[6]

Wahhabism is the official ideology of Saudi Arabia, but the ostentatious luxury of the large Saudi royal family, and of the Westernized elites linked to them by patronage, were in flagrant contrast to the austere Wahhabi creed whose puritanical adherents were the progeny of the desert Wahhabis. The consequent social tensions threatened the ruling dynasty. It would not be far-fetched to compare the situation to that of Iran on the eve of the Khomeini revolution. The regime's close alliance with the United States, perceived as a symbol of godless materialism, strengthens the analogy.

The rulers sought to appease the religious purists and mosque imams by supporting and financing Islamic causes and movements abroad: the mujahideen of the Afghan resistance; the Arab volunteers who fought on the Muslim side in Bosnia and in Kosovo; the Wahhabi-inspired fundamentalist movements in Central Asia; and the Taliban in Afghanistan. Saudi foreign policy has been facetiously described as 'ryalpolitik'. The most articulate exponent of Wahhabism was the Saudi rebel, Osama bin Laden, who broke with the Saudi regime on the issue of the presence of non-Muslim armed forces on Saudi soil during the Gulf War.[7]

Osama bin Laden: The 'Sheikh'

So much has been written about Osama bin Laden and al-Qaeda in the year that has elapsed since 11 September 2001 that it is advisable to gather up the threads by recapitulating as briefly as possible the personal odyssey of the man most frequently associated with al-Qaeda. He was born in 1957, the 17th of 52 children fathered by an immigrant from the Hadramaut in southern Yemen who had arrived penniless in Saudi Arabia in 1930. Mohammed bin Laden had first worked as a porter. Providing services to the hajj pilgrims was a principal source of income for Saudis at the time. But he soon started a contracting company which prospered. By the 1950s, Mohammed's company, which had branched out into construction activities (the Hadramis have been master-builders for centuries), outbid other contractors to work on King Saud's palaces, in a country that was becoming flush with petro-dollars. He had become close to the Saudi royal family, especially Saud's brother, Faisal. When Faisal became king in 1964, Mohammed served for a time as his minister for public works, and his company became known as' the king's private contractors'.[8]

The bin Ladens had become part of the Saudi establishment. The expanding construction company was awarded the prestigious contracts for renovating Islam's holiest sites: the rebuilding of the al-Aqsa mosque in Jerusalem after it was set on fire by a demented Australian tourist in the 1960s, and the renovation and expansion of the holy sites in Mecca and Medina. Mohammed died in a plane crash in 1967. One of his sons, Salem, who was educated in an exclusive prep school in England, took over the operation of the company and turned it into a conglomerate, with interests in industrial and power projects, oil exploration, mining and telecommunications, that was the largest of its kind in the region. The Saudi Binladin Group (SBG) built the US base in the desert, after the facilities housing US troops in Riyadh and Dharan were targeted in attacks attributed to al-Qaeda.[9]

Osama bin Laden's mother was an Alawite from Syria. The Alawites, a sect to which the Syrian ruling class also belongs, are considered heretical by mainstream Sunnis. As his mother was divorced from his father decades ago and had since remarried, she was not considered part of the family by the other bin Ladens. Osama has been quoted as referring to his mother as 'a concubine'.

The young bin Laden has been described as a 'loner'. In a country that sets great store on parentage and patronymics, bin Laden, despite his privileged upbringing among Saudi princes, might have felt an outsider, and doubly so: his father had been a poor immigrant from Yemen, and his mother was a Syrian and an Alawite to boot. She visited her son in the Sudan, and later in Afghanistan to celebrate the marriage of her grandson to the daughter of the Egyptian Mohammed Atef. On his father's death Osama had received his share of the family fortune, which was substantial.

At the age of 17, Osama married a Syrian relative, the first of his four wives. He attended the university in Jeddah and graduated with a degree in civil engineering. There he was drawn to two influential teachers of Islamic studies: Dr Abdullah Azzam, a Jordanian of Palestinian origin with a doctorate in theology from the Al-Azhar University in Cairo, and Mohammed Qutb, a brother of Sayyid Qutb, who had written, while in prison, one of the key fundamentalist texts of the jihadis, Ma'alim fi al-Tariq (Signposts), and was executed under Nasser in 1966. In 1981, bin Laden followed Dr Azzam to Pakistan to see what he could do in the cause of the Afghan jihad against the Soviets.

As recounted in Chapter 9, when Ronald Reagan was elected president of the United States in the year of the Soviet invasion of Afghanistan, he was determined, with a bellicose Congress behind him, to impose a maximum penalty on the USSR. In addition to huge infusions of cash and weaponry for the Afghan resistance, the United States enlisted the more than willing military dictator of Pakistan, Zia ul-Haq, and Saudi Arabia in a strategy – in Reagan's words – of rolling back 'the evil empire'. The agents for carrying out the plan were the CIA, Pakistan's Inter-Services Intelligence (ISI) and the head of the Saudi intelligence services, Prince Turki ibn Faisal.

The Saudis, accustomed as they were to sub-contracting their jobs to foreigners, from national defence (the Americans) to chauffeuring their Rolls-Royces (Sri Lankans), mobilized Islamic militants from across the Arab world to fight in a jihad against the invading Russian infidels. The notion of jihad, or holy war, had almost ceased to exist in the mainstream Muslim world after the tenth century until it was revived by those who fought in the Afghan resistance in the traditional religious context. Saudi Arabia could thus reinforce its position as leader of the Muslim world against the rival claims of Shi'ite Iran which had just overthrown a despotic monarchy in the Khomeini revolution.[10]

The charismatic and physically impressive firebrand, Dr Abdullah Azzam, who was born in a Palestinian refugee camp in Jenin, had studied Islamic theology in Damascus and Cairo, but could not hold on to his teaching job in Amman because of his provocative anti-secular attitudes. In 1980, he moved to Pakistan where he obtained a teaching job at the Islamic University in Islamabad. Later settling in Peshawar, he was the acknowledged 'emir' of the jihad against the Soviet invaders of Afghanistan: 'Jihad and the rifle alone, no negotiations, no conferences and no dialogues', he is quoted as saying.[11] His exhortations regarding jihad as the religious duty of every Muslim, the expulsion of infidels from the lands of Islam, past and present, and the unification of all Muslims in a restored caliphate, were to become an integral part of Osama bin Laden's political vocabulary, reflecting his particular view of the world and his mental universe.

Meanwhile the Afghan jihad had to be pursued. The young bin Laden assisted his mentor, Dr Azzam, in setting up a 'Services Bureau' in Peshawar. Bin Laden was assigned a role for which his background, including his wealthy Saudi family and Arab business and political contacts in the Gulf region, was particularly suited – to serve as a recruiting agent and paymaster, with Saudi, ISI and CIA encouragement and support, for foreign Islamic militants to fight in the anti-communist cause in Afghanistan. Both Azzam and bin Laden went on frequent fund-raising tours to the rich Arab states; Azzam's tours took him also to the United States, where he addressed Muslim rallies and set up a branch of his Services Bureau in Brooklyn.

The Saudi national airline granted discounts of 75 per cent to young men travelling to Pakistan to join in the jihad. Bin Laden paid a monthly allowance of $300 to the families of his Arab volunteers, a lordly sum if they were from poor countries. According to Milt Bearden, the CIA station chief in

Pakistan from 1986 to 1989, bin Laden and other fund-raisers for the Afghan jihad were bringing in between 20 and 25 million dollars a month from the Saudis and Gulf Arabs to underwrite the war.[12]

Altogether some 25,000 Arab, African and Asian militants are reported to have fought alongside the Afghan mujahideen. The Soviet 'defeat' in Afghanistan was generally seen in the Arab and Muslim worlds as a victory for jihad. However, Arab witnesses claimed that there were never more than 3000 Arabs in Afghanistan, and most of them were drivers, secretaries and cooks. The war was fought almost entirely by Afghans, not by Arabs. There were only some 500 Egyptians: 'They were known as the thinkers and the brains. The Islamist movement started with them.'[13]

In 1986, bin Laden settled permanently in Peshawar and set up a base for his Arab volunteers inside Afghanistan, in the mountains close to the Pakistani border. He built his first camp near the village of Jaji in Paktia province, a few miles from Parachinar, the 'Parrot's Beak' that juts into Afghanistan. The camp was called Al-Ansar – 'the helpers' who gave the Prophet and his followers refuge in their oasis of Yathrib (later Medina). The location was chosen because it was close to the Soviet front lines but close enough to the Pakistani border for re-supply (and for a speedy retreat). Bin Laden used the services and heavy machinery of his family construction company to enable his Arab jihadis to dig into the caves in the heights above the village. According to Essam Deraz, an eyewitness, 200 Russians, some wearing the uniforms of the Spetznaz, assaulted the positions held by some 50 Arabs in April 1987. The Arabs had to withdraw after losing 12 of their men.[14]

But the encounter at Jaji was celebrated as a victory in the Arab world, figuring in the dispatches about bin Laden's battlefield exploits that were widely published in Arab newspapers, along with stories of the wealth and comforts he had abandoned for the rigours of life in the Afghan jihad. Such tales became the stuff of the bin Laden legend which was crowned by the Soviet withdrawal, seen as a victory for jihad. US retaliatory actions, such as the missile attacks in Afghanistan and the Sudan after the 1998 embassy bombings in East Africa, contributed to the myth, making bin Laden a hero to the youth of the Islamic world.

The Soviet invasion of Afghanistan was the second of two events that marked 1979 as a watershed in the annals of Islamic militancy – the first was the Khomeini revolution in Iran. It was the lessons learned by the Arabs in the Afghan jihad, not their contribution to it, that was significant. As Gilles Keppel says: 'The Afghan jihad plays a central role in the evolution of the Islamist movement around the world. It replaces the Palestinian cause in the Arab imagination and symbolizes the movement from [Arab] nationalism to Islamism.'[15]

However, the true ideological roots of Islamic militancy have to be traced in the career of the Egyptian Dr Ayman al-Zawahiri, the founder of the Islamic Jihad organization in Egypt who was to become bin Laden's deputy in al-Qaeda. Zawahiri had practically burned his boats in Egypt. He followed bin Laden to Peshawar where he lodged his wife and two small daughters in a comfortable two-storey villa that was to be their home until the end of the Afghan jihad. He had been there before, on short stints in 1980 and 1981, as a volunteer doctor for the Red Crescent. Zawahiri would have found Pesha-war radically changed after his five-year absence, a provincial backwater transformed into a centre of international intrigue, awash with cash and corruption. He found himself among 'a great borderless posse' of disaffected young men who had found their mission of defending, in the Afghan jihad, the world of Islam.

But in Peshawar, Zawahiri had not placed himself under the patronage of the 'emir' of the Afghan jihad, Dr Abdullah Azzam, but developed instead a close relationship with bin Laden, an adjunct to his mainly nationalist moti-vations and interest, which was to reorganize his own Egyptian Islamic Jihad and renew its operations to carry out the first phase of his programme in his native Egypt. He was Stalin to bin Laden's Trotsky, not a good analogy at the end, but adequate enough for the time being. He recruited new members from among the Egyptian mujahideen, placed trusted members of his Islamic Jihad into key positions in bin Laden's entourage and obtained his much-needed financial support.

Members of the rival Egyptian Jaamah Islamiyya were also present in Peshawar, but the largest share of the bin Laden largesse went to Zawahiri and his organization. Bin Laden, who suffered from low blood pressure and had dizzy spells, also became dependent on Dr Zawahiri as a trusted personal physician. The doctor travelled from Peshawar when bin Laden needed medical attention at one of his fortified bases near Jalalabad or at his main base camp in a complex of caves near the Pakistani border named Masaada (the Lion's Den) – 'Osama' in Arabic means 'a young lion'. Bin Laden, as mentioned earlier, was addicted to the symbolism of names and dates. One of his camps was called 'Badr', evoking the Prophet's first victory against his Meccan enemies. Such symbolism fed his vanity. He saw himself also as a twentieth-century Saladin overcoming the Crusaders.

There were two crucial developments at the end of the Afghan Jihad in 1989 when Arab jihadi leaders were confronted with questions relating to the future of jihad. The first was a dispute between bin Laden, supported by Zawahiri, who envisaged the formation of an all-Arab legion that would wage a jihad in Saudi Arabia and Egypt to overthrow their respective regimes, and Dr Abdullah Azzam who strongly opposed waging war on fellow Muslims. Zawahiri had insinuated during the debate that Azzam was a spy. That same night in November, Azzam and two of his sons were blown up by a car bomb as they were driving to a mosque in Peshawar. Zawahiri read the eulogy at the funeral.

The second development stemmed from a meeting held in a mujahideen camp in Khost, Afghanistan. Jamal al-Fadl, a Sudanese defector who turned witness for the prosecution at the New York trial in connection with the 1988 embassy bombings in East Africa, was present. Among the ten men at the meeting, half were Egyptians, including Zawahiri. It was proposed by the chairman of the meeting, an Iraqi known as Abu Ayub, that a new organization be formed to wage war beyond the borders of Afghanistan. It was to be called al-Qaeda, or 'the Base' in Arabic. It was merely a loose association of like-minded individual Arab mujahideen and established groups like Zawahiri's Islamic Jihad. The evolution of al-Qaeda as an organization began after bin Laden was forced to seek refuge in the Sudan.

There, between 1991 and 1996, al-Qaeda became 'operational' as a global, clandestine network of terror. Osama bin Laden, with his private fortune and access to considerable funding sources, was the chairman of the board holding the purse strings. Dr Zawahiri and the members of his Islamic Jihad were to become the CEO and key staff in this evolution. As Strobe Talbott and Nayan Chanda described it in the introduction to their thought-provoking post-9/11 book of essays: 'al Qaeda flew no flag – it was the ultimate NGO'.[16]

The Vizier: Dr Ayman al-Zawahiri

A long essay by Lawrence Wright in a recent issue of The New Yorker focuses on the career of the key al-Qaeda figure who has often been described, somewhat marginally, as bin Laden's deputy. This very insightful essay, which attests to the writer's access to privileged information from CIA, FBI and other sources, significantly alters one's perceptions of al-Qaeda. It seems that the futile efforts to establish clear links between 'the Sheikh', as bin Laden was referred to by his followers, and the planning or organization of pre-September 11 terrorist attacks attributed to al-Qaeda, add up to barking up the wrong tree. It may be said in extenuation that journalism is the first draft of history. Wright's essay is a convincing second draft.[17]

Although Osama bin Laden has become, as Wright says, 'the public face of Islamic terrorism, the members of Islamic Jihad and its guiding figure, Ayman al-Zawahiri, have provided the backbone of the large organization's leadership. ... Bin Laden, an idealist with vague political ideas, sought direction, and Zawahiri, a seasoned propagandist, supplied it.' Wright quotes Essam Deraz, an Egyptian film-maker who produced several documentaries on the mujahideen during the Afghan–Soviet war: 'The people with Zawahiri had extraordinary capabilities – doctors, engineers, soldiers. They had experience in secret work. They knew how to organize themselves. And they became the leaders.'[18]

The association between Osama bin Laden and Ayman al-Zawahiri can be traced back to the beginnings of the Afghan jihad. Al-Zawahiri was an Egyptian nationalist and a radical political theorist: the objective of his Islamic Jihad was to overthrow the secular government and impose a theocracy that would become a model for the Arab world. His direct inspiration was Sayyid Qutb, the hero of his youth. Bin Laden was a dyed-in-the-wool Wahhabi who had acquired an international role in the Afghan jihad, and then, after the Iraqi war, focused his attention on the United States as 'the enemy of Islam'. Bin Laden had a background of immense wealth and privilege, with a pious Yemeni immigrant father who was the epitome of the self-made businessman. As bin Laden confided to a Pakistani journalist: 'My father was very keen that one of his sons should fight against the enemies of Islam. So I am the one son who is acting according to the wishes of his father.'[19]

Al-Zawahiri was an Islamic revolutionary whose parents belonged to the professional, intellectual and cultural elite of Egypt. His father, Rabie al-Zawahiri, was a respected professor of pharmacology who belonged to a medical dynasty: a 1995 obituary for a Zawahiri mentioned 46 names of relatives, of whom 31 were doctors, chemists and pharmacists. The others included an ambassador, a judge and a member of parliament. The father's uncle became the Grand Imam of Al-Azhar University in 1929 and was known as one of the great modernizers of that prestigious seat of Islamic learning. The elder Zawahiri's father and grandfather were also religious scholars. Ayman al-Zawahiri's mother belonged to the wealthy family of the Azzams. Her father was successively president of Cairo University, founder and director of King Saud University in Riyadh, and ambassador in Pakistan, Yemen and Saudi Arabia. Her father's uncle was a founding secretary-general of the Arab League. The Azzams were associated with government for 150 years, since the first Egyptian parliament, but always in the opposition.

The situation in Egypt that gave birth to the 'political Islam' of the Muslim Brotherhood has been sketched in Chapter 4. The Brotherhood was dissolved by the government in 1948 after some of its members resorted to violence in pursuit of their aims. Its founder, Hassan al-Banna, was murdered, allegedly by King Farouk's agents, in 1949, which was also the year of Ayman al-Zawahiri's birth. The year before, Sayyid Qutb, a well-known Cairo literary critic who was one of the first to recognize the literary talents of Naguib Mahfouz, the future Nobel Prize laureate, had left for the United States to study at the State College of Education in Greely, Colorado. Qutb had a sinecure at the education ministry. As a nationalist he had become too articulate in his opposition to the British hold on his country, and he was 'sent away' to cool his heels, apparently.

Qutb studied literature and popular culture at Greely. Like other forward-looking Egyptians of his generation, he had admired the United States as a friendly, neutral power with democratic ideals. He also wore his religion lightly. But he returned to Egypt in 1950 a completely changed man. He had encountered a post-war America quite unlike what he had understood from books and Hollywood films. As Qutb wrote after his return:

> It is astonishing to realize, despite his advanced education and his perfectionism, how primitive the American really is in his views of life. His behaviour reminds us of the era of the caveman. He is primitive in the way he lusts after power, ignoring ideals and manners and principles.[20]

Qutb was impressed by the number of churches – there were 20 in Greely alone – and yet the Americans he had met seemed completely uninterested in spiritual matters.

After what he saw as the spiritual wasteland of America, Qutb re-created himself as a militant Muslim, with a vision of Islam that would throw off the vulgar influences of the West. Islamic society had to be purified, and the only mechanism powerful enough to cleanse it was the ancient and bloody instrument of jihad. In a brief memoir that was published in a London-based Arabic newspaper in December 2001, al-Zawahiri quotes Qutb as saying: 'Brother push ahead, for your path is soaked in blood. Do not turn your head right or left but only look up to Heaven.'[21]

Egypt was in the throes of a nationalist revolution for which Nasser and his Free Officers enlisted the support of the still clandestine networks of the Muslim Brotherhood. Anwar al-Sadat served as liaison, and after a military junta seized power in July 1952 Qutb ran the Brotherhood's journal. But the Brotherhood had an agenda for Egypt that was radically different from Nasser's. Qutb's magazine was shut down after a few issues. Things came to a head in October 1954 when one of the Brothers tried to assassinate the hugely popular Nasser in Alexandria. Six of the Brothers were executed and a thousand others, including Qutb, imprisoned. Sadat was one of the judges at the trial that condemned Qutb to life imprisonment. His sentence was later commuted to 15 years because of ill health.

In prison Qutb wrote his manifesto, *Signposts*, which was smuggled out in instalments and circulated underground. In 1964 he was released, reportedly on the intervention of the Iraqi president, Abd al-Salaam Aref. This would show the extent of Qutb's reputation, and perhaps influence, in the Arab world at the time. Qutb's manifesto was published in Cairo in 1964. Some excerpts are worth quoting, since they provide insights into the ideology of al-Zawahiri and his Islamic Jihad, and later of Osama bin Laden and al-Qaeda. It begins:

Mankind today is on the brink of a precipice. Humanity is threatened not only by nuclear annihilation but by the absence of values. The West has lost its vitality, and Marxism has failed. At this crucial and bewildering juncture, the turn of Islam and the Muslim community has arrived.

Qutb divided the world into two camps, Islam and *Jahiliyya*. The latter encompassed not only the world of 'infidels' but also the so-called Muslim states and societies. 'We need to initiate the movement of Islamic revival in some Muslim country ... a vanguard which sets out with this determination and then keeps walking on the path.'[22]

Jahiliyya referred to the pre-Islamic conditions of religious ignorance. Qutb argued that since contemporary Muslim societies had lapsed into jahiliyya, it was lawful to wage jihad against governments that were Muslim in name only (bin Laden's 'Hypocrites'), and that the leaders of such governments should be considered infidels (*kafir*) and named or denounced as apostates (in a process called *takfir*, which involved the issuing of a fatwa by an acknowledged Islamic authority). The penalty for apostasy in Islamic law is death.

The literal meaning of jihad is 'effort' or 'struggle' against a believer's own moral shortcomings. This is 'the great jihad' as opposed to 'the little jihad' – the war against the enemies of Islam. But the Koranic sources that would justify a 'holy war' are quite ambiguous. Muslims are allowed to engage in a defensive war: 'Permission to take up arms is hereby given to those who are attacked, because they have been wronged.' Another verse states: 'But when the Sacred Months are past, then kill the idolaters wherever you find them.'

This was the verse cited by Osama bin Laden when he announced, on 22 February 1998, the formation of his World Islamic Front for the Jihad against the Jews and the Crusaders. On 12 March 1998, 40 Afghan ulema held a shura in Kandahar and issued a fatwa declaring jihad 'according to Islamic law', against America and its followers.[23]

For Qutb, and for al-Zawahiri after him, the home base for the revival of Islam was their native Egypt. They were the modern proponents of Salafism, movements for the re-establishment of an ideal Muslim state based on the shari'a. Qutb's book was banned. He was re-arrested and charged with conspiracy to overthrow the government by assassinating various public figures. He was hanged in August 1966.

Ayman al-Zawahiri was 17 years old. He was a quiet, well-spoken and exemplary student, but secretive. Two years earlier, he had formed a small cell of like-minded students who had heard stories of Qutb's sufferings in prison, and had been fired by his message. In the repressive political climate of the time, with political parties banned, small clandestine groups like al-Zawahiri's were forming all over Egypt. They consisted mainly of students, restless, alienated, disorganized and usually unaware of each other's existence.

The turning point for Arab Muslims in general, and for young students like Ayman in particular, was Israel's decisive victory in the Six Day War in 1967. As Wright states: 'They lost not only their armies and their territory but also faith in their leaders, in their countries and in themselves. For many Muslims, it was as though they had been defeated by a force far larger than the tiny country of Israel, by something unfathomable – modernity itself. A newly strident voice was heard in the mosques, one that answered despair with a simple formulation: Islam is the solution.'[24]

The year 1967 spelt the beginning of the end of Arab socialism, or Nasserism, as a political force in Egypt and the Arab world. After Nasser died of a heart attack in 1970, his successor, Anwar Sadat, needed allies. The leaders of the Muslim Brotherhood were in prison. Sadat offered them a deal: in return for their release from prison and their support, he would allow them to preach in the mosques as long as they did not resort to violence. Forbidden to act as a political party, the Brothers began to spread their influence widely, in the student unions, the trade unions and the professions.

But a younger generation of Egyptians had been radicalized. Islamic fundamentalists inspired by the preaching of Sheikh Omar Abdul Rahman, organized themselves into the Jaamah Islamiyya (Islamic Group). Sadat even supplied them with arms to defend themselves against Marxists and Nasserites. The universities also became radicalized. Al-Zawahiri, who was then completing his medical degree, was able to boast to a family friend, Dr Abdullah Schleifer, an American Jewish convert to Sufi Islam, that by 1974 his group had 40 members. His greatest recruiting successes were in Cairo University's elite faculties, the medical and engineering schools. These had been the strongholds of the Marxists in the 1960s.[25]

By the late 1970s, most of these radical student groups came together in al-Zawahiri's Islamic Jihad, which developed a two-phase programme based on Sayyid Qutb's manifesto: first, reform Egypt, chiefly through the imposition of the shari'a, and then use Egypt as the base or focus of a new caliphate that would be the rallying point of the Arab-Islamic world.

After graduating from medical school and being trained as a surgeon, Dr Ayman al-Zawahiri contracted a marriage in a very traditional manner with the exceptionally religious daughter of a prominent Cairo family. Both her parents were lawyers. He spent three years as an army surgeon before setting up his own clinic in his family home in the Cairo suburb of Maadi. In 1980, while standing in for another doctor at a medical clinic in Cairo run by the Muslim Brothers, he agreed to accompany its director on a humanitarian mission to Pakistan.

Al-Zawahiri spent four months working at a clinic in Peshawar operated by the Red Crescent for Afghan refugees who had begun to arrive in the province in large numbers. He returned again to Peshawar in 1981 but left after two months. His abrupt return to Cairo may have been prompted by considerations that had more to do with developments in Egypt.

The year 1979 had marked a watershed in the annals of Islamic militancy. The Ayatollah Khomeini had returned to Tehran after a long exile to lead the first successful Islamist take-over of a major Muslim country. When the exiled Shah sought medical treatment in the United States, student mobs attacked the US embassy in Tehran and held 52 Americans hostage, thus defying the superpower that had backed the Shah. But for President Sadat of Egypt Khomeini was 'a lunatic madman ... who had turned Islam into a mockery'. Sadat offered the ailing Shah a refuge in Egypt where he died the following year.

But as Lawrence Wright comments, for Islamic militants the Khomeini revolution reframed the debate with the West: 'Instead of conceding the future of Islam to a secular, democratic model, he imposed a reversal, by seeking a future within the Islamic discourse of the past.' Wright also quotes from one of Khomeini's earlier diatribes, which links up with the writings of Qutb and shaped the Islamist agenda of bin Laden and al-Qaeda: 'People cannot be made obedient except with the sword! The sword is the key to Paradise, which can be opened only for holy warriors.' As Wright concludes, 'The overnight transformation of a relatively wealthy, powerful modern country such as Iran into a rigid theocracy proved that the Islamists' dream was eminently achievable, and it quickened their desire to act.'[26]

Also in 1979, President Sadat signed a peace treaty with Israel and called upon Egyptians to endorse it in a referendum. It was a charade: 99.9 per cent of the voters were officially reported to have approved the treaty. In response to a series of demonstrations orchestrated by the Islamists, Sadat reversed his previous position by banning all religious student associations. In the 1970s, many female students had begun to wear the niqab (the Islamic veil that masks the whole face except for the eyes) as an outward sign of their piety. By banning the niqab at universities, Sadat exposed himself to charges of apostasy. He had signed his own death warrant.

Al-Zawahiri's plan was not to assassinate the head of state but to completely overthrow the existing order: it was a longer-term strategy consisting of infiltrating the armed forces, the bureaucracy and state institutions, acquiring weapons and then bringing about a coup d'état that would receive wide popular support. (It was strangely reminiscent of the strategy followed by the communists in Afghanistan who had come to power the previous year.)

But his plans were overtaken by events. In September 1981, alerted to the possibility of a conspiracy, Sadat ordered the arrest of more than 1500 persons, not only known Islamists, but others who had no connection with them – intellectuals, writers, journalists, students, Marxists and Coptic Christians, some of them prominent Egyptians. On 6 October 1981, Sadat was assassinated in full view of the public during a military parade. The assailants belonged to a military cell in the ranks of Islamic Jihad led by a young army officer, Khaled Islambouli. 'I have killed the Pharaoh', he shouted before the cameras. Zawahiri was among some 700 others arrested after the assassination. He testified later that he had nothing to do with the plot to kill Sadat. This was quite plausible. It was a premature action that had upset his carefully thought-out strategy for an Islamic revolution in his country.

Zawahiri was among the 300 defendants tried in December 1982. In a separate trial for 23 others, five were condemned to death, including Islambouli. As spokesman for his co-defendants, Zawahiri publicly avowed his Islamism, and was defiant: 'We are not sorry ... we are here, the real Islamic opposition against Zionism, Communism and Imperialism.' When he was released from prison in 1984, the gentler Ayman of before had turned into a hardened radical, with an 'overwhelming desire for revenge', according to a psychologist who had met him after his release. He had been tortured in prison, forced into betraying a fellow conspirator, an army officer who had helped him by assembling a cache of weapons, and was humiliated to the point of despair. In 1985, fearing for his safety because of his testimony in a case brought by former prisoners against the intelligence unit that conducted prison interrogations, Zawahiri left for Saudi Arabia to work in a medical clinic in Jeddah.

There he renewed his acquaintance with Osama bin Laden who was based in Jeddah. They might have met before in Peshawar. Bin Laden was then only 28 years old but already a seasoned fund-raiser for the jihad in Afghanistan, travelling to and from Pakistan prior to settling in Peshawar in 1986. Zawahiri was 35 years old, a committed Islamist who had operated in an underground cell for more than half his life and had come close to martyrdom in the single-minded pursuit of his mission: 'His political skills had been honed by prison debates, and he had discovered in himself a capacity – and a hunger – for leadership. He was pious, determined and embittered.'[27]

The evolution of al-Qaeda

After the Soviet withdrawal the United States turned its back on Afghanistan. The 'Arab Afghans' were of no further use to the US and its Saudi allies who were soon confronted with a new threat when Saddam Hussein invaded Kuwait in 1990. The USSR was also falling apart. The Islamic militants dispersed to their own countries or to fight other jihadi wars in Bosnia, Yemen or Kashmir. Large numbers still remained in Pakistan.

In 1989 bin Laden returned to Saudi Arabia. During the Gulf War he protested against the presence of American troops on Saudi soil. He had offered to organize for the Saudi rulers an international corps of Arabs to help defend the Saudi oil fields. They had instead preferred to activate the US defence umbrella, promising that the American troops would leave after the war. But a year after the end of the Gulf War, American troops remained on Saudi soil. Bin Laden felt betrayed.

He nursed what he believed to be a legitimate religious grievance against the presence of 'infidel' foreign troops on Saudi soil, based on the words of the Prophet: 'Let there be no two religions in Arabia.' The second caliph Umar had issued 'a final and irrevocable decree' that Jews and Christians be evicted from the 'holy land of Hijaz' and proceeded to expel or re-locate them, in an early version of ethnic cleansing. Bin Laden himself referred to a *hadith* (saying) of the Prophet on his deathbed: 'If Allah wills, and I die, God willing I will expel the Jews and the Christians from Arabia.'[28]

Threatened with arrest because of his public criticism of the Saudi rulers and his financing of Saudi dissidents in Britain, he flew to the Sudan in 1991 in his private jet, with his three wives, ten children and some followers. There a regime dominated by Islamic fundamentalists was in power. Bin Laden was warmly received by the *eminence grise* of the government, the brilliantly articulate Dr Hassan al-Turabi, a product of London University and the Sorbonne. Turabi was the leader of an Islamist party, the National Islamic Front. Its politics were the politics of Zawahiri's Islamic Jihad, but openly pursued. The country offered bin Laden a convenient and congenial base where he could develop al-Qaeda for international operations against American targets.[29]

In the Sudan, bin Laden combined the pursuit of new business interests with the pursuit of his jihad against the Americans in particular and in support of jihadi causes abroad in general. Each activity supported the other, but were kept strictly separate, with the jihadi dimension being confined to his loyal 'Arab Afghans', chiefly Egyptian veterans, who carried out their operations behind a veil of secrecy.[30]

Bin Laden had inherited his share of the $80 million of the colossal family fortune at his father's death in 1967, when he was ten years old. He now used his wealth, estimated to have increased to some $250 million by then, largely in foreign bank accounts, to establish nine holding companies in the Sudan with a wide range of commercial activities They included joint ventures with the Sudanese government on large infrastructure projects that greatly benefited the economy. One of these was a new 800-kilometre highway from Khartoum to Port Sudan to replace the old 1200-kilometre road.

Some of these activities were legitimate businesses, but some were also used as cover in support of the al-Qaeda network, to effect transfers of funds to jihadi causes through the bank accounts of Islamic 'charities' located abroad. For example, a Vienna-based agency, Third World Relief, funnelled millions of dollars raised from fund-raising efforts to the Muslims in the Bosnian conflict. Trained 'Afghan Arabs' were also sent to fight alongside the

Bosnian Muslims. Another example was a plane with a cargo of sugar for Afghanistan that returned to the Sudan with a consignment of guns and rockets.

But such operations were carried out in such secrecy that employees in bin Laden's commercial enterprises were quite unaware of al-Qaeda's existence. Bin Laden also financed three training camps in the north of the country as more and more 'Afghan Arabs' and other recruits arrived in the Sudan to support his operations. Some were employed as instructors in his camps, others to serve as liaison to militant Islamic groups abroad, and others as trusted management experts and economists to run his businesses. In May 1993, when Pakistan arrested 800 Arabs with a view to expelling them, bin Laden paid the travel expenses to the Sudan of 300 of them.

In 1994, the Saudi government stripped bin Laden of his Saudi nationality, froze his bank accounts and confiscated his assets. But to finance al-Qaeda, he received donations, as for the Afghan jihad, from wealthy businessmen in Saudi Arabia, the United Arab Emirates and Kuwait, tapped into Islamic charities, some of which, acting behind corporate shells, served as mere fronts for fund-raising, and so created the extensive but nebulous financial network that has proved so difficult to penetrate.

In the meantime, Ayman al-Zawahiri was pursuing his own nationalist agenda, with its focus on Egypt, in contrast to what already appeared in the Sudan to have become bin Laden's objective, to merge all national groups into some kind of multi-national corporation with specialized departments, under the al-Qaeda umbrella and subject to his direction. He became increasingly reluctant to fund the two rival Egyptian Islamist organizations, also because of their constant quarrels and conflicting aims and methods. But for Zawahiri, his association with bin Laden was a marriage of convenience. Strapped for funds, he travelled to the United States in 1993. He had been there before, in 1989, when he visited the Services Bureau in Brooklyn on a recruitment drive. This time he was on a fund-raising drive in California which was not much of a success.[31]

Thereafter, Zawahiri began working more closely with bin Laden, and his own committed followers went on the bin Laden payroll. In 1993, bin Laden sent an experienced member of Islamic Jihad, Mohammad Atef (also known as al-Hafs al-Masri) on exploratory missions to Somalia where US troops were engaged in a humanitarian mission. Atef may have planned the details of an anti-American operation with the Somali warlord, Mohammad Farah Aidid. The result of those visits was the shooting down of two Black Hawk helicopters with rocket-propelled grenades in October 1993. Eighteen US marines lost their lives.

The US peace-keeping force of 28,000 was withdrawn after that famous incident. It was a reason for bin Laden to boast, in his first interview on al-

Jazeera television in 1999, when he recalled: 'Based on the reports we received from our brothers, who participated in the jihad in Somalia, we learned that they saw the weakness, frailty and cowardice of US troops. Only eighteen troops were killed. Nevertheless, they fled in the heart of darkness, frustrated after they had caused great commotion about the New World Order.'[32]

He had claimed as much to Hamid Mir, his Pakistani biographer, the previous year. One could say that while bin Laden pointed, his operatives planned the attacks, leaving the task of execution to others. More usually, it was his rhetoric alone that pointed the direction, while trained operatives chose the targets and planned the operational details. This kind of *modus operandi* made it very difficult for investigators to trace bin Laden's personal responsibility for specific terrorist attacks and made his denials plausible. His personal responsibility has to be sought in his stated intentions and in his exhortations. It was also his style to praise those who had carried out terrorist attacks, especially if they had become 'martyrs' (*shaheed*) in the process.

Zawahiri's methods on the other hand were more 'linear', from designating targets through the planning and the execution. Sudan seemed ideal for launching terrorist attacks in Egypt, with its long, trackless and virtually unguarded borders, and the ancient caravan trails across the desert for smuggling weapons and explosives. Dr Zawahiri had developed an association with Dr Turabi whom he greatly admired as an Islamic intellectual. He could count on the active cooperation of Sudan's intelligence agency and military forces penetrated by Islamists. Islamic Jihad renewed its campaign in Egypt in August 1993, with an attempt on the life of the interior minister who was cracking down on Islamic militants. A passing motor cycle exploded next to the minister's car, killing only the bomber and his accomplice. Zawahiri's men also tried to kill the Egyptian prime minister in November 1993 with a car bomb as he was being driven past a girls' school: the prime minister escaped but the explosion injured 21 persons and killed a 12-year-old schoolgirl.[33]

The death of the schoolgirl outraged the Egyptian public which had seen 240 people killed in the previous two years, mostly by members of the Jaamah Islamiyya who targeted mainly Christians and their churches in the Islamic stronghold of Assyut in Upper Egypt. The crowds at the girl's funeral cried: 'Terrorism is the enemy of God.'

The use of suicide bombers broke the religious taboos against suicide and the murder of innocents. Zawahiri was a pioneer in the systematic use of suicide bombers. Another of his innovations was to record on video the bomber's vows of martyrdom on the eve of a mission. Zawahiri was also 'obsessed with secrecy and imposed a blind-cell structure on the organization, so that members in one group would not know the activities or the personnel in another. Thus a security breach in one cell should not compromise other units, and certainly not the entire organization.'[34]

These methods were to become the stock-in-trade of al-Qaeda when it went global. Unfortunately for Zawahiri, Islamic Jihad lost almost its entire Egyptian base when the authorities arrested the keeper of their membership records. They found a computer containing the entire database. Armed with this information, which included home addresses and the names used on false passports, the security forces pulled in a thousand suspects and placed 300 of them on trial in military courts on charges of attempting to overthrow the government. As Wright comments: 'The evidence was thin, the judicial standards weren't very vigorous.'

If Islamic Jihad was to survive, it would have to be outside Egypt. Zawahiri was reported to have travelled extensively in the early 1990s, visiting Austria, the Balkans, Dagestan, Iran, Iraq, the Philippines and even Argentina. (There is a very large Arab immigrant population in the 'Triangle', the region where the borders of Argentina, Brazil and Paraguay meet.) He often used a false passport. In April 1995, Zawahiri presided over a meeting in Khartoum that decided the assassination of President Hosni Mubarak of Egypt. The attack was carried out in June in Addis Ababa, when Mubarak was on a state visit. In a shoot-out with the president's bodyguards, two Ethiopian policemen were killed but Mubarak escaped unharmed.

The Egyptian government responded with a ruthless campaign to root out Islamic militants. New prisons were built to hold political prisoners whose numbers were estimated by human rights organizations at 15,000. Zawahiri's response was to bomb the Egyptian embassy in Islamabad on 19 November 1995: two cars loaded with explosives crashed through the embassy gates, killing the bombers, 16 others and wounding 60. This act of mass murder was Zawahiri's first success in conveying 'an eloquent and clear message', as he boasted in his memoirs.[35]

After his success in Somalia in 1993, bin Laden's 'pointing', in the pursuit of his main objective at the time – the forcing of US forces out of Arabia – resulted in two attacks. In November 1995, a car bomb outside a building used by US servicemen in Riyadh killed five Americans and two Indians. The alleged perpetrators were caught and beheaded before US intelligence agents could interrogate them. In June 1996, the explosion of a bomb placed in a fuel truck parked outside the Khobar Tower military complex in Dahran killed 19 US servicemen and injured hundreds of others, including Saudis.

In the Sudan, there were attempts by the Saudi and Egyptian intelligence services on the lives of bin Laden and Zawahiri. In the latter attempt, two young boys from families related to Islamists were blackmailed by Egyptian agents, in a particularly fiendish way, to spy on the father of one of the boys, a bin Laden operative, and to plant a suitcase bomb to kill Zawahiri. Sudanese security agents arrested the boys on suspicion when they were found in the vicinity of the Egyptian embassy. and put them in prison. Zawahiri obtained the temporary release of the boys so that he could interrogate them. The Sudanese, who were dependent on bin Laden's generosity, agreed. Zawahiri convened an Islamic court to judge the boys on a charge of treason and had them executed, but not before having a videotape made of their confession for distribution as a warning to others who might betray the organization. According to Wright's interlocutor: 'Many Islamists turned against Zawahiri because of this.'

The Sudanese authorities were furious at Zawahiri's behaviour. They were also under US and Saudi pressure to expel bin Laden. Without being given much notice, he left on a chartered jet with his family and entourage to find sanctuary with his old Afghan mujahideen allies in Jalalabad, and then with the Taliban, whom, as we have seen, he had generously supported in their drive to power. It was reported that the Sudanese government, through a back channel, had offered to arrest bin Laden and have him placed in custody in Saudi Arabia. But the US was unable to persuade the Saudis to accept him, and, lacking a case to indict him in a US court, allowed him to leave the Sudan unmolested.[36]

According to Wright, Zawahiri's own movements after his departure from the Sudan are not clear. He was variously reported to have been tracked to Bosnia, Holland and Switzerland. The Swiss police denied reports that he had taken up residence, or even arrived there. But an al-Qaeda computer obtained by a US journalist after the fall of the Taliban revealed that in December 1996 Zawahiri was on his way to Chechnya to establish a new base for the remnants of Egyptian Jihad there. The Russians had begun to withdraw after the failure of their first war in Chechnya and 'conditions there were excellent', he wrote in the computer memo. To the Islamists, Chechnya offered an opportunity to create an Islamic republic in the Muslim regions of the Caucasus from where they could wage jihad throughout Central Asia.[37]

Zawahiri and two of his chief lieutenants were arrested when they tried to cross into the Russian province of Dagestan. The Russians discovered false identity papers and a Sudanese passport that Zawahiri sometimes used. The passport showed that he had been to Yemen four times, Malaysia three times, Singapore twice and China (probably Taiwan) once – all in the previous 20 months. Zawahiri and his companions were brought to trial in April 1997 for entering Russian territory illegally and given a six-month sentence. As they had nearly completed their term in prison, they were released the next month. After the Russian fiasco, Zawahiri and his family had no other option but to join bin Laden in Afghanistan. The Taliban had taken power in Kabul the previous year. They had now found a new sanctuary and an ideal base in the first Islamic state totally committed to the implementation of the shari'a.

In Afghanistan, Osama bin Laden, with the collusion of the highly impressionable Taliban leader, Mullah Omar, hijacked a failing state. To seal his alliance, bin Laden took one of Omar's daughters as his fourth wife. The extent of the al-Qaeda hold on Afghanistan on the eve of Operation Enduring Freedom is revealed by an al-Jazeera television journalist: '260 Arabs in four bases around Kandahar, 145 Arabs in Uruzgan in two bases, 1,870 fighters in Kabul in seven bases, 404 around Mazar-i-Saharif, 400 in three bases around Kunduz, 300 in Laghman province, 1,700 in 12 bases in Nangahar Province opposite Pakistan's North-West Frontier Province, 160 in Kunar, 600 in Khost and 740 in Paktia.'[38]

It was not their numbers that counted but their discipline and their motivation. There were also the contingents from Pakistan, the militants from Central Asia and the Chechens. Al-Qaeda had become the occupying power in a failed state, and Afghanistan their base of operations for a global jihad.

Al-Qaeda at work: the evidence (1992–2001)

There was little to suggest that in the attacks or planned attacks on American targets before September 11 there was a mastermind that directed the choice of target or the operational tactics or even strategies. The operatives, however, were all Sunni Muslims who were either 'Arab Afghans' or were drawn from extremist factions of failed Islamic political movements in their countries of origin, or both. Many of them had also received training in al-Qaeda camps in the Sudan and later in Afghanistan.

In Algeria, returning 'Afghans' who had rallied to the Front islamique de salut (FIS) formed the Groupe islamique armé (GIA), after the government's repression of the FIS when they won the first round of the general elections in December 1992. The GIA resorted to pure terrorism, not only killing soldiers, policemen and officials, but carrying out unspeakable atrocities against defenceless civilians and village communities.

In Egypt, the Jamaah Islamiyya (Islamic Group) was a rival of Dr Zawahiri's Egyptian Jihad. It was also a fundamentalist movement whose 'spiritual guide' was the blind cleric Sheikh Omar Abdur Rahman, who was later to be convicted in a US court for his part in the 1993 bombing of the World Trade Center. The Jaamah Islamiyya, whose leaders were also 'Arab Afghans', had been responsible for terrorist attacks in Egypt that had killed 1100 people since 1992. Hounded by the Egyptian police, their original leaders had been imprisoned; those who remained had been driven to Upper Egypt where they had first begun their campaign of terror by targeting Coptic Christian communities. Their last major atrocity was carried out in Luxor in 1997 when they opened fire on foreign tourists, killing 68. The leader of the massacre was an 'Arab Afghan', Mehat Mohamed Abdul Rahman, as was another participant, Sayid Sayyed Salambe, whose extradition by the US at the request of the Egyptian authorities provoked an angry reaction from bin Laden. The latter had been equally furious at the imprisonment of Sheikh Omar.

Before September 11, the best sources of information on al-Qaeda, as well as insights into its organization, choice of targets and methods, were the highly publicized trials in US courts of those indicted for the bombing of the World Trade Center in February 1993, for the suicidal attacks of the two US embassies in East Africa in August 1998 and for the plot to set off a suitcase bomb at Los Angeles airport on Millennium Eve.[39]

Among the five convicted in the WTC bombing of 1993 was Sheikh Omar who had left Egypt, spent some time in the Sudan and had then settled in New Jersey. The ringleader was Ramzi Yousef, a Pakistani who had grown up in Kuwait. Their intention was to set off an explosion that would topple one tower against the other, and release cyanide gas at the same time. The attempt was botched. The bomb that went off did not have sufficient explosive force and caused relatively few casualties – six dead but many more injured. They were also accused of planning to blow up the United Nations headquarters, the FBI headquarters and key bridges and tunnels in New York, and to assassinate President Hosni Mubarak of Egypt.[40]

While his accomplices were apprehended, Ramzi Yousef was able to escape to Pakistan and then move to the Philippines, where he conspired with the local Abu Sayyaf group to assassinate President Clinton and the Pope. Ramzi also plotted to blow up 12 American passenger aircraft over the Pacific on a single day in January 1995. All these plans were thwarted when the Filipino police discovered damning evidence in Ramzi's Manila flat after a fire had broken out there. Ramzi escaped to Pakistan, where he was arrested in 1995 at the request of the FBI and extradited to the US. It was also disclosed at the trial that a Pakistani with a newly acquired commercial pilot's licence planned to crash a small plane into the CIA headquarters in Langley, Virginia.[41]

Insights into the al-Qaeda organization were provided at the trial by a highly placed defector, Osama bin Laden's Sudanese accountant, Jamal Ahmed al-Fadl, who had surfaced in Asmara, Eritrea, in 1996 after misappropriating some of his master's funds, following quarrels about the disparities in the salaries paid to favoured Saudi and Egyptian associates compared to others like himself. After being debriefed there by the CIA, al-Fadl was turned over to the FBI who placed him on their witness protection programme. He proved a goldmine of information on al-Qaeda. In his testimony Jamal al-Fadl described a complex organization, with business operations and three committees – military, religious and financial. Bin

Laden and his supporters used business fronts to move funds secretly by wire and computer.[42]

At the New York trial of those indicted for the August 1998 embassy bombings in East Africa, one of the accused, Wadih el Hage, disclosed that he had been ordered by bin Laden, who was then in the Sudan, to bring over surplus Stinger missiles in the hands of former Afghan mujahideen by air from Pakistan to the Sudan. Another of the accused, a Tanzanian, Khalfan Khamis Mohamed, admitted to his role in the bombing of the embassy in Dar es Salaam, but appeared to have no knowledge of who had planned it. Peter Bergen is quoted in an article in The Economist as saying: 'This confirms a pattern of foot-soldiers who knew very little of the wider plan, and master-minds who are spirited out of the country immediately after or even before the attack takes place.'

Further information was provided at the trial of a group of Canada-based Algerians who had planned to set off a suitcase bomb at Los Angeles airport on Millennium Eve. The suspicious behaviour at the Canadian border of one of the conspirators, Ahmed Ressam, whose knowledge of English was limited, led to his arrest and interrogation. Ressam gave evidence for the prosecution. He confessed to having received six months of training at a camp in Afghanistan in 1998, along with other volunteers from Arab countries and from Chechnya and France. They were taught to blow up the infrastructure of a country – airports, railways, large corporation buildings – as well as the techniques of urban warfare and the assassination of individuals. Ressam himself was given $12,000 to cover initial expenses for setting up the Los Angeles operation. When he asked for more cash, he was asked to finance himself by credit card fraud and similar means.

One of the four convicted in July 2001 for the embassy bombings in East Africa, Mohamed Rashid al-Owhali, also trained in Ressam's camp. He and Mohamed Odeh, who helped prepare the Nairobi bomb, testified that al-Qaeda was highly organized and professional. There was a military committee that was responsible for proposing and organizing attacks, and other committees for fund-raising, administration and political affairs. There were cells with a leader in charge for intelligence gathering, and three other members assigned to logistics, surveillance and other duties. The Nairobi operation used long-time 'sleepers', and 'cleanskins' who had never been on operations before. Bin Laden himself had never had contact with any of the Nairobi bombers, except that al-Owhali admitted to having had a chance meeting with him long before in Peshawar. The actual operatives were selected, briefed and supervised by senior aides, some from separate and affiliated organizations. It emerged that the key characteristic of al-Qaeda was that it acted mainly as a facilitator and coordinator but did not command or organize the individual operations.[43]

Reports were agreed that there were four al-Qaeda training camps in Afghanistan, teaching bomb-making, intelligence-gathering, security, disguise, sabotage and abduction. Intensive police work in Europe in the two years before September 11, particularly by the French and Italians, threw light on the selection process of prospective al-Qaeda operatives. Recruits, selected by al-Qaeda agents in many parts of the world, travelled to Pakistan where they handed over their passports, papers and cash, and waited in safe houses while they underwent background checks before being sent in groups to the training camps in Afghanistan. According to US, European and Pakistani intelligence sources, some 11,000 al-Qaeda recruits are estimated to have been trained in the Afghan camps in the five years before September 11, 2001 – 3000 of them in 'hard-core' terrorism, 8000 others in logistics, money transfers and other 'soft' operations.

The 'gatekeeper', said to have been responsible for the training of the recruits and their deployment after training, was the Palestinian Abu Zubaydah. He is believed to have been responsible for planning the attack on the USS Cole in Aden harbour on 12 October 2000, when suicidal militants steered a dinghy full of explosives into the side of the ship, killing 17 American sailors and seriously wounding 39 others. He was among the 25 Arabs and five Afghans arrested in raids on houses in two Pakistani cities at the end of March 2002. He was a major catch. He would be in a position, as gatekeeper, to reveal the identities of many key al-Qaeda operatives and 'sleepers' in Europe and elsewhere who passed through his hands.[44]

From the evidence available before September 11, one could draw some tentative conclusions about al-Qaeda. It was loosely organized, but multi-tiered and difficult to deconstruct. Its supporters were not card-carrying members of a party hierarchy but shared a common Islamic radicalism with diverse ideological roots, which gave them a sense of mission. They were inspired by a 'guru', Osama bin Laden, who gave coherence to the vision within an exclusively religious frame of reference, and a direction.

In a pre-recorded tape, released through al-Jazeera television in Qatar after the US bombing of Afghanistan began on 7 October 2001, bin Laden declared: 'Our nation has been tasting for more than 80 years this humiliation and contempt. ... [The United States will not] enjoy security before we can see it as a reality in Palestine (with Jerusalem liberated) and before the infidel armies leave the land of Muhammed.'

The humiliation 'for more than 80 years' refers to the period since the abolition of the caliphate by Kemal Ataturk in 1924.[45] In addition to his 'mission' since 1990 – the expulsion of US troops from Saudi Arabia – bin Laden referred to the most emotive issue in the Arab world: the plight of the Palestinians, dispossessed and defeated with the establishment of the state of Israel in their midst. In bin Laden's historically flawed, ill-informed and religiously inspired mental universe, he had helped topple the Russians in the Afghan jihad, just as the Arab armies of the Prophet had overcome the two greatest empires of his day: Byzantine Rome and Sassanid Persia. Only America remained – the 'Hubal of the Age' – and 'the Hypocrites', the Arab Muslim rulers 'propped up' by America. After the formal merger of al-Qaeda with Egypt's Islamic Jihad in early 1998, bin Laden included such rulers as legitimate targets in his global jihad against America.[46]

The 1999 trial in Cairo of members of Islamic Jihad, which had merged the previous year with bin Laden's al-Qaeda in the World Islamic Front for the Jihad against Jews and Crusaders, produced a rich trove of documents. Although Islamic Jihad had been fighting the Egyptian government for years, with little effect, it provided tactical support to al-Qaeda by forging travel documents, transferring money and arranging communications. After its leader, Dr Ayman al-Zawahiri, joined up with Bin Laden in Afghanistan in 1997, he merged his organization with bin Laden's al-Qaeda, gradually changing its focus from a national struggle to a global struggle against US interests.

During his interrogation by Egyptian security agents, one Jihad member stated: 'Osama wanted to launch a guerrilla war not only in the Arab and Islamic world, but in the whole world. ... He believed these attacks would force America to change their policy in the Middle East and the Islamic world, and this would fulfil the ultimate goals of the Front. It would show the weakness of these Arab and Islamic leaders compared to the Front.'[47]

The know-how, methods and experience of the Egyptians greatly enhanced al-Qaeda's organizational capacity. As reported by Susan Sachs:

> To support their terrorism, they skimmed money from a charity for Muslim orphans in Albania and robbed an Italian diplomat's home in Jordan. They acquired or forged seals from universities, border guards and the Saudi Arabian Interior Ministry. They brooked no dissent or deceit: suspecting that the 15-year-old son of one member was an informant, they murdered the boy. These were the hard-hearted often itinerant men of al-Qaeda at work. These men used the Muslim pilgrimages to Islamic holy sites in Saudi Arabia as a cover for recruiting new members or passing cash from one member to another. They moved money around the globe to bail members out of jail in Algeria or Canada, and to finance applications for political asylum and thus implant terrorist cells in Western Europe.[48]

The defendants at the Cairo trial, the biggest since the trials of the assassins of Anwar Sadat and the associated suspects, described a network of isolated cells throughout west Asia and Europe. There were references to bin Laden as the organization's financier, and to a safe house he maintained in San'a, Yemen. The network maintained bank accounts in many countries – England, Germany, Poland and Albania among them – and would send small amounts, less than $2000 at a time, through the accounts to support the activities of its members. Some of the 107 defendants had served time in prison after the Sadat assassination and had participated in the Afghan jihad. In what became known in Egypt as 'the trial of the Albanian returnees', the court convicted 87 of the 107 defendants, and sentenced ten of them to death, including their leader, Dr Ayman al-Zawahiri, tried in absentia. Zawahiri was bin Laden's deputy, and Mohamed Atef, another Egyptian (and his son's father-in-law), his chief of operations.[49]

Al-Qaeda groups together three generations: the founder-members who are all Arab veterans of the Afghan jihad; a generation that lived through the failure of Islamist parties in their countries of origin (Egypt, Algeria) or were radicalized by their life in Muslim ghettos in Europe; and Muslim youths in revolt who yearn for service in a global cause and who were recruited from mosques in the West and in Tablighi centres such as Finsbury Park in London or Mantes la Jolie near Paris. One such was the British-Jamaican 'shoe-bomber', Richard Reid, whose personal itinerary and travels, apparently as an agent of al-Qaeda, are quite instructive.

Many of the conspiracies linked to al-Qaeda were hatched by operatives based in Europe who found in these open and liberal societies an easier operating environment because of the ease of travel and communications. Once trained in Afghan camps, they were sent out as 'sleepers' and appear to have had considerable latitude in choosing their targets and executing their plans, in order to minimize communications and detection.

Police and intelligence operations that started after the discovery of a cell in Frankfurt on 26 December 2000 revealed the scope of the European networks of al-Qaeda. The cell members arrested in Frankfurt were two Iraqis and a French Muslim. Their leader was an Algerian, Mohammad Bensakhria, who escaped but was arrested in Spain in June 2001. The Frankfurt police found detailed handwritten instructions relating to the manufacture and use of handmade explosives and toxic substances. Corroborating evidence gathered by police in Milan revealed that the Frankfurt arrests may have averted some kind of chemical attack that was being planned, as well as the bombing of the European Parliament and other targets in Strasbourg.[50]

The police in Milan had planted listening devices and telephone taps in the apartment of a Tunisian, Esid Sami Ben Khemais, who had moved there in March 1998 after training for two years in Afghan camps. His activities and movements were documented in 300 pages of evidence presented to Italian courts, including police reports, arrest warrants and transcripts of bugged conversations and telephone calls, made available to *The Washington Post*. Khemais had telephoned and visited suspected terrorists in Spain, where eight were subsequently indicted; it was discovered that one group had planned to blow up the US embassy in Paris. The police found a telephone number that corresponded to a number in Mohammad Atta's apartment in Hamburg. Atta, the presumed ringleader of the WTC suicide bombers, had apparently visited Spain on two occasions.

The Spanish cells had begun to take shape as early as 1994 in a group called the Soldiers of Allah, led by a Palestinian and a Syrian. These two had left for Peshawar in 1995. Khemais and his deputy had also made calls to two of al-Qaeda's point men in Europe, Bensakhria in Germany and Hayder abu Doha, an Algerian who moved to London in 1999 after serving as a senior al-Qaeda operative in Afghanistan. Doha had been charged in London for organizing attacks in the United States and was fighting extradition to the US. A third point man in Europe, Tarek Maroufi – a Tunisian with Belgian citizenship – figured on a warrant issued by the Italian prosecutor, Stefano Dambruoso, but remained free because his Belgian citizenship prevented his extradition to Italy.

European investigators had observed that the structure of Arab terrorist networks in Europe had changed after 1998: violent, radical militants who had left behind conflicts in Afghanistan, Bosnia and Chechnya found a new organizing principle in bin Laden's campaign against the West. Initially cells were organized under two large umbrellas, one Egyptian (called Anathema and Exile), the other Algerian (Salafi Group for Preaching and Combat). These multi-national networks coalesced through the efforts of at least three key individuals mobilized by al-Qaeda, Abu Doha, Bensakhria and Maroufi.

Another pattern also emerged. Plots by North African groups against European and American targets appeared to be secondary: success or failure was unimportant as long as the attacks generated fear. They were also inept. Cells were penetrated before they could execute their plans. In 1994 Algerian hijackers of an Air France flight planned to crash the plane into the Eiffel Tower. But none of them was a pilot. They expected the French pilot to crash the plane with a gun at his head. The aircraft was stormed by French commandos when it was forced to land in Marseilles for refuelling. The Algerian Ressam expected to get through the Canadian border with a car-load of explosives and a smattering of English.

But al-Qaeda's signature operations, like the US embassy bombings in East Africa, the attack on the USS Cole and the September 11 attacks, were entrusted to select groups. Mohammad Atta was well educated, fluent in English and German, and had lived for several years in Hamburg where he held legitimate jobs. His associates were carefully selected and tightly insulated. They were English-speaking operatives from Egypt and the Gulf, supported by Saudis. According to a French official: 'Why Saudis? It's more difficult for North Africans to get visas. They can't move as easily in America. They don't have the language. And they don't control themselves as well.'

On 28 July 2001 Djemal Beghal, a French-Algerian, was arrested in the transit lounge of Dubai airport, taken to a prison cell, beaten and his family threatened until he poured out a wealth of information that enabled police investigators in Europe to act. Beghal's mission was to plan the suicide bombing of the US embassy in Paris. After months of training in Afghanistan, he had been summoned by the al-Qaeda 'gatekeeper', Abu Zubaydah, and instructed to return to France via Morocco and Spain.[51]

Beghal's personal history is also very instructive. Born in 1965, he was brought by his immigrant parents to Paris as a child where he grew up in one of those crime-ridden, low-cost public housing projects (HLM) that surround the French capital. He went through the French school system, married a Frenchwoman and appeared to have integrated well. But like many immigrants, he was stuck at the bottom, drifting between menial jobs, which was frustrating for someone of his intelligence and leadership potential. In the mosques the alienated Beghal discovered his vocation. In 1994 he was picked up in a police swoop after an attack on the Paris subway system by Algerian radicals. It is not clear whether he was imprisoned, but after this first encounter with the police he became a militant, speaking in makeshift mosques, raising money for Muslims fighting in Chechnya and Bosnia and for other Islamic causes. In 1997 he moved with his wife and children to London.[52]

It is surprising how often London turned up in investigations as a kind of clearing-house for Islamic radicals. British Intelligence officials and members of two London mosques testified that there Beghal met another Frenchman of his background, Zacarias Moussaoui, who is generally suspected to have been the 20th member of the September 11 hijacking team – a replacement for Mohammad Atta's flatmate in Hamburg, Ramzi Binalshib, who could not get a US visa.[53]

From London, Beghal made frequent trips to Spain, the Netherlands and Belgium and to France. Beghal and Moussaoui frequented the mosque run by Abu Qatada, a Palestinian cleric who had fought in Afghanistan and was sentenced to life imprisonment in Jordan for his involvement in bombings there. He was granted political asylum in Britain in 1994. British liberalism seemed to provide a soft environment for al-Qaeda operatives. The leader of al-Qaeda's Madrid cell, Eddin Barakat Yarkas, also known as Abu Dadha, who was arrested in November 2001, had made dozens of trips across Europe, including 20 visits to London. His telephone number was found among Mohammad Atta's papers and in the diary of one of his room-mates in Hamburg. In London, Beghal was part of a circle that included Moussaoui and Kamel Daoudi, another Algerian-born Frenchman whom he had included in his plot to blow up the US embassy in Paris. After leaving Afghanistan, Beghal was to pick up $50,000 for the Paris operation, rent a house, set up a business cover and buy a van at the Salon de l'Auto. A former

Tunisian-born soccer player living in Belgium was to drive the van loaded with explosives into the embassy compound and blow it up.

According to Louis Bruguière, the French *juge d'instruction* who specialized in investigating terrorist organizations: 'For these groups, there are no borders.' Those in the European cells had European passports, some of them false. Different responsibilities – the storage of explosives, the forging of papers and credit cards, financial support, logistics – were assigned to different countries. Different countries had different political and legal cultures, different traditions of police power, different levels of care about individual rights to privacy and protection from the state. The reach and sophistication of the al-Qaeda network were underestimated. 'The problem was bigger than we thought', said a senior British official quoted in the *International Herald Tribune*.[54]

When trying to make sense of the secretive international networks of Islamic terrorists that came to be known as al-Qaeda, their links with bin Laden were found to be tenuous and circumstantial at best. Many of their plans were thwarted by police arrests in various countries, and did not approach the levels of preparation and sophistication implicit in the September 11 attacks.

According to a former CIA official, intense surveillance efforts in the two years before September 11, 2001 had paid off: a plan by a Canada-based Algerian group to plant a suitcase bomb in Los Angeles airport on Millennium Eve, plans to blow up on the same night US warships and a hotel in Amman, Jordan, were pre-empted by the arrests in various countries of supposedly bin Laden operatives. So what went wrong? 'What went wrong was we fitted bin Laden and al-Qaeda into existing paradigms of terrorism and terrorist organization. But that doesn't work. He is something entirely different, entirely new.' What security experts came to realize was that al-Qaeda is neither a traditional hierarchical organization with a leader, deputies and a cell structure, nor merely an association of vaguely like-minded, loosely affiliated individuals. It is both and neither.[55]

The global reach of Osama bin Laden's influence, and links to al-Qaeda, were revealed by the arrests in Singapore, between 9 and 24 December 2001, of 15 Muslims belonging to a group called Jemaah Islamiya that was part of a larger, regional structure based in Malaysia. The arrests were prompted by a videotape found in a house in Kabul. At least eight of those arrested had trained in Afghan camps. Members of the gang were casing US ships, US company buildings and other American targets.

Following the Singapore arrests, an al-Qaeda-trained Indonesian munitions expert, Rohman Ghozi, was arrested in Manila just before he was about to board a flight to Thailand. He was charged with the illegal possession of a ton of explosives, and with being involved in the bombing of a local commuter train in December 2000 that had taken 20 lives. Ghozi had been travelling to the Philippines since 1996 and had contacts with the Moro Islamic Liberation Front – which in turn had contacts with the notorious Abu Sayyaf group. This group specialized in hostage-taking for ransom. Their penchant for decapitating some of their victims had a Saudi resonance.

According to a specialist in international terrorism, Rohan Gunaratne of St Andrews University in Scotland, 'Osama developed a strong relationship with the Abu Sayyaf founder, Abdulrajak Jaujalani, and sent his son-in-law, Jamal Khalifa, to establish a Qaeda presence in the region.' The prime minister of Malaysia himself, Mahathir Mohamad, acknowledged that Muslim extremists in Malaysia, the Philippines and Indonesia planned to overthrow local governments and establish a Muslim caliphate across three countries.

The smoking guns of al-Qaeda

The amateur videotape, date-stamped 9 November 2001 and found in a house in Jalalabad, shows an unscripted bin Laden receiving a Saudi dinner visitor and commenting on the September 11 attacks. It provides the most compelling proof of bin Laden's ultimate responsibility, the closest one can get to 'a smoking gun': he had foreknowledge of the attacks and a familiarity with the technicalities of the impact and the damage it would cause. 'We had calculated that the floors that would be hit would be three or four floors, but due to my experience in this field, I was thinking that the fire from the fuel would melt the iron structures of the building and collapse the area where the plane hit and all the floors above it only. This was all we had hoped for. [What actually happened] was a lot more than we expected. [The brothers] were overjoyed when the first plane hit the building, so I said, "be patient".'

What was most chilling in the tape was bin Laden's chuckle[56] when he recalled, 'the brothers who conducted the operation, all they knew was they have a martyrdom operation. We asked each of them to go to America, but they didn't know one thing about the operation, one letter.' His 'pilots' did not tell their fellow hijackers until they were 'walking fast' towards the airline gate, 'that the operation is, we are going to hit the building'. He also seemed to know personally the identity of two of the hijackers, the Alhazmi brothers, young Saudis whom he praised for understanding the law of the Prophet: 'killing oneself for the sake of God is better than the books and pamphlets'.

When considering the question of bin Laden's personal responsibility, direct or indirect, for al-Qaeda operations, it is useful to bear in mind what he said when questioned by a Pakistani journalist, Hamid Mir, whom he had commissioned as his biographer.[57] He admitted responsibility for assisting the Somali warlord, Mohamed Farah Aidid, to stage an ambush in which 18 US marines were killed. The harrowing sight on television screens of a dead marine being dragged through the streets of Mogadishu, with his body attached to a pick-up, ensured more than anything else that the United States would in future shy away from peacekeeping operations. The dead marine was after all engaged in an international humanitarian mission to provide food and medical assistance to starving Somalis in a failed state.

Bin Laden, however, denied responsibility for the June 1996 attack on the Khobar barracks in Dahran, Saudi Arabia, when 19 US soldiers died and some 500 others, including Saudis, were injured,[58] or for the East African bombings in 1998: 'I am not involved, but I praise the people that did it.' He may have been telling the truth. But bin Laden's responsibility for September 11 cannot be in question. According to the editor of the London-based Arabic newspaper Al-Quds al-Arabi, he had warned three weeks before that he would carry out an unprecedented attack on America: 'a very big one'.[59]

The September 11 attacks combined all the elements and ideas, and the lessons learned, in previous terrorist operations in Europe and the United States: the WTC explosion in 1993 showed up the mismatch between the means employed and the ambitious objective; the clumsy attempt in 1994 by Algerian hijackers to use a passenger aircraft as a missile against the Eiffel Tower showed the need for a discreet pilot-training programme for dedicated al-Qaeda operatives prepared to die in the attempt. The simultaneity of the 1998 suicide bombings of the US embassies in East Africa had sent a clear message, but what message could be clearer than the simultaneous targeting of the very symbols of American power on American soil? The element of surprise in East Africa was due in no small part to the use of 'sleepers' and 'cleanskins'. The hapless young Saudis, 'cleanskins' who were to be used as helpers in the hijackings, were informed of the suicidal nature of the operation only just before they boarded the aircraft.

September 11 was also a symbolic date, 79 years to the day that Palestine was brought under the British mandate, dashing the hopes of Arab nationalists who had dreamed of creating a unified state out of the Arab components of the former Ottoman Empire. As mentioned earlier, this explains bin Laden's reference to 'the humiliation for more than 80 years'.

In stark contrast to the feelings of horror experienced by millions around the world at the September 11 events were the scenes of rejoicing of Palestinians in Gaza, or of Muslim youths in the streets of Cairo and Karachi brandishing posters and photographs of their hero Osama bin Laden. These scenes were embarrassing and inexplicable. More understandable were the scenes of protest in the Arab, Pakistani and Indonesian streets when the US began bombing targets in Afghanistan on 7 October, the expressions of concern in Muslim capitals for civilian casualties, echoed also by the international media and human rights groups, and the talk of 'double standards' by

Arab politicians and journalists, that the killing of Palestinian, Iraqi and Afghan children counted for less in Western eyes than American casualties.

The scenes on the Arab streets must be seen as an expression of the sense of powerlessness among the youth of the Arab world. Professor Huntington has become somewhat unfashionable and politically incorrect these days, but he wrote in a 1993 article that today the world's billion or so Muslims are 'convinced of the superiority of their culture, and obsessed with the inferiority of their power'.[60]

Osama bin Laden's grand strategy was to harness the sense of despair and impotence among the youth of the Arab world and direct their rage outwards against the United States. The script had worked in his favour before: the embassy bombings in East Africa and the attack on the USS *Cole* had provoked the Clinton administration, acting hastily on flawed intelligence, to launch Cruise missiles against a terrorist camp in Afghanistan and destroy a Sudanese pharmaceutical company in Khartoum in September 1999. The ensuing anger in the Muslim world had made bin Laden an instant hero for many Muslims. Pakistani women began to name their male babies after him.

The US retaliatory bombing of Afghanistan following September 11 would, according to the bin Laden script, provoke Muslim outrage that would advance the cause of Islamic revolution within the Muslim world itself, polarizing that world between his version of the Muslim umma, or Community of the Faithful, and 'faithless' Muslim societies led by governments, considered corrupt, repressive, 'un-Islamic' and illegitimate, that were allied to and supported by America and the West. The bin Laden strategy was to win the hearts and minds of the umma, and this was also the thrust of his statement quoted at the beginning of this chapter.

As Michael Scott Doran argues persuasively, the United States was thus being drawn into 'somebody else's civil war'.[61] The cartoonist got it right. Danziger has one turbanned and bearded figure reading from a newspaper: 'Listen, O Great One – the Americans have divided the world into those who are for them and those who are against them.' The other figure (bin Laden) responds, 'Well, well, things are going according to plan.'[62]

As it turned out, the 'collateral damage' caused by the US bombings was remarkably low considering the circumstances, and some of the major incidents were duly investigated and acknowledged by the Pentagon. Without entering into the pros and cons of the issues raised by the mainly Muslim protestors, it must be mentioned for the record that the number of civilian casualties pale in comparison with the deaths inflicted by Muslims on Muslims in Afghanistan. During a short period in 1994, 25,000 civilians were killed in Hekmatyar's rocket attacks on Kabul, devastating a city that had remained largely intact until then, and thousands more were killed during the Taliban drive to power, including large-scale massacres in the Hazarajat, in the Shomali plains north of Kabul and in Mazar-i-Sharif.

The death toll in the September 11 attacks has been established at more than 3000 people, 2801 of them belonging to some 70 different countries. A large number of Muslims from the sub-continent and from Arab countries also died in the Twin Towers in Manhattan.

That Osama bin Laden was able to carry out his attacks of September 11 was widely attributed to a failure of intelligence. It was more due to a failure of the international coordination of intelligence. Readers of John le Carré are familiar with the rivalries within British counter-intelligence agencies as well as between them and their counterparts across the Atlantic. They have a natural inclination to guard their respective turfs. This is not fictional. But as we have seen in the case of European police operations in the two years before September 11, there was a lot of information on al-Qaeda that was successfully used to prevent many planned attacks through the sharing of intelligence and cooperation between national police forces on an ad hoc basis. But there were no permanent institutional arrangements because of conflicting sovereignties and police procedures even within the European Union. Europol had not yet begun to function.

In the United States a Counter-Terrorism Security Group (CSG) had been established under the Clinton administration. It was a close-knit group of experts, drawn from the CIA, the FBI, the National Security Council and the Defense, Justice and State Departments, which was presided over by Richard Clarke. Clarke was the national coordinator for counter-terrorism in the White House since the previous Bush administration. The group met every week in the White House Situation Room and would be briefed by John P. O'Neill, the legendary FBI agent with an obsession: the growing threat of al-Qaeda. O'Neill 'was not just the guy you turned to for a situation report. He was the guy who would say the thing that everybody in the room wishes he had said.'[63]

O'Neill had worked with Clarke to establish clear lines of responsibility among the intelligence agencies, and in 1995 a presidential decree designated the FBI as the lead authority for investigating and preventing acts of terrorism wherever Americans or American interests were threatened.[64] Thus the institutional mechanisms and procedures were established and functioning under the Clinton administration. Intelligence leads were painstakingly pursued, with major successes in many cases, both in the United States and in Europe.

But the global war against terrorism requires international action to create an institutional framework for information sharing and the coordination of police investigations, operations and judicial action. Some of the practical obstacles to cooperation have been mentioned in the present account. Indeed, they are best known to the police and intelligence operatives themselves. It would be the responsibility of the governments concerned to generate the will to remove the obstacles. Such an effort might even require amending existing national legislations. The Belgian citizenship of a prime al-Qaeda suspect that prevented his extradition to Italy is a good example.

When the Egyptian authorities began their campaign to stamp out Islamic fundamentalists in the early 1990s, they complained that their efforts were thwarted by the protection afforded to Islamist fugitives by Western countries. They alleged that more than 500 terrorists had found refuge in England, France, Germany, Austria, Denmark, Belgium, Holland and the United States. Many European governments refused to extradite suspects to countries where judicial standards were thought to be less stringent, or where suspects could be tortured during interrogation or face the death penalty in a trial.

There was, however, a new vigilance after bin Laden's open Declaration of Jihad in February 1998 followed soon after by a fatwa issued by a meeting of ulema in Afghanistan. This development prompted national police and intelligence agencies to intensify their vigilance, which paid off when many planned attacks were prevented, as we have seen.

In July 1998, CIA agents kidnapped two members of Egypt's Islamic Jihad in Baku, Azerbaijan, and found that the laptop computer belonging to one of them, Ahmad Salama Mabruk, contained some vital information about Jihad members in Europe. This enabled them to move against a cell in Tirana, Albania, that had been created by al-Zawahiri in the early 1990s. There were 16 members in the cell and the CIA succeeded in kidnapping five of them with the help of Albanian agents and sending them to Cairo after interrogation.[65]

On 6 August, a month after the break-up of the Tirana cell, Zawahiri sent a declaration from Afghanistan that was published in the London-based Arabic newspaper, Al-Quds al-Arabi, whose editor always seemed to have privileged access to the al-Qaeda leaders. The declaration read: 'We are interested in briefly telling the Americans that their message has been received and that the response, which we hope they will read carefully, is being prepared, because, with God's help, we will write it in the language that they understand.' The next day, suicide bombings carried out simultaneously destroyed the US embassies in Kenya and Tanzania. There was here, beside the clarity of the message, a clear connection, for the first time, between al-Zawahiri, if not bin Laden, and a specific terrorist action.

The retaliatory missile attacks of 20 August on an al-Qaeda training camp in Afghanistan turned out not only to be futile but counter-productive. When the voice of the target of the attack, Osama bin Laden, crackled across a radio transmission soon after – 'By the grace of God, I am alive' – anti-

American elements in the Muslim world had found their champion. As Wright comments: 'Here was a man whose defiance of America now seemed blessed by divine favour.'

A day after the missile attacks in Afghanistan and in the Sudan, which cost American taxpayers $79 million merely to expose the inadequacy of their expensive intelligence services, al-Zawahiri called a reporter in Karachi with a message: 'Tell the Americans that we aren't afraid of their bombardments, threats, and acts of aggression. We suffered and survived the Soviet bombings for ten years in Afghanistan and we are ready for more sacrifices. The war has only just begun; the Americans should now await the answer.'[66]

A year after September 11, 2001, in the uncertainty surrounding the whereabouts of bin Laden, or indeed whether he is dead or alive, it would be salutary to bear in mind the comments of a former official of the US State Department, David Long, in response to the question: 'Is Osama bin Laden the exclusive font of terrorist evil?' His answer was No. 'Bin Laden is a facilitator – a practitioner of the most ancient way of doing things in the Middle East. He does not have the brilliant top-of-the-art international structure of Abu Nidal' – the Palestinian terrorist of the 1970s and the mid-1980s – 'If you were to kill Osama tomorrow, the Osama organisation would disappear, but all the networks would still be there.'[67]

The odour of al-Qaeda has been detected in further terrorist attacks that have taken place since September 11: the bombing of a synagogue in Tunisia, the attacks on Christian targets in Pakistan, the attack on a French warship off the coast of Yemen that is reminiscent of the attack on the USS *Cole*. These are perhaps the work of loose cannons, carried out by operatives possibly linked to al-Qaeda.

The clues lie, however, in the nature of the targets chosen – if one were to apply the strategy of detection in murder stories where the investigator seeks clues to the identity of the unknown murderer in the profile of the known victim. Looked at in this way, the mass murder of more than 180 tourists in the Indonesian island of Bali in October 2002 could be the harbinger of an ominous new development: the application of the fundamentalist bin Laden/Zawahiri ideology of jihad to wider, softer targets. The target here was a popular nightclub filled with Western tourists in a location where any 'collateral' local victims would likely be Balinese Hindus, not Indonesian Muslims. Here the al-Qaeda inspiration, including the method, is fairly clear.

However, there could be other explanations, such as a particularly horrible manifestation of local xenophobia. The Sari Club in Kuta was exclusive, inaccessible to the locals unless they were invited, or accompanied by foreigners.[68] But the Balinese are a gentle people, and their beautiful island has become so dependent on the tourist trade for its prosperity that such an expression of anger would be suicidal to their livelihood, their prosperity and their future.

Al-Qaeda remains the candidate. The Indonesian Riudan Isamuddin, known as Hambali, who has been linked to every terrorist activity against foreign targets since he returned from the Afghan jihad, remains at large. Given the mind-set of al-Qaeda, the further danger is that its followers would not hesitate to use weapons of mass destruction, even a crude nuclear device, if they could lay their hands on them. In the current state of the world's politics the prospects are mind-boggling.

CHAPTER 17

Winning a War, Building the Peace

T he extraordinary thing about September 11 is that for many around the world, from nations to individuals, it concentrated minds. People were forced to take a stand, and there could be no moral drift. It was not that civilization was at stake, or was in mortal danger. But September 11 showed up the fact that civilization is a fragile edifice, a human construction, built up over centuries of civic struggle, of human effort to transcend 'Nature, red in tooth and claw'. September 11 also showed that there was such a thing as civilized values, at the core of which was respect for human life, the first of the commandments, 'Thou shalt not kill'.

Some commentators have suggested that September 11 was comparable to the fall of the Berlin Wall. But that event clarified only what happened before it. With hindsight, the spread of communism and the Cold War took on a quite different aspect. It was a mere episode in human history, quite an aberrant one, but still an *accident de parcours*, a wrong turning and a false direction, a dire warning of the dangers of utopianism, not more. From that perspective also, the term 'post-Cold War era' has no particular meaning, except for those victims of 'the evil empire' who had to pick up the pieces of their shattered lives and hopes in their sorely wounded countries.[1]

But the collapse of the Soviet Union did produce one incontrovertible new reality. It left the United States as the world's only superpower, with an enormous political, economic and military potential to exercise a power unprecedented in history. With its innovative technologies, its competitive industries, and its dynamic international bankers and businessmen, the United States was at the cutting edge of economic globalization. Its national interests would be paramount in the exercise of its new imperial power. No one could quarrel with that in principle. But it is now the great task of its leaders and strategic planners to decide, in the spirit of their republican traditions, where those national interests lie, when they exercise their virtually unlimited, but not necessarily unchallenged, power beyond their national frontiers. How the United States now chooses to manage its responsibilities as a superpower in the short and long terms is bound to define the contours of the post-September 11 era. Given the wisdom, the will and the vision, the windows are wide open for opportunities without precedent.

To begin with, isolationism is no longer an option available to US leaders. That old policy represented the refusal of the young American republic to become embroiled in the civil wars of Europe. The corollary of that policy was the Monroe Doctrine, which put the states of the Old World on notice that the US would not brook their intervention in the internal affairs of the New World, north or south. The US abandoned its isolationism on two notable occasions in the twentieth century; first, when it intervened on the side of the European allies against German militarism in the Great War, and again during the Second World War, when it was itself attacked by Japan. The US retreat into isolationism after the Great War, when Congress failed to ratify US membership of a League of Nations that its visionary president Woodrow Wilson had done so much to create, is generally agreed to have been a costly mistake.

In the weeks following the outrage of September 11, the United States did not immediately 'lash out in a vengeful rage'. Instead, it channelled the universally expressed empathy and support into concrete actions in a 'coalition against terror' that had many dimensions: the coordination of international police investigations, the sharing of intelligence, the tightening of institutional controls to trace and interdict the flow of al-Qaeda finances. But the most skilful of the short-term achievements was the rapid mobilization of support for the military campaign in Afghanistan, carried out with energy and finesse by the US Secretary of State, Colin Powell.[2]

The diplomatic success was due in the first place to the reaction of sheer horror at the events of September 11. Even China's communist leader telephoned President Bush as the horror was unfolding in New York, and two candlelight vigils of solidarity were held by Iranians, in a country that the US had taken every opportunity to insult and vilify in the past. Besides obtaining the unconditional support of its natural allies in NATO, which invoked Article 5 of its constitution for the first time, the US obtained the acquiescence of China and Iran and, most importantly, the support of the front-line states – Pakistan, Uzbekistan and Tajikistan – for easing the logistics of the military campaign. Most remarkable was the support of President Putin of the Russian Federation that may represent a real turning point in post-Cold War Russo-American relations. President Putin waived his objections to the US using airfields in Uzbekistan and Tajikistan for military purposes after his defence minister had previously limited their use to purely humanitarian operations. Implicit in the coalition against terror was an acknowledgement of America's superpower status. But there was also a large measure of self-interest involved, especially on the part of some states that courted US acquiescence in their campaigns, criticized by human rights groups, against their own home-grown terrorists.

After initially announcing two targets in its military campaign – the al-Qaeda training camps and installations in Afghanistan and the Taliban – the United States downplayed the latter objective in deference to concerns expressed by its partners in the coalition regarding civilian casualties and refugee flows. As in all military campaigns whose outcomes are difficult to predict once they are launched, the results in this case went beyond the most optimistic expectations. Not only was the al-Qaeda presence practically eliminated in Afghanistan, but the Taliban as a political force evaporated virtually into thin air, leaving room for an interim government to be formed and installed by December 2001.

The military campaign in Afghanistan, what came to be called Operation Enduring Freedom, was carried out after meticulous planning in which the British played a key role. As Prime Minister Tony Blair expressed it, there was no point in 'bombing sand' in order to retaliate against al-Qaeda.[3] A major ground offensive was ruled out, not because of American reluctance to engage combat troops and face unacceptable levels of casualties, as some commentators inferred, but for sound military reasons dictated by the topography. Heavily armed and equipped coalition troops dropped into static positions would have been vulnerable to attacks by Taliban and al-Qaeda forces operating in small, mobile units from the surrounding hills. It would mean being drawn into a possibly interminable war against guerrillas who were familiar with the terrain. Ground combat troops would also require considerable helicopter support for the large-scale movements of troops and supplies. Supply lines from bases in Central Asia would be long, involving hazardous flights, in bad winter weather and low visibility, over the high ranges of the Hindu Kush.[4]

A second option was a heavy bombing campaign to destabilize the enemy, allowing the forces of the Northern Alliance to advance against them. But intelligence available to the British had revealed the essential weaknesses of the Alliance, both as a cohesive political group and a military force. It was well known that the Alliance consisted of mainly ethnically based rival groups, led respectively by Ismael Khan (Herati), General Dostum (Uzbek), Karim Khalili (Hazara) and Massoud (Tajik). After the assassination of the charismatic Massoud by al-Qaeda on 9 September, the command of his Panjshiri veterans had passed into the hands of an untested deputy, Mohammad Fahim. The forces of the Alliance consisted of some 15,000 regulars, assisted by an equal number of armed peasant militias. Together they had at their disposal some 200 barely serviceable Soviet-era tanks and a few pieces of artillery and heavy mortars. Facing them would be Taliban forces numbering from 40,000 to 50,000 men, a large percentage consisting of Pakistani and other foreign volunteers, and Osama bin Laden's contingent of some 4–5000 trained fanatics from around the Muslim world known as

Brigade 55. They had at their disposal about 200 tanks and some powerful artillery.[5]

It was the third option that was implemented, very successfully as it turned out, in what amounted to a classic textbook operation, inspired also by the lessons learned from Operation Desert Storm and the air war in Kosovo: a blistering air offensive to weaken or destroy the Taliban's operational capacity, followed by a ground offensive executed by Northern Alliance forces with American, British and Russian assistance.

In the run-up to the second phase, the Russians provided the Northern Alliance with 60 T-55 battle tanks, 12 T-62 K command tanks and 30 infantry fighting vehicles; other coalition partners supplied weapons and ammunition, including new uniforms that would give fighters from the disparate, rival groups a semblance of psychological cohesion. Behind a veil of secrecy, US Special Forces and CIA agents were dropped by helicopter into northern Afghanistan to guide the bombers to their targets, to assist in communications and impose field discipline in conformity with a coordinated plan of action.

The execution of the first phase, the air war, began on Sunday, 7 October, when some 50 Cruise missiles were launched from US ships and British submarines; 25 carrier-based aircraft and 15 land-based bombers destroyed Taliban air defences, communications infrastructure and airports in Kabul, Jalalabad, Kandahar and Herat using 'smart' bombs' that hit their targets, including the small Taliban fleet of parked planes and helicopters, with precision. By the second week it was clear that coalition aircraft were unchallenged in the air: roving navy bombers began to seek out what US Defense Secretary Donald Rumsfeld, in his daily press briefings at the Pentagon, called 'targets of opportunity' – tanks, military vehicles and fuel depots. A powerful low-flying gunship (the Airforce AC 130U, or 'Spectre') made its appearance over the Taliban stronghold of Kandahar, and on 19 October US ground combat troops (Army Rangers and the elite Delta Force) carried out a night raid to take out a housing complex in Kandahar used by the Taliban leader, Mullah Omar, an airstrip and an al-Qaeda training camp. The first US casualties were two servicemen who died in a helicopter crash in Pakistan in the course of the operation.

The pattern of bombings thereafter – airstrikes throughout Afghanistan, including the al-Qaeda stronghold of Kunduz in the north, Taliban defences around the strategic city of Mazar-i-Sharif, the Shomali plains north of Kabul, carpet-bombing of Taliban forces around the Bagram airbase, the use of cluster bombs and the dreadful 'daisy-cutter' (the BLU-82, weighing 15,000 lbs, that could destroy hundreds of the enemy at a time) – suggested that the air war was intended to 'hollow out' the Taliban front lines before the Northern Alliance was allowed to engage them. After four weeks of relentless air strikes, the air offensive appeared to be interminable and the bombers running out of credible targets.[6]

In the first weeks of the air campaign, which mainly targeted the offensive capabilities of the Taliban and al-Qaeda emplacements, 'regime change' did not appear to have been a war aim. Holding back on front-line strikes against the Taliban also appeared to have been deliberate. There were fears that, given the past record of some of the Alliance leaders like the Uzbek General Rostum, their forces would sweep into Kabul and wreak vengeance on the Pashtuns, who were the chief supporters of the Taliban. There was also some misinformation involved, through leaks to the press that the US did not trust the Northern Alliance and that the campaign on the ground would be conducted by US Special Forces operating behind Taliban lines.[7]

The ground had to be prepared for the rallying of the Pashtun tribes against the Taliban. Pashtun leaders like the legendary mujahideen commander, Abdul Haq, and Hamid Karzai, the tribal leader of the Popolzai Pashtuns and a supporter of the exiled king, were already active behind Taliban lines in the east and south respectively. Abdul Haq was caught and executed by the Taliban on 26 October, and Karzai himself nearly fell victim to a misdirected American air strike in the vicinity of Kandahar.

When it emerged that the air campaign had worked so well that Taliban resistance was quickly overcome when Alliance forces began capturing the main cities, the longer-term strategy for an orderly, negotiated transfer of power to a broad-based, representative provisional government (from which moderate Taliban leaders were not in principle excluded) was overtaken by events. On 9 November, Alliance fighters occupied Mazar-i-Sharif; on 12 November, Ismail Khan returned triumphantly to his old fiefdom of Herat; on 13 November, Alliance troops entered Kabul and were welcomed by a jubilant populace; on 15 November, the important Pashtun city of Jalalabad was also recovered, this time by local Pashtun warlords. This was a repetition of the classic Afghan scenario of local power-brokers and warlords shifting their loyalties to the winner of the moment.

Outbreaks of looting and casual executions of Taliban stragglers prompted the United Nations to announce plans, on 13 November, for the deployment of a multi-national force to Kabul, a city with a mixed but largely Pashtun population that was now occupied by Tajik forces. The first contingents of the International Security Assistance Force (ISAF) began to arrive at the end of the year. The initial force of 3000 was drawn from 18 member-states of NATO and deployed for a period of six months under British command. The endorsement of the ISAF mandate was one of the first official acts of the provisional Afghan government.

Meanwhile, the war remained to be won. The decisive breakthrough had occurred in Mazar. With the US deploying its high-tech arsenal to attack enemy positions from the air, the Uzbek General Rostum sent 1000 horse-men charging uphill through the mountains west of Mazar to get inside the range of the Taliban's heavy artillery and capture their positions. This latter-day 'charge of the light brigade' – 300 of the horsemen were killed – took the Taliban completely by surprise. They simply ran away.

Taliban and foreign al-Qaeda fighters who had fled Mazar and other locations in the north escaped to their stronghold of Kunduz where they prepared for a last stand. But the 15,000 fighters found themselves hopelessly surrounded and besieged by far superior forces. Some escaped to the south, but the majority negotiated their surrender through a trusted intermediary, Amir Jhan. At a meeting with Dostum at his fortress-headquarters of Qala-i-Jangi, where some American and British personnel were present, Jhan con-veyed an offer from the Taliban to surrender their weapons and be allowed to go home, while the foreigners would surrender and be handed over to the UN. Defense Secretary Donald Rumsfeld reportedly intervened at this point to demand that the entire Taliban force surrender to the Northern Alliance in return for a pledge that their lives would be spared, while those identified as foreign or al-Qaeda elements were to be taken to the fortress to be incar-cerated and await their interrogation by the CIA. The arrangement was concluded on 21 November. But those incarcerated at Qala-i-Jangi attempted an uprising on 23–25 November that resulted in a bloodbath: among the 470 prisoners, only 85 survived the gunfights and airstrikes called in by US and British special forces who participated in the counterattacks, in full view of the television cameras. Others killed were 30 guards and a CIA agent.[8]

The journalist Jamie Doran alleges that some 5000 of the 8000 Taliban who surrendered to the Northern Alliance at Kunduz are unaccounted for. The prisoners were taken to a large fort, Qala-i-Zeini, which escaped media attention because of the excitement created by the uprising in Qala-i-Jangi. According to the intermediary who negotiated the surrender, Amir Jhan: 'I counted them one by one; there were 8000. Now there are only 3015 left. And among these 3015 are local Pashtun people from Kunduz, Shibargan, Balkh and Mazar who were not even among the original persons I handed over. Where are the rest?' According to other eyewitnesses found during Doran's six-month-long investigation, the prisoners at Qala-i-Zeini were literally packed into 25 containers of 200 persons each and were to be taken to a prison in Shibergan, located in the Uzbek region of Jowjazan. Some did not arrive there, and most of those who did arrive were found to be dead or dying when the containers were opened, and disposed of in the desert known as Dasht-i-Leili outside Shibergan. There was a mound in the desert where human remains were found by Doran. If this report is substantiated, the atrocities are a throwback to the horrendous treatment meted out to Taliban prisoners by Uzbek militias after their failure to occupy Mazar in 1997 and the similar fate suffered by Hazara prisoners after the Taliban finally captured Mazar in 1998.[9]

UNHCR reported in February 2002 that some 20,000 refugees, mainly Pashtuns, had fled the north as a result of harassment by their non-Pashtun neighbours. Accommodated in a transit camp south of Kandahar, they were awaiting an opportunity to cross into Pakistan, in a new kind of exodus caused this time by ethnic cleansing.[10]

On 6 December, following the formation of the interim government negotiated in Bonn the previous day, the Taliban leader, Mullah Omar, negotiated the surrender of his forces in Kandahar to local tribal chiefs, through an intermediary.[11] With the annihilation of the Taliban as a political and military force in Afghanistan, the US-led coalition forces concentrated on flushing out al-Qaeda. A major operation begun in December was the relentless attacks by B-52 bombers on the complex of caves in Tora Bora, high up in the mountain ranges of the Safid Koh (the White Mountains) overlooking the Pakistani border.

But the US forces here displayed a failure of nerve, a reluctance to engage ground combat troops in strength and incur casualties. Instead they used bombs and drones in the air and Afghan mercenaries on the ground, assisted by 30 American military advisers, in a failed attempt to cordon off a very large and virtually inaccessible region. Hundreds of al-Qaeda militants may have escaped unnoticed into the contiguous tribal agencies of Pakistan where the local population had showed themselves sympathetic to their cause. By the US reliance on Afghans as proxy ground forces in Tora Bora, important al-Qaeda leaders, including bin Laden, may have eluded the net. Similarly, another attempt to encircle remnants of Taliban and al-Qaeda forces in the Shah-i-Kot Valley near Gardez in March 2002 was a missed opportunity because of an excessive reliance on Afghan militias. In the midst of the operation, code-named Anaconda, the United States had to call in 1700 British commandos for help.[12]

When 28 Afghan delegates representing the Northern Alliance and the so-called Rome, Cyprus and Peshawar shuras gathered on 28 November at Königswinter near Bonn, under the auspices of the German Chancellor, Gerhard Schröder, the meeting was not as spontaneous a gathering as it appeared to be. The shuras had met several times before to plot their respective strategies; the foreign ministers of the '6+2 Group' (the six geographically contiguous states, the US and Russia), had met in New York on 13 November to discuss a post-Taliban Afghanistan. Working tirelessly behind the scenes was the UN's Lakhdar Brahimi who also presided over the Bonn meeting.

Hard bargains were driven in the allocation of the 29 ministerial portfolios, such was the level of mistrust between the ethnically based groups. The intransigence of Burhanuddin Rabbani, head of the Jamiat and nominally president of Afghanistan, who refused to accept any arrangements made in Bonn, was overcome through a quiet revolt on the part of his Tajik representatives, notably Yunus Kanouni and Abdullah Abdullah. By 5 December, agreement was reached on the constitution of a transitional Afghan authority for six months, with Hamid Karzai as chairman, until the convening of a Loya Jirga in June 2002 that would elect a provisional government and a president for 18 months. The holding of nationwide elections at the end of the period would be preceded by the adoption of a new constitution.

The election of delegates to the Loya Jirga of 13-16 June in Kabul was organized and closely supervised by the United Nations. The delegates represented a cross-section of the whole nation and included clerics and women. It was opened by the ex-king Zahir Shah who had returned to Kabul after having offered to serve as nominal head of state. The deadlock that arose in the bitter debates on this question was broken when the ex-king renounced any official role for himself. The assembly then elected Karzai as head of government by a large majority, thus conferring a political legitimacy that all Afghans were henceforth obliged to respect.

There were in these developments important implications for the future of Afghanistan. The political role of the monarchy had apparently come to an end. Secondly, Rabbani's intransigence reduced him to irrelevance, and his political demise could signify the demise of 'political Islam' in Afghanistan, as the eviction of the Taliban had thrown 'Islamic fundamentalism' into the proverbial dustbin. A shadow that hovered over the meeting room in Bonn was that of Commander Ahmad Shah Massoud, murdered on 9 September 2001 by two Arabs posing as journalists – bin Laden's last gift to his Taliban protectors. The independent-minded Massoud had become for many of his countrymen the embodiment of Afghan nationalism. During his long years of struggle, first against the Soviets and then against the Taliban, he had refused to be the pawn of foreign powers.

But the formal implementation of the Bonn Agreement left many questions unanswered. Would the new transitional government, representing the collective will legitimized by a Loya Jirga, have the necessary muscle and the material resources to build a new Afghan state that might emerge, Phoenix-like, from the ruins and still-smouldering embers of the old? Would the plans for the political, economic and social reconstruction of Afghanistan envisage the possibility of building, from scratch, the first 'civil society' in the Muslim world?

That peace and security is the necessary precondition for the reconstruction of the country was strongly emphasized by Chairman Karzai in his first public statements. Richard Holbrooke, writing in *The Washington Post*, spelled out the requirements for a post-Taliban Afghanistan: elimination of the terrorist structure, the creation of viable political structures, a mandate to the UN's chief representative that would be similar to those given to Bernard Kouchner in Kosovo or Sergio Vieira de Mello in East Timor, the deployment of about 3000 UN staff for two to four years before local government institutions are established, and, the most essential, a multilateral security force that would allow the new political authorities and the international administrative structure for reconstruction to succeed.[13]

A multi-national force (MNF), as Holbrooke clarified, is a force sanctioned by the Security Council, as distinct from a UN peacekeeping force such as the ones that failed in Rwanda, Somalia and Bosnia, 'almost bringing the UN down with them'. Such UN forces take a long time to assemble, are invariably weak and un-coordinated in their command and control structures, and are far too politicized. But an MNF receives its legitimizing authority from the Security Council, as in East Timor, where Australian troops were able to move in within 96 hours of the enabling Security Council resolution. The International Security Assistance Force in Afghanistan (ISAF), which was set up after Holbrooke wrote his article, is such a force. The mandate of the ISAF was renewed in June for another six months and Turkey has taken over its command from Britain.

As regards American participation in an MNF (such as the ISAF), Holbrooke's thinking was that the US role should be limited to logistics and communications support troops – an American presence on the ground would be too tempting a target for terrorists, suicide bombers and warlords. US objections to the extension of the ISAF presence, now limited to Kabul, throughout Afghanistan, now appear to have been waived. Holbrooke recommends that the United States should be prepared to cover a good portion of the costs of the MNF: 'It isn't cheap, but it will be in the long-term US national interest.' The MNF would be gradually replaced as and when a national police force, fully trained and credible, becomes available to the central government. The training of a truly national multi-ethnic army, loyal only to the representatives of a national government, would also be part of the reconstruction effort, for which some $4.5 billion for a five-year period was initially pledged in Tokyo.

But the training of a sizeable national army would take at least four years to accomplish. So far only 600 men have been trained. Germany has undertaken the training and equipment of a national police force. It seems that in the absence of a pervasive international security presence throughout the country, President Karzai is no more than a glorified mayor of Kabul. He may have been saved in the attempt on his life in September 2002 because of the precaution he had taken, after an earlier bomb blast in Kabul that left 30 dead and 167 wounded, to have US Special Forces personnel assigned for his protection. The danger was not only from recalcitrant Taliban and al-Qaeda elements. The warlords are also flexing their muscles. The assassination of his vice-president and minister, Hajji Abdul Qadir, the head of the Jalalabad shura and governor in pre-Taliban days, may have been due to local feuds involving perhaps drug-related issues.

The last 120 years of Afghan history surveyed in this book provide many object lessons to be kept in mind by the builders of a new Afghan state. It would be essential to avoid setting bad precedents. The responsibility of the international community, in close cooperation with Afghan leaders, in setting the right objectives and tasks, is immense. An underlying objective would be to prevent the country from lapsing into the status of a 'rentier state', as defined in earlier chapters of this book; that is, a state that permanently relies on foreign aid to maintain, develop or expand its infrastructure. This depends very much on the quality of international assistance in the initial years.

The Afghan delegates at the Bonn meeting variously estimated the total costs of reconstruction, including immediate humanitarian assistance, at between $22 and $45 billion. The UNDP, the World Bank and the Asian Development Bank had jointly prepared a needs-assessment report for the pledging conference held in Tokyo on 21–22 January 2002. The report estimated total requirements at $15 billion, to be spent over the next ten years. The priorities that were identified were de-mining, without which large agricultural tracts could not be safely brought under cultivation, as well as schools, hospitals, water supplies and roads. At the Tokyo Conference of potential donors from 60 states, as well as NGOs, a total of $4.5 billion for Afghan reconstruction was pledged for five years, with $1.8 billion to be made available in the first year.

A year after the United States and its allies set out to destroy al-Qaeda and effect a regime change, only about half the amount pledged has been delivered, mainly to meet urgent humanitarian requirements and to start up relatively small reconstruction projects. The needs were exacerbated by the return of 1.7 million refugees. UNHCR, which had expected the return of no more than 1.2 million refugees from Pakistan and Iran, faced acute funding problems. WFP also had great difficulty in meeting its commitments to the millions of Afghans who were facing the consequences of the prolonged drought of the previous years.

Despite the efforts of the UN's Lakhdar Brahimi to obtain a formal endorsement at the Tokyo meeting of a multilateral approach to development funding, coordinated by the UN, donor states preferred to retain control of three-quarters of the budget. Thus, President Bush announced on 13 September 2002 a joint aid package of $180 million from the US, Japan and Saudi Arabia for the reconstruction of the Kabul–Kandahar–Herat highway. The World Bank announced a contribution of $460 million for two years. Other contributions have also been made on an ad hoc basis: in response to President Karzai's urgent appeals: some donor states meeting in Cordoba, Spain, in July 2002 pledged $1 billion for humanitarian assistance and reconstruction projects; during Karzai's first official visit to Islamabad on 8 February, Pakistan pledged $100 million towards reconstruction costs, including the improvement of the roads between the two countries, and a further $10 million towards the administrative expenditures of the Afghan government. During Karzai's visit to Tehran on 26–27 February 2002, Iran pledged $560 million over five years for reconstruction needs; the European Union pledged 9.25 million euros for the return of refugees from neighbouring countries; during Secretary of State Colin Powell's visit to Kabul in February 2002, he had pledged $1 million towards a UN fund for the payment of salaries and the purchase of office equipment for the Afghan administration.

It is essential that the strengthening of national institutions at the central, provincial and district levels be considered a priority, with a strong, long-term commitment by donors to institution building rather than the provision of rapid infusions of cash for the visible projects favoured traditionally by aid-givers. A corollary to this policy is that the salaries of public officials, including teachers and medical personnel, be borne by donors for a reasonable period until the Afghan government is in a position to pay for such recurrent costs from its own resources. In this respect the United Nations Development Programme (UNDP) took a praiseworthy initiative, in advance of the Tokyo meeting, by providing the Karzai government with $6 million in cash to pay its civil servants, many of whom had not been paid for months. This was done despite the fact that in principle UNDP does not fund salaries in its development projects. There is nothing like a guaranteed monthly income to motivate public officials and to keep them on the straight and narrow.[14]

International funding would be required, in the Afghan context, to assist a process whereby a truly representative government can restore social trust and be seen to be providing essential public services and enforce the law. Considerable international assistance and funding would of course be required initially in all these areas. In the meantime it is inadvisable that aid policies are set by outsiders before credible political structures emerge. Bosnia offers some cautionary lessons. In that situation, aid policies favoured wartime Muslim, Croat and Serbian nationalists and their followers; aid served to enrich local fiefdoms and was largely wasted; hasty infusions of cash fostered corruption; and seven years after the Dayton Accords, there is still no credible functioning government at the federal level. The recent elections have confirmed these results.

It is noteworthy that the World Bank, after the costly failures of the 1980s, has come round to the idea, long advocated by the UNDP and experienced NGOs, that it is desirable that projects are planned and implemented at the grassroots level, with the active participation of the target communities. Communities thus empowered would use the initial international resources channelled through NGOs to supplement their own inputs towards projects that would be self-sustaining. Projects implemented since 1997, in the framework of the UNDP's PEACE programme described in Chapter 15, could serve as models. These would bring immediate and tangible benefits, while longer-term policies, aimed at nation-building for modernization and democratization, would have time to work themselves through Afghan society.

The president of the World Bank, James Wolfensohn, has himself endorsed 'quick-action' projects that would enable 1.5 million children to be enrolled in primary schools over the next two years, and food-for-work projects that could generate 100,000 jobs in a short time. He also refers to the country's 'strong and resilient entrepreneurship culture' based on small and medium enterprises, an agricultural sector that can be encouraged to develop traditional farm products that have export markets, such as fresh and dried fruit and nuts, and a vibrant informal economy in cross-border trade.[15]

During the years of war and hardship, the free operation of markets, albeit linked to illicit activities like smuggling, played an important role in sustaining ordinary Afghans, simply as part of a circular flow of income in a trading economy. The application of a framework of rules for the free operation of private enterprise, tied to a banking system and a secure currency, would be a priority task for the interim government.[16] A beginning was made in October 2002 when a new currency was introduced, with a thousand new afghanis exchanged for a million of the old, replacing a confused welter of banknotes issued, or rather printed, by various authorities in the past.

Another priority would be the establishment of a comprehensive system of rural credit, with international funding and technical assistance to safeguard farmers from becoming chronically indebted to unscrupulous money lenders and landowners when they require seeds and tools, as they became in the past, or from selling opium to dealers in return for ready cash, as they seem to be doing now.[17]

A novel approach to economic development, through capitalizing the assets of the poor, was pioneered by the Peruvian economist, Hernando de Soto. In studies of the urban poor who migrated to the cities from the impoverished countryside in search of employment, his research revealed that the poor themselves had created small enterprises in an informal economy. But without legal title to their assets, such as homes, land and workshops, they could not use them as collateral to obtain bank credits. In Peru the terrorists of the Shining Path movement protected peasant land claims as part of their politics. By reforming the laws that made it easier for the poor to gain legal title to their homes and lands, the state itself became involved in protecting title, thereby undermining the guerrillas' support among the peasants. The new appeal was to the entrepreneurial instincts of the poor, to their aspirations, rather than to their stomachs alone. This is development focused at the micro level, encouraging free-market capitalist growth from below.[18]

The philanthropist George Soros, drawing on his experience as a private donor aiming to foster free-market economies and democracies in the former Soviet Union and in ex-Yugoslavia, underlines the dangers when donors compete among themselves in an un-coordinated manner: all aid goes to the same recipient government which can divert resources for its own purposes, or siphon it off for patronage, as in Bosnia. Soros makes a strong case for the United Nations overseeing all reconstruction efforts in Afghanistan, not least because of the multilateral character of its mission. UN agencies already have an extensive presence on the ground as well as a strong core of local staff. Staffing could be expanded by recruiting qualified Afghan expatriates who could later be absorbed to form the backbone of the government bureaucracy.

Soros also thinks that the UNDP has the necessary experience, political openness, transparent budgeting and financial controls to minimize the chances of misallocations and misappropriations. It is also equipped to deliver 'quick-impact' (QI) projects that can be directly administered at the community level. 'By delivering aid at the community level, donors would help the political process by removing some of the urgency for artificial, short-term political solutions. This would also avoid the ugly fight for spoils that has corrupted politics in other countries. Warlords would stick to their territories rather than fight for control of Kabul, as they have done in the past.'[19]

Chris Patten, the European Union's commissioner for external relations, also stresses the need for disciplined donor coordination, steered by the UNDP, the international financial institutions and the Afghan Finance Ministry. He cites the exemplary case of East Timor. He believes, like Soros, that aid should be channelled through the NGOs in Afghanistan who have had field experience for many years, sometimes operating in the most difficult conditions during the Taliban years. Before the Afghan administration begins to function fully, Patten insists that a clear message should be sent to the warlords, local tribal leaders and militias that reconstruction efforts will take place only where there is active support from local players to provide security and stability.

Investor confidence in the future of Afghanistan has emerged in a hopeful sign, the conclusion of an agreement between the governments concerned towards the implementation of the previously aborted UNOCAL project: the construction of a 1500-kilometre gas pipeline from Turkmenistan to Pakistan of which 765 kilometres would be built through Afghanistan. Total costs are projected at $3.4 billion. The project would create 12,000 jobs in Afghanistan, provide training and earn the country 12 per cent of the profits.

There remains the extremely problematic issue of eradicating the cultivation of the poppy - that has often meant survival for peasant families when all else failed - and the production, sale and export of the drugs that kept the warlords in business. Much has been said about the subject in earlier chapters of this book. Both the peasants and the drug barons are not likely to give up easily.

On the eve of September 11, fresh opium was selling on the markets of Afghanistan at $700 a kilo. Two weeks later the price dropped to $100 a kilo. Given the effective ban on opium cultivation imposed by the Taliban in 2000, this development meant, given the extreme sensitivity of the drugs market to fluctuations in supply and demand, that the Taliban were selling off opium from their stockpiles. UN officials believe that after a series of bumper harvests ending with the ban, 2800 tonnes of raw opium, convertible to 280 tonnes of processed heroin, was in the hands of the Taliban, the al-Qaeda network and Afghan and Pakistani drug lords. 'On the wholesale market in Pakistan, this deadly harvest could be worth $1.4 billion. On the streets of London and Milan, processed into white powder, its wholesale value is estimated by Interpol and UN officials at between $40 billion and $80 billion. To put these figures in context, the actual turnover of the European heroin trade is estimated at $20 billion a year. The Afghan stockpile was enough to keep every addict in Europe supplied for three years.'[20]

Enforcing a ban on poppy cultivation and eliminating the drug lords and the smuggling networks running through Pakistan is one of the greatest challenges that face the Afghan administration and the international community. It is desirable that the incentives given to farmers are attractive enough to stop them from planting a crop that has often meant sheer physical survival for their families. On the other hand, the campaign against the drug barons call for very muscular measures indeed.

The cultivation of the poppy resumed in 2002 on a large scale. The production of opium has reportedly risen from 185 tonnes in 2001 to 2700 tonnes in 2002. Three laboratories for the processing of raw opium into heroin have been reported to be operating in the lawless hills south-east of Jalalabad and close to Pakistan. Heroin and the chemicals required to process the opium were being openly traded in the local markets, with prices varying from $500 per kilo for low-quality 'brown' heroin for smoking, and $1500 per kilo for highly refined heroin for intravenous use. The latter could fetch $50,000 per kilo in Britain. A British-led eradication programme, at a cost of $20 million, has led to the destruction of 16,500 hectares of poppy fields out of a total of 80,000 hectares cultivated The programme, however, which involves also the payment to farmers of $1750 for each hectare destroyed, has had no immediate or perceptible impact on the production of heroin, owing to the existence of stockpiles of opium that is used as a form of credit in rural Afghanistan.[21]

Iran's efforts in combating the drug trade have been impressive. Forty-two thousand soldiers, police and militia are deployed along the eastern border, in a front that extends 1950 kilometres from Turkmenistan to the Indian Ocean. In an investment totalling some $1 billion since 1979, Iran has built 200 observation posts, walls to block mountain passes, with trenches and barbed-wire fences extending hundreds of kilometres. Some 3140 members of the security forces, including two generals, have lost their lives in skirmishes with well-armed smugglers. International smuggling networks avoid the Iranian route.

But the battle is far from being won because of the involvement of the Baluchi tribes. The Baluchis, among whom clan loyalties predominate, are found in large numbers in Iran as well as in Afghanistan and Pakistan. They ignore national frontiers. Iran, which for many years denied that there was a drug problem in its Islamic society, has admitted to the presence of some 1.2 million drug addicts and 800,000 occasional users, in a population of 73 million. Drug-related offences account for more than 80,000 prisoners in Iran's total jail population of 170,000.[22]

An issue that has bedevilled Afghanistan's relations with Pakistan in the past has been the status of the Durand Line as an international frontier. As noted in Chapter 3, the Line was demarcated by the British in 1893 in accordance with the Treaty of Gandamak (1879) – the Afghans were obliged to accept humiliating terms, including the cession of large chunks of territory west of the Indus. For British India's successor state of Pakistan, the problems arising from Afghan irredentist claims, which reached a climax under Daoud in 1953–63, were compounded by the existence of a curious historical anomaly: the status of 'the tribal areas lying between the outer boundary of the Province and the line recognized by the Anglo-Afghan Treaty of 1921'. The quotation is from a secret British Foreign Office document, dated 28 April 1949, uncovered as recently as 1998 by a veteran specialist on Afghan affairs.[23]

The 'Province' refers to the North West Frontier Province (NWFP) created by the British in 1901, 'the line' to the Durand Line, and the 'tribal areas' to the five autonomous Tribal Agencies of Malakand, Khyber, Kurram, North Waziristan and South Waziristan. While the so-called 'settled districts' of the NWFP were directly administered by the British (and later became an integral part of Pakistan), the tribal area was not. Since independence the area comes under the purview of the Federally Administered Tribal Agencies (FATA) with a specially constituted frontier constabulary exercising the

flimsiest of controls over an otherwise lawless region. The conclusions of the
Foreign Office legal adviser merit quotation in full:

> On the 15th August 1947, therefore, the tribal areas of the North-West Frontier
> Province became a sort of international limbo, not being part of any state. This
> being so and the tribal areas being independent of Pakistan, though having certain
> treaty relations with her as regards customs, communications and similar matters,
> it would appear that Pakistan could not have inherited either the frontier fixed by
> the Treaty with Afghanistan of 1921 or any right under Article 2 of that treaty.
> This does not mean to say that the Durand Line ceased to be the international
> frontier of Afghanistan. The new situation did not give Afghanistan any right to
> extend her territories to include the tribal areas without the consent of the tribes
> any more than it gave Pakistan the right to do so; but it may well be that Pakistan
> would not have been able to raise any legal objection if the tribes had placed
> themselves under the protection of Afghanistan or if, with the consent of the
> tribes, the tribal areas have been annexed by Afghanistan.[24]

As noted in Chapter 3, the jirga of tribes organized by the British in 1947
requested and obtained affiliation with Pakistan – the choice was between
affiliation with Pakistan or India, not the right to vote for independence or
affiliation with Afghanistan. And so, the legal adviser concludes, 'This gives
Pakistan the conduct of their foreign relations and enables Pakistan to claim
observance of the boundary on their behalf. There was provision in Section
2/3 of the Indian Independence Act for the inclusion in Pakistan at any time
of areas additional to those parts of British India allotted to Pakistan under
Section 2/2 of the Act.'[25]

A review of the arrangements unilaterally carried out by imperial Britain
could now be the proper subject of negotiations between the Afghan interim
government and Pakistan. The conclusion of a treaty that would first recognize the Durand Line as the international frontier, and secondly enable
Pakistan to annex and bring within its jurisdiction the five Tribal Agencies
could be the starting point of a solid new relationship between the two
countries.

There is no doubt that the extension of full Pakistani sovereignty over the
agencies would be strongly resisted by the tribes who have used their special
status illegally to their advantage, through smuggling, the drug trade and
outright extortion. They were among the principal beneficiaries of anarchy in
Afghanistan, and also of the Taliban regime. They may even now, at the time
of writing, be harbouring and protecting recalcitrant elements of the Taliban
and al-Qaeda. But there is little they can do if Pakistan, backed up by its
armed forces, and with the endorsement of the Afghan state, were to extend
its jurisdiction over them. It would be a muscular but gradual process. One of
the benefits accruing to both countries would be the elimination of drug

trafficking, in which the existence of autonomous tribal areas on the frontier has been an important factor.

Negotiations between Pakistan and Afghanistan would also afford the opportunity for reviewing the Afghan Transit Trade (ATT), which was the subject of an agreement between the two countries concluded in 1950. As we have seen in Chapter 14, the ATT became subject to massive abuse by Afghan warlords, the frontier tribes and the Taliban, to the detriment of Pakistan's economy and institutions. The conclusion of a comprehensive treaty that would then be endorsed by the United Nations according to the usual procedures would remove the surviving anomalies and enable the two states to better exercise control over their own territories.

In conclusion, nation-building policies and the related reconstruction efforts will have to be guided by the past. From 1747 to 1973, the old tribal structures were the basis of a crude but workable federalism headed by a king whose central authority was seldom very strong. These structures have survived after two catastrophic decades of war and anarchy. But the tribal mindset based on patronage – warrior prowess and the dispensation of favours from the top down – has also survived. It would run counter to the implementation of policies, fostering a civil society and free-market mechanisms, that would be required to construct a viable and modern state. For this to take place, the population has to be first disarmed and the warlords put out of business, and secondly, a federal system established under which tribes and ethnic groups become the partners, and not the rivals, of a national government.

Epilogue

In his foreword to this book, the late Prince Sadruddin Aga Khan posed a question that remains rhetorical: 'Can Afghanistan emerge, Phoenix-like, as a viable and stable state ...?'

At first all seemed to augur well for the launching of a process of nation-building in a country where the state – which had functioned less than optimally it must be said, with imperfect institutions and a precarious infra-structure – was destroyed by over 20 years of continuous civil war and anarchy, as narrated in this book. In this pre-modern 'zone of chaos', the Taliban had imposed, by force of arms and with foreign help, a threadbare, regressive, religiously motivated regime of the most primitive kind, nihilistic and totalitarian. A ruthlessly like-minded syndicate of Islamic zealots of foreign origin hijacked the country for use as a convenient base for its world-wide terrorist operations. The armed intervention of the United States in response to the 9/11 attacks of al-Qaeda on its soil, endorsed and supported by the international community in a 'coalition against terror', was successful in attaining not only its primary objective of destroying the al-Qaeda infra-structure but also in bringing about a relatively painless change of regime that came as a relief to the long-suffering population.

The political process that began in Bonn in December 2001, with the constitution of an Afghan Transitional Authority (ATA), acquired domestic legitimacy in the traditional Afghan manner through the Loya Jirga of June 2002. In keeping with the time-table agreed upon in Bonn, a new Afghan Constitution was adopted in January 2004, and both the presidential and parliamentary elections were scheduled to be held not later than June 2004. At the international conference held in Berlin in April 2004 to re-assess Afghanistan's reconstruction needs, it was declared that an elected president should be accountable to an elected parliament, with the implication that the elections should be held simultaneously. This may have been at the insistence of the Bush administration, for its own domestic reasons.[1]

But it was obvious to responsible observers and analysts on the ground, including interim President Hamid Karzai, UN officials and NGOs, that while the fairly straightforward presidential elections could be held earlier, pending completion of the Herculean task of voter registration undertaken by the United Nations, the credibility of the results of the considerably more complex elections to the two houses of parliament could be badly compromised were they to be held prematurely. The overriding reason was the risk of voter intimidation by the warlords and their militias.[2]

Credibility in a democratic process does not only mean that voters should be able to choose between their options without constraint, in an electioneering environment that is reasonably free of violence, intimidation and corruption. Credibility also requires that an elected government should emerge from an inclusive, representative process in order to function. This was implicit in the political process that began in Bonn, where the Afghan delegates, representing all ethnic groups and political, religious and other interests, including warlords, negotiated hard bargains to gain seats at the table in the transitional government. The main political drama that has been playing out since then is the resistance of regional power holders and local militia commanders to the Kabul government's centralizing agenda. President Karzai's delicate task has been to confront these challenges to his authority (not to his legitimacy) from a position of weakness. Lacking a monopoly on the use of force, he has had to depend on the cooperation and the goodwill of the warlords.

The greatest failure of the international community in general, and the Bush administration in particular, was the failure to provide President Karzai and his interim government with the international forces required, in the absence of a national army and police force, to sustain the momentum of securing and stabilizing post-war Afghanistan.

The Afghan warlords bore the primary responsibility for the anarchy that prevailed after the fall of the communist regime in 1992 but had performed poorly in resisting the rise of the Taliban. They were given new opportunities to rebuild their power when they were armed and re-equipped in the run-up to Operation Enduring Freedom. It was the fear of reprisals by the mainly non-Pashtun anti-Taliban forces of the Northern Alliance that occupied Kabul after the collapse of the Taliban that prompted the UN Security Council to authorize the dispatch of the International Security Assistance Force (ISAF). But the ISAF mandate, endorsed by the provisional Afghan government in its first official act, was limited to the policing of the multi-ethnic city of Kabul.

Local warlords and militia commanders in the rest of the country were thus able to take *de facto* control of their respective areas. They were initially useful to the coalition forces in maintaining some kind of order in the cities and in the countryside: there was neither the large-scale looting nor the general anarchy that occurred in Iraq after the overthrow of Saddam Hussein. But the Pentagon resisted ISAF deployment outside Kabul, fearing interference in the US-led coalition's efforts to capture Osama bin Laden and his cohorts, including hardline Taliban remnants. The excessive reliance on opportunistic militia commanders for this purpose and a reluctance after the Iraq adventure to commit more US ground combat troops have had disastrous practical consequences, both for the war against terror and for the stabilization of Afghanistan.

In the first place, the balance of armed force was weighted heavily on the side of the warlord militias, variously estimated at between 60,000 full-time fighters to over 100,000, if one includes 'part-timers' drawn from the swollen ranks of the unemployed. To date, some 10,000 men have been trained for a national army with the assistance of the US military. But this embryonic corps lacked a sufficiently broad ethnic base and was subject to high rates of desertion. In an international division of labour, Germany took responsibility for training and equipping a national police force, Italy for legal reform and the UK for dealing with the drugs problem.

As before, warlords have been able to expand their financial base by imposing customs duties and other taxes on their own account. Some have benefited substantially from smuggling and drug trafficking. One year after the formation of the interim government the opium crop earned Afghan farmers and traffickers some $2.3 billion, or around 50 per cent of the gross domestic product. According to the World Drug Report for 2004, published by the UN Office for Drugs and Crime Prevention (UNDCP), the crop in Afghanistan accounted for over 75 per cent of the world's illicitly grown opium in 2003. The area under poppy cultivation was expected to rise to 120,000 hectares in 2004 (from 90,000 hectares in 2003), increasing the dependence of farmers on this crop and providing rich pickings for local militia commanders through taxes on crops and trafficking. Need and greed drive farmers and the drug mafia: a hectare of land planted with the opium poppy yields the equivalent of US$10,500, whereas the same land planted with wheat yields US$180. The 2004 crop is expected to be the biggest in the country's history.

The New-York-based Human Rights Watch has produced detailed documentation on the abuses committed with impunity by militia leaders and their followers. The general lack of security outside the Afghan capital has seriously endangered the lives of UN and NGO personnel engaged in relief and reconstruction projects. Projects had to be abandoned and staff withdrawn. One of the most dedicated of European NGOs, Médecins sans Frontières (MSF), which had courageously soldiered on through 24 years of conflict in the country, announced its withdrawal in June 2004, after five of their employees were killed by Taliban elements in the north-west of the country.

The re-emergence of unreconstructed elements of the Taliban, to undertake armed attacks against foreigners and Afghans engaged in the peace and reconstruction process, has been another alarming consequence of the failure to stabilize the country. These groups appear to have re-established links with al-Qaeda operatives who had escaped into the untamed tribal areas of Pakistan's frontier agencies or had found refuge among sympathizers in that country. One of the most notorious of the Afghan warlords, Gulbuddin Hekmatyar, openly declared his alliance with these groups from his hiding-place somewhere in the region. The resurgent Taliban were emboldened enough to engage US and Afghan forces in a pitched battle in the southern province of Zabul in August 2003, leaving 200 of their number dead.

The situation on the ground has deteriorated to such an extent that remedial measures taken by the international community may have come too late. In August 2003 NATO took command of the ISAF in its first 'out-of-area' mission, and in October 2003 the Security Council authorized the ISAF to expand its presence throughout the country, with the further mission of providing security for the elections. Some 6500 troops make up the ISAF force: 5000 drawn from NATO member-states, with small contingents from several non-NATO countries making up the rest. These modest numbers contrast with the 20,000 US troops of the coalition against terror. At its summit meeting in Istanbul in June 2004, NATO pledged to increase its commitment by 2000 more troops. Afghanistan is NATO's most important current operation and a test of its new 'out-of-area' mission. In another test-case, the European Union's chief military arm, Eurocorps, which was formed in 1992 as a rapid-reaction force, was deployed in August 2004 for the purpose of safeguarding the presidential elections set for 9 October 2004 and the parliamentary elections which were postponed, in a more realistic general consensus, to the spring of 2005.

By focusing on security, the ISAF worked fairly well in Kabul. Provincial Reconstruction Teams (PRTs) were formed to provide security for aid workers engaged in relief and development projects outside Kabul. Working with local authorities and the police, the PRTs are also meant to serve as a mechanism for extending the interim government's authority over the provinces. The UK-led PRT in Mazar-i-Sharif was effective in defusing conflicts between the local Uzbek warlord, General Dostum, and the forces of a Tajik general that might have erupted into a full-scale local war.

This episode shows up the complexity of a situation where warlords, who represent real power in the provinces and were coopted into the governmental structures, have themselves become a threat to stability. As a leader of the anti-Taliban Northern Alliance, Dostum was assigned the post of deputy at the Ministry of Defence, which was headed by another war leader, General Mohammad Qasim Fahim, a Tajik. The latter assumed the title of 'Marshal' and transformed his ministry into a personal fiefdom, delaying the reforms that had required him to replace his Tajik commanders with a more ethnically balanced officer corps. The efforts of one of his generals, a fellow Tajik, to establish central governmental authority in Mazar, were seen as an intrusion on his native turf by Dostum. Both he and Fahim are men of the past who believe that power can only be exercised through the barrel of a gun.

The vulnerability of his position was such that President Karzai, delving deep into his impressive reserves of tact and diplomacy, had to state that his government did not use the term 'warlords' to refer to those whom the media labelled as such: they were 'respected leaders of the Afghan resistance' to the Soviet invasion.[3] The contrast between Karzai's democratic vision and the mindset of the Afghan warlords can be best illustrated by a story related by Karzai himself to the journalist and author Ahmed Rashid. When General Fahim walked up to the aircraft that had brought Karzai to Kabul, he was surrounded by about 100 armed bodyguards, loyalists and new ministers. He 'looked confused' at seeing the new president with just four companions. 'Where are your men?' he asked. 'Why General', Karzai replied, 'you are my men – all of you are Afghans and are my men – we are united now – surely that is why we fought the war and signed the Bonn agreement?'[4]

President Karzai's tolerance of the warlords has been seen by Afghans in general as a weakness that undermines their confidence in his power and authority. This is fatal for an aspiring national leader in the Afghan context. There was a particularly serious lapse in the application of the rule of law in April 2004 when Karzai ordered the execution of a self-confessed murderer and war criminal, a certain Abdullah Shah, who was well known as a subaltern of Abdul Rasul Sayyaf. The latter is the ferociously anti-Shi'ite Wahhabi leader of a militia that was associated with mass murders, mass rapes and the disappearance of hundreds of people during the civil war. He is particularly remembered for master-minding the massacre of Shi'ite Hazara civilians in Kabul in 1993. As a member of the interim government with his own private army, Sayyaf leaned on Karzai to appoint the conservative head of a religious school in Pakistan, Maulavi Fazl Hadi Shinwari, as chief justice of the Afghan Supreme Court. Shinwari has since appointed like-minded fundamentalist mullahs as judges throughout Afghanistan. Even before Abdullah Shah's trial was over, Shinwari had declared that he should be executed. Shah had been interviewed by human rights observers and had offered to show them the location of mass graves in Paghman, west of Kabul, where Sayyaf maintained his own jails at his headquarters there. According to Amnesty International, the hasty execution 'may have been an attempt by powerful political players to eliminate a key witness to human rights abuses'.[5]

Officially the government was committed to demobilizing at least 40 per cent of the militia forces before the elections. But estimates vary widely on the numbers involved. To assist in this process, the UN set up a Disarmament, Demobilization and Re-integration programme (DDR) in October

2003. The programme has scarcely had any impact. By targeting the civilian followers of militia commanders – the 'part-timers' – DDR staff try to convince volunteers that the demobilization process was not about giving up their weapons, often obsolete, but about offering them alternative civilian job opportunities, which are scarce anyway. After being disarmed and demobilized, they sometimes came under pressure from their commanders to hand over their severance payments. The real obstacle, however, is the disarmament of full-time fighters armed with sophisticated weaponry, whose commanders have links to powerful warlords. In one example, Karzai had little leverage when faced with the refusal to disarm of a commander whose 3500 fighters were implicated in terrorizing the population in the western districts of Kabul. He commanded the so-called 10th Division of the Afghan Army controlled by the Ministry of Defence. A warlord in Jalalabad, Hazrat Ali, is also nominally accountable to the Defence Ministry. He fought his rivals to extend his control over four eastern provinces, but is a law unto himself. Some officials enrich themselves by illegally felling eastern forests to extract the high-grade local timber and have it trucked to Pakistan.

In an interview with the *New York Times* on 16 July 2004, Karzai was forced to concede that the warlords were the greatest threat to Afghanistan's future. He may have issued his first major challenge to the warlords by snubbing his powerful minister of defence, General Fahim, in his choice of Ahmad Zia Massoud, a younger brother of the national hero, Ahmad Shah Massoud, as his running mate for first vice president. The Bonn consensus required that the president, an ethnic Pashtun, choose his deputy from among the political heirs of Massoud, mainly Tajiks who had fought long and hard with him in the Panjshir Valley, now a province. Fahim had flouted the Bonn requirement that he withdraw his own Tajik militias from Kabul. His commanders elsewhere have also resisted demobilization. Karzai's move has also been shrewd: the younger Massoud is a son-in-law of former President Rabbani, the Tajik leader of the leading mujahideen political party, the Jamiat-i-Islami. Rabbani has since declared his support for Karzai's candidature.

Among the 17 other candidates, including Dostum, a strong contender in the presidential stakes is Karzai's erstwhile education minister, Yunus Qanooni, who had to give up his portfolio in accordance with the electoral rules. Fahim and other Panjshiris have declared their support for Qanooni, who might be a rallying point for the Tajiks, the second largest ethnic group, and some other factions of the non-Pashtun mujahideen opposition to Karzai. This would suggest the possible line of division between governmental and opposition parliamentary parties in the future elected legislature, which could be a good beginning for a multi-party democracy.

But elections do not a democracy make. In the short term, the Afghan people will need all the help that they can get to ensure the integrity of the electoral process and the integrity of the results, so that the government that emerges merits their trust. Another aspect of trust, very important in the Afghan context, is the involvement of ethnic and other minorities in the political structures, so that their interests are legitimately represented through their political parties in a national parliament and not through warlords. The rest is a long haul, with the government taking the lead in imposing the rule of law and developing, with international assistance, the institutions that go with it – an independent judiciary and civil courts that uphold human rights, gender equality, and the rest. High on the agenda should be the eradication of mass illiteracy, the indispensable precondition for the modernization of tradition-bound societies and without which a progressive political culture that could in the long run bring about a civil society cannot be implemented or sustained.

The restoration of social trust also implies that an elected government addresses the basic needs of the people, including the provision of schools, health care and employment for the poor and destitute. At the Berlin Conference in April 2004, some 60 donors pledged US$8.2 billion for Afghanistan's reconstruction and recovery over the next three years. The assistance package represents an aid programme that is unprecedented in the country's history. In the past, foreign aid has been associated with patronage and corruption. It is to be hoped, in the spirit of the Nobel Laureate Amartya Sen, that a democratically elected government that has to answer unfriendly questions in the national parliament and confronts criticism from a free press and voters in other future elections will be sufficiently transparent and accountable in the use of such funds.

The overall success of the PRTs in general, as a mechanism for providing security in their operational areas and so protecting the local population from the depredations of warlord commanders, remains to be seen. The two German-led PRTs in Kunduz and Fayzabad in the north-east are precluded by German Federal Parliament directives from taking on combat roles. The principal mission of the PRTs is to provide a secure environment for the implementation of humanitarian relief and reconstruction programmes by UN agencies and NGOs. But the military personnel in the US-led PRTs in south-eastern Afghanistan – Pashtun areas where the Taliban drew their support – are directly involved in implementing US-funded projects. They are thus dangerously blurring the distinction between humanitarian aid workers, who have to be perceived as politically neutral and impartial, and military personnel. Such confusion of mandates makes aid workers vulnerable to attack by neo-Taliban insurgents and terrorists who have openly declared war on the coalition forces and on the Afghans associated with them.[6]

Support for the Taliban appears to be still strong among some of their old allies in Pakistan, including renegade elements within the intelligence services (ISI), and, as some observers believe, within the government and army establishment. What is clear, however, from recent al-Qaeda-related arrests in Pakistan, the UK and elsewhere, is the existence of a communications and supply network supporting terrorists in Afghanistan. Pakistan has become more cooperative with US and other intelligence agencies in the war against terror and more muscular in its efforts to track down and arrest al-Qaeda operatives, particularly since General Musharraf himself became a prime target of assassins twice in December 2003. But Musharraf's position has been ambiguous. While pursuing al-Qaeda in the frontier tribal agencies, particularly south Waziristan, where bin Laden is believed to be hiding, and receiving millions of dollars of US aid in return, he has wooed and received political support from the coalition of Islamist parties that came to power in the two provinces that are contiguous with Afghanistan. They share with the Taliban a common religious ideology and are fiercely anti-American. By also controlling the activities of his opponents in the two secular parties, whose leaders have been prevented from ending their exile, Musharraf's policies are strongly reminiscent of those of his military predecessor, Zia ul-Haq. According to a Pakistani analyst, 'America is backing the military that is backing the mullahs that are backing the jihadis'.[7]

One of the far-reaching consequences of the Iraq war has been the spread of anti-Americanism in the Muslim world in particular, giving its disaffected youth a new jihadi cause to fight for and providing fresh recruiting fields for al-Qaeda. Computer records, e-mail addresses and documents seized after the arrest of a Pakistani al-Qaeda operative, a computer engineer by profession, have led analysts to believe that 'a new generation of operatives appear to be filling the vacuum created when al-Qaeda leaders were killed or captured ... al-Qaeda is regenerating and bringing in new blood'.[8] The Madrid bombings suggest that 'sleeper cells' can be activated at will against targets selected in advance. A bin Laden tape was issued on 15 April 2004, after the Madrid bombings, which had the intended effect of causing Spain to withdraw its troops from Iraq. Bin Laden offered 'a truce' to European states if they would pull out their forces from Iraq: 'The door to a truce is open for three months. ... The truce will begin when the last soldier leaves our countries. ... Stop spilling our blood so we can stop spilling your blood ... this is a difficult but easy equation.' The voice may have been bin Laden's, but the terse, precise sentences are couched in the language of his educated deputy, Dr Ayman al-Zawahiri, particularly when he refers to the Madrid bombings as 'your goods delivered back to you.'[9]

It is outside the purview of this epilogue to examine, however briefly, the motivations of key decision makers in the Bush administration in turning their attention away from Afghanistan and the continuing threat of Islamic terrorism to a target that did not pose an immediate threat to the security of the United States.[10] One of Bob Woodward's revelations was that on 21 November 2001, exactly 72 days after 9/11, and while the war in Afghanistan was still being waged, President Bush queried his Secretary of Defence on his war plans for Iraq. Another revelation was the secret diversion of US$700 million of funds approved by the US Congress for the Afghan operation to finance preparations for the war in Iraq. The war in Iraq had the perverse effect of both destabilizing Afghanistan through neglect and giving a new lease of life to Islamic terrorists both in Afghanistan and the rest of the world.[11]

Notes

Introduction

[1] Afghan incursions into northern India had begun with Mahmud of Ghazni, a fanatically Muslim Turkic ruler of Central Asian origin whose annual raids in the first quarter of the eleventh century were purely predatory and iconoclastic. A more permanent Afghan presence was established by the conquests of Mohammad, the Turkic ruler of Ghor in Afghanistan, towards the end of the twelfth century. He had left his Indian possessions in charge of a slave general, Qutb-ud-din Aybak, who founded what is known as the Slave Dynasty of the Delhi Sultanate. The sultanate of Delhi, under successive dynasties and subject to fluctuating fortunes, remained the focus of political power in northern India until the arrival of Babur. These dynasties were Turkish and dominated by Turks of Central Asian origin but their armies included large numbers of Afghan mercenaries, as well as Turks and Persians, while the language of the court was Persian. In 1451 a provincial governor of purely Afghan origin, Buhlul Lodi, took over the sultanate, leading to the eclipse of the Turkic nobility. See Romila Thapar, A History of India, vol. 1 (London: Penguin Books, 1990), chapters 10 and 12.

[2] Mountstuart Elphinstone, An Account of the Kingdom of Cabaul (London, 1815; reprinted by Indus Publications, Karachi, 1992), vol. 2, p 283.

[3] Such situations in the Muslim dynasties of west Asia developed their own novel solutions, as at the Sublime Porte, the seat of the Ottoman sultan, where potential rivals were strangled with a silken cord by black eunuchs at the Topkapi.

[4] Ibn Khaldûn, The Muqaddimah: An Introduction to History, translated by Franz Rosenthal; abridged and edited by N.J. Dawood (London: Routledge and Kegan Paul, 1967), chapter 3.

[5] Quoted by George Arney, Afghanistan (London: Mandarin Paperbacks, 1990), p 7.

[6] There were some survivors, not only the solitary survivor of legend, the surgeon William Brydon, who staggered pitifully into Jalalabad on his haggard horse, but a number of British officers, women and children, who had been given up as hostages or captured during the skirmishes, but who had been well treated under the circumstances, and restored to the British avenging forces the next year. The surviving Indian sepoys and camp followers on the other hand had taken to begging on the streets of Kabul.

[7] 'Historical Note by Sir Olaf Caroe', in J.C. Griffiths, Afghanistan: Key to a Continent (London: André Deutsch, 1981).

8   Actually the phrase was coined by a young British army officer, Arthur Conolly, spying on Russian activities in Central Asia, who, with his companion, Charles Stoddart, came to a sticky end at the hands of a notoriously cruel amir of Bukhara.

9   The term 'Afghan' may have been derived from the Pashtun word 'afghani' that refers to a knitted or woven shawl or to the sheepskin coat with the furry side worn inside, and with trimmings of fur, that was part of the traditional garb of the people of Afghanistan. No-one, however, can be certain of its etymology.

10 Louis Dupree, *Afghanistan* (Karachi: Oxford University Press, 1997), pp 57-65.

11 Many of the Hindus and Sikhs, important as merchants, traders and money changers in the laissez-faire economy of Afghanistan, left for India after the collapse of the Najibullah regime in April 1992. Nothing is known in the extant literature of the fate of the Jews of Bukharan origin, pursuing similar occupations, and mentioned by Dupree as consisting of 'several thousand' in the main cities. Some of them had emigrated to Israel after the creation of that state, and then returned to Afghanistan. It is obvious that the demographic patterns described by Dupree and other field researchers have been immensely disrupted after the Soviet invasion and the subsequent civil war, resulting in massive outflows of refugees and migrants, and vast movements of the internally displaced.

Chapter 1

1   Quoted in Rosanne Klass, 'The Great Game Revisited' in Klass (ed), *The Great Game Revisited* (London: Freedom House, 1987), pp 2-3.

2   Quoted in Arney, *Afghanistan*, p 12.

3   The British could not but respect Dost Mohammad, as can be gathered from this extract from a letter addressed to Lord Auckland, the governor-general of India, by Sir William Macnaghten, one of the principal hawks on his staff who had advocated intervention, and who was then assigned to Kabul as principal adviser to their puppet, Shah Shuja, during the First Anglo-Afghan War: 'I trust that the Dost will be treated with liberality. His case has been compared to that of Shah Shoojah ... but surely the cases are not parallel. The Shah had no claim upon us. We had no hand in depriving him of his kingdom, whereas we ejected the Dost, who never offended us, in support of our policy, of which he was the victim.' (Quoted in Dupree, *Afghanistan*, p 382.) Macnaghten's assassination precipitated the British intervention.

4   The annexation of Sind was controversial. The question raised in some British circles was whether 'the "blessings of civilisation" justify war and annexation of backward regions in defiance of international usage and the principle of self-determination'. (See Percival Spear, *A History of India*, vol. 2 (London: Penguin Books, 1990), p 133.) Such high-mindedness had still a place in British attitudes before the unfurling of imperialism in full panoply in the second half of the century. Apart from some strategic considerations, the conquest may have been inspired by a fervent wish to restore the British name in India after the Afghan fiasco the previous year. It was carried out apparently on the personal initiative of General Sir Charles Napier, who sent to his disapproving superiors in London,

after the conquest of Sind, perhaps the most famous one-word telegram in history: 'Peccavi' (I have sinned).

[5] A phrase that was to be re-used in an altogether ignominious context by another British prime minister 60 years later.

[6] In 1875 he had purchased from the debt-ridden Khedive Ismail of Egypt £4 million sterling's worth of shares in the Suez Canal, to protect the 'lifeline' to India, another insurance policy for an enhanced imperial future. In 1877 he had persuaded a reluctant parliament to create the title 'Empress of India' for his sovereign, Queen Victoria, whose friendly patronage was of great value to him in his political career. As he said, 'Everyone likes flattery; but when it comes to Royalty, you should lay it on with a trowel.'

[7] Bismarck said that the Balkans were not worth the bones of a Pomeranian grenadier.

[8] There were, however, grounds for treating such Russian assurances with some scepticism, as they had been volunteered before in respect of the Russian annexations of Samarkand, Khiva and Kokand. (See Firuz Kazemzadeh, 'Russia and the Middle East', in Ivo J. Lederer (ed), *Russian Foreign Policy* (New Haven and London: Yale University Press, 1962), pp 498–500).

[9] Quoted in Dupree, *Afghanistan*, p 411.

[10] The novelist Fyodor Dostoievski, in an article written after the Russian capture of Goek Tepe in 1881, involving the notorious massacre, expressed his nation's 'manifest destiny' in these terms: 'The Russian is not only a European, but also an Asiatic. Not only that; in our coming destiny, it is precisely Asia that represents our main way out. In Europe we were hangers-on, whereas to Asia we shall go as masters. In Europe we were Asiatics, whereas in Asia, we too are Europeans. Our civilising mission in Asia will bribe our spirit and drive us thither.' (Quoted in Ahmed Rashid, *The Resurgence of Central Asia: Islam or Nationalism* (London and New Jersey: Zed Books, 1994), p 18.)

[11] Dupree, *Afghanistan*, p 424.

[12] Olivier Roy, *Islam and Resistance in Afghanistan* (Cambridge: Cambridge University Press, 1986), chapter 1.

[13] Quoted in Dupree, *Afghanistan*, p 419.

[14] Since the time of Ahmad Shah, the rebellious Ghilzais have often been distrusted by the Durrani rulers as a fifth column, whenever there were internal conflicts or uprisings.

[15] The Marquess Curzon of Kedleston, 'The Amir of Afghanistan', in Peter King (ed), *A Viceroy's India: Leaves from Lord Curzon's Notebook* (London: Sidgwick and Jackson, 1986).

Chapter 2

[1] A practical result of the Comintern and Baku Congresses was that the USSR was able, within a short period in 1921, to conclude bilateral treaties of 'Friendship and Co-operation' with its southern neighbours who were ready for Soviet assistance in their ongoing national revolutions. The contracting parties agreed to refrain from entering into any political or military agreements with a third party

that were directed against the other. Soviet diplomacy was also successful in bringing about the conclusion of bilateral treaties between Afghanistan, Turkey and Iran, in which the contracting parties agreed to give assistance to the other in case either of them was attacked by an outside power. Thus by the summer of 1921 a system of bilateral treaties linking Turkey, Iran and Afghanistan with Soviet Russia, and with one another, was put in place through Soviet initiatives. The system ensured the security of its southern borders, from the Black Sea to the Oxus. The obvious target was British imperialism, which had been very active in the whole area, as well as in the USSR itself, through its support of the anti-Bolshevik armies of the White Russian generals, Denikin and Wrangel. (See Harish Kapur, *Soviet Russia and Asia, 1917–1927* (Geneva: Institut de hautes études internationales, 1965), pp 40-6, for an account of the Comintern and Baku Congress debates, drawn from Soviet sources, and on early Afghan–Soviet relations, pp 240-6.)

2   Quoted in Dupree, *Afghanistan*, p 450.

3   Quoted in Arney, *Afghanistan*, p 21.

4   Musahiban, or Companions, so designated by Habibullah when they returned from India after a long exile. Their ancestor was the brother of Dost Mohammad who was governor of Peshawar during the Sikh invasions.

5   'Hindu-Killers', in view of the numberless Indians captured in wars over the centuries, who perished in the snows on their way to be sold in the slave markets of Central Asia, particularly in Khiva. *Kush* was more probably a corrupt form of the Persian word for a mountain range, *koh*.

6   Quoted by Fazal-ur-Rahim Marwat in *The Frontier Post*, Peshawar, 12 March 1993.

Chapter 3

1   Leon B. Poullada, 'The Road to Crisis, 1919-1980', in Klass (ed), *The Great Game Revisited*, p 42.

2   *Ibid.*, p 41.

3   *Ibid.*, p 43.

4   Winston Churchill, *My Early Life* (London: Fontana Books, 1959).

5   In 1931 the seat of the viceregal government was moved from Calcutta to the splendid new imperial capital of New Delhi, designed by Sir Edwin Lutyens.

6   Dupree, *Afghanistan*, p 487.

7   Henry S. Bradsher, *Afghanistan and the Soviet Union* (Durham, Mass.: Duke University Press, 1984), p 25.

8   Dupree, *Afghanistan*, p 516.

9   Arney, *Afghanistan*, p 35.

10   S.M. Burke, *Pakistan's Foreign Policy: An Historical Analysis* (London: Oxford University Press, 1973), pp 68-90 for a historical analysis of the Pashtunistan issue.

11   Quoted in Bradsher, *Afghanistan and the Soviet Union*, p 27.

12   Dupree, *Afghanistan*, p 533.

Chapter 4

[1]   Dupree, *Afghanistan*, p 581. In the drafting of this chapter, I have relied heavily on Dupree's very informative first-hand account of the proceedings of the Loya Jirga, and on his insightful comments, inspired by his field researches over many years as a resident social anthropologist in Afghanistan that were his life's work. My overall debt to the late Louis Dupree is more than I can acknowledge in the referenced material.

[2]   Dupree, *Afghanistan*, p 590.

[3]   Griffiths, *Afghanistan: Key to a Continent*, pp 99–101.

[4]   The college was established in 1875 by Sir Sayyed Ahmad and called the Mohammadan Anglo-Oriental College, reflecting the anglophile founder's aim to bring about a synthesis of the modern and the rational, and the core Islamic values shorn, as he was fond of saying, of 'fanaticism and charlatanism'. The college is now the Aligarh Muslim University.

[5]   Barnett R. Rubin, *The Fragmentation of Afghanistan: State Formation and Collapse in the International System* (New Haven and London: Yale University Press, 1995), p 69.

[6]   *Ibid.*, p 70.

[7]   Dupree, *Afghanistan*, p 599.

[8]   Rubin, *The Fragmentation of Afghanistan*, p 76.

[9]   Dupree, *Afghanistan*, pp 601–7.

[10] As Wahid Tarzi observes in a personal note to the present writer: 'The King was reluctant to sign it and this may have led to the strengthening of the leftist movement.'

[11] Raja Anwar, *The Tragedy of Afghanistan: A First-Hand Account*, translated from the Urdu by Khalid Hasan (London and New York: Verso, 1988), pp 28–9.

[12] *Ibid.*, p. 178.

[13] *Ibid*, p 43.

[14] Christian fundamentalists are still very influential in the US 'Bible Belt'. They are at the origin of the various proselytizing evangelical sects that send out missionaries all over the world, are associated with the so-called 'creationists' as opposed to the 'evolutionists', and form the backbone of the 'Christian Right' in contemporary US politics.

[15] Bernard Lewis, 'Islamic Revolution', *The New York Review of Books*, vol. XXXIV, nos. 21–22, 21 January 1988.

[16] Olivier Roy, 'Has Islamism a Future in Afghanistan?', in William Maley (ed), *Fundamentalism Reborn? Afghanistan and the Taliban* (New York: New York University Press, 1998).

[17] In May 1916 the British and the French had secretly concluded the Sykes–Picot Agreement, designating in advance their respective spheres of control in the Arab lands of the Ottoman Empire. The official guardian of the Islamic holy places in the Hejaz, Sherif Hussein, had supported the Allied war effort - duly romanticized in the exploits of Lawrence of Arabia - in the hope of establishing an independent

state uniting the Arab components of the empire. In the actual post-war dispensation, however, Syria and Lebanon became virtual French protectorates, Palestine
became a British mandated territory under League of Nations auspices, and the
British carved out the new kingdoms of Iraq and Transjordan, with two of the
sons of the sherif of Mecca as their respective heads, as a sop to Arab aspirations.

[18] Anwar Sadat had served as liaison between the Free Officers and the Brotherhood
during the revolution.

[19] Hekmatyar was imprisoned for allegedly murdering a Maoist student, a harbinger
of his bloody-minded activities in the future.

[20] Nadir Shah had to abandon his project to establish a state central bank in view of
the opposition of the ulema, who cited the Koran's injunction against the charging of interest.

[21] Anwar, *The Tragedy of Afghanistan*, pp 184-5, quoting as his source an Afghan
government publication written by Mahmood Baryali (a brother of Babrak Karmal), *Afghanistan: Multifaceted Revolutionary Process* (Kabul, 1982 or 1983).

[22] Rubin, *The Fragmentation of Afghanistan*, chapter 4.

[23] Barnett R Rubin, 'The Political Economy of War and Peace in Afghanistan',
Online Center for Afghan Studies, June 1999 (www.afghan-politics.org).

Chapter 5

[1] Arney, *Afghanistan*, p 65.

[2] *Ibid.*, p 67.

[3] *Ibid.*, pp 70-1.

[4] Anwar, *The Tragedy of Afghanistan*, pp 73-5.

[5] Quoted in Arney, *Afghanistan*, p 72.

[6] Daoud's domestic and foreign policies were summed up wittily by an American
official: 'He didn't lean leftward or rightward, but "Daoudward"', and 'Daoud was
happiest when he could light his American cigarettes with Russian matches.'

[7] Anwar, *The Tragedy of Afghanistan*, pp 73-5.

[8] *Ibid.*, p 81.

[9] *Ibid.*, p 77.

[10] *Ibid.*, p 86.

[11] The oft-quoted and sagacious observation of the late President Sekou Touré of
Guinée is apt in this regard. He said that he preferred to send his students for
higher education to countries in the Soviet Bloc, whence they returned utterly disillusioned with the communist system, than to send them to the West where they
became dangerous communists.

[12] Arney, *Afghanistan*, pp 55-7.

[13] Quoted in Anwar, *The Tragedy of Afghanistan*, p 89, from Taraki's biography.

[14] Anwar, *The Tragedy of Afghanistan*, p 91, quoting from Baryali, *Afghanistan: Multi-
faceted Revolutionary Process* (Kabul, 1982 or 1983). In the narration of this chapter
and the next, the writer is very largely indebted to Rajah Anwar's unique and indispensable first-hand contribution to the history of the period. As a pro-Bhutto
exile from the Zia ul-Haq regime in his native Pakistan, Anwar lived in Afghani-

stan from June 1979 to January 1984, spending the period from October 1980 to March 1983 in jail: 'These were the most painful, the most trying years in Afghan history. I am glad to have been there to observe events at close quarters before, during, and after my imprisonment. In jail, I came to know many rebels, as well as members of Hafizullah Amin's family and his former Ministers. During the nine months I spent in Kabul after my release, I heard many inside stories and met a large number of important figures. I have tried to transfer this knowledge and experience to the pages that follow with detachment and honesty.' (From the author's foreword to *The Tragedy of Afghanistan*.)

Chapter 6

[1]   Babrak Karmal, when he came to power after the Soviet invasion, accused Hafizullah Amin of being responsible for the murder. The real identity of the gunmen was never known. But two brothers associated with the Khalqis were tried and executed for the deed, although no hard evidence was produced by the Parchami prosecutor. But if it had been Amin's intention to emasculate the Parchamis, their leader Karmal, towards whom he bore a visceral hatred, would have been a more plausible target than the harmless Khyber.

[2]   The two most senior of the rebel officers had the rank of lieutenant-colonel: Mohammad Rafi of the Fourth Armoured Corps and Abdul Qadir of the air force. They were Parchamis who had been briefed on the crucial roles they were called upon to play in Amin's plan, apparently on a strictly need-to-know basis. The Parchamis in general were kept in the dark regarding Amin's overall plans. This may explain Qadir's reluctance, like Achilles sulking in his tent, to enter immediately into the fray, and Karmal's query, 'Where to?' when the PDPA leaders were released by rebel officers from the detention centre near the Arg palace, to which Amin laughingly replied: 'If you do not wish to come, you are welcome to stay.' (Anwar, *The Tragedy of Afghanistan*, p 100.)

[3]   According to Anwar, citing Khalqi sources, when the ambassador called on Taraki the next day, he handed over the protest note he had been unable to deliver and they both burst out laughing. As Taraki said later: 'The news of our Revolution took both superpowers by surprise. The Soviet Union was ecstatic and the United States went into shock.'

[4]   The Czech writer Milan Kundera begins his novel *The Book of Laughter and Forgetting* with a fascinating story of how the communist leader Klement Gottwald stood bareheaded in the snow on the balcony of a baroque palace in Old Prague with his comrade Clementis at his side. A solicitous Clementis took off his own fur cap and placed it on Gottwald's head. Photographs were taken of this famous occasion in February 1948 when a totalitarian 'people's state' replaced a democratic republic. Four years later Clementis was charged with treason and hanged. His picture in the widely diffused photograph was eventually 'airbrushed out of history' and all that remained of Clementis was his hat on Gottwald's head.

[5]   Anwar, *The Tragedy of Afghanistan*, p 112.

[6]   *On the Saur Revolution* (Kabul: Political Department of the Armed Forces, 1978).

[7] Amin's personal involvement was to bring him dividends in the future. As Anwar says: 'Amin was also to use this incident to denounce Taraki and Karmal, later spreading the story in the army and Party ranks that Taraki and Karmal had run away to the airport to be able to fly out of the country in case the Revolution failed, while he was willing to die fighting.' (Anwar, *The Tragedy of Afghanistan*, p 101.)

[8] Anwar states that, according to the prison and security staff at the Pul-i-Charki jail, some 400 to 500 Parchami leaders and activists were imprisoned after the exposure of the Eid conspiracy. Of these, nearly 250 Parchamis and Badakhshi's Sitm-e-Melli activists were executed. Rajah Anwar, who was himself an inmate between October 1980 and March 1983, remains a primary source on these and other events of the period. He provides a graphic table of how the Afghan revolution devoured not only its own children, as Voltaire would have said, but its parents too: 'The Saur Revolution was unique in the sense that all its major and minor figures had either been murdered, jailed or executed.' (Anwar, *The Tragedy of Afghanistan*, pp 103–9.)

[9] According to government statistics released in 1978 and cited by Anwar, 5 per cent of the landowners held from 25 to 50,000 acres, comprising 45 per cent of the cultivated land, 15 per cent held from 10 to 25 acres, adding up to 20 per cent of the land, while the remaining 35 per cent was owned by peasants holding from five to ten acres of largely uneconomical land. In 1978 there were 30 families in the whole of Afghanistan who held 500 to 50,000 acres of agricultural land. Among these wealthy landowners were the leading families of the two major Sufi orders, the Mujaddidi and Gailani clans. Those landowners who were affected by the land reforms did not exceed 400, between them owning some 20,000 villages. These statistics have to be treated with caution but they do give some indication of the magnitudes involved.

[10] Afghan 'feudalism' does not correspond to feudalism in the accepted sense. Its origins can be traced back to the importance of water, the source of life and sustenance in a country that was largely mountainous and arid. If a tribe successfully occupied the water source of another tribe, it was tantamount to occupying that tribe's lands. Forts were built to protect the precious water. With the passage of time both the forts and the water sources became the personal property of the tribal, clan, or sub-clan chief who began to charge the farmers for the use of the water. Landholdings were initially of equal size. But in times of drought or loss of livestock, the farmers were forced to borrow money from the tribal chief on interest, giving up their land as collateral. Gradually much tribal agricultural land came to be possessed by the tribal chief and its cultivators became his tenants. However, no member of the tribe was entitled to sell his land, which could only be used as collateral within the tribe. But rivers, mountains and pastures within the tribal territory remained under communal ownership, their use being subject to decisions by consensus in the tribal jirgas or shuras where all members of the tribe were social equals. Anwar points out that a dispossessed farmer felt that his landlord was holding his land on trust because he or his forebears had failed to honour a debt. To claim ownership of mortgaged land was considered 'un-Islamic'. The landlord in the circumstances described was also the chief or khan of

his tribe, clan or sub-clan, and tenants were fellow tribesmen who were joined to him in a social contract of long historical standing.

[11] Roy, *Islam and Resistance*, p 90.

[12] The American-educated Marxist Hafizullah Amin did not himself comply with Decree No. 7 when it came to the marriage of a daughter. She was forced to marry a cousin against her will. (See Anwar, *The Tragedy of Afghanistan*, pp 144-5.)

[13] Sarwari imputed his change of heart to the visits made by Amin's son, Abdul Rahman, to Japan, allegedly taking with him priceless antiques from the Kabul Museum and precious stones from the palace, and Amin's alleged overtures to the US by using Japan's good offices. (Anwar, *The Tragedy of Afghanistan*, p 162.)

[14] See Anwar, *The Tragedy of Afghanistan*, pp 165-81.

[15] Quoted in Arney, *Afghanistan*, p 105.

Chapter 7

[1] Quoted in Arney, *Afghanistan*, p 110.

[2] The transcripts from the Soviet archives that are cited extensively in the current chapter have become available through the Online Center for Afghan Studies at www.afghan-politics.org, one of the Afghanistan websites on the Internet. But there is no means of being certain that these transcripts are a complete record, and it is possible that they have been released into the public domain on a selective basis.

[3] Taraki, in his response to Prime Minister Kosygin's warning in a telephone conversation on 17 or 18 March that a Soviet intervention in Herat would be 'a very complex matter', suggested naively that Afghan markings could be placed on Soviet tanks and aircraft, and 'no one will be any the wiser. ... Why can't the Soviet Union send Uzbeks, Tajiks and Turkmen in civilian clothing? No one will recognise them ... we have all these nationalities in Afghanistan.'

[4] The transcript of the meeting contains a detailed inventory of the equipment and supplies that were being delivered.

[5] In a transcript dated 10 July, there is a cryptic reference by Taraki expressing to Puzanov his satisfaction over 'the arrival and deployment in Bagram of the Soviet special group'.

[6] Anwar, *The Tragedy of Afghanistan*, pp 187-9; see also Arney, *Afghanistan*, pp 112-13.

Chapter 8

[1] Anwar, *The Tragedy of Afghanistan*, p 215.

[2] What happened in fact was that rebels and refugees in Pakistan sent back harmless members of their families to reclaim their properties, mortgage them to local residents (to rule out any further take-overs), and then return to Pakistan, their pockets lined with money.

[3] Anwar, *The Tragedy of Afghanistan*, p 210. Anwar himself was jailed in October 1980 for his critical journalistic views on Karmal's and Brezhnev's policies. His prison term gave him the unique opportunity of being able to converse at leisure

with former Khalqi officials and cadres who were his fellow inmates at Pul-i-Charki, gathering material at first hand for his future book.

4   See Anwar, *The Tragedy of Afghanistan*, p 208, and Arney, *Afghanistan*, p 183.

5   Arney, *Afghanistan*, pp 187ff, gives a succinct account of the process of Sovietization. He was the BBC's resident Pakistan and Afghanistan correspondent from 1986 to 1988.

6   Stalin's policies in Central Asia had twin objectives: to politically divide the population along ethnic and linguistic lines as an antidote to the anti-Russian pan-Islamic movement of the 1920s and 1930s; and to integrate their economies irreversibly with the rest of the USSR. Thus the monoculture of cotton was developed in Uzbekistan to the exclusion of all else so that its economy became wholly dependent on markets elsewhere in the USSR for its exports of raw cotton and for its imports of consumer goods. Incidentally, the drainage of the two major rivers, the Syr Darya and Amu Darya, to sustain an elaborate irrigation system for the growing of cotton has brought about one of the world's biggest ecological disasters in the Aral Sea region.

Chapter 9

1   Mohammad Yousaf and Mark Adkin, *The Bear Trap: Afghanistan's Untold Story* (Lahore: Jang Publishers, 1992), pp 25-6.

2   Kurt Lohbeck, 'Money is the Root of All Evil', in Rosanne Klass (ed), *The Great Game Revisited*.

3   Anwar Sadat was indiscreet. He disclosed before his assassination in 1981 that he was asked 'please open your stores for us so that we can give the Afghanis the armaments they need to fight'. (Quoted in Arney, *Afghanistan*, p 151.)

4   Later described by Casey's successor, Robert Gates, as 'the bank of crooks and criminals international'.

5   Because of the strict separation of powers between the three branches of government enshrined in the US constitution, the executive branch – the presidency – was hamstrung by the requirement that all government agencies, while reporting to the president, were accountable to Congress, the legislative branch.

6   According to Kurt Lohbeck ('Money is the Root of All Evil', p 186) who was translating Eden Pastora's Spanish for the benefit of the Afghan mujahideen commander, Abdul Haq, when comparing notes at a meeting, the famous Commandante Zero of the Nicaraguan Contras said he knew that the CIA, who thought he was not subservient enough, were cutting him off from their supply network when Kashoggi's representatives stopped socializing with him over drinks in Costa Rica. Kashoggi also played a key role in the initiatives of Oliver North of the National Security Council to supply arms to Iran in exchange for the release of the American embassy hostages.

7   Yousaf and Adkin, *The Bear Trap*, pp 95-6.

8   *Ibid.*, p 85.

9   *Ibid.*, p 86.

10   *Ibid.*, p 42.

[11]   An important exception to this general rule was the Jamiat forces of the two most effective commanders revealed by the resistance: Ahmad Shah Massoud in the north-east and Ismail Khan in the west. They were able to organize not only more effective fighting forces but also political administrations in the areas under their control, as will be examined in a later chapter. They were also the least favoured for the largesse distributed through the ISI.

[12]   UNHCR, *Refugees: Focus on Afghanistan*, vol. 108, II-1997.

[13]   The extraction of oil, gas and mineral deposits.

[14]   Yousaf and Adkin, *The Bear Trap*, pp 57-8.

[15]   Arney, *Afghanistan*, p 178.

[16]   *Ibid.*

Chapter 10

[1]   Quoted in Arney, *Afghanistan*, p 206.

[2]   For details see Riaz Mohammad Khan, *Untying the Afghan Knot: Negotiating Soviet Withdrawal* (Durham, Mass.: Duke University Press, 1991), and Diego Cordovez and Selig S. Harrison, *Out of Afghanistan: The Inside Story of the Soviet Withdrawal* (New York: Oxford University Press, 1995).

[3]   Arney visited one such group in Paghman province in March 1987 that had already been supplied with wheat, sugar, blankets and household utensils.

[4]   Arney, *Afghanistan*, p 195.

[5]   *Ibid.*, pp 145-6.

[6]   Amin Saikal, 'The UN and Afghanistan: A Case of Failed Peacemaking Intervention?' in *International Peacekeeping*, vol. 3, no. 1 (Spring 1996), pp 19-34.

[7]   Arney, *Afghanistan*, p 211.

[8]   Quoted in Arney, *Afghanistan*, p 214, from a British newspaper report.

[9]   *Ibid.*, p 215.

[10]   *Ibid.*, p 218.

[11]   Quoted in Arney, *Afghanistan*, p 234.

[12]   When Pakistan's ISI outlined its battleplans, one commander is reported to have asked: 'Why should we who have never lost a war take advice from people who have never won one?' (Quoted in Arney, *Afghanistan*, p 235.)

Chapter 11

[1]   The pir himself, Sayyed Shah Naderi, was vice-president of the Afghan parliament under King Zahir Shah and later lived in exile in London.

[2]   In the summer of 1989 President Rafsanjani of Iran reminded the Shi'ite parties that the jihad was over, and that they should seek a political settlement with Najibullah - advice that they did not heed.

[3]   See Rolf Bindeman, 'Der politische Aufstieg und der Fall der Hazara' (The Political Rise and Fall of the Hazara), *Afghanistan Info*, March 1999.

[4]   Massoud was a product of the French-sponsored Lycée Istiqlal in Kabul and was popular with the French media, whose documentaries on his activities had a wide international distribution.

[5]   Zia, who had been a military adviser in Jordan during the Black September episode, when the Palestine Liberation Organization nearly overthrew King Hussein, may have drawn a lesson from that situation: the first Arab Summit in Cairo in 1964 had established a single, unified PLO with its own treasury, tax system, and diplomatic identity. The main Palestinian guerrilla organization, Al-Fatah, was then able to wrest control of the internationally constituted apparatus from its sponsors and use it for its own ends in Jordan.

[6]   The prevalent mood in Washington was expressed by a leading pro-mujahideen lobbyist, Congressman Charles Wilson: 'I viewed this as an opportunity to defeat the Soviets on the battlefield. We lost 58,000 men in Vietnam. The Russians have maybe lost 25,000 dead in Afghanistan. I figure they owe us 33,000 dead.' (Quoted in Arney, *Afghanistan*, p 157.) The hardliners were known as 'bleeders'.

[7]   Rubin, *The Fragmentation of Afghanistan*, p. 253.

[8]   The nationalist mood in Moscow was best expressed in a prophetic 1991 essay by Alexander Solzhenitsyn calling for the break-up of the Soviet Union and the rebuilding of Russia. As he wrote in *Rebuilding Russia*: 'We don't have the strength for the peripheries either economically or morally. We don't have the strength for sustaining an empire – and it is just as well. Let this burden fall from our shoulders, it is crushing us, sapping our energies, and hastening our demise.' (Quoted in Ahmed Rashid, *The Resurgence of Central Asia*, p 39.) It is ironic to contrast this statement with the quotation from Dostoievski cited in Chapter 1.

Chapter 12

[1]   A wild game played by two teams of skilled horsemen with the headless carcass of a sheep or goat. The winner is the player who manages to carry and deposit the carcass inside a circle in the middle of the field, where the game also starts. To the foreign spectator the whole game looks chaotic, but it is played according to some rules. It is interesting to note that the winner is an individual, not the team to which he belongs. The game was very popular in the Central Asian steppes. It is said to be the forerunner of polo, which was pioneered by British officers in the NWFP and in the Punjab.

[2]   Amin Saikal, 'The Rabbani Government, 1992-1996', in Maley (ed), *Fundamentalism Reborn?*, pp 29-42.

[3]   After the conclusion of the Geneva Accords in April 1992, the United Nations launched an ambitious programme for the post-war rehabilitation and reconstruction of Afghanistan. The programme was headed by Prince Sadruddin Aga Khan and was named Operation Salaam (Peace).

[4]   Ahmed Rashid, in his *Taliban: Islam, Oil and the New Great Game in Central Asia* (London and New York: I.B. Tauris, 2000), gives the fullest and most authoritative account to date of the Taliban, the circumstances surrounding their rise to power, and of the wider, regional issues.

[5]   See Anthony Davis, 'How the Taliban Became a Military Force', in Maley (ed), *Fundamentalism Reborn?*, for a blow-by-blow account of how the Taliban became a victorious force.

[6]   Ejaz Haider, 'Pakistan's Afghan Policy and Its Fallout', *Central Asia Monitor*, no. 5, 1998.

[7]   According to evidence that has since come to light, the looting and the atrocities were actually carried out by forces directed by the virulently anti-Shi'ite Wahhabi, Abdul Rasul Sayyaf, who was then a member of the Kabul government.

[8]   Davis, in Maley (ed), *Fundamentalism Reborn?*, p 62.

[9]   See Sreedar and Mahendra Ved, *The Afghan Turmoil: Changing Equations* (New Delhi: Himalayan Books, 1998).

[10]   During the ten weeks of fierce fighting between May and September 1997, the Taliban suffered over 3000 casualties, killed or wounded, with 3600 others taken prisoner. These included 250 killed and 550 captured who were identified as Pakistanis. According to the ICRC, more than 7000 troops and civilians were wounded on both sides. Unspeakable atrocities were committed by both sides.

[11]   Ahmed Rashid, *Taliban*, p 73.

[12]   *Ibid.*, quoting from a Human Rights Watch Report: 'Afghanistan, The Massacre in Mazar-i-Sharif', November 1998.

[13]   Dost Mohammad himself wound up in jail in Kandahar when his wife complained to Mullah Omar that he had brought back with him two Hazara concubines from Mazar. It was reported that some 400 Hazara women had been kidnapped and taken as concubines by the Taliban.

[14]   Sreedar and Mahendra Ved, *The Afghan Turmoil*, chapter 8 and appendix 5.

[15]   See map.

[16]   Ahmed Rashid, *Taliban*, pp 160ff.

Chapter 13

[1]   General Roberts, who commanded the British forces of occupation in Kabul after the Second Anglo-Afghan War, suggested to his superiors in Calcutta that in Abdur Rahman, who had appeared in the north to lay his claim to the Afghan throne, 'it was just possible might be found our most suitable instrument' (cited by Nazif Sharani, 'The State and Community Governance in Afghanistan', in Maley (ed), *Fundamentalism Reborn?*). Afghan rulers thereafter were not puppets, except during the communist interlude, but they were heavily dependent on foreign aid for their state-building efforts.

[2]   The peace settlement was preceded by a meeting in Moscow of Russia and the CARs called after the temporary seizure of Mazar-i-Sharif by the Taliban that prompted Pakistan, Saudi Arabia and the UAR to hastily recognize the Taliban. The notable absentee at this meeting, as at the October 1996 meeting in Almaty, was Turkmenistan which had a strong interest in seeing its oil and gas exported through Afghanistan, had initiated contacts with the Taliban, and took up a neutral stance.

[3]   See Ahmed Rashid, *The Resurgence of Central Asia*, for a well-researched account.

[4]   There were altogether some 10 million such settlers and immigrants in the CARs at the time of their independence, with heavy concentrations in Kazakhstan, where they constituted nearly a third of the total population of 17 million, as well as in Uzbekistan and in Kyrgyzstan. Russia could not be indifferent to their fate.

5   The Egypt-based Muslim Brotherhood had created a number of cells in Soviet Central Asia that operated secretly but came out into the open with the advent of *perestroika* in the form of Islamic Renaissance parties. These became politically active in Tajikistan and Uzbekistan, organizing and even arming their supporters against the entrenched ex-communist rulers.

6   Wahhabism was brought earlier to Central Asia by a native of Medina, Sayed Sharie Mohammad, who set up secret cells in Tashkent and in the overpopulated Ferghana Valley. Seven million people, or a third of the population of Uzbekistan, live in the Uzbek part of the Valley, where an acute land shortage and an unemployment rate of 35 per cent make it a hotbed of extremist dissent. The Wahhabis became very active after *perestroika*, openly preaching Islamic revolution and the overthrow of President Karimov. They received lavish funding from their supporters in Saudi Arabia to build mosques and madrasas, and to distribute Korans.

7   Saudi Arabia's expenditures in Afghanistan in 1991–93 amounted to the very substantial figure of $2 billion, Hekmatyar being the main beneficiary, according to Anwar-ul-Haq Ahady, 'Saudi Arabia, Iran and the Conflict in Afghanistan' in Maley (ed), *Fundamentalism Reborn?*, p 123.

8   Bernard Lewis, 'Islamic Revolution', *The New York Review of Books*, vol. XXXIV, nos. 21–22, 21 January 1988.

9   Ahmed Rashid, *Taliban*, p 200.

10 See map.

11 See Sreedar and Mahendra Ved, *The Afghan Turmoil*, for details.

12 Richard MacKenzie, 'The United States and the Taliban', in Maley (ed), *Fundamentalism Reborn?*

13 Rashid, *Taliban*, p 179.

14 From a speech to the Asia Society in New York, quoted in Rashid, *Taliban*, p 205.

15 Quoted in Rashid, *Taliban*, p 164.

16 Dmitri Trenin, Carnegie Moscow Center, 'Central Asia's Stability and Russia's Security', PONARs memo no. 168, November 2000, Online Center for Afghan Studies (www.afghan-politics.org).

17 *Ibid.*

18 *Ibid.*

19 Echoing the czarist General Aleksei Yermolov's famous characterization of Chechnya in the first half of the nineteenth century. In fact the overall vision is reminiscent of the justification by Russian apologists of czarist imperialism in Central Asia, such as the Dostoievski quotation cited in the Introduction.

20 Trenin, 'Central Asia's Stability and Russia's Security'.

21 Observatoire géopolitique des drogues (OGD), 'Afghanistan–Tajikistan: La Route de L'Opium', *Afghanistan Info*, September 1998.

Chapter 14

1   Olivier Roy, 'Le mouvement des Taleban', *Afghanistan Info*, February 1995.

2   An Afghan scholar, the late Professor S.B. Majrooh, characterized the content of the teaching in madrasas as meaningless. His description of the absurd traditional

   'art of disputation', or theological 'debates' between talib, with prepared answers to prepared questions, or between two maulvis armed with donkey-loads of Arabic texts and commentaries, would have provided, as Arney comments, 'perfect material for a Monty Python sketch' (Arney, *Afghanistan*, pp 47-8).

3   The order was founded in Bukhara by Baha'uddin Naqshband (1318-89) and has many adherents in Afghanistan and Central Asia.

4   The greatest of the Moghul emperors did not think of himself as a purely Muslim ruler governing in the interests of his Muslim subjects, but as a kind of universal emperor, responsible also for the welfare of his overwhelmingly Hindu subjects. He conceived of India, vast areas of which he had brought under his rule, as potentially greater than the sum of its parts: 'For an empire ruled by one head, it is a bad thing to have the members divided among themselves and at variance with one another' expressed the basic policy that he followed. He assembled Muslim and Hindu scholars, Jains, Zoroastrians and learned European Jesuits from Portuguese Goa at his new capital of Fatehpur Sikhri, a glorious amalgam of Persian and Hindu styles of architecture, where he presided over their debates. What he caused to emerge from these debates was not the victory of one system of beliefs over another, but his own syncretic Din-i-Illai (Divine Faith) which he sought to propagate.

5   The 'millennium' in question was the Islamic one, dating from the hijrah in CE622.

6   It was Shah Waliullah who called for a jihad against the Hindu Marathas who were in the military and political ascendancy in northern India. Also, at his urging, the Afghan ruler Ahmad Shah Durrani invaded India to lay claim to the conquests of Nadir Shah whom he had served until his assassination. This action had long-term historical consequences: the Persian conquests west of the Indus and in Kashmir were brought into the Afghan domain by Ahmad Shah; by defeating the Marathas and eliminating them as serious contenders for power in a weakened and fragmented Moghul Empire, he also paved the way for the British to eventually fill the power vacuum.

7   See Chapter 2, pp 17-18.

8   The somewhat outworn cliché to describe British imperialism should be balanced by the no less apt comment by an Indian journalist: 'We divided, they ruled.'

9   One may add here that prominent twentieth-century political figures like Mohammad Ali Jinnah and President Mohammad Ayub Khan of Pakistan were heirs to the modernist Muslim intellectual tradition of British India.

10   Contrary to the purist and puritanical Wahhabism of Saudi Arabia that rejected Sufism in all its forms.

11   Quoted in Ahmed Rashid, *Taliban*, p 89, from Asta Olsen, *Islam and Politics in Afghanistan* (Richmond, Surrey: Curzon Press, 1995).

12   Of the 28 members of the senior Taliban leadership listed by Ahmed Rashid, eight were educated at the Haqqania school, and one, the attorney-general who served as education minister in the Rabbani government, studied at Deoband. Eight of the Taliban leaders were former members of the extremist breakaway faction of the Hizbi-i-Islami led by Younis Khalis, and ten others were former members of Nabi's Harakat. (Rashid, *Taliban*, appendix 2). Rashid is an indispen-

sable source for much of the material re-worked in this chapter, material drawn
from extensive personal interviews conducted in Afghanistan and Pakistan.

[13] Rashid, *Taliban*, p 191.

[14] Quoted in Lawrence Liftschultz, 'Pakistan, the Empire of Heroin', in Alfred
McCoy and Alan Block (eds), *War on Drugs: Studies in the Failure of US Narcotics
Policy* (New York: Westview Press, 1992).

[15] See Alain Labrousse, 'Les Drogues et les conflits en Afghanistan (1978-1995)',
Afghanistan Info, March 1996, for an interesting account of the CIA's attempts to
prevent publication of the UNDCP's 1994 report – the US estimates were scan-
dalously below the UN figures. Labrousse, who is the director of the Observatoire
géopolitique des drogues in Paris, states that the CIA may also have wanted to
cover up its own, not so insignificant, role in producing the situation that permitted its creature, Pakistan's ISI, and the Afghan mujahideen parties and warlords to
become major operatives in the narcotics trade. This was another of the 'blowback' effects of past US policies.

[16] Traditionally *zakat* is a 2.5 per cent tax on wealth, obligatory for all Muslims, to
pay towards charity and for the destitute.

[17] Ahmed Rashid, 'Afghanistan: The Year in Review – 2000', Online Center for
Afghan Studies, January 2001 (www.afghan-politics.org).

[18] Rashid, *Taliban*, pp 191-2.

[19] According to the Islamic canon, jihad is legally permissible only against non-
Muslim opponents of Islam, and it can be declared only by an acceptable, that is,
learned and highly qualified religious authority. Similar legal considerations apply
to the issuing of fatwas.

[20] I once struck up a conversation in a Lahore park with a boy, about 10 or 11 years
old, who was assiduously practising his batting as his friend bowled. He said that
he wanted to become a professional cricketer, play in the national team, and 'become famous'. 'But I can't', he said. When I asked him why, he said simply, 'I am
a Christian.'

Chapter 15

[1] Olivier Roy, *The Failure of Political Islam*, translated by Catherine Volk (London:
I.B. Tauris, 1994), p 12.

[2] Gilles Dorronsoro, 'Les Talibans: Dynamique révolutionnaire et environnement
regional', *Afghanistan Info*, March 1999.

[3] Ahmed Rashid in *Le Monde diplomatique*, English edition, *Guardian Weekly*,
November 1999.

[4] The Afghan diaspora in the West was estimated at 120,000 migrants and asylum
seekers, with some 45,000 in the United States. Between 1989 and 1998, there
were 59,570 asylum seekers in Germany, 15,924 in the Netherlands and 24,000 in
other European countries. Of these, 39,436 Afghans were granted asylum under
the 1951 Refugee Convention or permitted to remain on humanitarian grounds –
15,247 in Germany and 15,924 in the Netherlands. In 1999 the number of Afghans seeking asylum in Europe rose to 23,299, an increase without precedent in
previous years. There were also close to 20,000 Afghans in India, over 20,000 in

the Russian Federation, and tens of thousands in the Central Asian Republics, some of whom may have acquired citizenship locally. (See Pierre Centlivres in *Afghanistan Info*, October 1997, and Micheline Centlivres-Demont in *Afghanistan Info*, March 2000.)

[5]   For the record, the largest in fact was the temporary escape into India of some 10 million refugees from the former East Pakistan (now Bangladesh) when the Pakistani armed forces clamped down brutally on the independence movement led by Sheikh Mujibur Rahman.

[6]   UNHCR, *Refugees: Focus on Afghanistan, the Unending Crisis*, No. 108, II-1997.

[7]   Fabrice Gaussen, 'The Evolution of UNHCR Repatriation Assistance', *Afghanistan Info*, March 1996.

[8]   The website www.pcpafg.org offers very comprehensive documentation on all current UN and NGO assistance programmes and projects in Afghanistan.

[9]   See William Maley, 'The UN and Afghanistan', in Maley (ed), *Fundamentalism Reborn?*, for an analysis of UN mediation in Afghanistan.

[10] Barnett R. Rubin, *Afghanistan: Persistent Crisis Challenges the UN System* (London: Writenet, 1998).

[11] Alfredo Witschi-Cestari, 'Coordinating Aid in Afghanistan', *Afghanistan Info*, October 1997.

[12] In the United States, vigorous lobbying by women's groups forced US policy makers in a presidential election year to rethink their hitherto complacent attitude to the Taliban. The UN International Women's Day on 8 February 1998 was dedicated to the plight of Afghan women.

[13] See Chapter 3, pp 56-7, for an overview of the social and economic conditions when the communists took power.

[14] But it can also be argued conversely that foreign aid, by keeping the population alive, absolved the Taliban of the responsibility of having to provide for the people, and allowed them to use their resources largely to maintain their war machine. The legality of their 'resources' - derived also from drugs and smuggling operations on which they imposed taxes - was also very much in doubt.

[15] Michael Keating, 'Dilemmas of Humanitarian Assistance in Afghanistan', in Maley (ed), *Fundamentalism Reborn?*

[16] Alfredo Witschi-Cestari, 'Coordinating Aid in Afghanistan', *Afghanistan Info*, October 1997.

[17] For example, the successful micro-credit schemes for income-generating activities by socially disadvantaged women, pioneered by Mohammad Younus in Bangladesh, which are being emulated elsewhere in the world.

[18] Nazif Sharani, 'The State and Community Governance in Afghanistan', in Maley (ed), *Fundamentalism Reborn?*.

[19] Bernt Glatzer, 'Is Afghanistan on the Brink of Ethnic and Tribal Disintegration?', in Maley (ed), *Fundamentalism Reborn?*.

[20] Rashid, *Taliban*, p 213.

[21] Some observers regarded the decree and its enforcement as a marketing ploy to offset falling world prices as a result of the 1999 glut in opium production in Afghanistan, 97 per cent of the crop having been grown in Taliban-controlled areas.

22   Rubin, *Afghanistan: Persistent Crisis*.

23   Bernard Lewis, 'Islamic Revolution', *The New York Review of Books*, vol. XXXIV, nos. 21–22, 21 January 1988.

24   Ahmed Rashid, 'They're only sleeping', *The New Yorker*, 14 January 2002. I am indebted to Rashid's informative essay for this updated account on the Taliban's links to fundamentalist groups outside the country.

25   *Ibid.*, p 40.

26   Olivier Roy, 'Les Talibans et L'Asie centrale', *Afghanistan Info*, March 2001.

27   Ahmed Rashid, 'Taliban Stir up Regional Instability', *Le Monde diplomatique*, English edition, *Guardian Weekly*, November 1999.

28   Pierre Centlivres, 'Le mouvement Taliban et la condition feminine', *Afghanistan Info*, March 1999.

29   Quoted in Bernard Lewis, 'Islamic Revolution', *The New York Review of Books*, vol. XXXIV, nos. 21–22, 21 January 1988.

30   Olivier Roy, *The Failure of Political Islam*.

31   See Olivier Roy, 'Les Contours flous de l'"internationale" islamiste', *Le Monde diplomatique*, October 1998, for an excellent review of the nebulous international terrorist networks that sprang up in the aftermath of the Afghan wars.

Chapter 16

1   From *Meditation XVII*, 'No man is an island'.

2   See Chapter 15, p 204.

3   Islam literally means submission to Allah.

4   Cyril Glassé, *The Concise Encyclopedia of Islam* (San Francisco: HarperCollins, 1999). Glassé comments that while the gods of the Greeks were treated by their adherents as symbols of a reality that transcends the idols themselves (as Critias expounds in Plato's *Timaeus*), the paganism of the Arabs of the jahiliyya, who attributed miraculous psychic powers to the idols themselves, was *'the end-point of religious decadence and hardening, not unlike the present hardening of the monotheism with reductive fundamentalism'* (my italics).

5   *Ibid.*

6   Saudi Arabia and the Yemen generally adhere to the Hanbali School of Law, the most rigid of the four orthodox schools, named after their founders, who developed their respective legal systems based on the shari'a by applying analytical principles through *ijtihad* (interpretation). The other schools are the Maliki, dominant in the Arab west and in West Africa; the Hanafi, prevalent in countries that were formerly part of the Ottoman Empire, in Afghanistan and the subcontinent; and the Shafi, followed in South East Asia. Officially the age of ijtihad is considered to have ended after the four orthodox schools had been established by the tenth century. This is not the case with Shi'ite Islam, which developed its own schools of Islamic jurisprudence, and continued the practice of ijtihad, which can also be interpreted to mean adaptation of the law to the changing circumstances of the age. This practice has intensified in the last 200 years, and in Iran

contemporary developments are carrying the Iranians into completely uncharted territory. (See Glassé, *The Concise Encyclopedia of Islam*.)

[7]   The forerunner of the Wahhabis was Ibn Taymiyyah (CE1263–1328), a jurist of the Hanbali school whose literalist interpretations of the Koran outraged the Islamic scholars of his day, and earned him several spells in prison and even denunciations as a heretic. He was in fact a kind of thirteenth-century bin Laden, angrily responding to the conquest of much of the Islamic world by the infidel Mongols. The Wahhabi creed, compared to traditional Islam, is religion reduced to a set of rigid rules enforced by religious police and a primitive penal code, as in Saudi Arabia and Taliban Afghanistan. Ibn Taymiyyah's writings have much influenced Islamic radical movements in the twentieth century as well as preachers in the mosques of the Muslim world.

[8]   See Peter L. Bergen, *Holy War Inc., Inside the Secret World of Osama bin Laden* (London: Weidenfeld and Nicolson, 2001) for a well-researched account. Bin Laden's father also jumpstarted the career of another Saudi billionaire, Adnan Kashoggi, who figured prominently as Saudi Arabia's financial agent in the Afghan resistance against the Soviets. His sister's son was Dodi al-Fayed.

[9]   *Ibid.* Salem bin Laden, who died in 1988 when the plane he was piloting crashed in Texas, had married into the British aristocracy. His wife's stepfather was the Marquess of Queensberry, whose namesake, it will be recalled, brought the charges against Oscar Wilde in that famous *fin de siècle* case that ruined the great writer.

[10] It is interesting to note that the word 'jihad' was given a wider global application by President Carter's National Security Adviser, Zbigniew Brzezinski, when he spoke of a jihad against communism in front of the cameras at the Afghan–Pakistan border. It is in this sense that bin Laden and his cohorts declared a jihad against America and the West and their Muslim allies – which is quite unorthodox or even considered heretical in Islam. Brzezinski's stated aim was to 'sow shit in the Soviet backyard', and when the Soviet army entered Afghanistan he wrote exultantly to President Carter: 'Now we can give the Soviet Union its Vietnam War'. The policy was carried out with crusading zeal by the Reagan administration. Osama bin Laden and the 'Arab Afghans' were one of its by-products.

[11] Bergen, *Holy War*, p 57.

[12] Quoted by Mary Anne Weaver, *The New Yorker*, 24 January 2000.

[13] Bergen, *Holy War*, p 61. In a book to be published in Beirut by the Qatar-based *al-Jazeera* television's correspondent in Islamabad, the Syrian Ahmed Zeidan, there were 2742 'Afghan Arabs', or foreign Muslims who came under bin Laden's umbrella. They comprised 1660 north Africans, 30 Americans, 62 Britons, 270 Egyptians, 180 Filipinos, eight Frenchmen, 80 Iraqis, 430 Palestinians, 680 Saudis, 520 Sudanese, 33 Turks and 480 Yemenis. Zeidan states that the Taliban provided roughly the same breakdown. (See *The Independent*, London, 23 October 2002.) Zeidan's figures relate obviously to the later period of Taliban rule, prior to the start of the US air war in October 2001.

[14] *Ibid.*

[15] Quoted in Bergen, *Holy War*.

16   Strobe Talbott and Nayan Chanda (eds), *The Age of Terror* (New York: Basic Books, 2001).
17   Lawrence Wright, 'The Man behind bin Laden', *The New Yorker*, 16 September 2002.
18   *Ibid.*
19   Quoted in Bergen, *Holy War*, p 56.
20   Wright, 'The Man behind bin Laden'.
21   See also Chapter 4, p 52, for Qutb's view of the Muslim world.
22   *Ibid.*
23   Bergen, *Holy War*, pp 104-9. Bergen also refers to a press conference called by bin Laden at his Badr camp in Afghanistan, referring to the formation of his Front and hinting at some sort of major action. The simultaneous bombing of the two US embassies in East Africa took place nine weeks later.
24   Wright, 'The Man behind bin Laden'.
25   *Ibid.*
26   *Ibid.*
27   *Ibid.*
28   Quoted in Bergen, *Holy War*, pp 103, 107.
29   He had sent his Sudanese accountant in advance to scout the terrain and to purchase a farm for which he had given him $250,000.
30   See Bergen, *Holy War* and Chapter 4 for details of these activities.
31   Wright, 'The Man behind bin Laden'.
32   Quoted in Bergen, *Holy War*, p 90.
33   Wright, 'The Man behind bin Laden'.
34   *Ibid.*
35   *Ibid.*
36   The *Washington Post* article quotes Samuel Berger, the then National Security Adviser, as saying: 'In the United States, we have this thing called the Constitution, so to bring him here is to bring him into the justice system. I don't think this was our first choice. Our first choice was to send him someplace where justice is more' - he paused a moment - 'streamlined'.
37   Wright, 'The Man behind bin Laden'.
38   *Independent*, London, 23 October 2002.
39   *The Economist*, 22-28 September 2001.
40   Sheikh Omar is believed to have 'approved' the assassination of President Anwar Sadat in 1982. In 1990 he had obtained a US visa in Khartoum, and then a Green Card after he set himself up in New Jersey, where the local mosque became a gathering place for Islamic radicals.
41   In 1993 another Pakistani, Mir Aimal Kansi, had opened fire on CIA employees as they entered their headquarters in Langley. He escaped to Pakistan, from where he was extradited to the US in 1997. In November that year four American employees of a US oil company were gunned down in Karachi, in an attack claimed by a local terrorist group, Ansar al Hamza, in retaliation for Kansi's condemnation in the US. Hamid Gul, the former Islamist head of the ISI, demanded a court martial for the Pakistani officials who had been responsible for Kansi's extradition.

[42] According to bankers and regulators, shares in three large European reinsurance companies fell sharply in the days before September 11, raising suspicions that al-Qaeda financiers placed advantageous trades in the stock and derivative markets before the attacks (*The Economist*, 22–28 September 2001).

[43] The military wing was headed by Mohamed Atef who was chief of al-Qaeda operations. A former Egyptian policeman, he had a hand in the planning of the ambush of US marines in Somalia and the embassy bombings in East Africa. He was reportedly killed in the US bombing of Afghanistan.

[44] *Guardian Weekly*, 20–26 September 2001.

[45] The abolition of the caliphate provoked a major religious and political crisis in the Sunni Muslim world, comparable to the crisis in the thirteenth century, when the Mongol hordes of Hulagu Khan sacked Baghdad and killed the last Abbasid caliph in CE1258. Thereafter the title was nominally held by the descendants of the Abbasids in Mameluke Cairo. The Ottoman Turks claimed that the title had been ceded to their Sultan Selim I when he conquered Egypt in 1517.

[46] After the merger, the full text of bin Laden's 'Declaration of the World Islamic Front for the Jihad against Jews and Crusaders' was published in the London-based Arabic newspaper *Al-Quds al-Arabi* on 23 February 1998. (See Bernard Lewis, 'Licence to Kill', *Foreign Affairs*, vol. 72, no. 3, November/December 1998.)

[47] *International Herald Tribune*, 22 November 2001. The confessions and investigative reports were made available to *The New York Times* by the Egyptian lawyer who represented most of the 107 defendants at the trial.

[48] *Ibid.*

[49] The partnership between Islamic Jihad and al-Qaeda was sealed in the tribal Arab manner by the marriage of Atef's daughter to bin Laden's son in Kandahar.

[50] *International Herald Tribune*, 24 September 2001.

[51] *International Herald Tribune*, 29–30 December 2001.

[52] Social workers estimate that 70 per cent of those in French prisons are of North African origin. According to a French Interior Ministry official, 'Prisons are good indoctrination centres for Islamic radicals. There are about 300 Islamic radicals in prisons in Paris, and they spend a lot of time converting criminals to Islam' (*International Herald Tribune*, 29–30 December 2001).

[53] See Seymour M. Hersh, 'The Twentieth Man', in *The New Yorker*, 30 September 2002, for an interesting profile of Moussaoui.

[54] *International Herald Tribune*, 29–30 December 2001.

[55] *Guardian Weekly*, 20–26 September 2001.

[56] A cruel, thin-lipped visual version of the reptilian image conjured up in words by V.S. Naipaul when he described his meeting in Qom, Iran, with the notorious 'hanging judge' of the Khomeini revolution, the Ayatollah Khalkhalli, as he reminisced about the murder of the shah's last prime minister, the honest, upright and blameless Abbas Hoveyda: 'His mouth opened wide, stayed open, and soon he appeared to be choking with laughter, showing me his gums, his tongue, his gullet' (*Among the Believers: An Islamic Journey* (London: Penguin Books, 1982)).

[57] There is an element of megalomania in this. He has been compared to the terrorist Ossipon, in Joseph Conrad's *The Secret Agent*.

58 Iran, most implausibly, was blamed. One of the suspects was a Shi'ite Saudi who had spent some time in Qom, Iran.

59 *International Herald Tribune*, 27 September 2001.

60 Samuel P. Huntington, 'The Clash of Civilisations', *Foreign Affairs*, vol. 72, no. 3, Summer 1993.

61 Michael Scott Doran, 'Somebody Else's Civil War', *Foreign Affairs*, vol. 81, no. 1, January/February 2002.

62 *International Herald Tribune*, 10 October 2001.

63 O'Neill's profile ('The Counter-Terrorist', *The New Yorker*, 14 January 2002) would make for a superlative screenplay. O'Neill was dedicated, single-minded, intense and energetic, but 'a loner', unconventional, flamboyant and flawed, like a Graham Greene character. His potential screen character if imaginatively created would be more human and convincing than James Bond's. O'Neill's modest Irish-American background, his highly private home-life, his romantic attachments, his lifestyle and expensive tastes are all elements that could be well exploited in a movie. Some of the episodes mentioned in the essay, such as when 300 FBI investigators and support and security staff ('a bunch of six-foot-two Irish-Americans') arrived in the Yemen ('a country of eighteen million inhabitants and 50 million machine guns', according to O'Neill), the conflicting diplomatic concerns of the US ambassador, a woman, and 'the FBI way', and all the other fascinating details of that and other intrusions (in Saudi Arabia) would, in the hands of a competent director, provide material for an absorbing film. Because of disappointments in his prospects of promotion, O'Neill took up the better-paid post of chief of security at the World Trade Center on 23 August 2001. When O'Neill told an ABC News producer of his decision to work at the WTC, the latter joked: 'At least they're not going to bomb it again.' 'They'll probably try to finish the job', O'Neill replied. He died on September 11 in the line of duty.

64 *Ibid.*

65 Wright, 'The Man behind bin Laden'.

66 *Ibid.*

67 Quoted by Weaver, *The New Yorker*, 24 January 2000.

68 Sunanda Datta-Ray, 'Blazing Open a Color Chasm', *International Herald Tribune*, 29 October 2002.

Chapter 17

1 In 1932, George F. Kennan, then a young diplomat at the US mission in Riga, Latvia, wrote a short analysis of the Soviet Union for his chief of mission in which he stated, with canny prescience, that for internal reasons 'an ultimate failure and collapse of the Russian-Communist system, while perhaps long in the coming, was inevitable'. (See *The New York Review of Books*, vol. xlviii, no. 7, 26 April 2001.) Kennan was one of the chief architects of President Truman's policy of 'containment'. He set out his views in a famous 1947 article, 'The Sources of Soviet Conduct', in *Foreign Affairs*. One of his deeply held beliefs is that, in the conditions of modern warfare, there are no winners.

2 *The Economist*, 29 September 2001.

3   Jason Burke et al., 'The Rout of the Taliban', *Observer*, London, 18 November 2001.

4   The overt use of Pakistani bases was politically unwise at the time, and the cooperation of neighbouring states such as Uzbekistan and Tajikistan considered unreliable. According to a British military official, 'Islam Karimov is not so much leading a one-party state but a one-person state. We didn't know how he would go from one day to the next. We couldn't rely on people like that for the safety of our troops'. (*Ibid.*)

5   *Afghanistan Info*, no. 49, October 2001.

6   Burke et al., *Observer*, 18 November 2001.

7   *Ibid.*

8   Jamie Doran, *Le Monde diplomatique*, English edition, *The Guardian Weekly*, September 2002.

9   See Chapter 12.

10 *Afghanistan Info*, March 2002.

11 Mullah Omar himself was reported to have escaped (on a motorcycle) with a handful of his followers to a hideout in the province of Zabul. His present whereabouts may be known to some intelligence agencies but have not been revealed.

12 According to official US sources, to date only eight of the 40 identified as key leaders of al-Qaeda have been caught.

13 Richard Holbrooke, 'Send a Multilateral Security Force to Afghanistan', *International Herald Tribune*, 15 November 2001.

14 Astri Surke and Susan L. Woodward, 'Make Haste Slowly in Assistance for Afghanistan', *International Herald Tribune*, 21 January 2002.

15 James Wolfensohn, 'With a Lot of Money, Country Can Be Fixed', *International Herald Tribune*, 21 January 2002.

16 William Maley, 'Reconstituting State Power in Afghanistan', *Afghanistan Info*, March 2002.

17 See Chapter 6 on the problems of rural debt in Afghanistan.

18 Hernando de Soto, *International Herald Tribune*, 17 October 2001. See also his *The Mystery of Capital* (New York: Basic Books, 2000) for a detailed treatment of his thesis.

19 George Soros, 'The United Nations is the Best Tutor for Afghanistan', *International Herald Tribune*, 4 December 2001.

20 'Another Powder Trail', *The Economist*, 20 October 2001.

21 Jason Burke, *Observer*, 11 August 2002.

22 Cedric Gouverneur, 'Iran Loses its Drug War', *Le Monde diplomatique*, English edition, *The Guardian Weekly*, March 2002.

23 Ludwig Adamec, 'Greater Afghanistan - A Missed Chance?', *Afghanistan Info*, March 1998.

24 *Ibid.*

25 *Ibid.*

Epilogue

[1] These were generally perceived as amounting to an exit strategy that consisted in declaring a victory for democracy in Afghanistan, to compensate for the debacle in Iraq, and returning sovereignty to the Iraqis so as to enable the US forces to focus on fighting the insurgency there as an ally of a sovereign government – all this before the US presidential elections of November 2004.

[2] By mid-August 2004, the UN had registered just over 10.35 million voters (of whom 58.6 per cent were men and 41.4 per cent were women), against their target of 10.5 million – a considerable achievement, even as registration centres became subject to murderous attacks by neo-Taliban insurgents.

[3] Karzai made this statement at a news conference in Washington on 15 June 2004, after calling on the US President and addressing a joint session of Congress. (*Afghanistan Report*, 18 June 2004, at www.rferl.org.)

[4] Ahmed Rashid, 'The Mess in Afghanistan', *New York Review of Books*, 12 February 2004.

[5] Quoted by Patricia Gossman, *International Herald Tribune*, 6 May 2004. Sayyaf was generously funded by Saudi Arabia when he was a leader of the anti-communist mujahideen. He had once lived in that country where he married a Saudi princess.

[6] House of Commons, Foreign Affairs Committee, *Foreign Policy Aspects of the War against Terrorism* (London, July 2004).

[7] Quoted in *The Economist*, 13 March 2004. US$700 million has been earmarked for Pakistan, out of $5.7 billion of assistance in 2005 to countries 'that have joined us in the war against terror', as requested from Congress by Secretary of State Colin Powell.

[8] David Johnston and David E. Sanger, *International Herald Tribune*, 11 August 2004.

[9] The language is so reminiscent of the language in the al-Zawahiri statements quoted towards the end of Chapter 16 of this book.

[10] Donald Rumsfeld was one of the signatories to a letter addressed on 26 January 1998 to President Clinton urging him to wage a pre-emptive war to remove Saddam Hussein from power. Among the others were Richard Perle, Paul Wolfovitz, Richard Armitage and Zalmay Khalilzad. A 'Statement of Principles', made at the inception of the neo-conservative Project for the New American Century (PNAC) in June 1997, bears in addition the signatures of Dick Cheney and Jeb Bush, among others. These documents can be read on the PNAC website. Anatol Lieven ('The Bush Blip', *Prospect*, August 2004) provides a thought-provoking essay on the Cold War background of key members of the Bush administration which blinded them to the threat of 'stateless' terrorism. Zalmay Khalilzad, now US Ambassador in Kabul, is of Afghan origin. As an official in the Reagan administration, he helped channel US assistance to the Afghan mujahideen during the Soviet occupation and later served as a consultant to UNOCAL.

[11] Bob Woodward, *Plan of Attack* (Simon and Schuster, 2004). See Brian Urquhart's 'A Cautionary Tale' (*New York Review of Books*, 10 June 2004) for a balanced and insightful review.

Bibliography

Adamec, Ludwig W.A., *Historical Dictionary of Afghanistan* (Mehichen, NJ, and London: The Scarecrow Press, 1991)

——, 'Greater Afghanistan – A Missed Chance?', *Afghanistan Info*, March 1998

Ahmed, Akbar S., *Pakistan Society: Islam, Ethnicity and Leadership in South Asia* (Karachi: Oxford University Press, 1986)

——, *Discovering Islam: Making Sense of Muslim History and Society* (London and New York: Routledge and Kegan Paul, 1988)

——, *Postmodernism and Islam: Predicament and Promise* (London and New York: Routledge, 1992)

Amnesty International, *Afghanistan: The Human Rights of Minorities*, Report ASA 11/14/99 (London, November 1999)

Anwar, Raja, *The Tragedy of Afghanistan: A First-Hand Account*, translated from the Urdu by Khalid Hassan (London and New York: Verso, 1988)

Arney, George, *Afghanistan* (London: Mandarin Paperbacks, 1990)

Arnold, Anthony, *Afghanistan's Two-Party Communism: Parcham and Khalq* (Stanford, California: Stanford University Press, 1983)

Bacharach, Jere L., *A Middle East Studies Handbook* (Cambridge: Cambridge University Press, 1984)

Bakhash, Shaul, *The Reign of the Ayatollahs: Iran and the Islamic Revolution* (London, Boston and Sydney: Unwin Paperbacks, 1986)

Balta, Paul, *L'Islam*, (Le Monde, 1998)

Bindeman, Rolf, 'Der politische Aufstieg und der Fall der Hazara' (The Political Rise and Fall of the Hazara), *Afghanistan Info*, March 1999

Bradsher, Henry S., *Afghanistan and the Soviet Union* (Durham, Mass.: Duke University Press, 1984)

Brockelman, Carl (ed), *History of the Islamic Peoples* (London and Henley: Routledge and Kegan Paul, 1948; first published in German, 1939)

Burke, S.M., *Pakistan's Foreign Policy: An Historical Analysis* (London: Oxford University Press, 1973)

Byron, Robert, *The Road to Oxiana* (London: Macmillan, 1937)

Caröe, Sir Olaf, *The Pathans, with an Epilogue on Russia* (Karachi: Oxford University Press, 1990; first edition, London: Macmillan, 1958)

Caryl, Christian, 'Tyrants on the Take', *The New York Review of Books*, vol. XLIX, no. 6, 11 April 2002

Centlivres, Pierre, 'Le mouvement Taliban et la condition feminine', *Afghanistan Info*, March 1999

Centlivres-Demont, Pierre and Micheline, *Et si on parlait de l'Afghanistan? Terrains et textes, 1964–1980* (Neuchâtel: Institut de l'Ethnologie, 1988)

Chadda, Maya, 'Talibanisation and Pakistan's Transitional Democracy', *World Affairs*, vol. 3, no. 3, July–September, 1999

Churchill, Winston, *My Early Life* (London: Fontana Books, 1959)

Cordovez, Diego and Selig S. Harrison, *Out of Afghanistan: The Inside Story of the Soviet Withdrawal* (New York: Oxford University Press, 1995)

Curzon of Kedlestone, Marquess, 'The Amir of Afghanistan', in Peter King (ed), *A Viceroy's India: Leaves fom Lord Curzon's Notebook* (London: Sidgwick and Jackson, 1986)

De Soto, Hernando, *The Mystery of Capital* (New York: Basic Books, 2000)

Dorronsoro, Gilles, 'Afghanistan. Du "djihad" à la guerre civile', in *L'Islamisme* (Paris: Les Dossiers de l'Etat du Monde, 1994)

——, 'Les Talibans: Dynamique révolutionnaire et environnement regional', *Afghanistan Info*, March 1999

Dupree, Louis, *Afghanistan* (Karachi: Oxford University Press, 1997; first edition, Princeton, NJ: Yale University Press, 1973)

Dupree, Nancy Hatch, *An Historical Guide to Afghanistan* (Kabul: Afghan Tourist Organisation, 1970)

Elphinstone, Mountstuart, *An Account of the Kingdom of Cabaul* (first edition, London, 1815; reprinted by Indus Publications, Karachi, 1992)

Etienne, Gilbert, *De Caboul ä Pekin* (Geneva: Librairie E. Droz, 1959)

——, *L'Afghanistan, ou les aléas de la coopération* (Paris: Presses universitaires de France, 1972)

Fraser-Tytler, W.K., *Afghanistan* (London and New York: Oxford University Press, 1950)

Friedman, Thomas, *From Beirut to Jerusalem* (Glasgow: Fontana/Collins, 1990)

Fry, Maxwell J., *The Afghan Economy: Money, Finance, and the Critical Constraints to Development* (Leiden: E.J. Brill, 1974)

Gabrieli, Francesco, *Muhammad and the Conquests of Islam* (New York and Toronto: World University Library, McGraw-Hill Book Company, 1968)

Gause, Gregory, 'The Kingdom in the Middle', in Hoge and Rose (eds), *How Did This Happen? Terrorism and the New War* (New York: Public Affairs, 2001)

Gaussen, Fabrice, 'The Evolution of UNHCR Repatriation Assistance', *Afghanistan Info*, March 1996

Glassé, Cyril, *The Concise Encyclopedia of Islam* (San Francisco: HarperCollins, 1991)

Glatzer, Bernt, 'Ethnizität im Afghanistankonflict' (Ethnic Features in the Afghan Conflict), *Afghanistan Info*, September 1999

Gouverneur, Cedric, 'Iran Loses its Drug War', *Le Monde diplomatique*, English edition, *The Guardian Weekly*, March 2002

Gregorian, Vartan, *The Emergence of Modern Afghanistan. Politics of Reform and Modernisation, 1880–1946* (Stanford: Stanford University Press, 1969)

Griffiths, J.C., *Afghanistan: Key to a Continent* (London: André Deutsch, 1981)

Guillaume, Alfred, *Islam* (London: Penguin Books, 1956)

Haider, Ejaz, 'Pakistan's Afghan Policy and Its Fallout', *Central Asia Monitor*, no. 5, 1998

Harrison, Selig S., 'Inside the Afghan Talks', *Foreign Policy*, no. 72, Fall 1988

Hill, Charles, 'A Herculean Task: The Myth and Reality of Arab Terrorism', in Talbott and Chanda (eds), *The Age of Terror* (New York: Basic Books, 2001)

Hiro, Dilip, *Islamic Fundamentalism*, Paladin (London: Grafton Books, 1989)

Hitti, Philip K., *Makers of Arab History* (New York: St Martin's Press, 1968)

Hoge, James F. and Gideon Rose (eds), *How Did This Happen? Terrorism and the New War* (New York: Public Affairs, 2001)

Hoodbhoy, Pervez Amirali, *Muslims and Science: Religious Orthodoxy and the Struggle for Rationality* (Lahore: Vanguard Books, 1991)

Hourani, Albert, *A History of the Arab Peoples* (London: Faber and Faber, 1991)

Huntington, Samuel P., 'The Clash of Civilisations', *Foreign Affairs*, vol. 72, no. 3, Summer 1993

Inderfurth, Karl F., 'Afghanistan at a Crossroads', US Senate Foreign Relations Committee, Statement, 14 April 1999 (Online Center for Afghan Studies, www afghan-politics.org)

Kakar, Hasan Kawun, *Afghanistan: A Study in International Political Developments, 1880–1896* (Lahore: Punjab Educational Press, 1971)

Kapur, Harish, *Soviet Russia and Asia, 1917–1927* (Geneva: Institut de hautes études internationales, 1965)

Kazemzadeh, 'Russia and the Middle East', in Ivo J. Lederer (ed), *Russian Foreign Policy* (New Haven and London: Yale University Press, 1962)

Khaldûn, Ibn Abdul Rahman, *The Muqadimmah: An Introduction to History*, translated by Franz Rosenthal; abridged and edited by N.J. Dawood (London: Routledge and Kegan Paul, 1967)

Khan, Ansar Hussain, *The Rediscovery of India* (Hyderabad: Orient Longman, 1995)

Khan, Riaz Mohammad, *Untying the Afghan Knot: Negotiating Soviet Withdrawal* (Durham, Mass.: Duke University Press, 1991)

Klass, Rosanne, (ed), *The Great Game Revisited* (New York: Freedom House, 1987)

Labrousse, Alain, 'Les Drogues et les conflits en Afghanistan (1978-1995)', *Afghanistan Info*, March 1996

Lamb, Christina, *Waiting for Allah: Pakistan's Struggle for Democracy* (New Delhi: Viking Penguin India, 1991)

Lane-Poole, Stanley, *Medieval India under Mohammedan Rule* (New York: G.P. Putnam's Sons, 1903)

Lewis, Bernard (ed), *The World of Islam* (London: Thames and Hudson, 1976)

——, 'Islam', *The New York Review of Books*, 30 June 1983

——, 'Islamic Revolution', *The New York Review of Books*, vol. XXXIV, nos. 21–22, 21 January 1988

——, 'The Enemies of God', *The New York Review of Books*, 25 March 1993

——, 'Licence to Kill', *Foreign Affairs*, vol. 72, no 3, November/December 1998

Liftschultz, Lawrence, 'Pakistan, the Empire of Heroin', in Alfred McCoy and Alan Block (eds), *War on Drugs: Studies in the Failure of US Narcotics Policy* (New York: Westview Press, 1992)

Lippman, Thomas W., *Understanding Islam: An Introduction to the Muslim World* (Meridian (Penguin Books), 1995)

McCoy, Alfred and Alan Block (eds), *War on Drugs: Studies in the Failure of US Narcotics Policy* (New York: Westview Press, 1992)

Majrooh, Sayyed Bahanuddin, 'Past and Present Education in Afghanistan: A Problem for the Future', Lahore

Maley, William (ed), *Fundamentalism Reborn? Afghanistan and the Taliban*, (New York: New York University Press, 1998)

Marsden, Peter, *The Taliban: War, Religion and the New Order in Afghanistan* (London and New York: Zed Books Ltd, 1998)

Matinuddin, Kamal, *Power Struggle in the Hindu Kush* (Lahore: Wajidalis, 1991)

Miller, David W. and Moore, Clark D. (ed), *The Middle East, Yesterday and Today* (Toronto, New York, London: Bantam Pathfinder Editions, 1970)

Mishra, Pankaj, 'Jihadis', in *What We Think of America*, Granta 77, Spring 2002

Moorehouse, Geoffrey, *To the Frontier* (London: Hodder and Stoughton, 1984)

Naipaul, V.S., *Among the Believers: An Islamic Journey* (London: Penguin Books, 1982)

Observatoire géopolitique des drogues (OGD), 'Afghanistan–Tajikistan: La Route de L'Opium', *Afghanistan Info*, September 1998

Olsen, Asta, *Islam and Politics in Afghanistan* (Richmond, Surrey: Curzon Press, 1995)

Pounds, Norman J.G. and Kingbury, Robert C., *An Atlas of Middle Eastern Affairs* (London: University Paperbacks, Methuen and Co. Ltd, 1966)

Rasanayagam, Angelo, 'Taliban Fundamentalism: Afghan Turmoils', *World Affairs*, vol. 3 no. 3 (June 1999)

Rashid, Ahmed, *The Resurgence of Central Asia: Islam or Nationalism* (London and New Jersey: Zed Books, 1994)

——, 'Taliban Stir up Regional Instability', *Le Monde diplomatique*, English edition, *Guardian Weekly*, November 1999

——, 'The Taliban: Exporting Extremism', *Foreign Affairs*, vol. 78, no. 6, November–December 1999

——, *Taliban: Islam, Oil, and the New Great Game in Central Asia* (London and New York: I.B. Tauris, 2000)

——, 'Afghanistan: The Year in Review - 2000', Online Center for Afghan Studies, January 2001, (www.afghan-politics.org)

——, 'They're only sleeping', in 'Annals of Terrorism', *The New Yorker*, 14 January 2002

Robinson, Francis (ed), *The Cambridge Illustrated History of the Islamic World* (Cambridge: Cambridge University Press, 1996)

Roy, Olivier, *Islam and Resistance in Afghanistan* (Cambridge: Cambridge University Press, 1986)

——, *The Failure of Political Islam*, translated by Catherine Volk (London: I.B. Tauris, 1994)

——, 'Le mouvement des Taleban', *Afghanistan Info*, February 1995

——, 'Les Contours flous de l'"internationale" islamiste', *Le Monde diplomatique*, October 1998

——, 'Les Talibans et l'Asie centrale', *Afghanistan Info*, March 2001

Rubin, Barnett, *The Fragmentation of Afghanistan: State Formation and Collapse in the International System* (New Haven and London: Yale University Press, 1995)

——, *Afghanistan : Persistent Crisis Challenges the UN System* (London: Writenet, 1998)

——, 'Testimony on the Situation in Afghanistan', US Senate, Council on Foreign Relations, 8 October 1998 (Online Center for Afghan Studies, www.afghan-politics.org)

——, 'The Political Economy of War and Peace in Afghanistan', Online Center for Afghan Studies, June 1999 (www.afghan-politics.org)

Said, Edward W., *Orientalism* (London: Penguin Books, 1991)

Saikal, Amin, 'The UN and Afghanistan: A Case of Failed Peacemaking Intervention', *International Peacekeeping*, vol. 3, no. 1, Spring 1996

Saikal, Amin and William Maley (eds), *The Soviet Withdrawal from Afghanistan* (Cambridge: Cambridge University Press, 1989)

Shah, Safia (ed), *Afghan Caravan* (London: The Octagon Press, 1991)

Soros, George, *On Globalisation* (New York: Public Affairs, 2002)

Soviet Archives (1978–1989), Online Center for Afghan Studies (www.afghan-politics.org)

Spear, Percival, *A History of India*, vol. 2 (London: Penguin Books, 1990; first published, 1965)

Sreedar (ed), *Taliban and the Afghan Turmoil* (New Delhi: Himalayan Books, 1997)

Sreedar and Mahendra Ved, *The Afghan Turmoil: Changing Equations* (New Delhi: Himalayan Books, 1998)

Stiglitz, Joseph E., 'A Fair Deal for the World', *The New York Review of Books*, vol. XLIX, no. 9, 23 May 2002

Surke, Astri and Susan L. Woodward, 'Make Haste Slowly in Assistance for Afghanistan', *International Herald Tribune*, 21 January 2002

Talbott, Strobe, and Nayan Chanda (eds), *The Age of Terror: America and the World after September 11* (New York: Basic Books, 2001)

Thapar, Romila, *A History of India*, vol. 1 (London: Penguin Books, 1990; first published, 1966)

Toynbee, Arnold J., *Between Oxus and Jumna* (London: Oxford University Press, 1961)

Trenin, Dmitri, 'Central Asia's Stability and Russia's Security', PONARs memo no. 168, November 2000, Online Center for Afghan Studies (www.afghan-politics.org)

Trevor Roper, Hugh, 'Naipaul's Islam', *The New York Review of Books*, 5 November 1991

UNHCR, *Refugees: Focus on Afghanistan*, vol. 108, II-1997

Von Grunenbaum, G.E., *Medieval Islam* (Chicago: The University of Chicago Press, 1953)

——, *Classical Islam* (London: George Allen and Unwin Ltd, 1970)

Watson, Francis, *A Concise History of India* (London: Thames and Hudson, 1979)

Watt, W. Montgomery, *The Majesty That Was Islam: The Islamic World, 661–1100* (London: Sidgwick and Jackson, 1974)

Witschi-Cestari, Alfredo, 'Coordinating Aid in Afghanistan', *Afghanistan Info*, October 1997

Yousaf, Brigadier Mohammad and Major Mark Adkin, *The Bear Trap: Afghanistan's Untold Story* (Lahore: Jang Publishers, 1992)

Index

307